THE
MALLING
OF
AMERICA

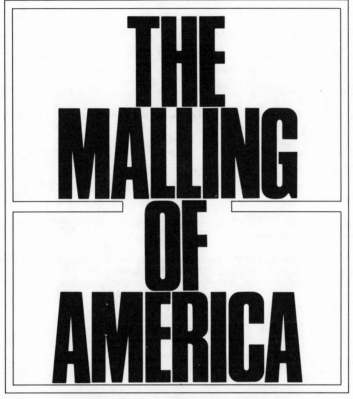

THE MALLING OF AMERICA

An inside look at
the great consumer paradise

WILLIAM SEVERINI KOWINSKI

William Morrow and Company, Inc
New York

Portions of this book appeared in a different form as "The Malling of America" in *New Times* magazine, *American Film, The New York Times Magazine* and *West*.

Grateful acknowledgment is given for permission to reprint the following:

Portions of the poem "Dreaming America" from *The Fabulous Beasts* by Joyce Carol Oates (Louisiana State University Press, 1975).

"Rockin' Shopping Center" copyright © 1976 by Modern Love Songs. Written by Jonathan Richman.

Selections from "A Farewell to France" by Richard Eder copyright © 1982 by The New York Times Company.

Photographs courtesy of Tom Cramer, Gruen Associates, Alice Moulton-Ely, Suzanne Opton, The Rouse Company, and Westcor.

Library of Congress Cataloging in Publication Data

Kowinski, William Severini.

The malling of America.

Includes index.

1. Shopping malls—United States.   I. Title
HF5430.3.K68   1985   381'.1'0973   84-22597
ISBN 0-688-04180-9

Printed in the United States of America

First Edition

1 2 3 4 5 6 7 8 9 10

BOOK DESIGN BY JAMES UDELL

This book, being my first, is dedicated to the memory of my mother, Flora Severini Kowinski; the memory of my grandfathers, Ignazio Severini and Frank Kowinski; to my father, Walter Kowinski; and especially to my grandmother, Gioconda Severini, the best storyteller I know.

Acknowledgments

The people I met on my mall treks, articles and books I read, movies and plays I saw, and even music I heard, directly contributed to this book's being about more than shopping malls. It is a book also about America. My gratitude goes to friends named in the book, and to the people (named and not) who generously related their impressions and experiences, as well as to those in various professions who shared their expertise. I'm grateful also for the aid and comfort provided by my sisters and their husbands, Kathryn and James Duffy, and Deborah and Gerald Boice; and by friends and hosts, especially Michael Shain, Suzanne Opton, Judy Field, Mark Jenkins, Larry Jackson, Elizabeth Offner, Terry Corey, Joyce Morgan, and Douglas and Sharon Wilson.

Several magazine editors aided this project in various stages, notably Jon Larsen and Ken Emerson, but the major share of credit and thanks goes to John Lombardi, who was the first editor at *New Times* to respond with encouragement and ideas to the weird notion of writing about shopping malls. Special credit and thanks also to Jeanne Drewsen, the literary agent whose initial enthusiasm and continued support were vital to this book's publication.

Although they are of course not responsible for my interpretations, I am grateful for the insights and information I found in published works of authors named in the text, especially Richard Francaviglia, Neil Harris, Robert Hughes, Jane Jacobs, Ralph Keyes, Richard Lingeman, Philip Slater, Calvin Trillin, and William H. Whyte. Other works of special helpfulness and inspiration were written by John Cheever, Joan Didion, Herbert J. Gans, Suzanne Gordon, John Janovy, Samuel Kaplan, Stanislaw Lem, William Manchester, Marshall McLuhan, Herman Melville, Peter Muller, Moshe Safdie, Richard Sennett, Sam Shepard, William Irwin Thompson, John Updike, Kurt Vonnegut, Jr., and Tom Wolfe.

Thanks also to the International Council of Shopping Centers for access to their library and their convention, and to the people in the mall industry who gave me interviews or arranged them.

For the usual range of reasons, the names of some people in this book have been changed. Malls themselves change—I've described them as they were when I visited (and revisited) them from 1977 to 1984. I've compressed some incidents, but what people said— mostly to me, but otherwise in print or broadcast—I've presented as accurately as I can.

Since this is my first book, I thank the teachers and believers of earlier days, especially Carol and Joni. Thanks, too, to the waitresses who provided coffee and indulgence at Lee's, the Court Jester (especially Kathi and Kathy), and elsewhere across America, without whom this book would not have been fueled. Finally, thanks to Mary, for the moments of her treasured attention.

Contents

The adventurer
In humanity has not conceived of a race
Completely physical in a physical world.
The green corn gleams and the metaphysicals
Lie sprawling in majors of the August heat,
The rotund emotions, paradise unknown.

—WALLACE STEVENS
Esthétique du Mal

Part 1

THE MALLING
OF MAIN STREET

*I hear the ruin of all space, shattered glass
and toppling masonry, and time one livid
final flame. What's left us then?*
—JAMES JOYCE
Ulysses

1

Loomings

She floated out of the dimness, the iridescent fog. Behind her were the sounds of battle: the shrieking, crashing, ringing, and staccato screaming, piercing the churning, turgid, rolling roar. Inside the electronic cave, adolescents manned the rows of panels as fluorescent flashes roiled the darkness.

She was the guardian at the gate, wearing a red-and-white vertically striped smock over jersey and jeans. She was like a candy cane in a den of electric mayhem. Her name was Carol, and she dispensed change and kept order among the kids playing air hockey and Death Race, the clerks on their breaks relieving frustration by pounding the pinball machines, and the video warriors at the screens of Zaxxon and Berzerk, Pac-Man and Galaxan, their fingers twitching as they peered into the relentless, regulated abyss. This was the game arcade at Greengate, an enclosed mall at the edge of

Greensburg, the small western Pennsylvania town where Carol and
I both were born. In her twenties, Carol was a few years younger
than I, and we had never met before.

After an absence of more than fifteen years, I'd been back in
Greensburg long enough to notice that Main Street wasn't what it
used to be, and that most of the town's retail business—and therefore its shoppers—were out on the highway at malls that hadn't
existed when I was growing up. At first the malls seemed to mean a
simple relocation from Main Street to Route 30, but I was beginning to see it was more than that. Now each new bit of evidence
about the malls and their part in changing the town and the lives of
its people came to me as a kind of jolt.

I wasn't used to malls. I especially wasn't used to the mall being
normal, just taken for granted as a fact of everyday life in my hometown. But for someone even as close to my age as Carol, the mall
had pretty much always been there. I left for college in 1964;
Greengate opened in 1965, when Carol was just entering her teens.
That was the first real jolt: The only experience I had of Greensburg
was being young there. Now the young people I saw were living in
a different town, with a new Main Street.

I started understanding that when I kept seeing Tommy, a
younger brother of one of my closest high-school friends, hanging
out at Greengate. On Friday and Saturday evenings Tommy met
his high-school friends there, sometimes just to find out where the
parties would be that night, or to hook up for car caravans to Pittsburgh for a rock concert. But often the mall was itself where the
weekend happened, and Tommy would get dressed up just to
cruise its courts.

Tommy spent afternoons after school and days in the summer
there, too, glowering over coffee in the hippest fast-food restaurant, or memorizing all the records in the racks of the National
Record Mart. Or he and his friends would simply sit together on
the large polished-wood bench that was wrapped around three sides
of a planter full of glossy-leaved greenery. It was their special place.
They fooled around and watched people go by, and baited the security guard they called Sarge because of his thick neck and drill-
sergeant demeanor. On his mall patrol, Sarge would always stop to
tap his nightstick on their shoes when they had their legs up on the
bench, and would bite out the terse command "Feet Down!" He
did it so regularly that they would wait for him, as he approached
they would move their legs to the floor in military dance-step uni-

son and shout, "FEET DOWN!" Then, when he was past them but not out of sight, they would return to their former postures in the same synchronized movement. Then they would laugh.

It didn't take long for me to notice that every time I was at the mall, Tommy was already there. He was always there. So were his friends. If they weren't in the mall they were out in a car in the parking lot, or toking up behind the Dumpsters. Mostly it was all harmless—*normal*—but sometimes it wasn't. Tommy had seen one teenager pull a gun on another and shoot him at a mall entrance. A young woman he knew had been raped in the parking lot. "Everything that was happening," he told me, "happened at the mall."

There hadn't been a Greengate when his brother and I were Tommy's age, but for life patterns to be quickly altered by something called the shopping mall was not just a quirk of personal or local history. I was about to get an indication of that—with another perceptual jolt—when I talked to Carol at the threshold of the arcade, and she told me about her life and travels across America.

Carol ran away from home at seventeen and hitched across the country to California, then back again, and down the East Coast to Florida. "I learned more about life in three months than I would have in twenty years in this town," she said. As we talked, I recognized the rites of passage familiar since the 1960s and not all that different from those of my own youthful wanderings, when many of us explored the places where things were happening, seeking new experiences and the meaning that was missing from the conventional agenda. So when Carol mentioned places we'd both visited, like Berkeley and Boulder, Chicago and Atlanta, I assumed we could compare our adventures and what it was like to be back in our little town. But not only was the town Carol left different from mine because of the mall—so was the America she found in her travels.

When Carol left Greensburg, she had actually been leaving Greengate Mall. So when she traveled it was completely natural for her to seek out not only cities and university communities (as I had) but shopping malls as well. She went to malls for shelter from the storms, the heat and cold that batter the carless voyager; she accompanied friends she visited to their local malls for shopping and entertainment (people, she said, like to show off their new malls as points of local pride); or she simply wandered around in malls on her own when she was broke or blue or when she just felt like

walking and watching the promenade of strangers while medi-
tatively munching on an ice-cream cone.

When Carol returned to Greensburg to assimilate her experiences and decide what next to do with her life, she came back to
Greengate Mall. She got the job in the games arcade because, she
said, "Since I'm always in the mall anyway, I may as well get paid
for it."

Looking into Carol's surprised eyes when I told her that in my
own travels I couldn't remember a single time I'd been in a mall, I
suddenly saw how blind I had been. How could I have been to
Denver and not seen Tamarac Square, or in San Francisco without
going to The Cannery? What was Wheeling, West Virginia, without the Mountaineer Mall, or Boston without Faneuil Hall Marketplace? Even in Manhattan, the new species of malls like the
Market at Citicorp Center, the South Street Seaport, and the shops
at Trump Tower were as essential to know as any of the other
monuments. The truth was—and I soon found I wasn't the only
one who hadn't seen it yet—that in terms of economic and cultural
power, as well as impact on the physical and social ecology, the
malling of America was a fact of life.

Their names are the litany of a new America, an inventory and
an incantation: Northland and Southdale, Eastridge and Westgate,
Fox Valley and Fox Hills, Fashion Square and Fashion Island, the
Galleria in Atlanta, Dallas, Fort Lauderdale, Glendale, Houston,
Sherman Oaks, White Plains . . . Powder Basin Mall, Ponderosa
Shopping Center, Camel Plaza, Battlefield Mall.

There is a Manoa Marketplace in Hawaii and a Manoa Shopping
Center in Havertown, Pennsylvania. Rainbow Mall is just a block
away from the river in Niagara Falls, New York. Brooklyn has
Kings Plaza; Staten Island has the Staten Island Mall; Queens has
Queens Center; Manhattan has the Herald Center. Yazoo City,
Mississippi, has the Yazooville Shopping Center, and Amityville,
New York, with or without its horror, has a bright new mall. Even
Hibbing, Minnesota, Bob Dylan's hometown up in northernmost
nothingness, has a 225,000-square-foot mall with three major de-
partment stores. Rand McNally puts shopping malls on some of its
maps, right alongside cities and towns.

There are more shopping centers in the United States than
movie theaters (and most movie theaters are now in shopping centers). There are more enclosed malls than cities, four-year colleges,
or television stations, and nearly as many as county courthouses.

There are more shopping centers than school districts, hotels, or hospitals. One mall—the Del Amo Fashion Center in Southern California, with more than three hundred stores in two complexes connected by a glass bridge that spans a six-lane freeway—is larger than the principality of Monaco. It employs a special staff just to show people around: its own tourist bureau.

Plaza Del Sol in Del Rio, Texas. The Beverly Center in Beverly Hills. Paramus Park in Paramus, New Jersey. The Hickory Hollow Mall in Shreveport, Louisiana. Olde Mistick Village is an entire shopping center representing a New England village, circa 1720, in Mystic, Connecticut. The Reverend Jerry Falwell, head of the Moral Majority, owns his own shopping center. His radio program, *The Old Time Gospel Hour,* is broadcast from it. After being paroled from his sentence for his participation in the My Lai massacre in Vietnam, William Calley worked at his father-in-law's jewelry store at the Cross-Country Plaza Shopping Mall in Columbus, Georgia. Bruce Springsteen (who has a verse about mall shopping in one of his songs) cut his first record at a studio in the Brick Mall Shopping Center in New Jersey.

Linda Vista Shopping Center in San Diego, Bel Air Mall in Mobile, Towne West Square in Wichita, Manzanita Plaza in Tucson, Big Town Mall in Dallas: The malling of America is happening wherever stores like Sears Roebuck, Neiman-Marcus, J. C. Penney, and Bloomingdale's glare down long corridors of Slack Shacks, Thom Mc Ans, Nina Riccis, Courrèges, Magic Pan Crêperies, Waldenbooks, and Bath Trends, or even where stalls selling fresh bread and fruit kabob rub up against the reconstituted walls of historical buildings. Most of America's retailing is done in shopping centers now; the vast majority of department stores are in malls, and there are national chains of shops, restaurants, and services (including law and medicine) that have virtually all of their outlets in shopping centers. As of 1984, the biggest real estate deal in U.S. history was the sale of nineteen shopping malls in eight states for more than $700 million. The previous record holder was New York's Pan Am Building.

Since retailing and real estate are two of the most potent elements of the American economy, with service and entertainment fast becoming growth industries of the future, shopping centers represent a major economic force. But malls have more than financial significance; they are becoming a way of life.

You can get anything from diamonds to yogurt in the mall; you can attend college classes, register to vote, go to the library, see topless dancers and male strippers, give blood, bet, score, jog and meditate, and get a room or a condo and live there. Someday it may be possible—if it isn't already—to be born, go from preschool through college, get a job, date, marry, have children, fool around, get a divorce, advance through a career or two, receive your medical care, even get arrested, tried, and jailed; live a relatively full life of culture and entertainment, and eventually die and be given funeral rites without ever leaving a particular mall complex—because every one of those possibilities exists now in some shopping center somewhere. These meticulously planned and brightly enclosed structures, these *ideas* conveniently located just off the great American highway, have taken the concept of one-stop shopping, as old as the ancient public markets, and turned it into a virtual one-stop culture, providing a cornucopia of products nestled in an ecology of community, entertainment, and societal identity.

Finger Lakes Mall in Auburn, New York. Mayfair-In-The-Grove in Miami. Gleason's Corner Mall, Winrock Center, Snug Harbor Square, The Mall of New Hampshire, the Plaza at Aurora. The mall has entered the language as a metaphor ("The term 'office automation' is a convenient roof over a shopping mall of technologies," says an advertisement for the International Data Corporation), and it has become a familiar reference in topical humor. ("The Allies are on the outskirts of the city!" says an aide to Hitler in a *Saturday Night Live* sketch. "In the suburbs!" Hitler cries. "They've taken the shopping malls! Now where will I get my records and tapes!") One survey showed that Americans were spending more time in malls than anywhere else except home, job, or school. They make 7 billion trips in and out of shopping centers every year.

Empire Park Shopping Center, Cherrywood Commons, Pierce Street Village, Bonanza East, Rapids Mall, Crystal Mall, Brand Plaza Shopping Center, the Eden Prairie Mall. Once confined to the highway, the mall has taken its suburban alchemy—its middle-American magic—beyond those original boundaries to make sorcery in the small town, to add the shimmer of its fantasies to giant city towers, and to encircle historical structures with its glistening image. More than mere locations for consumption, the malls have become the signature structures of the age. The mall is Our Town's year-round carnival, the cathedral of the postwar culture, the Garden of Eden in a box. It is a mirror held up to contemporary

American dreams and a fantasy haven from American nightmares—
a circus in a fallout shelter. It is the strange achievement of the
American Way: a utopia fashioned by the not-quite-invisible hand
of merchandising. It is our latest attempt to cure the great endemic
American disease of loneliness. Malls are everywhere, and everywhere they are, they are expressive and emblematic.

But the mall is not even confined to the United States anymore.
There are malls throughout the Western Hemisphere—in Canada
(where some mall styles later copied in the United States were pioneered), Mexico, and South America. There are new malls in Western Europe, Africa, the Far East, and even one in the Soviet Union.
Tokyo, Japan, boasts an underground mall that features 46 movie
theaters, more than 1,500 restaurants, 15 discos, and 699 Mah-
Jongg parlors. Barney Kiernan's pub in Dublin, Ireland, was the
location for a scene in James Joyce's *Ulysses;* it is now part of a
shopping center. If negotiations are successful, visitors may someday find an American-style shopping mall in Jerusalem, not far
from the Wailing Wall.

Talking to Carol made me realize that I was a member of the
last generation that remembers an America without the mall. That's
an intriguing thought for a writer. John Updike and his generation
saw the change as it happened—a middle-aged character in an Updike short story, for example, looked at a mall and recalled the bean
field that had been cultivated there since his grandfather's day.
Joyce Carol Oates observed the change in a poem:

> Where the useless stretch of trees lay
> an orange sphere like a golf ball
> announces the Shopping Mall, open
> for Thursday evening shopping.
> There, tonight, droves of teenagers hunt
> one another, alert on a memorized pavement.

Even one of my contemporaries, Chrissie Hynde, songwriter and
lead singer of the Pretenders rock group, recorded her astonishment
at returning to her hometown and finding its landscape dominated
by shopping malls, in her song "My City Was Gone."

But those of Carol's age, or Tommy's, and of course those born
in the sixties and after, have never known a world without the
world within the shopping mall. They did not see these landscapes

go from stands of trees or fields of corn, beans, or wild weeds to parking lots and access roads, shopping-center strips and malls. Instead they grew up roaming the enclosed miniature streets of an era in which shopping (as a former director of Manhattan's Museum of Modern Art observed) had become the chief cultural activity in America.

Until I returned to my hometown I hadn't really noticed this large-scale incursion of the mall, and what I saw of it had made no impression. Now I realized I might be in a peculiar position both to look back into mall-less memory, and to become engaged in the mall world of the present. For I had been born at a crucial moment: in 1946, the first year of the postwar Baby Boom, the beginning of many of the changes that defined the postwar American experience and created the context that permitted—even demanded—the shopping mall's conquest of the American landscape.

I was, for example, one of the first of the first generation to grow up with television. Although I can recall listening to Baby Snooks and Jack Benny on my grandparents' radio, I can also vividly remember waiting all morning for the fifteen minutes of experimental programming a day being broadcast by WDTV in Pittsburgh. Soon I was watching old Flash Gordon and Dick Tracy movie serials that were the beginning of a new institution: Saturday morning children's TV. Then the Dumont network began broadcasting original programming, and *Captain Video* became as much a part of my life as dinner and homework. Pretty soon there were three networks and educational TV to choose from, and Walt Disney—the first "Uncle Walt"—became our television teacher, bard, and magician.

But I can also remember things that linked my childhood to the small-town life of previous generations, like Saturday afternoons at the downtown movie palace watching twenty-four-cartoon shows and a double feature (all for 25 cents). I am just old enough to remember the trolleys that linked local towns, and the driver carrying his wooden stool from one end of the car to the other when he reversed direction at the end of the line. I remember when a Sunday drive meant counting cows in pastures along the two-lane roads we took to the homes of relatives; "visiting" was another Sunday institution, like the family dinner.

It had already been a long time since small towns existed in a complete vacuum. I was well aware of the atomic bomb by the time I was in grade school, when we had regular "duck and cover" drills, and I remember moodily discussing with my neighborhood friends what we understood about the debate over radioactive fall-out during the second Eisenhower-Stevenson presidential campaign. When I was at the age of joining things, I signed up with the Ground Observer Corps, a Civil Defense volunteer group that was supposed to scan the skies for enemy bombers, before intercontinental nuclear-tipped missiles made that a laughably futile exercise.

Of course, as one of the first Baby Boom children, I was myself part of a great catalyst for change in the era of postwar prosperity. As infants, our numbers helped create suburbia; as youngsters, we needed huge new schools; as teenagers, we made the car and the highway our home. The culture followed our progress, as in many ways it still does.

When I returned to Greensburg and began wandering through the new world of Greengate Mall, it seemed clear to me that television, suburbia, the Highway, the Baby Boom, and the Bomb had all prepared the way for the mall—had even conspired somehow to create it. It was an intuition more physical than intellectual at first; just the way the mall sat on the landscape, the way it looked and felt inside—the way it *glowed*. I felt that somehow, for good or ill or quite possibly both, *this* was *it*, the embodiment of it all. The aura of something that's been *perfected* was so strong—the mall seemed to be the fruition of so many of the prophecies, promises, dire warnings, and false starts that I could remember. I couldn't analyze it yet, but I was captivated by the idea: The mall was where all the postwar changes were tied together. It was the culmination of all the American dreams, both decent and demented; the fulfillment, the model of the postwar paradise.

But what *is* it? I thought that maybe a person like myself, straddling the cusp of change, should take a crack at finding out. So in a sense I was dispatched from Carol's shrieking cave of electronic storms by her blithe acceptance of an America I had not seen, to begin my own mall odyssey, to boldly go where few writers had gone before: into the heart of mallness.

Before I traveled in the great American spaces, I would begin here at home in a journey through time. I would seek the mall's essential nature before looking for its manifestations and elaborations across the land, its greater impact and meaning; its future, and ours.

Mallingering

If you had to pick one thing that would typify civilization in the U.S. in the twentieth century, a frontrunning candidate would be the suburban shopping mall.

—Tom Walker, business editor
of the *Atlanta Journal*

On low-clouded nights in Greensburg, Pennsylvania, there are two glowing strips in the sky. The one in the west, which is orange, hovers over Greengate Mall. The one in the east, which is white, is the aureole of Westmoreland Mall. These are the signatures written across the darkness, signing the decree of Greensburg's fate.

On a Friday evening, for instance, the crowded flow of cars on Route 30 edged gently into the off-ramp at Westmoreland Mall. The streams of paired white lights cut into the twilight as the cars wound around the perimeter of the parking lot, heading for separate destinations in the wide expanse of asphalt. In the dim light dispersed from high stanchions, the chuffing and coughing of engines stopping and the last blinks of headlights winking out yielded to the smaller sounds of footsteps and muted voices, as people walked quickly through the cool air and the overwhelming quiet.

Inside the mall it was Michael Jackson Night. He wasn't going to be there, of course, but one of the many Michael Jackson look-alikes fanning out to malls across America was on the center-court stage, with the wet-permed hair, the red-and-black jacket, and the silver glove, duplicating the dance moves from the Jackson videos. A crowd watched from both levels, girls screamed, and a few younger children thought they were seeing the real thing. Meanwhile, the National Record Mart was playing the Jacksons at full volume, Camelot Music displayed the albums and videos, clothing stores had racks of the appropriate fashions, the bookstores had the Jackson bios and picture books, and even a furniture store had a wooden Michael Jackson dummy out front holding a sign that said TRY AND BEAT IT—IT'S A THRILLER.

As I got into the foyer at the main entrance, two teenaged girls who seemed to be leaving did an about-face when they saw two of their friends entering behind me. "God, we've already been here *three hours*," one of them cried. The small court just inside this entrance is where the teenagers first congregate; it's where the swarm gathers, buzzing and swirling with the smell of sweat and hot cologne, the hive in heat. Tonight it was as crowded as a high-school hallway outside the gym at half time of the biggest basketball game of the year.

A little further into the mall itself, two boys were quietly talking about their body-building progress, while one girl sharing a bench with another suddenly shouted emphatically, "I *hate it* when people do that—I *hate it*!" A mixed group of teens in a shifting circle listened to a girl say to a bemused boy, "I *never* said that about her. What did she say about me?"

I made my way past the spectators at the second-level railing around center court who were jostling the card table filled with literature on abortion rights and black women in history, sponsored by the National Organization for Women. Two women were sitting there patiently while people bobbed their heads against the ERA NOW! balloons, trying to get a better look at the dancing clone below.

I stopped at the National Record Mart, where a friend of mine had recently become the store manager. "One kid who works here told me why he likes the mall," Jim said. "It's because no matter what the weather is outside, it's always the same in here. He likes that. He doesn't want to know it's raining—it would depress him."

Hearing this, another teenaged boy who worked there added,

"It's better for looking at girls, too. They aren't all bundled up in coats and stuff even in the winter."

I told them that Bobbi (a friend of Jim's and mine who worked in one of Westmoreland women's clothing shops) told me she was convinced the glass doors at the mall entrance are purposely tinted dark so that it always looks gloomy outside, and customers will decide to stay inside the mall.

The young clerk looked amazed. "We have paranoid friends," Jim explained. On the other hand, it was true that I'd just heard a disc jockey on the radio say, "Outside it's cold and rainy—a great day to spend at the mall." Then he announced the malls where other DJs from his rock music station were hosting promo parties.

I walked toward the other end of the mall, past two older men sitting on a bench in front of the organ store requesting their favorite tunes from the woman playing the display model closest to the doorway, as teenagers passed by, worrying aloud about their popularity. I trotted down the stairs at Kaufman's department store to my favorite place in Westmoreland Mall. It's just under the stairs, where a bench is built into a planter in a kind of sunken patio, a few steps below the mall court. There is a static lawn-sprinkler fountain sending thin layers of spray into a small pool that reflects elements of surrounding light; the silver rods of the sprinkler parse the red neon from the Radio Shack logo with a diffusion of blue from Command Performance. The bricks around it are tinted an oddly glowing shade of dark red. Green branches of small trees hang over the bench, and above it is a skylight, one of the few sources of natural light in this mall. The place is clearly designed to be a kind of retreat, a cool nook away from the bustle, and people sit there silently, as if no one could see them. It is strange that such a small space could seem so set apart, with an aura of peace and isolation, like a garden. It is the best place in the mall to read, and I was not the only one who sought it out for that purpose.

Farther down the first level a buxom middle-aged couple was walking blandly down the court, wearing identical camouflage battle fatigues, complete with berets. The only difference was that he wore combat boots and she wore running shoes. Two girls were sitting on a bench positioned where they could hear music blaring simultaneously from Camelot record store and through the two-way acoustic suspension speakers on sale at Radio Shack next door: ZZ Top mixing with Paul Simon singing "Still Crazy After All These Years."

There was a Friday-night crowd in the court in front of the three-screen cinema, which at Westmoreland is contained within the mall itself. Kids streamed out of the theater lobby, heading for hamburgers and Cokes at Lums, while the older dating crowd checked the movie times. Westmoreland has two game arcades and more restaurants than Greengate, so entertainment is more of a factor here. That makes Westmoreland the mall of choice for family excursions on the weekend—everyone can go to the movies, either the same film or different ones, with the kids making up the extra time at the video arcades, or their parents with shopping. In fact, a divorced father I knew often brought his daughter here during his weekend visitations. He could take her to a movie, have lunch, and buy whatever guilt-gifts he could afford, without wasting time and energy on driving, parking, and getting in and out of cars and coats.

Westmoreland is the newer of the two malls, slightly larger than Greengate and done in the style prevailing in the late seventies—dimly lit dark-brick tile and wood and nostalgic globe lights, contrasted with gleaming high-tech fixtures and a shiny glass elevator as its centerpiece. Westmoreland also has a strip center out back, with a supermarket, Murphy's Mart, and other stores that supposedly have more of a quick-purchase, in-and-out clientele. The enclosed mall is for more leisurely shopping—that, at least, is the theory that now prevails in the mall industry.

Greengate had opened a decade earlier; in the style of an earlier age, it had a supermarket inside it for a long time, and still contains a Murphy's. But Greengate has changed with the times, too. There is a satellite strip center now, and a cluster of buildings out back that houses its cinemas, a bank, offices, a Lady Venus spa, and a V.I.P. nightclub. Because Greengate had been around so long, it had the greater claim to community loyalty, and it plays up that image. Westmoreland was sponsoring more community events than it used to, especially those of a show biz kind, like the Miss Pennsylvania pageants, personal appearances by soap opera stars, and the regional scholastic cheerleading competitions, where junior-high and high-school girls could be rated by university experts on appearance, cheer execution, creativity, and difficulty, and be introduced by a television game-show host. But Greengate was still "the mall" to many people.

Greengate is only a couple of miles down the highway from Westmoreland Mall, on the other side of Greensburg. Inside on this

Friday evening, the parade into Greengate began in the fluorescent latitudes of the side-court entrance. Here, every kind of western Pennsylvania citizen that it is possible to assemble or even imagine poured into the mall in their life-costumes: business suits, or overalls and factory-logo baseball caps, frilly blouses and buckskin jackets; in high-heeled shoes, work boots, ballet slippers, and sneakers. The stream clotted briefly outside the video game arcade, where knots of teenagers pattered restlessly, and then divided to flow around a tall birdcage (the aviary) and the indoor picnic area of the food court.

As soon as they hit the mall itself, a brother and sister separated from their parents and took off, racing each other to the same parental disapproval shouted in different pitches. On one bench near the aviary a three-year-old girl in a red jacket, with matching red barrette in her long brown hair, ate a pink ice-cream cone beside her father, who was eating a yellow one and naming for her the birds she pointed to. To the thinly echoed calls of the birds, a young woman strode past, her blond curls touching the shoulders of her sea-green sweater. She was holding hands with a young man in a gray sweatshirt and jeans; in their free hands they were both carrying their coats.

The wrought-iron lawn tables and chairs of the food court were interspersed with sparsely green trees growing out of metal grilles in the lacquered brick floor. At one table a family of three generations huddled around soft drinks from Burger King; at another a middle-aged man with a loud voice argued enthusiastically with two women, pausing to acknowledge greetings from numerous passersby. "How do you know all these people?" one of the women demanded.

Across from the Stuft Potato, a middle-aged man in striped jersey and black cap, reminiscent of French sailors in old movies, talked quietly to a woman in a peach blouse. An old man with crew-cut hair and a huge belly sat on a bench glaring off into the forlorn blankness beyond Thrift Drugs. A girl of seventeen or so sat alone at a white table leafing through *Cosmopolitan* magazine, chewing gum, and dreaming dreams. At the next table a young woman, maybe eighteen or twenty, wearing a crisp skirt and vest with her store's ID card on her blouse collar, munched fries and gossiped with co-workers, launched on a career at the mall.

A bearded young maintenance man wheeled his dark-blue cart of brooms, cleaning solutions, and canvas refuse-pouch to an empty white table. His girl friend, wearing a black T-shirt with the insignia of R.E.O. Speedwagon, talked to him between mouthfuls of pizza from the Pizza Place. At the farthest table a circle of old men, all wearing hats, passed around sections of the local newspaper, occasionally commenting on the news of the day, what the President and the Pittsburgh Steelers were up to, and what was interesting in the classifieds. Nearby was a mall perennial, a former teenager whose habitual presence at the mall had turned sullen. Once I heard a shop manager refer to him as The Vulture; he leaned against a planter, ready to pounce.

Jeannie is in her early twenties; she purveys monstrous chocolate chip and peanut butter cookies, funnel cakes, and other baked goods at the Cookie Cupboard, one of the small storefronts on the food court. She tries to mitigate the general boredom of standing here all day by keeping an eye on what's going on. "There goes the pharmacist from Thrift, over to the flower shop again," she said. "He's going over there a lot. Looks like the latest mall romance."

But Jeannie's main field of vision covers the clusters of teenagers outside the video game room, and their strategic conferences held near the aviary. She's not too charmed by them, but she remembers it wasn't so long ago that she was among them. "But we didn't stand around like that," she said with evident distaste. "They look terrible." Then she laughed.

"Yeah, I used to come to Greengate once a week, on Friday," Jeannie admitted. "And then I started to come on Saturdays, too. And then I started coming on weeknights—I'd call my girl friend or she'd call me and we'd say, 'Want to go to the mall?' We even started coming right after school. We did our homework sitting on a bench." She laughed again.

"But I know somebody who had a real romance here," she added. "A girl friend of my sister Delores met her husband here. They met accidentally on purpose. He'd seen her someplace and he wanted to meet her but he didn't want to ask her out. So they arranged to sort of be at the mall at the same time. I think maybe Delores was the one who arranged it. That kind of thing happened a lot. Anyway, she met the guy at Greengate and now she's married to him."

But not everyone was there for fun and romance. "I went back in the supply tunnel with the trash the other night," Jeannie said, "and I turned a corner and there was this couple on the floor. I sort of jumped and said excuse me, and I was getting out of there when

I realized that sex wasn't what they were into. They were putting all this stuff they had shoplifted in a big trash bag. It was their stash. I got out of there in a big hurry. I thought about reporting them but they were probably long gone before I even got back out here."

On the other side of the tables and chairs farther up the side court is the place where older people primarily gather at Greengate. They sit at the tables and on the benches there, though some brave the set of benches closer to the games arcade and the kids. There is bus service to Greengate from surrounding towns now, and some is designated for senior citizens. Some older people are here on doctor's orders: the sheltered, comfortable, and consistent mall is ideal for walking. There are so many of them, in fact, that Greengate's management has instituted a kind of walker's club for senior citizens, and gives them certificates for the miles they walk. That's become a fairly common practice in malls all over the country, and some malls even open their doors a little early to accommodate morning constitutionals.

Greengate's public relations director told me once that the elderly are sometimes frightened by the young, especially when they are rowdy or running. I've heard kids complain about old people being intolerant, but the two groups coexist as those who most regularly use the mall for social purposes. In the outside world, each group is usually confined to its own age-segregated institutions and activities, so the mall is also about the only place these days that the old and the young seem to see each other.

On the corner of the side court is Animal Crackers, a card and gift shop that is one of the minority of independently owned stores in the mall. (Greengate, however, has more of these than most malls.) Inside, a young clerk named Lori was helping a shy father select a stuffed animal for his son. Lori's husband works for a chain of jewelry stores. When he was transferred from their home in Ohio to Westmoreland Mall, Lori found a job at Greengate. "I wouldn't want to work at the *same* mall," Lori said. "This is close enough." Meanwhile, Mary Gilbert, Animal Crackers' owner, was writing up an order for a gorilla to deliver a dozen blue balloons to a birthday party. Mary will be the gorilla. Kate, Mary's eight-year-old daughter, drifted back from Murphy's, where she had been visiting the parakeets.

Near the railing around center court, a grandfather and his grandson consulted a bulletin-board kiosk of tacked-up announcements: craft shows, a quit-smoking class, jazz-ercise, the Elks festival, the Seton Hill College evening degree program, the St. Vincent College lecture series on "The Future," a ballroom and Latin dancing class, the March of Dimes Wine and Cheese Gala, a community medical seminar, black lung clinics, a Pennsylvania State Police recruiting poster, and a number to call to report UFO or Bigfoot sightings.

At the head of the escalator a tall blond-haired young man in black velvet jacket and jeans leaned against the railing; it is the traditional spot, held for many years by another long-haired boy until he became embarrassingly older, of the mall regular most likely to be peddling drugs. The uniformed security guard passed him, seemingly oblivious as he mildly walked his beat—the neighborhood cop.

At The Athlete's Foot, a young woman clerk named Marina waved hello. She was not looking forward to the weekend here; her store is in a high-traffic location at the head of the stairs and not far from the corner of side and central courts, so people tend to congregate there. "I just hope it isn't as bad as last weekend," she said. "It was a full moon, and all the crazies were out. Right out in front here, a bunch of young guys locked arms and stood across the aisles and wouldn't let anybody pass. We had to call the police."

Marina stared at the guy at the head of the escalators. "Mall rats," she said. As defined by people who work at the mall, the species known as *mall rat* consists of people who seem to do nothing else but hang out at the mall, all day, every day. Mall employees are also there all the time, not always willingly but at least productively, and therefore in a position to notice and disdain them.

Some mall rats are women, but they are the hardest to spot if they look like regular shoppers, Marina said. Eventually they are seen too often and seen buying too infrequently. They are the mall's kempt equivalent of shopping-bag ladies, except that they must be prosperous and together enough to drive. Most mall rats, however, are young men who may have been regulars as teenagers but somehow never graduated from the mall. One of Greengate's most famous was a former mall maintenance and security employee who lost his job but kept coming back anyway. Another was the aforementioned most-likely-to-be-a dope dealer, who also accumulated a measure of fame for always being accompanied by a very young teenaged girl—always a different one, but always a blonde.

Some mall employees count the teenaged regulars themselves as
mall rats, but if these kids at least go to school and spend some
money in the mall, they may earn a more decorous designation,
like "the mallies." According to Marina's definition, the classic mall
rat is unable to hold a job, and simply comes to the mall as something to do every day. "I thought maybe you were one," Marina
says, "until I saw you taking notes."

On the other side of the second level above central court, two
teenaged girls noticed they were being casually followed by two
teenaged boys; they stopped to inspect Country Hits of the 70s at
the National Record Mart entrance, to let the boys catch up. The
boys lost their nerve and walked past. Looking at cassettes inside,
Chris, not yet sixteen, was waiting for her boyfriend. They were
going to a movie at the Greengate theaters out back. Since they are
both too young to drive and the mall is midway between their
homes, they are each dropped off here. Their choices are limited to
the three movies showing; often they see one they've seen before. I
said hello to Chris; she's my niece.

At the foot of the escalator on the first level, two veteran mall
salesmen from neighboring stores met at the planter in front of
Florsheim Shoes and complained about the condition of the greenery. "I told him about those plants," one said. "And you know
what he said? They grow that way. Can you believe it? They *get*
that way, I told him, but they don't *grow* that way. Those plants are
dead." In Standard Sportswear, David waited on an attractive young
woman who was buying a sweater for her boyfriend's birthday.
David told me later that he asked her out and she accepted. He
claimed this isn't too unusual.

Meanwhile in center court, customers gathered for the evening's
attraction: a Hawaiian Dance Show, apparently sponsored by the
mall's travel agency. Men in checked hunting jackets, women holding blond babies, old men leaning on canes, and couples holding
hands sat on benches and folding chairs in front of the stage to
watch a woman playing the ukulele and a younger woman dancing
in a modest outfit that seemed to owe as much to mainland pom-
pon girls as to island traditions. As the performers sang and danced
and talked to the crowd, shoppers kept passing by, some joining
the audience for a moment or two. Others were confused about
what was going on. "It's *Hawaii,* Ellen," one explained.

The performers asked for volunteers to learn the hula but the
only taker was a not entirely self-possessed man in a blue wind-

breaker who climbed onto the stage and gyrated crazily to the music, grinning at the audience while the performers smiled wan Hawaiian smiles. Meanwhile one of the teenagers watching from above along the second-level railing—a girl wearing a red T-shirt that said SOFT IN THE RIGHT PLACES—did her own dance, a kind of funky hula, for the amusement of her friends. The show ended with the performer's thanks for being invited to "your beautiful mall." The audience applauded, but the reviews by those walking away were mixed. "Not as good as *Love Boat,*" one boy said with a shrug.

There is a strong temptation to concentrate on mall weirdness, since there is plenty of it. Besides the mall rats, there are the mall crazies, like the woman with striking blond hair cut at a severe angle across her luminous forehead who makes continuous circuits of Westmoreland Mall, clinging to the walls; or the middle-aged woman who suddenly stood up on a bench at Greengate, tore off her clothes, and jumped into the fountain. I also heard at Greengate about an elderly woman at a New Jersey mall who showed up every morning with an urn containing the ashes of her husband and father, which she kept all day in a mall locker.

But for the middle-class patrons (including teenagers and the elderly) who make up its majority, the mall has become normal, and by and large they like it. I heard them say why in basically the same terms all over the country, sometimes in response to my questions, sometimes into the cameras and microphones of media doing stories on the mall and my mall trek, or on the phone to radio call-in shows.

"The mall's the greatest thing to bring families together," one woman said. "Father, mother, children—they've got to talk to each other, even if it's at the mall."

"When I have to buy clothes or shoes for my kids in different age brackets, I can come to one place and just go from store to store without fussing with getting the kids in and out," another woman said. "It's just so much more convenient and pleasant."

"I just come to look around and enjoy myself," said a young mother. "To get away from the house, and sometimes the kid."

"The mall is wonderful for senior citizens with no one in their homes and no places to go," said a middle-aged woman. "They can go and see people and be with people. I think that's the greatest thing that's ever happened."

"We meet our old cronies, we go 'round, spend a couple of dollars here and there," said an old man, laughing. "If I have a stroke at home there's nobody there to help me," another man said. "But at the mall, maybe somebody will help me."

"The reason young kids come to the mall is they're too young to do anything else," said a teenaged girl. "Like in seventh and eighth grade we're old enough to be on our own but not old enough to go to like a bar or anywhere, so we walk the mall with our new jeans and our combs in our back pockets and pretend we're hot."

"We come to play video games and pick up girls," a teenaged boy said. "Sometimes the girls pick up the boys but me and my friends aren't that lucky."

"You can sit in the mall and watch all the strange people go by and make comments on them," said another teenager. "Everything's there—the movies and stuff, and all your friends are there."

"I come to the mall to walk around and get some exercise because I have a heart condition," said a middle-aged man. "But also to keep my wife company, so she doesn't spend too much money."

"Usually you meet somebody," said another middle-aged man. "Some days you meet three or four people, some days nobody. Sometimes I meet somebody I haven't seen in ten, fifteen years."

"Walking around," said a young man, holding his girl friend's hand. "Yeah," she said. "We like to walk around."

That the mall has become not only normal but essential is illustrated in a somewhat crazy way by my favorite Greensburg mall story. It was just a small item in the Police Blotter of the local newspaper, but it said everything. A woman shopper was abducted from Greengate Mall by a young man with a knife, but at a stoplight a few miles away she jumped out of the car and escaped unharmed. Her teenaged assailant fled, but nevertheless he was caught the very next day. This quick triumph of justice was accomplished because the very next day he went back to Greengate Mall and so did the woman he kidnapped. She spotted him, alerted a security guard who called the state police. Since both perpetrator and victim had returned so promptly to the scene of the crime, the police got her identification on the spot, and took the guy away.

But even on a Friday night, for all the fun, romance, craziness, and crime, most of what the mall is about is buying and selling. So through all the entrances the parade continues, as the customers come marching in to the infectious beat of products: the dads shrugged into flannel shirts and down vests, the moms munching yogurt cones, followed by clutches of fiber-filled kids . . . the stringy sophomores in letter jackets and the girls in corduroy gaucho skirts, harness-style boots, and acrylic knit sweater-coats, out on shopping dates . . . the wandering gangs of teenaged girls with identical post-Farrah Fawcett blowy-curl permanents in every imaginable shade . . . the blank-browed men in three-piece suits of polyester or natural blends, their eyes focused somewhere above the crowd . . . the smartly suited businesswomen, their squints ticking off an invisible shopping list, their heels clicking to an internal drummer on the terrazzo tile. . . .

They are all here at the malls, moving brightly through the big bazaar and making the bleep-blip-bleep cash registers sing, and the brap-clack-clack-brraaap money processors burp with satisfaction, ringing up all those electric woks, Coleco Arcade microprocessors, Atari space games, Watta Pizzeria electric pizza-makers, Marie Osmond fashion dolls, tube sox, smoke detectors, leisure slippers, champagne charmeuse tucked-front wing-collar blouses with matching parachute pants, wicker-look bench hampers, microwave popcorn poppers, time/date readout ballpoint pens, black leather bomber jackets, cable knits, sherpa-lined Trailblazers, Star Wars digital wristwatches, Barbie Disco radios with special seat for Barbie, handbags "crafted from the finest man-made materials," and ceramic jars of Aramis Muscle Soothing Soak that carry the inscription: "Life is a joy and all things show it/I thought it once but now I know it!"— only $22, soak included.

Coming Home

I was crossing the court in front of the automated teller machine at Greengate Mall when I ran into Vince, a man in his seventies who had been part of the lives of three generations of my family. I hadn't seen him in years, but that I saw him at the mall wasn't a complete surprise. Already I was getting used to running into people there. At Christmastime in particular, the mall could be literally like a dream, a blurred and crowded chaos out of which suddenly emerged bright figures from several unrelated parts of my past and present. People I hadn't seen in a long time waved and spoke with the resumed familiarity of another purpose and experience we were now to have in common—maybe we weren't going to school or running around together anymore, but here we were at the mall, in our united states of shopping.

Vince and I had coffee together at his favorite place, the lunch counter at Murphy's. "They make it the way I like it," he said. "Not too strong." Vince was a tailor, and for his last several years of employment he'd done alterations in the men's department at Horne's in Greengate mall. He'd retired a few years before, but he still came to the mall for an hour or so almost every day. "It's like therapy for me," he said. "I have friends here. Sometimes I don't see anybody I know but lots of times I do. You'd be surprised. The other day I talked to two couples I hadn't seen in years. Sometimes I go around to all the stores where I know people. I make the rounds from one end of the mall to the other. I don't go into Greensburg. There's nobody there I know," he added, grimacing to indicate that the kind of low-life old guys who hang out downtown are not the kind he is used to knowing, or would want to know.

Vince was one of three friends from a mountain village in Italy who left for America together just after World War I. One of the others was Ignazio Severini, my maternal grandfather, who was also a tailor. They all moved to Greensburg, a town of some 16,000 inhabitants then as now, layered on rolling hills about thirty miles east of Pittsburgh, toward the Laurel Mountains, foothills of the Alleghenies. Other Italians were already here, including many from their village of Manopello—enough, eventually, to build one of many local ethnic clubs and mutual-aid organizations of Irish and Eastern Europeans as well as Italians.

Vince and my grandfather got work, saved money, and sent for their wives and children. Throughout the next half-century their families remained close, and I can remember many Sundays when we all gathered at my grandparents' house. When my grandfather died suddenly on a summer Sunday in 1966, Vince was one of the first to come to the house—he had already been planning to visit, because it was the anniversary of the day he and my grandfather had arrived in America.

Over several cups of coffee, Vince told me stories about parties he went to with my grandparents when they were young, vacations they took in the forties and fifties, and about my mother as a young girl. He talked about his own family, his views on life and death, and he related the story of the one mystical experience of his life, which he said he had never told anyone but his priest. I realized that after knowing him all my life, this was our first adult conversation. It was happening in the neutral intimacy of the mall.

The mall was not part of my past, but Vince was. That past was part of what I was doing back in Greensburg. After campuses and cities, writing and editing for Baby Boom weekly newspapers and national magazines, I was going to be around town for a while, to write on my own in inexpensive isolation. But I also wanted to see what had become of my little town. Very quickly I began to feel like the character in the movie *Coming Home* who tells Jane Fonda: "I went back home once. There was nothing there. They tore down my past and put up a shopping center."

It wasn't quite that bad in Greensburg yet, but the town was clearly different. Of course, it had changed several times before. Greensburg began as a colonial settlement in the last county in America to be established by the British, and the first county court west of the Appalachians. The town was incorporated in 1799, and named after Nathanael Greene, the Revolutionary War general in whose command many of the town's soldiers had served.

Greensburg was a town of inns and taverns, the midpoint of a two-day ride on horseback from Fort Ligonier west to the smaller settlement of Pittsburgh on the road opened by Colonel Henry Bouquet and the young George Washington. Later, thanks to a new state road that passed through it, Greensburg became the seat of Westmoreland County when the original courthouse a few miles away was burned down by Indians.

Nearly a century later the railroad was transforming America, and some old towns were dying while others sprang up overnight. But the railroad routed through Greensburg and made it a principal stop, so the downtown did not die. It boomed as never before. A magnificent new train station was built, and the coal and coke of western Pennsylvania fields and ovens chugged out, while passengers and prosperity tooted in. From the turn of the century through the Roaring-Twenties, Greensburg grew quickly and Main Street was the center and the crossroads of the county's social, political, and business activity.

My grandfather's first job in the New World was in a tailor shop across the street from the train station. Greensburg's two best hotels were built nearby. Things slowed down but didn't stop in the Great Depression, and by the 1940s the downtown glittered. The train station was busy and even glamorous, with big bands like the Glenn Miller orchestra arriving to stay at the Penn Albert Hotel and play in its Crystal Room, or the nearby Coliseum ballroom.

The downtown that I remember from my childhood in the 1950s was still the center of commerce, not only for Greensburg but for what was still one of the larger and more prosperous counties in Pennsylvania. Main Street had five department stores then: a large Sears, a smaller J. C. Penney, and three locally owned stores. A. E. Troutman's, which had opened on Main Street in 1897, was the largest department store in the county. Troutman's was at its height in the early 1960s, when it filled a six-floor building and an appliance annex across the street. The four-story Bon Ton opened in 1925 and was refurbished in 1949, when a Main Street landmark of my youth was added: a neon sign that hung over the sidewalk, vertically spelling out BON TON, with a clock in its first "O" and a temperature gauge in the second. The third department store of local origin was Royer's, the newest and most fashionable, with an art deco facade and (of particular fascination to children) a pneumatic tube system that shot sales slips up and across the ceiling. Whenever anyone of my age recalls Royer's, they invariably remember the swoosh and clatter of secret messages sent through those tubes.

My mother shopped in all these stores, and as a child I walked around in them with her, and into the small shops, restaurants, and lunch counters on Main Street and surrounding avenues. My father worked on Main Street, at the Singer Sewing Machine store, and became its manager.

Soon I was in town on my own, walking to Main Street from home or school. I spent time at the public library, first in the children's room, then sneaking into the adult stacks. The department stores were good for pranks and fooling around, but the five-and-tens were where my friends and I did our actual commerce, which principally involved model airplanes—shopping for red Messerschmitts and silver F-100's and black Marauder jets in Murphy's basement, and buying airplane glue and decals. We bought our hamburgers and vanilla Cokes at the lunch counters of these five-and-tens, and at Thrift Drugs—our true "corner drugstore"— which had the special advantage of booths; they gave us more privacy to rig the salt shakers to dispense pepper. We often went there after the double features at one of downtown's two movie theaters.

I can remember an event on Main Street that may well have been its final moment of mass glory. It was a time when the city buses still ran twice an hour, and county buses linked surrounding towns. My guess is that it was in the mid-1950s. It was Old-fashioned Bargain Days, and the sidewalks of Main Street were packed with people. They spilled over the curbs and along the edges of the bumper-to-bumper traffic. People were lined up to buy hot dogs and soft drinks at 1910 prices from clerks dressed up in period costumes. Boards were placed on the concrete sidewalks, in order, I suppose, to simulate the wood sidewalks of that 1910 era, which some scholars call the apotheosis of the American small town and the source of most of our nostalgic images of small-town life.

The feeling of that day was magical, not only for its fantasy of a time gone by but for the sheer spectacle of the crowd itself on this otherwise familiar street. I never saw a crowd like that on Main Street again; I never saw anything like it in Greensburg at all . . . except now, every Christmas shopping season, at Greengate and Westmoreland malls.

This time the changes had circumvented Main Street—that was the crucial difference in the post-World War II period. It meant the town had lost its heart. For the Main Street that I traversed countless times had been the center of everything here long before I walked along it. Federalists and Anti-Federalists had debated on Market House soapboxes, and preachers preached the Great Awakening there. The only elephant present in the United States in 1808 was exhibited in the courthouse square. There had been slave auctions and public hangings on this street; traveling repertory companies had performed Shakespeare; there were vaudeville theaters, and the first movie house in town showed *Birth of a Nation*. All the things—good and bad—that made this a community, year after year, happened on Main Street.

There was an invisible history here, unimaginable anyplace else. Numberless parades had undulated down the hilly length of this Main Street, as town military units marched off to all the wars; or citizens rallied under their party's banner on election eve, or celebrated the Fourth of July and Christmas. People of some importance had known this street: General Arthur St. Clair, the first president of the Continental Congress that elected George Washington President of the United States was from Greensburg, and the park honoring him is near Main Street. Andrew Carnegie, industrialist and library-builder, walked this Main Street as a boy and was impressed both by the railroad that ran under its bridges, and by the library of a prominent citizen who lived in one of its grand homes. American songwriter and folk-song collector Stephen Foster lived in Greensburg for several years.

But shortly after my return to Greensburg I overheard two middle-aged women talking as they left a downtown bar after their Friday afternoon Happy Hour. One of them stopped, blinking as her eyes adjusted to the twilight, and assessed the empty street.

"Remember when everybody came to town on a Friday night, and Saturday, and Saturday night?" she said to her friend. "To go shopping and have dinner and go to a movie? *Everybody* did."

Now the department stores of Main Street were gone, including Troutman's, which held on as a forlorn and somewhat tawdry three floors of merchandise until early 1985, when it closed completely. Most of the old shops and nearly all the restaurants, coffee shops, and tearooms had closed. But there was a brand-new Troutman's (now owned by a national department store chain) opening at Westmoreland Mall. Sears had already moved there; Penney's and Royer's had long since been at Greengate. Two of the five-and-tens had closed, and the other—Murphy's—had new stores at both malls. Many other small businesses relocated at the malls, including a women's store called the La Rose Shop, which left after fifty-five years on Main Street under the going-out-of-business-sale banner of THE FUTURE DECIDED. Even the corner drugstore had closed, and Thrift moved to Greengate. The train station was boarded up and abandoned, and the hotels were empty. The fate of downtown retailing was more than symbolized one spring day shortly after I came back, when the facade of the long-abandoned Bon Ton literally fell onto Main Street.

It's a short drive from Main Street to Greengate Mall, especially if the driver takes the Route 30 bypass just west of downtown. This east-west bypass was built in the 1960s to make it possible to zip from Ligonier to Pittsburgh without passing through Greensburg's downtown. Few at the time thought it was going to affect Greensburg except for the better. There were too many stoplights in town that slowed the efficient traffic flow, and the impatient cars wanting to get through made walking on Main Street more dangerous than before. But now the sad truth was obvious: Main Street had been totally bypassed. People can drive from Westmoreland Mall to Greengate without crossing Main Street at all, and they do.

But it is also possible to approach Greengate from downtown on a small surviving section of the old Route 30, winding up and down the last big hill from town instead of cutting through it, as the bypass does. This road is very quiet now. But it is an instructive route to take in order to understand what a difference Greengate has made to this town.

The effect is even better if you stop at the last turn in the road and walk. There are high trees on both sides, arching a little above the steep roadway. Birds hidden in the branches rustle and chirp. The road had real traffic a generation ago but this is basically how it was: the winding wideness and this steepness through the trees. Even then, this hill was far enough from other streets that at night you could see the stars. Now, instead, you approach the glow.

As you get to the bend and the road slopes downward, there is a sound like rushing water. The trees part and through low branches and above high brush there is the steady, efficient flow of cars along the bypass. And then, as the foliage clears altogether, you can see it: the low white apparition of Greengate mall, with its gray wrap of parking lot.

As a structure it is starkly amazing—to be here, on the edge of this old town and the implacable landscape of cascading hills and ancient trees, just a few minutes from the faded brick and stone buildings solidly weathered into the landscape of downtown, and the neat, compact houses that crowd the hills. Out here the mall's presence is at once indisputable and ethereal—long, low, faceless; floating in an asphalt sea, mysterious and beckoning. How did it get here, to dominate what was recently a soft flow of gently rolling farmland? Was it assembled overnight, like the circus? Or, one dark midnight, did it just settle from the sky?

"Hey," an old school friend said when I was lamenting the sad state of our little town, "downtown was practically dead even when we were in high school. Don't you remember?"

He was right. The mall may have appeared overnight, but the ground had already been prepared for it. Downtown's retail may have been cleaned out by the mall's appearance, but downtown had already been changing. For although Tommy's older brother and I drank coffee in the Hi Boy on Main Street and he worked as a sales clerk at Troutman's for Christmas seasons during high school, we didn't really spend most of our adolescent leisure time downtown. We were going out on the highway.

It was the early 1960s, the precise years of *American Graffiti,* when the highway strip was king. There was no public transportation in Greensburg anymore—the trolleys, the buses had all vanished; even the taxicab company had gone out of business—and everything was dependent on the driver's license, the wheels, the car.

Even earlier, our family drives had changed to include stops at the frozen-custard stand or the pizza place with the thirty-five-foot-high sign on the new four-lane highway, with bright gaudy neon to catch the eyes zooming past. Sometimes these automobile outings included parental perusals of the new cars shining under necklaces of hot white lights at the car lots, or the latest circuslike opening of a big new highway supermarket or freestanding store. The downtown movie theaters were beginning to close but the drive-ins were flourishing—there had been only 300 of them in all of America in 1946, but they reached their peak of 4,700 in 1958.

By the time I was in high school some of the highway restaurants, like the Eat & Park, had become such important teenage hangouts that special auxiliary police had to be assigned to their parking lots on weekends just to direct traffic. In part this was made necessary by changes in the high schools themselves. Because of improved roads, suburbanization, and the huge number of Baby Boom kids reaching high-school age, the trend was for several communities to combine their school districts and build huge high schools that drew students from a large area. So our classmates and friends no longer lived just in Greensburg. To see them—or to try to meet someone spotted in school halls—was no longer a matter of hanging out on anybody's Main Street. The places on the highway became a more natural meeting place than any downtown.

Now the wide multilaned ribbons of white were becoming environments in themselves: The highway was becoming a destination—a place. But it wasn't just a teenage phenomenon. An economic and social life, and now the beginnings of a culture, kept expanding throughout the sixties and seventies, and began to supplant the old town-based way of life. How far this had gone by the time I returned to Greensburg was most dramatically evident on Sundays. The churches on Main Street were still filled on Sunday morning, and the cars of worshipers still cluttered the closed service stations and surrounded the drive-in banks. But after that, it was all highway.

Instead of going home to family dinners, families were lined up to get booths and tables at Eat & Park. Instead of visiting friends and relatives, they headed for the flea markets in shopping-center lots, or the freestanding discounters and specialty retailers, and of course, the malls. As recently as the mid-1970s, commerce on Sunday was unheard of, but the malls led the way by opening from noon to five P.M., and soon Sunday shopping was not only accepted, it was a favorite rite. Meanwhile, downtown Greensburg has been shut tight all day. The American flag doesn't even fly on Main Street on Sunday, but it flies at Elby's out on Route 30. This is the new America—the Neon Democracy.

Over the years the highway places have not only grown more numerous (between Greensburg and the vicinity of the Latrobe Shopping Center some eight miles east on Route 30, there are at least thirty-five fast-food and sit-down restaurants, not counting the fifteen or so at Westmoreland Mall) but they have also become more sophisticated. There is more than McDonald's out there now: There are two Chinese restaurants (one of them authentic) and a host of theme restaurants, such as Sorry Charlie's, which serves cleverly named sandwiches (the Oral Fixation, the Mary Heartburn) and the now-paradigmatic Bloody Mary with the huge stalk of unkempt celery growing out of it. The theme is the sea (as inhabited by television commercial character Charlie the Tuna) and so, alongside its laminated seaworthy booths, vinyl seaweed clings to banisters and there are thin walls of dribbling water, three-quarter-scale life preservers, and portholes to nowhere. Above the exit is a sign announcing that Sorry Charlie's will host parties celebrating Anniversary, Birthday, Divorce, and Graduation.

This is the culmination of the postwar Highway Comfort Culture which has matched the aspirations, obsessions, social mores, and upward mobility of the middle class every step of the way. Quick 'n Easy isn't enough anymore: The Highway Comfort Culture has gone beyond mere hamburgers and wash 'n wear to a veneer of sophistication. So even on the outskirts of a town like Greensburg, you will find the Naugahyde restaurants with ersatz Tiffany lampshades, antiqued mirrors, and the bric-a-brac of mass-produced nostalgia, selling foreign beers and exotic foods that a decade or so ago were the exclusive preserve of big-city life. It's lobster and Löwenbrau out here now, although the lobster is microwaved and the German beer is made in Texas. Even the fast-food places have hanging plants and salad bars; the discount stores have designer labels. The stores and restaurants have dressed up their interiors with motifs that suggest high fashion and *haute cuisine* and sometimes they even deliver it, but they do so while maintaining and refining the same basic delivery system as McDonald's. The highway has created new forms that continue to mold the culture while responding to changing wants and needs.

Looking at the dense thickets of highway development, it's easy to imagine that the mall could have been created by a kind of spontaneous generation—a cluster of cells that inexorably combined to form single superorganism. For it seems almost inevitable that these replicated highway outlets would draw together and unite under one roof in the one-stop oasis of splendor: the shopping mall.

It would happen because the Neon Democracy was sloppy, wild, and, perhaps most telling, inefficient. The hint of its next era of development came with the first shopping centers. In Greensburg, the very first was on the far edge of Main Street itself, outside the downtown. The next was built a little farther away, at the precise location of Greensburg's first public hanging. The third was built farther away still, out on the highway—*out there*.

Out there was the place called the Highway, and everyone was getting into their cars to see what was happening *out there*. For a while the new shopping centers were convenient but not very exciting. They were simple elaborations of supermarkets with a few other stores in a strip. Then the strips got longer, and in Greensburg there was talk about a huge new one opening in Monroeville, some twenty miles away, called the Miracle Mile. But this was just the first step, producing tantalizing images only later to be realized. "I remember my father saying, 'Get in the car—we're going to the Miracle Mile,'" reminisced Francine Costello, a Pittsburgh broadcast journalist and contemporary of mine. "I thought—Wow! I'd never even heard of Monroeville, but the *Miracle Mile*—it sounded fabulous! I guess I expected an enormous amusement park. I thought it really was going to be a miracle, and a mile. But it wasn't either one, so I was disappointed."

But then the Highway got its organizing principle: the enclosed mall, and the whole became more than the sum of its parts. Soon the Monroeville Mall opened, the first and still one of the largest in this area, and this time Francine was not disappointed. "When I went to Monroeville Mall for the first time, I thought—Now *this* is it! *This* is what I expected when I heard those words *the Miracle Mile*."

From a dead start, the number of shopping centers in America grew to twenty-five thousand in thirty years. In the 1980s they continue to be built at the rate of a thousand a year. Among them are a few thousand officially defined shopping malls which, together with even more unofficial hybrids, have been dominating the form and content of the consumer culture.

The mall became the magic place where the Highway Comfort Culture achieves its critical mass. The mall didn't completely clean up the highway clutter—if anything it took the best and left the rest—but it centralized and concentrated the concepts while creating a remarkable energy, putting so much of what the highway had to offer in one place.

The mall also changed the highway by bringing the traditional big department stores out from downtown and the city—which was its major triumph and the final evidence of its legitimacy. The presence of the department stores meant that the mall could provide a relatively sumptuous environment for smaller stores and eventually for deeply specialized outlets that charmed the middle-class customers who prowled the highway in quest of the new and the cute.

Agoraphobia (literally "fear of the marketplace" and, by extension, of all public places) is a personal psychological problem not unknown in Greensburg, especially since the advent of mental health clinics. But when Greengate Mall arrived in 1965, the vast majority of the local citizenry was immediately infected by its opposite: agoramania. They couldn't get enough of the marketplace. The mall courts were constantly jammed, the stores flooded with gawking and buying humanity. According to stories I heard from reliable sources (like my sisters, who both worked there, and my father, who was the first manager of the Singer store at Greengate), the sheer quantity and accessibility of products in such a concentrated space seemed to push some people over the edge. There was a man who suddenly grabbed an entire rack of suits from a Greengate store and tried to run out of the mall with it. Another man scooped up an armload of record albums at the National Record Mart and charged down the escalator with a security guard in hot pursuit; tellers in the Dollar Savings Bank saw albums flying in the air as the two men disappeared on their way to the first level.

No sooner had Greengate settled down and become the normal shopping place for local communities than Westmoreland Mall opened in 1977, erasing the woodlands where Thomas Edison and George Firestone once camped out together on their trek along the Lincoln Highway. Westmoreland boasted a more fashionable array of shops, and there were skeptics who couldn't believe that this basically working middle-class area could possibly support them. Nevertheless, from the day Westmoreland opened to mammoth crowds, the mall attracted its market—the super-coiffed women in skintight fashion jeans and thigh boots or tweed blazers and slit skirts, with smudged cheekbone makeup and glossy lipstick; as well as the men in expensive jogging suits or wool sport coats and razor-cut hair. It seemed that the mall had virtually called these customers into existence—and in a way it had.

One afternoon at Westmoreland, a man who had worked as a salesman in the Sears store there and had previously worked in the old Sears on the highway (which had succeeded the store on Main Street; both now gone) talked to me about the amazing differences he saw as soon as the new mall opened.

"At the old store we'd get a guy who comes in with cow shit on his work boots, picks out a TV, and pulls out a wad of cash," he said. "I'm exaggerating, but that's the idea. But at the mall we got people who cleaned their nails once a week and ordered Harvey Wallbangers at Sorry Charlie's, and they paid with plastic."

But it wasn't just the customers—he saw changes actually happening within the mall. "We had a fashion store here, Hughes and Hatcher, that absolutely set the tone for everyone who worked at the mall. All the salesgirls adopted the same look, the same attitude and posture—it was the Hughes and Hatcher look. It was really interesting to see some of the women who got jobs in the mall—housewives who hadn't worked for a long time or maybe ever, and now for the first time in years they had to dress up every day. They had to deal with men every day—and deal with being looked at by men, and by other women. You could just watch personalities change before your eyes."

The culture that both accomplished this prosperity and gave it its particular character was linked to the highway. Readily available and cheap petroleum fueled the new American way of life; it meant that the automobile would be the key to America's manufacturing might, that petroleum-based synthetics and plastics could create a new mass-production consumer economy. It led to the Highway itself, and to the federal highway program, which literally paved the way to suburbia. The highway also changed the way America moved its goods, where they were manufactured, and even how and where our food would be produced: Thanks to the highway (and to petroleum-based insecticides) the trend toward centralized, mass-production farming accelerated, and trucks full of food connected every American supermarket with distant farms and orchards, thereby freeing nearby farmland for housing tracts, industrial parks, and shopping malls.

But all of it began with a booming economy and its new characteristics. Western Pennsylvania's dependence on agriculture and mining gave way to a larger emphasis on steel, glass, and product manufacturing, with attendant increases in white-collar and service occupations. As workers reaped the benefits of sometimes violent labor-union struggles, more families moved swiftly into middle-class income brackets, accompanied by images of a middle-class way of life. It was generally the same in the rest of the country: By the mid-1950s, nearly 60 percent of all Americans had incomes qualifying them as middle class, a historically mind-boggling statistic. Thanks to prosperity, union contracts, and white collars, they also had the time and taste for spending.

Suburbanization and the Baby Boom created and defined the needs and desires of this culture; the highway finally defined how and where that culture would flourish. The highway didn't need the town, or the cities. They only slowed things down. The Highway Comfort Culture was growing too fast to be contained within old limits. The highway led straight to the new centers of consumer commerce, the place where the good life was on sale.

An additional factor helped shape the Highway Comfort Culture, and changed the psychological map of America as the highway changed the physical. The shopping mall's magic, its transformative power, simply would not have been possible without that other new element of postwar America: television. In the blink of an eye—in just the first five years after World War II—the number of television sets in America grew from six thousand to 15.5 million. Soon virtually every home in the country had at least one. For the small town, TV provided a window on a bigger world, and there was a great hunger for it. The major news that TV brought was about all the neat stuff there was to buy. Television was the first visual, dramatic advertising medium, and it sent those moving, speaking, and singing images into the home itself. The images turned out to be amazingly persuasive, as advertisers quickly learned. While early commercials, derived from radio, were heavy on claims and arguments for a product's usefulness and quality, television commercials soon evolved into minidramas, comedies, and a visual mélange of suggestive images that operated almost entirely outside of logical persuasion.

Eventually television was advertising the burgeoning consumer culture not only in commericals but in the programs themselves. A study made when the average American income was $12,000 a year indicated that the families portrayed on television as average—like the Andersons of Springfield, the Nelsons, the Cleavers—would really need an income of some $40,000 a year to pay for the homes and cars and consumer accoutrements they possessed. The underlying message of TV was that when families chose which products and services to conspicuously consume, they were choosing a particular way of life—this was the way to display their participation in the American dream. And everybody wanted to keep up with the Nelsons.

Television helped to create instant national demand, everywhere, all at once. So there had to be places to buy all this stuff, everywhere, all at once: outlets for televised goods and services that bypassed local differences. Mobility helped to create demand—the Organization Man transferring from suburb to suburb—but even in a place like Greensburg, where people had a tendency to stay put, there was this need to participate in the national definition of the good life.

Enter the Highway Comfort Culture, with its new, fast way of selling products, and the new products brought by national chains to the outskirts of every village, hamlet, and town. The highway network bypassed the filtering process of individual towns; there was no local storekeeper who didn't get the word, or who doubted that people around here will really buy this stuff.

It was a perfect partnership: The national network of the big chain stores offered this array that people everywhere knew about because of those other national networks, the ones on television. The Highway Comfort Culture is everywhere, but it is from no place in particular. It isn't the city, the suburb, or rural America, although it takes themes and images from those places and turns them into its own. It is just . . . *out there.*

The shopping mall completed the link between the highway and television; once the department stores and the national chains and franchises were inside, just about anything advertised on the tube could be found at the mall. The mall provided the perfect and complementary organization for the nationally replicated and uniform outlets of the Highway Comfort Culture. The mall, too, was national, and it was also replicated and uniform in management as well as appearance—the chains knew what to expect just about everywhere. They could slip easily into any mall; one size fits all. Meanwhile, people didn't have to drive all over the highway to find stores and products. They just drove to the biggest parking lot in sight and walked into consumer wonderland.

Greensburg's Main Street became obsolete not only because it was physically bypassed by the highway and its new institutions, but because the new national culture had supplanted the local one with a way of life implied (if not dictated) by consumer products and services. The national consumer culture controls the images of the good life, even of what a small town is supposed to be. Television advertising goes directly into every home; the television networks feed the highway networks. The cars in front of every home are driven to places that are like little dots connected by the highways of the nation to form the picture of a new culture. Television, the highway, the mall . . . what they all add up to is that the small town can't be a small town anymore. It's a twinkle in the highway's eye.

4

King Harry O

When I asked people about how the mall really worked they usually
said, "You should talk to Harry."

They meant Harry Overly, for years the manager of Greengate
Mall and something of a local legend. Just before Greengate opened
in 1965, Harry was summoned to clean its floors. He had a well-
known local maintenance company and his last-minute blitz to get
Greengate in shape for its grand opening impressed the Rouse
Company, Greengate's developer and one of the major mall development companies in the country. Overly was contracted to handle
all of Greengate's maintenance from then on: snow removal, window washing, floor care, and garbage collection. Harry will tell
anyone that his career began with garbage.

In fairly short order Overly became the manager of Greengate.
He continued to impress the Rouse Company and they gave him

other assignments, eventually promoting him to a vice-presidency in the corporation and installing him in their headquarters in Columbia, Maryland. But Harry wouldn't stay in Columbia; he wanted to come back to Greensburg. After their efforts at persuading him to remain finally failed, the Rouse Company relented and gave Greengate back to Harry, although he retained his vice-presidency and continued to have corporate duties. He simply made Greengate his own personal corporate headquarters.

Harry was known around town (and, thanks to the other Rouse Company malls he worked on, around the country) as a character. His name often prompted smiles and anecdotes, but many people—especially current and former mall employees and store managers—were intimidated by him as well. Some people called him colorful, others an egomaniac. Some people didn't smile when they heard his name; their faces turned red with anger, but in tribute to his power they usually kept silent. But everyone was sure of one thing: Few people knew how malls work better than Harry O.

I met Harry in his spacious office, hidden away at the end of the management suite at Greengate. He sat behind a huge desk in his stuffed swivel chair, restlessly swinging back and forth, occasionally toying with a pencil, yet direct and precise in telling how he runs his mall.

Overly looked to be in his fifties, with thinning red hair, a stocky build, and the mischievous expression of a man who seemed happy to be wearing a suit but wasn't really comfortable in one, as if it were a masquerade. His bluntness seemed natural, but I'd also seen him take boyish pleasure in causing a little discomfort, maybe even dismay, with his plain talk, especially when he threw in a string of obscenities—which was reasonably often.

My ignorance of the basic mall system was almost total, but Harry patiently explained how it all worked. The company responsible for building the mall, and signing up all the stores and other facilities that go into it, is called the developer—in Greengate's case, the Rouse Company. All the department stores, shops, restaurants, banks, video arcades, and law offices in the mall are called tenants, because they pay rent to the developer. And rent is not all they pay.

Besides the basic monthly rent, the tenant stores also pay something called "overage" rent, which is a percentage of the store's profits over a certain set amount; the percentage and amount are stipulated in the store's contract with the developer. Every tenant also pays "common area" charges, which are applied to the costs of maintenance and management of the mall outside the specific stores—that is, the areas held in common.

There are other charges, too, and costs that tenants must cover (like the cost of repairing a broken water pipe in the store). The tenants must also adhere to a number of specifications imposed by the developer and must obey an entire list of rules. The reason they do all this, even if grudgingly, is simple: They make a lot of money being in the mall, more than they would anyplace else.

Even before a tenant store goes in, the developer must approve all aspects of design and construction, including storefronts, colors, the store logo, and sometimes even the name of the store (some malls have been known to force tenants to change their names in order to conform to the mall's standards and image). But that's only the beginning. When the stores open, they must contend with Harry's rules.

I'd been briefed by a couple of past and present mall store employees about Harry's extensive list of edicts, which they regarded as practically fetishistic, if not evidence of outright megalomania. Harry, they said, will not permit a handwritten sign to appear anywhere in a mall store. He sends his security people around with an actual Black Book to take down the names of stores violating his rules, especially the stores that do not open promptly at 10:00 A.M. or that close earlier than 9:30 P.M.—even if they violate this schedule by only a few minutes. Violators may be reprimanded, fined, or even asked to leave the mall.

They said that Harry would even try to regulate the private lives of his own staff by forbidding intra-office dating. But there were limits to his omniscience, if not his omnipotence; they smiled with satisfaction when they said that two of his office employees got married before Harry even realized they'd been seeing each other on the sly.

With this background of in-mall controversy, I was a little surprised when, in response to my questions, Harry not only admitted that the rules existed but justified them as basic to the special nature of the mall. They were in fact more than Harry's fetishes; they were corporate policy, and shared to a great degree by other mall developers and managers.

Yes, there is a Black Book and a strictly enforced policy about all of the mall being open at the same time, Harry said, because customer's expectations must not be disappointed. Yes, there is a rule about signs, but it's only a small part of the continuous effort to maintain a standard image of quality and newness. All tenants are required to keep their stores looking fresh and new, completely clean and bright. More than that, they have to keep up to date stylistically, even if that means major remodeling, which the tenants pay for themselves. "We don't want a store that looks old," Harry said.

These and other rules are spelled out in the tenants' leases with the developer. In a Greengate lease I managed to see, the tenant was required to maintain clear windows without surface decoration; even window displays were subject to management approval. The store could not alter its exterior without the mall's permission. It was forbidden to have a going-out-of-business or fire sale (mall stores that would be gone tomorrow nevertheless had to be completely and normally here today). The lease also stated that the tenant store could not sell products inconsistent with the mall's standards of quality or "the moral character or image of the shopping center area."

These stipulations are unique to shopping malls; no downtown has this kind of control over the appearance, products, and procedures of its businesses. But this difference, as I was to see later when I thought about the reasons behind the rules, is crucial to the mall's success.

After the rules are spelled out in the lease, it is up to managers like Harry to enforce them. What made Harry a particular case was his rigor and attention. Sometimes this caused bad blood; he was too authoritarian and bureaucratic and just plain nitpicking for some shop managers.

But others supported Overly's efforts. Shortly after this first meeting with Harry, I struck up a conversation with a young management trainee at one of Greengate's stores who had worked at several other malls before. (He was, in fact, the first person I met who'd never worked outside a mall. He would not be the last.) He thought Overly was a good manager. "He's tough and he sees everything," the young man said. "I've been at other malls where they let things go and it can really degenerate quickly. Stores start accusing each other of lowering standards and ruining the mall. Somebody had to take charge."

The relationship among the stores, and between each tenant and the mall management, can be delicate. Without rigorous controls uniformly enforced, a mall can become chaotic and disorganized. But in turn, management has certain responsibilities to the tenants.

Much of Harry's time (including some of the time I spent with him, when he interrupted our conversation to take phone calls) is in fact devoted to keeping the mall itself running smoothly. This means all the maintenance and repair—Harry's original expertise. He is responsible for keeping the supply lines into the mall functioning and the garbage going out; for keeping the parking lots clear and maintained, the mall's floors clean and its light bulbs bright; for, in effect, keeping the mall looking always new.

Harry is also responsible for the mall's machinery, especially the Heating, Ventilation, and Air-Conditioning system known in mall parlance as HVAC, and in adspeak as "comfort control." Besides keeping the mall comfortable, Harry is charged with keeping it safe. He has a security staff, and procedures to cover acts of crime and emergencies. Beyond these basics, mall management also initiates and coordinates public relations, promotion, advertising, and marketing for the mall as a whole, and with the mall tenants as a group. To the basic bread of stores and the environment of the mall itself, management also adds circuses.

I left Harry Overly's office confirmed in my impression that the mall was not simply an informal collection of stores inhabiting a common building. It wasn't a single business either, like a department store. The shops were owned by others, by big chains and franchise holders and a few local individuals and partnerships.

Organizationally, I decided, the mall was like a federation—only in the United States of the Mall, those who violate the rules might find themselves on the outside looking in. It was as if North Dakota could be kicked out of America for closing too early, or Massachusetts could be dispensed with for not staying new enough. Of course, this federation had something pretty close to an absolute monarch. When I saw Harry Overly walking out in the mall, I no longer wondered why he gave up his office at corporate headquarters in Columbia. Here at Greengate, Harry O is king of all he surveys.

What Harry told me added up to the fact that the mall doesn't just *seem* like a single environment—it is managed as one. But what were the reasons behind the rules? What did they add up to? That was the next step in investigating the mall's nature as a whole and special entity, an integrated phenomenon, a real thing—a new thing, a new force—on the American physical and psychological landscape.

5

Secrets of the Shopping Mall

At this point an event of such glamour and such ra-
diance occurred that you forgot the name all over
again. It could be compared to arriving in an unknown city at night, intoxicated by the strange
lighting and the ambiguities of the streets. . . . At
once the weight of the other years and above all the
weight of distinguishing among them slipped away.
You found yourself not wanting to care. Everything
was guaranteed, it always had been, there would be
no future, no end, no development, except this
steady wavering like a breeze that gently lifted the
tired curtains day had let fall.

—JOHN ASHBERY
Three Poems

A little overwhelmed by the swirl of sights and sounds, by the
information I'd been collecting from Harry Overly and others
about how the mall operates, I sought sanctuary one night in
McSorley's, the only bar at Greengate. McSorley's keeps later
hours than the rest of the mall, so after the shop managers have
banged down their electro-shutters and made their night deposits,
and after the last extraterrestrial teenager has abandoned the video
game panels and phoned home, and all the shoppers have melted
into the night, mall people and other regulars meet and mingle for a
while at the bar, grousing about rents, talking merchandising strategy, gossiping, flirting, and raising a little hell. Some may honor
the Greengate tradition of sliding down the railing of the dormant
escalator on their way out. One spring night, as legend has it, a

somewhat sodden group slid right into an Easter display of live ducks, causing the whole mall to quack.

I sat among the menagerie of mall rats, barflies, and potential duck terrorists, treating my mental wounds with cognac, and then wandered out into the empty mall alone. The mall courts were dimmer than usual (all the stores were dark) but there was enough light for the maintenance crew to clean the floors and empty the refuse containers. They even kept the piped-in music on; they Muzaked while they worked.

I sat on a bench on the second level and looked across the court. Since the lighting was different, the court looked different. Green-gate's basic layout is the model of the American shopping mall: It is fully enclosed, with two levels, three big department stores, and about a hundred shops, services, and eating places. The large central section has a two-level department store at each end and two parallel rows of shops on each level, separated on the first floor by a wide, plazalike central court, with the space above it open to the high ceiling; and on the second level by the railings that surround the central court, making the aisles in front of the second-level shops into a kind of continuous balcony.

Jutting off the central court is a long side court, again with two parallel rows of shops, the food court (the area of tables between fast-food outlets), and another department store at the end. (Because department stores are typically at the ends of the courts, they are often called "anchors.") Greengate has benches and planters in several places, and a central-court fountain that shoots water nearly to the ceiling. It has some interesting architectural touches, due perhaps to the relatively unusual conjunction, for a small town, of a major mall developer—the Rouse Company, known for its innovativeness—and a major designer—Victor Gruen Associates, the premier mall-design firm in the country.

Now when the mall was devoid of people and movement, I could take note of that architecture; I could look at the mall simply as space, and try to see what had been done with that space. I looked at its size and scale. It felt comfortable, intelligible, not overwelmingly large but big enough to be a bit mysterious, to warrant walking around and exploring. I saw the wide shiny courts, the gleaming silver escalator ending in the kind of tile you associate with the outside, in a plaza or a sunny path around a garden. There was a staircase, too; it looked like a staircase that should be inside a building, even a house, yet its wide landings overlooked a broad square and two rows of storefronts along an indoor street. All the elements that didn't seem to belong together were here, nevertheless, in a kind of harmony, with a strange feeling—perhaps inevitable in the emptiness of night—of magic.

Then suddenly I knew why, or anyway I started to find my way to why. My next perceptual jolt was the sudden realization that this space was special, that it could break so many rules and preconceptions because it was completely separated from the rest of the world. It was its own world, pulled out of time and space, but not only by windowless walls and a roof, or by the neutral zone of the parking lot between it and the highway, the asphalt moat around the magic castle. It was *enclosed* in an even more profound sense—and certainly more than other mere buildings—because all these elements, and others, psychologically separated it from the outside and created the special domain within its embrace. It *meant* to be its own special world with its own rules and reality. That was the first and most essential secret of the shopping mall.

Its space is also special because it is *protected*. The mall banishes outside threats of disruption and distraction: No cars are allowed in the mall, no traffic, noise, or fumes. The natural world can't even intrude; there's no rain or snow, heat or cold, no seasonal changes—not even gathering clouds to cause concern. This space is protected so that people will not be distracted or feel threatened; they'll relax and open themselves to the environment, and trust it. That must be part of the reason why very little is allowed in the mall that is larger, faster, or more powerful than a person.

The mall is also *controlled* space. This essential element is clearly implied in the official definition of a shopping center that I read in a publication of the Urban Land Institute, an organization that works closely with the mall industry. The operative part of that definition is: "a group of architecturally unified commercial establishments built on a site which is planned, developed, owned and managed as an operating unit . . ." Unity, preplanning, single and centralized management (and Harry's rules) are the instruments by which the mall creates its special conditions, by which it controls the environment created by enclosure and protection.

The process begins with the mall's careful design: The developer selects what goes into it, from concrete to conceptual statement, from tenants to trees. Then the process continues in the day-by-day management: the control of temperature, lighting, merchandise, and events.

The mall's special space is achieved by enclosure, protection, and control. Those are its secrets, the keys to the kingdom, the whole mall game. Within the environment established by those elements, a mall can contain five department stores or none, one level or six; it can be a brand-new building or deposit itself in the shell of an old one; it can thrive in Alaska or Hawaii, in the desert or on the beach; it can put in skating rinks and roller coasters and historical markers; it can be as small as a garage or as big as a country, and it will still be a mall.

These are also the elements that make the mall an extremely efficient and effective selling machine—but that is a subject for the daytime. At night the mall reveals other implications that contribute to its selling success; but they are also intriguing to consider on their own. For when you have a space that you have separated from the outside world, and the ability to create your own world inside, governed by your own rules, what you have is the ability to make magic. You've got yourself a house of fantasy.

For after all, isn't this sense of separated, protected privileged space common to the special worlds of history and myth, from the castles and walled cities of medieval Europe and the Forbidden City of China to the enchanted wood, the city in the sky or under the sea, the Shangri-La in the mystic mountains of fantasy? These are the necessary conditions for magic places apart from the ordinary world: through the looking glass, up the beanstalk, down the rabbit hole, off to the Emerald City. Such magic places may also be separated by time (whether places that time forgot or places in the far future or the distant past accessible only by time travel) and by a combination of time and space (as in the *Star Wars* saga—"long, long ago in a galaxy far, far away . . ."). So it is no wonder the mall is full of themes and suggestions of the past and an intergalactic future.

But of course the mall is not completely inaccessible from the real world—in fact, it's convenient, with plenty of free parking. It is instead a special space within the usual world where the imagination is given strong suggestions for fantasy. And there is a model for that kind of environment.

I saw that, too, on this night in the empty mall, as I stood at the second-level railing and looked down into center court. I saw the white pools of light, the areas of relative darkness, the symmetrical aisles and gleaming escalator, the bracketed store facades, the sudden strangeness of live trees and plants indoors. It was as if I were standing on a balcony, looking down on a stage, waiting for the show to begin.

That was it. This is theatrical space. The mall is a theater.

At Greengate the theatrical element is fairly explicit. Over the center court are a series of arches—a subtle proscenium—lined with double rows of white lights in marquee array. These lights also surround the cupola over the landing of the center stairs, and are incorporated into the design of many mall stores. In comparison to downtown, the stores are brighter and glitzier; even the banks, staid and sturdy on Main Street, are sprightly and open at the mall. On Halloween, the vice-presidents and loan officers dress up as ghouls and goblins, and on the mall's Country and Western Days the tellers wear cowboy hats. The mall environment is itself a magic theater—trees grow out of the tiled floor! Plants flourish without sun or rain!

But even before the theatrical effects, the conditions for theater are set by design and management. For a space to be a theater, the outside rules of time and space must be banished. The mall keeps out such reference points—not only its windowless enclosure but its very uniformity (one mall resembling another) means it could be anywhere. It is placeless. Many malls banish all sense of time by eliminating clocks, and although Greengate has a large but unobtrusively decorative clock above center court, it neutralizes time by controlling light and sound—morning, noon, and night, they are the same. The mall doesn't allow the appearance of aging—the stores are forever new in an environment that is forever now. It is timeless.

The mall is kept squeaky clean, the stores bright, the fountains gushing, the greenery fresh—or at least those are management's goals. The effect is one of almost unreal perfection. Moreover, this continuous, flowing environment with no reference to the outside—this sense of a special world—permits a kind of unity of experience within an effortless enclosure that is something like the classical theater's unities of time, place, and action. It's all here, now. The mall concentrates the drama, suspends disbelief.

For theater, after all, is largely a matter of light and darkness. The mall at night suggests this most strongly. The idea is to darken all distractions and to focus audience attention with light. For the mall, the process begins with excluding the outside in order to concentrate on what is happening inside. To do that, the basic environment must be created and maintained. The audience must not be distracted; it must be lulled into receptivity by a comfortable, sweet neutrality.

Then comes the shaping of what is in the spotlight, what's on the stage. For once the mall's space is enclosed, protected, and controlled, it can be further designed to create almost any fantasy within it. Like a theater in which *King Lear* might be followed the next night by *Camelot* and the next by the Jacksons in concert, the mall is a Never-Never-Land that says let's pretend. What is pretended can be virtually anything. The mall is, in a word, malleable, and that becomes another key to its success.

There are essential differences between theater and the mall, too; between the kind and intent of the fantasies created in each. But the similarities were fascinating as I gazed out over the mall: silent and still, with its dramatic lighting, its props and staging, and the costumed mannequins in store windows. It looked liked a stage anticipating the play, a movie set on down-time, waiting to be brought alive.

6

Mousekatecture on Main Street

So much for the theater—what is the show? Greengate Mall looks like a set for many potential plays, movies, and television shows—a little *Our Town,* a bit of *High Noon,* a touch of *Star Wars,* a piazza from Fellini thrown into an atmosphere out of *Ozzie and Harriet,* as well as a little of *The Twilight Zone* (or maybe a lot). But what is the central image that pulls all these other images together?

Pondering this problem at home, I happened on help. I saw a tiny wire-service story in the local paper, not much more than a filler in a page of advertisements. It was about how shopping malls were becoming community centers. By now that wasn't news to me, except perhaps that it was happening elsewhere and to an impressive extent. The article quoted a few mall industry people, a public relations director or two, and one writer. His name was Ralph Keyes, and the quote selected was from his book *We, the*

Lonely People. "Malls aren't part of the community," he wrote. "They are the community."

That was a pretty strong statement. Keyes evidently also saw something special in malls, something that made them more than shopping centers. I got in touch with Ralph Keyes, and it turned out that although his interest in malls began when he was a reporter for *Newsday* on Long Island, he now lived across the state of Pennsylvania from me, near Allentown. He was kind enough to send me a copy of his book and an earlier article he'd done on teenagers at Walt Whitman Mall on Long Island.

He also put me in touch with Richard Francaviglia, a young professor of geography at Antioch College. Geography is one of the old disciplines (like landscape architecture) that studies such new phenomena as the organization of cities and the nature of theme parks, phenomena that have escaped or transcended traditional academic categories. Even so, as Francaviglia told me in a letter, he had a tough time getting his academic colleagues to take malls seriously. When he read one of his papers on malls at a Popular Culture Association convention in Chicago, "It nearly started a riot," his letter said. "Quite literally, scholars were yelling back and forth at each other—and me. It was all very stimulating, but while we were arguing, 20 million people were shopping in malls and generally enjoying themselves."

What Francaviglia apparently wanted to know was *why?* Why were all those people at malls? What were the malls doing to attract them? In two articles for scholarly journals that he sent me, he came up with some ingenious answers.

Two of the now conventional observations about the mall are that, because it has become such a community center, it is "the new Main Street," and, because of the bright array of consumer products, it is a "Disneyland for adults." Francaviglia not only demonstrated deeper meaning in each of these ideas, he showed how they were connected. In the process he answered my question: What is the central image that brings all the mall theatrics together?

Francaviglia began by analyzing "Main Street U.S.A.," the centerpiece of Disneyland and Disney World, the world-famous amusement parks. These parks are, it should be noted, commercial environments that are preplanned, enclosed, protected, and controlled (and therefore might just as well be called "shopping malls for kids").

Francaviglia was interested in how Walt Disney took the popular mythology about small towns and created a brilliant but artificial design for Main Street U.S.A. Francaviglia began by pointing out that there are two basic kinds of Main Street in the real America. The most common kind is the Main Street that is not only the principal business district but also the "main drag"—the road that leads through town. Essentially this Main Street is both for pedestrians conducting business and social affairs, and for cars and trucks passing through. This, in fact, is the kind of Main Street that Greensburg's is—it's part of Route 66, the principal north-south artery, and has a substantial amount of truck traffic rumbling along it for that reason.

The other and much less frequently encountered type is the Main Street that has only one way in and out; the other end of it leads to a town square or village green. So the destination of cars on this Main Street has to be Main Street itself. As Francaviglia pointed out, this is the kind of Main Street most often portrayed in movies and on television, especially when the purpose is to evoke small-town nostalgia. The reasons for that are obvious: This kind of Main Street is quieter and more peaceful; it doesn't have the roar of traffic crashing through town on its way from somewhere to somewhere else. The town square itself makes it even more peaceful, pedestrian-oriented, and probably prettier.

But Disney took this second and rarer kind of Main Street and did it one better: He put town plazas at both ends, enclosing it completely. Furthermore, cars and trucks were banned altogether from Disney's Main Street, and as Francaviglia noted, such clearly enclosed space creates a strong, if mostly unconscious, psychological confidence that no car *could* ever be on this street. It is a toy street, a fantasy, a Main Street of dreams.

So Disney, who had already outdone inventors who merely try to build a better mousetrap by inventing a better mouse—the sweet, lovable, suburban-head-of-household Mickey Mouse—now evoked small-town nostalgia by building a better Main Street. He based Main Street U.S.A. on the Main Street of Marceline, Missouri, as it was when he was a boy growing up there. But besides enclosing it, he encased it in the mistiness of memory. Part of Disney's genius was his ability to make fantasies concrete, and he did this with Main Street U.S.A. by improving on reality.

Marceline's Main Street had been (in Francaviglia's words) ". . . rutted and rilled and horse manure helped turn it into a soupy quagmire in wet weather. . . . Gaunt telephone poles with many cross arms, rather than trees, bordered the sidewalks." But Disney's Main Street U.S.A. was lined with shapely trees, and not only the occasional horse droppings but everything else was cleaned up immediately, to keep this street as pristine as any gold-paved avenue of paradise.

There were also no sleazy bars, dingy luncheonettes, seedy pool halls, or dirty jail cells arrayed along Disney's Main Street. There were only pleasant, clean, colorful, and nostalgic small-town stores which seemed to shimmer with remembered magic.

Disney employed another device to achieve his effects which I found particularly intriguing. The buildings along Main Street U.S.A. are not only better than life, they are smaller; according to Francaviglia, they are five-eighths the size of actual stores on real streets. This scaling-down appeals psychologically to both children and adults; children find the smaller spaces more comfortable and comprehensible—more their size—while the adults, as Francaviglia writes, "are reminded of trips back to childhood haunts; everything is much smaller than one remembers."

Francaviglia goes on to make the connection with the enclosed shopping mall. The rows of stores are set up as on a street, but the street of the mall is also clearly enclosed. Except for auto shows, a car in the mall is unthinkable, and the mall's street is bounded by plazas or courts. Francaviglia claims that so-called pedestrian malls in real downtowns that are created by blocking off real streets never really succeed in subliminally convincing customers that they are safe from traffic. But the mall does, because its street is obviously— theatrically—enclosed and artificial.

Like Disney's street, the shopping mall plans and carries out a consistent design so that the mall's street looks unified, quaint yet familiar. The mall also excludes the rougher elements of real downtowns—no dives or pool halls here—and like the Disney versions, the stores are smaller than stores on town streets.

So the resemblance goes beyond enclosure, protection, and control. It struck me that the basic image the mall delivers—what this stage was set up to be—is a simplified, cleaned-up, Disneyfied fantasy version of Main Street U.S.A. Francaviglia doesn't claim that mall designers copied directly from Disney, but mall people that I met all praised the Disney parks. Still, it's worth noting that Disneyland and the first enclosed malls were being built at about the same time.

Suddenly it seems so obvious, and all too ironic: The "new

Main Street" for Greensburg was not just a metaphor for the mall as the major retail and community center of town. It was literally true: The mall was the new "Main Street."

The mall not only acted like a Main Street, it was designed to be one. But not the real one—an archetypal Main Street, designed to fulfill wishes and longings and to allay fears; it was meant to embody a dream and keep out the nightmares. So Greengate Mall's Main Street was an idealization of Greensburg's Main Street, with just the right touch of obvious artificiality to make it permanently extraordinary. It was also cleaner, dryer, more comfortable, more convenient, better scaled and designed for walking, apparently safer, brighter—and in the final irony, more nostalgically reminiscent of small-town Main Street life. The mall was Old-fashioned Bargain Days, every day of every year.

7

Cosmallogy

The Main Street of Greengate mall confirmed what Francaviglia was saying. The store facades and signs impart a kind of friendly quaintness, a nostalgic peaceful brightness. But not only do stores like Hickory Farms, the Plantation Country Store, or Tobacco Village suggest a sleepy country town in an era before the roar of cars and the hugeness of steel and glass high-rises; so do the scale and design of the street itself. That's why this atmospheric creation can turn Video Concepts, the Program Store, and Radio Shack into the equivalent of the butcher, the baker, and the candlestick maker.

The mall design conveys an image, an ideal, of a small, controllable environment that is quiet, prosperous, and neighborly, where good citizens keep the streets clean and safe and the storekeepers take scrupulous care of their shops and their customers. This may be a technologically controlled kingdom, but Big Brother is invisible behind the friendly haze of nostalgic, suggested, half-enacted dreams.

The mall shops have appropriated not only the nostalgic look of Disney's Main Street but their smaller size as well. This happens to make physical sense here, for with the mall itself providing exterior walls and roof, the shop's structure doesn't have to do as much. These stores are essentially partitioned spaces within a building.

The smaller size also makes economic sense for tenants who need to get as much productivity out of high-rent space as possible. Fortunately, they've generally found they can generate more business in a smaller space than they could on a real street. They can leave it to the mall itself to provide a sense of openness and peacefulness, while the shops create a sense of excitement by squeezing the merchandise together into a continuous crush of color, texture, and product. This contrast is also carried out in lighting—the stores are usually much brighter and brasher than the more demure mall courts.

The coincidence of physical requirements and fantasy-producing design is seen in other aspects of the mall—for example, why mall shops don't have doors. Because of enclosure, they actually need doors only when they are locked up for the night. There is no snow or wind to keep out. All that's really necessary is the locked shutters that most mall shops use. But psychologically the absence of doors makes looking in and entering the store practically effortless. For even more friendly than an open door is no door at all. The entrance positively beckons; it is a surprise and an invitation.

The mall also incorporates other fantasy elements found on Disney's Main Street U.S.A. The mall courts function as public squares, the greenery as gardens and parks—all scaled down to a quaint and comprehensible size. Just as Disney's street eventually leads to Sleeping Beauty's castle, the mall's Main Street leads to the department stores, the consumer equivalent of a citadel of wonders.

The courts are often the most blatantly theatrical sections of the mall, and they serve many fantasy functions. When displays are here they are the public markets or the fairgrounds; when a performance is under way, they are the bandstand in the park. Greengate's major center-court attraction is the fountain shooting water high in the air, as in an outdoor park. The court is large enough to have a plaza atmosphere, with its tiles and terraces, benches and greenery, suggesting a European village square.

There is an innate theatricality about such places; Giorgio de Chirico in particular caught this quality in his supposedly surrealistic paintings in the early twentieth century. Of Chirico, art critic Robert Hughes wrote, "What fascinated him in the squares and arcades of Perrara and Turin—the cities from which most of his motifs came—was not their solid architectural reality but their staginess."

But for all this effective stage setting, there is something at work here that goes beyond clever design. The question arises: Can these parallel strips of stores on a toy Main Street of polished brick really work magic? How can this be such a powerful and attractive fantasy that it compensates for what's missing—like the sky, or a little bit of fleshly disorder? How can people accept roofed-over trees, patently artificial effects, and outdoor cafés that aren't really outdoors?

There is perhaps one more element that explains this acceptance, that accounts for the believability of the mall's fantasy world. The idea began with Ralph Keyes. It was his explanation for why people buy the mall fantasy. "Television," Keyes said. "The mall *is* television."

He didn't mean just that the mall is TV's delivery system: that what TV proposes, the mall disposes. He was talking about the management of people's perceptions of space and reality, the elements that persuade people to suspend their disbelief. *The magic of television!*

The mall is a visual experience. It's TV that you walk around in. "People-watching" is what people do in the mall when they aren't "looking for something" to buy. The images they see in the mall are from television; and how they see and accept these images has been conditioned by watching television.

"People have gotten used to two-dimensional effects, to cardboard reality," Keyes maintained. "That's what they see on television, and they accept it."

In particular, television shows from *Ozzie and Harriet* to *Happy Days* produced visual dramatic images of small towns. They were simplified and cosmeticized: a few endlessly repeated sets, characters, and relationships, all encased in squeaky-clean nostalgia, but since they all appeared complete, in everybody's living room every week, they assumed an undeniable reality. It was all there, scaled down to the small screen.

From family sitcoms and homey westerns to the sixty-second

and thirty-second dramas of commercials, television makes the mall's relentlessy upbeat and minimalist Main Street easier to accept. For millions of urban and suburban viewers, the television image may be the only visual idea they have of small-town Main Street. For residents of real small towns, this Main Street may be equally convincing on another level: It may be what they wish their reality was, and they wish it hard enough to make it so.

Advertising uses this kind of suggestion (as opposed to suggestiveness) even more extensively, and more pointedly. TV commercials try to communicate quickly with a repertoire of visual images that suggest places and the feelings associated with them. They didn't invent all these images and associations, but through repetition they've made a virtual iconography of them. In advertising talk, the image "says" something. If you want to "say" glamour and romance, you "say" Paris, and if you want to "say" Paris with an image, you show the Eiffel Tower. The Eiffel Tower "says" Paris, which "says" all kinds of glamorous and exciting things about the product, and what will happen to you if you buy it.

The mall shrewdly makes use of these perceptual habits created by TV. It "says" Main Street with some Disneyesque design elements and a few props. The same technique is used in theme restaurants and shops. It's relatively cheap to do, and it works great.

What is true of the perception of Main Street is also true of the perception of many other kinds of places, from western towns and sailing ships to grand hotels and space ships: All these places have been seen in movies and on television—and perhaps *only* there. Media images dominate ideas about these places. The mall can make use of these simplified images to create its own fantasies, even beyond the principal one of Main Street.

It occurred to me that perceptual habits learned through hours and hours of television watching may also account for something else the mall seems to manage easily: its incongruities. The mall jumbles so many kinds of stores and services, from brokerage offices to cotton-candy stands, singles bars to interfaith chapels, that otherwise don't go together. But to a population used to seeing a bloody murder followed by a candy-bar commercial, followed by soap opera sex, a religious revival, and a public TV fund drive, nothing much would seem incongruous. Compared to what is shown in sequence on one TV channel, or what is available at any moment on many channels as the viewer switches through them, the eclecticism of the mall has to be considered mild.

The similarities of television and the mall go on and on. Both of them lull and stimulate simultaneously. Watching TV, we can be everywhere without being anywhere in particular. And basically, television and the mall are in the same business: entertainment in order to sell products. Advertisers pay for TV programs so people will watch the commercials, and the commercials themselves try to sell products by being entertaining. In the mall, product sales are also based on how attractive and entertaining the mall environment and its stores are. The mall is like three-dimensional television.

Television advertises attractive ways of life and the products associated with them in its programming, and its commercials tell little stories; the line between programs and ads is therefore often blurred. At the mall, the line between "programs" and "advertising" is almost nonexistent. The fantasy of Main Street is there to sell products. Because that's what all of this—the theater, the sets, the costumes and props—is for. The mall industry even has a name for what it's all about: They call it The Retail Drama.

8

The Retail Drama and the Management of Fantasy

Especially give action its full share;
They come to gaze and they prefer to stare.
—GOETHE
Faust: Prologue to the Theatre

Alte Faust, promotional director for Tysons Corner Center in Virginia, personally dyed baby elephants pink for the mall's Christmas parade. Her job, she told a reporter, was "show business."

I was beginning to search out articles written about malls and to peruse some of the trade publications produced for mall industry people. I was surprised by how many trade magazines there were. *National Mall Monitor, Shopping Center World, Shopping Center Age,* and *Shopping Centers Today,* the monthly newspaper published by the International Council of Shopping Centers, itself one of the largest trade organizations in America. This was the mall industry talking to itself, and I was intrigued by the abundance of theatrical images.

The theatrical aspect is pretty obvious in the plethora of promotions these magazines described: Rock-a-thons for crippled children, Ben Franklin Birthday kite-flying competitions, spaghetti-eating contests, bluegrass jamborees, hypnotists, and petting zoos. The Hudson Valley Vagabond Puppets presented *The Silly Jellyfish* at The Market in Manhattan's Citicorp Center, while the Spruce Up for Spring Program at Paramus Park in New Jersey included tennis and golf clinics and home-improvement shows.

The show business analogies went beyond promotions. Obviously the mall industry itself considered malls to be theaters of a sort, but since these were the people putting on the show, they could talk about their intent. What exactly is the production all about? The mall industry's answer is: The Retail Drama.

"The Retail Drama" is a term actually used in these trade magazines to describe what the mall is doing. The ultimate goal of everything in the mall is to persuade customers to buy. This fantasy world is managed in order to orchestrate The Retail Drama, and the roar of the cash drawer is its ultimate music.

The Retail Drama is a responsibility of the mall itself, not just of the stores, because the mall provides the basic environment that can attract customers, keep them shopping, and bring them back again. "Customers shop centers rather than stores," Robert Bearson, managing director of a business consulting firm, warned readers of *Shopping Center World*. "Loyalty is developed to your center."

Besides maintaining a comfortable and subtly exciting environment with the plash of fountains and the lilt of Muzak, the mall preplans The Retail Drama through the selection of its stores and services. This selection is called "the tenant mix" and it is considered crucial to the success of the show. Because of its importance, not every store that wants to get into a particular mall always does, nor do tenants always get the particular location in the mall they might want. Big department stores can quite often cut their own deals, but malls increasingly try to shape an overall image, or at least skew their tenant mix to their target customers.

An ad I saw said it perfectly: PERL-MACK'S LONNIE KLINE IS "CASTING" HIS NEXT EPIC! the headline screamed, but it wasn't in V*ariety*—it was in *Shopping Centers Today*. The epic that was being cast was Southwest Plaza, a major mall in Colorado. According to the ad, "Lonnie has already cast' Sears, Wards, the Denver, May and Joslins to star in Perl-Mack's next box office smash." The ad featured a picture of Lonnie in a director's chair.

For a mall like Greengate, the tenant mix is more likely to be balanced for breadth, with something for everybody. Greengate is a bread-and-butter kind of mall, serving a mostly middle-class and working middle-class market with a basic array of stores and services, and it is conscious of being a community center. Greengate is where Florence Henderson and the Walton family are supposed to go for shoes and sheets, panty hose and lunch boxes.

Westmoreland Mall—like many malls that go into the area that already has one—is a little more specialized. Its decor is flashier and its tenant mix is slanted toward younger and more affluent customers. This is where the law partners and television news anchors, along with the local versions of John Travolta and Victoria Principal are supposed to shop for tailored suits, designer dresses, the latest in cosmetics, expensive exercise outfits, and video cassettes.

The tenant mix of each of these malls also reflects the geographic and demographic characteristics of their chief customers: Greengate, west of Greensburg, gets much of its clientele from the more working-class towns of Jeannette and Irwin to the west; Westmoreland, east of Greenburg, goes after a more affluent customer in Ligonier in the Laurel Highlands, which was for years the summer home territory of the industrial magnate families of Pittsburgh. Both malls draw from the appropriate groups within Greensburg itself. This division is not simply assumed, either; both malls began with detailed marketing studies, and update them frequently. Both malls also hedge their bets with stores of different appeal. Greengate has Horne's, one of the better Pittsburgh department stores; Westmoreland has Sears.

The tenant mix also has to do with the internal drama of the mall, so the malls strive for variety and completeness too. They also go for the hot trends in mall outlets (the latest retail stores, like computer stores in the early eighties, and the latest fast-food fads) both to keep on top of the market and to promote a sense of novelty and excitement.

Much of The Retail Drama is up to the stores themselves—their merchandise and displays, their management and customer relations. But the mall management continues to organize and prod and keep the show moving; it takes care of the basic environment, encourages tenants to merchandise effectively and aggressively, puts together advertising campaigns and themes, and sponsors special events in the form of mall promotions. Some of these promotions are simple crowd-gatherers; some try to attract a special crowd (families to the school art shows, women to see the soap opera stars); others have a direct merchandising goal, such as mall-wide sales. From Bozos to blood banks, the mall provides all manner of pleasing sideshows and carefully calibrated special audience attractions to lure the customers to the mall, keep them there, and implant the idea in their heads that they had a great time and ought to come back soon.

Other techniques of The Retail Drama are concerned with creating a maximum buying frenzy while the customers are treading the courts. In The Retail Drama, it seems, the customers are not only the audience; they are the action and the actors. The mall environment itself gives them the script. All the mall's a stage, and they are but players in it.

Apparently it's very consciously done. Another advertisement in a mall trade magazine says it all in one visual image: a drawing of a pair of nyloned legs, a woman's sleek foot sheathed in a smart high-heeled shoe, but around her tender ankle is a steel band connected to a ball and chain. The legend with the picture says simply, "The Captivated Shopper." The copy (advertising the Shopco Company, a developer based in New York City) begins: "Getting CAPTIVATED shoppers is not simply a matter of luck, but rather a science."

The people who practice this science are the mall's management, and I saw them at work as they created their most important moment of the year: Christmas at the mall.

Greengate was known throughout western Pennsylvania for its elaborate Christmas displays, which saturated the entire mall and turned it into a single Christmas fantasy. Greengate had spent some $50,000 on decorations over the years, resulting in a grab bag of holiday images. The train that children rode around center court, for example, was called the Sugar Plum Express, and there the kids could (according to the sign at its entrance) "learn the true meaning of Christmas from the Wizard of Oz." But this year all the decorations were going to be new, and all tied into one Christmas theme: the story of the Nutcracker.

"This is the first time we've done a completely coordinated theme," said Karen Kozemchak, who, in her mid-twenties, was Greengate's director of marketing, advertising, and promotion.

"We wanted something special this year because we're just finishing a major remodeling of the mall. We have a new floor, new fixtures, everything's been repainted, lots of new lights. We want to bring people in to see what we've done. Also, we want to create a classier image. Our demographics show there's a more upscale market for us out there now. But we don't want to lose our old market either—the decorations came in with lots of purples and pinks, but we're mixing in red and green. This is a very red-and-green area."

"Don't tell him we spent seventy-seven thousand dollars on them," Harry Overly said.

The Christmas season has become a holiday celebrated, more than anywhere else in America, in the shopping mall. Downtown department stores by and large don't do it up as big as the malls now do, and this is where people come not only to shop but to experience the season.

The reason for this, apart from the relocation of community to the malls, is that Christmas is crucial to the mall economically. At least a quarter of annual retail sales and half of the retailers' profits are chalked up in these few weeks. More than a third of what consumers spend during the year is spent for Christmas. The mall environment is expensive to maintain—without a good Christmas, most malls could be in trouble. So they deck the halls of Maplewood Mall in Minnesota with pink angels dangling from the ceiling around huge simulated ice-cream cones spinning over the central court; they hang huge green-and-gold banners at the Sunrise Mall in Massapequa, Long Island; they come donning and blitzing with the Los Angeles Premier Chorale Strolling Christmas Medieval Feast Ceremony in Costume at Promenade Mall in California. And at Greengate Mall, they get ready for the Nutcracker.

Harry led the way to the large workroom where the actual displays were being built. Working from designs prepared by Walter Schwartz of The Design Group in New York City, middle-aged men in green work clothes hammered and sawed, while teenaged girls with bright orange-handled scissors in the back pockets of their jeans applied details to dozens of already completed components that would be assembled into a number of large displays. There were wooden castles, cardboard arches, tubular towers, and oversized boxes swaddled in gift wrap. It was part Cecil B. De Mille, part junior prom.

"We build all our stuff right here," Overly explained. "We usually just build freestyle, but we're building from blueprints this year because the Rouse Company wants to be able to duplicate this at other malls next year. Other centers around here spend as much as we do or more, but they don't have as much to show."

Harry beamed at all the activity and introduced me to one of the men working on the displays who had the size and some of the appearance of John Wayne. In fact, his name was John. "John's been here about as long as I have," Harry reminisced. "Yeah," John said, "but I'm still poor."

Next, Harry led me to center court, where some of the decorations were already going up. The latest addition was the thirty-five-foot-high artificial Christmas tree itself. Harry was going out to inspect it. It was late in the day; the mall was closed and mostly dark, although center court was brightly lit.

Harry looked up and around. "Everything looks great so far," he said to the assembly of management and maintenance staff, and others hired specifically for the Christmas decorating job. "Everything, except for that damn tree."

There was a certain nervous stirring among the assembled, who for the most part pretended to be doing something else.

"I hate that tree," Harry said flatly. "Did you ever see a real tree like that? The branches don't stick out like branches."

He was assured that it would look more treelike when the branches were properly fluffed and decorated, but he was apparently unconvinced. The discussion among the inner circle of four or five moved on to other subjects, but Harry kept returning his gaze to the tree, and sour comments about it punctuated every couple of sentences.

Then Harry began to ask questions about a large decorative golden ring, several feet in diameter, suspended from the ceiling over center court. He wanted to know what size screws were holding it and where they were placed into the support beams and ceiling struts. He asked how much the ring weighed and how the weight was distributed.

"I don't want the damn thing to fall," he said. Everyone assured him that it couldn't possibly fall. The support was adequate for a much heavier load, many times what the ring weighed. The weight was evenly distributed. It had been checked and rechecked.

"If it falls, it wouldn't fall straight down," Harry continued, as if no one had spoken. He kept looking up at the ring. "It would sway a little. Probably it would hit the train track and derail the train. Or it could hit a train full of kids."

By now everybody in center court was standing still and looking up at the ring. Someone else calculated how the ring would fall. It might hit the tree. Or sway into a storefront.

But in fact Overly had already concluded that the ring was more than adequately supported, and with a wave and a final okay—and with everybody else still looking up at the ring—he began to walk back to his office, out of the circle of light in center court and into the semidarkness. "Somebody has to ask these questions," he said with a shrug.

Then in the shadows he stopped and turned back again for a final look. "I hate that tree," he said.

In the management office downstairs, back in the corridor behind the management-office reception area, Harry overheard a discussion between Karen and Stacey Smith, the mall's receptionist and Karen's assistant for the Christmas preparations. Stacey explained to Harry what had just happened: A truck she had dispatched from the mall to pick up a load of materials needed for the displays returned full, but with only half the boxes it was sent to fetch. There hadn't been enough room for the rest.

"I asked the guy at the warehouse how much there was," Stacey said, "and he told me that one small truck could carry it all." Now the warehouse was closed and the rest of the boxes wouldn't be available until after the weekend.

"What did I teach you?" Harry said quietly.

"I should have sent a bigger truck anyway?" Stacey said.

"No," Harry said. "What do I always say? Don't take anything for granted. You ask them: How many boxes are there? How big is each box? Is it big enough for a man to fit in it? . . . You ask questions."

This was another of Harry Overly's functions within the Rouse Company: to groom employees for larger responsibilities in other Rouse malls and for the main office in Columbia. After three or four years of tutelage and raffish abuse—known in the company as "Harry's School of Charm"—they would be ready for bigger jobs. Stacey and Karen were Harry's latest pupils; in fact, in a few months Karen would be moving on.

For now, however, they all had to deal with Harry. But Karen had already managed a modicum of revenge for Harry's mall-treatment. Every Christmas season Harry Overly's house, a rambling ranch homestead on a rural road near Greensburg, becomes a local legend. White lights outline every inch of it, as well as the fences around the grounds and some objects strewn in the yard, like a Christmas sleigh. On the nights before Christmas, a costumed Santa (usually a Greengate employee) is posted at Harry's gate to give small gifts to children in the many cars that line up to see the decorated house, and to take donations for a local charity. Like townsfolk coming to the lord's castle, carloads of people come to his gate every year.

All of this is well known within the Rouse Company. On this particular evening at Greengate, after Harry had left, Karen was told that he'd made off with another box of the mall's Christmas lights for his house. So Karen told me about the corporate practical joke pulled on Overly at a meeting the previous year in Columbia, to which she had been a willing party.

Karen's part in the joke was to make a short film that her co-conspirators would show at the end of the company's conference on mall energy conservation at their headquarters, after all the statistics and graphs had been presented. Karen's film began with a shot of an extension cord being plugged into an outlet at Greengate mall. Then the cord was followed out of the room, winding down the supply tunnel and into the mall parking lot, then across the highway and down portions of various roads, until finally it snaked down a long driveway and was shown being connected to a string of Christmas lights.

The last shot was of Harry Overly's house, all lit up.

"The snow is thinner this year," Karen told the fifty or so people assembled in the mall community room at three o'clock in the morning. "So be careful, because once it tears, that's it." The crew—some regular mall part-timers mixed in with community-college students majoring in retail, and relatives of the mall staff—nodded, put down their soft drinks and coffee, and headed back to center court.

Karen Kozemchak's duties ranged from coordinating market studies and writing radio ads, to counting the number of staples that would be used in a year's promotions. Some malls have two or three people to do what she did. In fact, her immediate predecessor at Greengate had lasted about a month. One morning his resignation was found on his desk and he was never heard from again—he simply disappeared. But for Karen, no time was busier than these few weeks, and these few days in particular. While the decorations were going up, she would be at the mall for forty-eight continuous hours.

After Harry's unfavorable reaction to the tree, Karen began replacing lights and starting the fluffing process, getting up high in the basket of the Snorklelift 40—a big noisy machine that extends a hydraulic arm upward and side to side from a tractorlike cab on wheels. Then the tree lights were tested in the silent mall, causing the fragments of glittery stuff dangling from the ceiling to spangle shadows across the darkened storefronts.

Then out of the shadows the parade of elves began: the boys in sweatshirts, the girls in sweaters and fresh jeans, carrying some of the thirty animated figures from the workroom and stacking them against the storefronts. Then they brought out the huge gift-wrapped boxes—large but empty, so that each elf could carry several of them, and those working at center court turned to see this prodigious parade and smiled.

Then a crew of outsiders arrived to set up the tracks and kiddy train. They were a motley group that usually works for carnivals. One of them was an extremely grizzled man past his sixties, wearing a beat-up logo cap with bill turned up that said CHRISTY'S BAR B QUE and an ancient T-shirt that said 4 × 4 FORD. "You crazy old man!" one of the other crewmen shouted at him at one point. "You put the wheels on backwards!" Karen watched them carefully, nursing a bottle of Squirt. "They're wild men," she said. Yet there was something absurdly evocative about them: large men hammering spikes into tiny ties, like some strange parody of the building of the railroad in the American West.

After the carnival crew disappeared back into the night, the next task was to lay a base of chicken wire over the entire court inside the train tracks. Then a crew of girls began cutting and laying down the Dacron snow carpet, inserting tiny lights underneath to create an effect of snow gently illumined by moonlight.

This work continued after the 3:00 A.M. break. A girl gathered a string of tiny bulbs already turned on; she held them like a bouquet of light. Amidst the strings of lights, two women stapled down the snow.

Then the big displays were installed. By 5:00 A.M. the final elements were being assembled—the flags of starched felt, the hot-pink dusted Styrofoam balls. A boy threw loose plastic snow around the castle and the towers, which were tubes covered with vinyl in shades of azalea and American Beauty rose. One girl was off by herself, very carefully arranging the Dacron snow carpet on a hill of wire, bending forward from the waist with her feet flat on the floor. Her work was as delicate and as seemingly effortless as that supple physical movement, yet she was completely absorbed. And when she was finished, her particular area could not have looked more like wind-driven snow.

It continued on through the morning—25,000 yards of ribbon, 150 pounds of diamond dust, 850 pounds of scattered snow, 4,000 sets of miniature lights, and 24,000 feet of snow blanket. Several crews came and went, working diligently, fighting fatigue, getting silly, getting angry, making friends.

By early afternoon the towers were topped with snow cones, the figures were all in place and animated, and the train was moving smoothly through the displays with its first load of enchanted kids. Already customers were exclaiming and taking pictures. Some participants from earlier crews returned to look at the finished results. A television crew from a Pittsburgh station arrived to film the displays for the Greengate Christmas commercial, using the Snorklelift as a makeshift movie crane.

The light-up of the tree and decorations occurred on the next weekend, followed a week later by the Christmas parade, with the Hempfield High School band and majorettes and color guard marching around the parking lot and through the mall. The parade ended in center court, where the Nutcracker (played in costume by Stacey) and the wooden soldiers cracked open the Nut, out of which emerged who else but Santa Claus.

The pay off for all the hours of effort, all the quiet artistry and gimmickry, all the money and calculation and enthusiasm and care was the ballet of cars at the traffic lights leading to the mall. As Christmas came nearer, there were constant lines on the highway, and lines of parents and children at center court to get onto the miniature train, lines to get pictures taken with Santa on the side court, lines at the pizza place, and lines at the ladies' room.

It's the Christmas Paradise Parade, the Captivated Shopper's mad clanking of her ankle bracelets, the finest hour of The Retail Drama, when the customers go after the Phillipe designer handbags, Pant-Her Coordinates, Bromley opossum-trimmed nylon coats, and misses' White Stag Outerwear, the Oneida flatware and Nikko Ming Tree twenty-piece service dinnerware, the oral water jets, Pastamatic 700, battery tooth polisher kits, energy boots, Crazy Foam, pulsar quartz watches, Fantasy Ultima II makeup kits complete with cell renewal lotion, M★A★S★H identity bracelets, plush-touch velours, Vanity Fair French Flirts, Swiss Army shirts, Maidenform Delectables, personalized blazer buttons, Izod Lacoste nylon bicycle jackets in navy, kelly, or eggplant, blueberry sleepware Jammies Nightshirts in a Jar, Wintuck orlon fisherman sweaters, the Buns Calendar, Ciao garment bags, ceramic pagodas, Intellivision video game systems, and Activision game cartridges, plus 20 percent off all chemical services at Great Expectations Hair Salon, their Christmas special.

Meanwhile, down the highway at Westmoreland Mall, flamenco Muzak plays as people line up at Orange Julius and at the glass elevator that goes from one floor to the other. One of the *Star Wars* sound tracks animates teenagers in Camelot Music, as well as their older siblings, knotted in spontaneous reunions with dimly recalled high-school classmates home for the holidays. The serious shoppers—heartbreaking young women with modified wedged haircuts and perms, their frankly svelte figures in pullover split-neck tops and black polyester-knit flared pants, each dragging three blond kids and a double-knit sloppo husband who looks like he's been drinking beer in a laundromat for twenty years—are spinning through aisles of genuine walnut jewelry boxes with sardonyx Incolay stone tops, Infinity Model Qa speakers with optional pedestals, TV Action News Team dolls, financial planning programs, imitation Christian Dior velours, anti-cling crepeset lounging pajamas, wrap-tie shawl cardigans, electric crock pots, handsome wall dividers, multi-option video games . . . while old men sit on benches in the non-shade of the non-palm trees.

The sheer numbers are stimulating, exciting, from the rarely filled but now overflowing parking lot to the jammed courts where old acquaintance is renewed amid the shopping din. All the elements that the mall manages start to click and the energy takes over—people exciting people in a visual and aural riot of images:

products, colors, light, music, and sentiment, the climax of The Retail Drama.

"It's a madhouse," one customer at Greengate said, not complaining. Another turned from the center court display. "Isn't it something?" she said. "Hurry up," her companion told her. "We've still got two more malls to hit today."

Neighbors in Never-Never-Land

It is when people are toiling and trading . . . that they best reveal themselves and the character of their society. It is when they are spending the money they have earned, when they are feeling easy and relaxed, when they are most impressionable, that the pattern blazes out.

—J. B. Priestley
Journey Down a Rainbow

There isn't an official Christmas parade in downtown Greensburg anymore. For competitive reasons the Greensburg merchants thought they had to have their parade on the same day as Greengate's, but they found that if they had it later in the day than the mall's no one would come, and if they had it earlier, people would watch it and then round up the kids and head out to see the mall's parade anyway. Either way it wasn't adding up to business for downtown retail, so the Christmas parade was dumped as a waste of money. It was left to a group of citizens to organize their own parade.

Still, downtown Greensburg wasn't dead. Main Street had gradually reorganized around the courthouse and a white-collar and service sector, with lawyers, doctors, dentists, accountants, brokerages, government offices, social services, and education, from the business academies to the beauty academies.

Like the structure of the human brain (which piles the new cerebellum on top of the old reptile brain), but in reverse, Main Street changes its street-level facades to the latest fashions in business—the portrait photographers, boutiques, computer and video stores—while leaving the upper floors of old buildings untouched. The faces of these buildings above the street are eloquent reminders of the past: the turquoise art deco facade of the defunct La Rose Shop now hangs over an office-supply store, the columns and arches of the old Masonic Temple now surround a shoe store.

But there is no theme, no packaged charm to this Main Street. It's just a town. It is also filled with townlike inefficiencies. Local politicians and downtown merchants continue to grouse about the malls and the downtown's deficiencies and to engage in the lethargy and squabbling that is normal for a Main Street of independent souls. Solutions are discussed, and some in due time are tried, in that slow evolution that is sometimes known as the political process. Town government and the merchant association simply can't function or respond as efficiently as the single management of the malls can. They also aren't linked to large outside developers and management firms—at least not yet.

Some new businesses try to take advantage of the town's traditional virtues in a traditional way. I chatted with the young owner of a new shoe store on Main Street on the day he officially opened. As we stood sipping complimentary soft drinks at a table laden with a good-luck cake sent over by his former colleagues at Troutman's, he spoke optimistically about combining loyal town customers with the new constituencies who worked or went to school in town.

"There's been a long line of shoe stores in this spot," he said. "That old lady who just came in—she's always bought shoes here, and we're going to try and see that we keep her as a customer. At the same time we're getting in new styles that the girls who work at the bank across the street say they like. We can give personal service. We know our customers. The mall has too many part-timers."

His name was Jack, and his business was called Jack's Shoes. All he said was true, but a few years later Jack's Shoes was gone.

Occasionally, downtown Greensburg sprouts new kinds of

businesses that display the kind of personality that seldom survives at the mall. The Woodshed pioneered a new generation of shops that opened downtown after Greengate's competition had cleared out many of the old ones, and the rents had gone down. Bruce Adamson, its originator and owner, sold handmade and imported wood furniture and, later on, an assortment of playful curios. Another of these shops that brought new products and a new style to downtown was Nature's Way, a health food store that was begun by a young couple as much as an expression of their way of life as a business venture. A third was Animal Crackers, a colorful mélange of cards, gifts, children's clothes and toys, and whatever else Mary Gilbert, the owner, wanted to sell.

I had drinks one afternoon with Bruce Adamson, Mary Gilbert, and Pamela Slezak (who worked at Nature's Way). All in their mid-thirties, they often visited one another's stores and were friends during off-hours. I asked them to talk about their businesses, Greensburg, and the malls.

"There's no future for retail downtown," Bruce said flatly. "Our businesses are just making it. Unless the product is super or special, you can't go on and expand. We're the oddballs. I make toys and write children's stories. Mary has a goat."

"The city won't cooperate," Mary said. "They won't hire a promotional person—"

"—Like a mall would," Bruce said. "Right now the malls provide the essentials and we provide the frivolous. The only way downtown will survive is if they bring in a mall, and they'll take over little stores like ours. Right now some of our customers are going to the Station Square mall in Pittsburgh to buy the kinds of things we sell." Bruce turned to Mary. "I know you don't like malls, but how many people have goats?"

"Everybody I know does," Pam said.

"If I moved my store to the mall, it would be a different store," Mary said. "It would become instantly more successful—more people would be coming in, I'd order more stuff and do more business, but I'd be so much busier. Even if I hired more people, I'd have to oversee everything. I wouldn't have the time to keep thinking of new things, like the Valentine deliveries. It wouldn't be as much fun."

"You'd triple your business at the mall," Bruce said. "Even fourple it."

"If downtown merchants would just get together and hire a promotion person—" Mary began again.

"But they won't," Bruce said. "People are downtown because they're independent. That's why I'm here. At the mall everything's done as a unit. Independence doesn't matter to them."

"So that's what's going to be the death of us," Mary said. "Our independence."

"Greensburg is just another downtown," Bruce said. "It isn't picturesque. It's architecturally divided."

"Look at West Alexandria," Mary said. "It was a bad town. Now it has all those new shops—they got together on that. It's a tourist place now."

"It's a tourist attraction because it's another mall," Bruce said. "They'll go to look at pictures of a goat, not a goat."

Mary talked about the most important clientele of her store and other small shops downtown: mostly the wives of doctors and other professionals. "They go to New York City once or twice a year," Mary said. "They know what's going on. There's only a few of them but they spend a lot—as much as everyone else put together that day. There are so few of them that we know them all. We know what their friends have bought their other friends for gifts, so we can advise them. They are totally delighted with our life-style. They love what they see as the gypsy in us. The goats. They tell me, 'I'd love to have a store like this.' They're buying the aura. They say, 'The thing I'd like to do more than anything in the world is work in your store.' I say, 'Great—give me your husband.' But they never do."

"Most of their husbands look like mashed potatoes," Bruce pointed out.

"We get a lot of the same people," Pam said. "They make a special trip into town just to come to our store and then that's it. They go home. They won't go to the malls."

"Yes, I get some wonderful rich old ladies who refuse to go to malls," Mary said. "One of them told me, 'I know the children sneak in, but I never go.'"

"They come for personal service," Bruce said. "Everything is too rushed at the malls. They come to see Mary."

"They come for what we sell, too," Pam said. "I shopped at your stores before I knew you. I liked your stuff."

"There's a lot of money in Greensburg," Mary said. "If these people were appealed to on the basis of sentiment or history—if they could do something with the train station, for instance. If the city, or somebody, the merchants or all our rich customers maybe, would just give me a hundred thousand dollars, I could turn this town around. In a year, I know I could."

"The city talked about bringing in an expert, but—" Bruce said.

"No, it wouldn't work," Mary said. "I could do it better. People here want a personality."

"But a lot of these businesses wouldn't go for it if it cost them anything," Bruce said. "They're just making it now, and if they're doing pretty well, why should they contribute to building up the businesses that aren't doing as well? Besides, the only downtowns that are making it now around here are the ones where there aren't any malls nearby."

"But we've had some successful businesses start here," Mary said. "A woman—K. Barchetti—started a shoe store with special styles and sizes. She moved to that little mall in downtown Pittsburgh, the Bank, and she started advertising in national magazines. She's going to be in that new mall in downtown Pittsburgh—Oxford Centre. She's doing very well."

"Yeah, but she didn't do so well here," Bruce said. "I suppose the truth is that without the malls drawing off business, there never would have been room downtown for businesses like Mary's and mine. I started with a total working capital of four thousand dollars. That's ridiculous. I couldn't have done it without low rent. I definitely couldn't have started at the mall."

"I'm going to stay in town," Mary said. "I'd like to expand. I'd like to have an ice-cream and candy store. We do have people who make a point of shopping downtown. People who work downtown will come back here on a Saturday to shop."

"There are people who just don't like malls," Bruce said. "They don't like the lights or they've heard about car thefts and rapes out there. And we get people with romantic notions about shopping where you can walk out of doors once in a while."

"Yes, especially at Christmas," Mary said. "They like to breathe the cold air, look at the sky and snow, along with the lights and decorations."

"But I don't know," Bruce said. "We've got one mall to the east and one to the west. They're talking about another one south. Then they'll build one north and seal off the town. People on the highway will stop and ask, 'Where's Greensburg?' And they'll say,

'Greensburg? There's no Greensburg. There's Greengate and Westmoreland and the other malls, but no Greensburg.' And we'll be sitting here, wondering where everybody is."

Some time after this conversation, Bruce Adamson sold the Woodshed and went into another, nonretail business. Nature's Way had originally been located in the old General Greene Hotel, which was first registered as a historical building so the owner could rehabilitate it and fill it with new businesses, but it was later deregistered when these plans fell through, and demolished. Nature's Way then moved out of the downtown, into its own one-building mall called Paradise Village.

Mary Gilbert kept her store in town, but she also opened up a new Animal Crackers at Greengate Mall. Downtown, she had been the absolute master: She shelved and painted the store herself, and in its beginning stages she was the only employee, the only one with customer contact. She had a store cat, which pleased her customers, and she had space enough for friends to gather around a table in the back room. But going to Greengate meant hiring a lawyer, obtaining a large loan, and contracting with an architect to design her store, which had to be approved by the mall. It meant paying out the equivalent of her monthly downtown rent just in advertising, to meet the requirements of her mall contract. Her bills were sent to an accountant, who tabulated them with his new computer. Because of the mall's long hours and the fact that there were now two stores, Mary had to hire several more people, which meant she was less accessible to customers, and she had to spend considerably more of her time dealing with inventory and cash flow. There was a lot more money going out as well as coming in at the mall. The Greengate store was smaller and more densely filled with merchandise; there was no room for a table and chairs, or time for long talks on slow nights.

America has always cherished the small town, at least as an ideal. It is where the mythic constituents of the American character were to be found: simplicity, idealism, decency, and a down-to-earth intelligence. Our heroes were supposed to spring from its soil, nurtured by the intimacy of its streets and the deep moral lessons and perhaps magical strength derived from closeness to nature. It was the place for the young to dream before they went into the larger world to achieve; it was lso where old dreamers returned, to pass on their dreams. "As Thornton Wilder's *Our*

Town reminded us," John Updike writes, "small-town people think a lot about the universe (as opposed to city people, who think about one another)." Even today, Americans routinely tell pollsters that the small town is the ideal place to live, and in a sense many have tried to get back to it, in suburbia.

But the small town is almost impossible to find now. The highway, the mall, and television—which, in Updike's words, "imposed on every home a degraded sophistication"—became only the most recent and most effective agents of its destruction. Still, the dream of the small town remains, and these same postwar phenomena have appropriated it for their own purposes, sometimes perverting it in the process.

In the last decade, television advertising has refined its ability to manipulate viewers, going so far as to use research on the hemispheres of the human brain to isolate the elements it can use to bypass the brain's logic and make a direct connection with the emotions. That's one reason there is so much small-town imagery in commercials: The small-town dream has powerful emotional appeal. The ads tap the same elements the malls do: the small-town virtues on a small scale, familiarity and security. But some of these ads go further; they ingeniously substitute the Highway for the Hometown as the place where small-town relationships exist.

Consider the ads that contrast the friendliness and quality to be found at national chain outlets with the sleaziness and sloppiness of small-time independents, usually depicted as shiftless rubes and rude incompetents. These commercials turn the assumption of small-town community on its head: It is now the anonymous chain that "cares about you" and offers personal service, not a business from your own town run by somebody who knows you personally. Such ads respond to the facts: Most Americans live in large cities or suburbs, and see small towns only as they are passing through. They are accustomed to dealing with strangers, so when they search for a shock absorber or a motel room, they crave the security of a known chain where there are "no surprises."

So now TV advertises "your hometown Pizza Hut," although about the only thing hometown about it is that there is probably one on the highway near where you live, pretty much like every other one in the country. Even the idea of a pizza "hut" is neutralizing; not only is it devoid of ethnic content (unless you're thinking Polynesian), it doesn't even make sense.

The highway chain outlets with the dependability supposedly

guaranteed by national advertising and centralized management, and the carefully designed imagery of nostalgia, friendliness, and personal service, make up what Ralph Keyes has called our "National Hometown," and it is just about the only kind of hometown we have left. Television may be the disembodied bedrock of the National Hometown, but the mall is its greatest physical manifestation.

When I was growing up, there was still a living downtown not yet completely replaced by the National Hometown. It was a mostly dying organism by then, but there was yet a discernable cycle of change: Some things got old, some aged gracefully and usefully, and some decayed. Some were replaced by something new. But most of what was new wasn't happening in town anymore, so this openness to uncontrolled change became a kind of tragic flaw. The Main Street of Greensburg was not enclosed or protected, and so without the infusion of the new, it simply got old and empty. It wasn't a street that began at a castle and ended in a village square. It had dirty, noisy trucks adding to the heat of summer or splashing slush in the winter.

It had its inconveniences, but what I remember best about growing up mall-less in Greensburg is the weather, and how it related to the world of the town and added its character to my experiences there. As an adolescent, I played off my moods against the wind and rain and sunshine, the contours of clouds and the colors of the sky, the part of every day ruled by the stars, and the months made by the moon. I saw it where my life took me, including Main Street. Weather changed and it was worth watching, as were the cycles of day and night and the seasons. The gradations of weather and time taught me something about the gradations and complexities of emotions.

An irony of my return was that I had sought to escape the staginess of the city, the blotting out of the sky by buildings and high electric lights. I wanted again those reassuring glimpses of the moon and stars through a window, the feel of a bright sky widening my eyes. I found those sensations again—but I also found my hometownspeople flocking to enclosures isolated from their hills and trees and as separated from nature and weather as any city street.

You don't learn much about cycles and change in the mall, except perhaps for the nearly secret way one store replaces another. There is no reference to the triumphs or disasters of history, unless you count Presidents Day sales. It is unchanging, ideal, and neutral, except that everything is linked to commerce. It becomes as addictive as junk food—pretty soon we can't accept any environment unless it has shopping. The absence of weather—of anything larger than the mall itself and its commerce—intensifies the shopping experience until it assumes a disproportionate importance. The mall is the universe! There's no relief, no contrast, no cosmic *caveats;* just the mall.

The mall's neutrality is in some ways democratic; nowhere else, at least before the mall came, was absolutely any style of clothing appropriate for everything and at every time of the day. The mall, being everything, is nothing in particular. Still, there is the sense in which the artificial dream world of the mall is like an artificial flower: It will never die because it was never alive.

Probably the mall-goer wants it just that way. After all, nobody goes to the mall to be depressed, or even to learn anything; certainly not to face reality. The real world is too troubled, and even the small town sees that, not only on television but in the hospitals, the divorce courts, the shelters for battered women, the drug and alcohol rehab programs, the child abuse agencies, the welfare office, the Unemployment Compensation lines; in the homes that need repair, the cars that need to be replaced, or with the children whose college education promises to cost a small and nonexistent fortune. It's better to escape to a place where, in the parlance of the eighties, everything is "positive." The real world drives the mall-goers inside, where they are sold a superficial dream. They go looking for novelty but they want to be protected, passively embraced, brought home.

Still, even before the mall, Greensburg was not an idyllic place to be young. In many ways it was a classically crushing small-town environment. I *yearned* for a wider world. In particular, growing up here in the 1950s and 1960s was hardly ideal. It wasn't Clark Kent's Smallville of the twenties—it was too large a place and too late in history for that. But as prosperity took hold, the new ideas and fresh visions of the 1960s that might have countered an empty materialism were adamantly resisted at the same time that every new gadget and fast-food invention was excitedly embraced. Then, when the degraded styles associated with the sixties finally became financially profitable, they, too, were eagerly accepted.

The typical blandness and provinciality of a small town were in some ways made even worse by industrial prosperity. As long as anyone put in the hours and played the game, attainment of the American Dream was apparently automatic. Taking risks to achieve a special dream was considered foolhardy. The dreamer was called conceited. There was little incentive to learn for the sake of learning, to think and feel more subtly and appreciate more deeply, to speak and move through life more gracefully, or act more compassionately. Those who tried to connect with that kind of wider world faced the censure of the certain. For all the new stuff and styles the malls brought, they didn't change this.

Now that the willingness to punch a time clock no longer guarantees a life of two cars and a new house filled with microwave ovens and color TVs, some Greensburg people are in shock. Their certainty has been taken from them, along with their work and earning power. You can see them sometimes, dazed, angry, and exhausted, sitting in the malls—the castles of the middle-class kingdom that has used and callously abandoned them.

By the 1960s, there were few places left for the young to be together informally or to be alone in pleasant and evocative circumstances, as there would be when the malls came. But even if its golden age could be recaptured, few Greensburgers of any age would really want to go back to the old small-town Main Street. By now it would be far too dull. Out at the mall they can have it both ways, for the mall's Main Street—the Highway Comfort Culture in the guise of the small town—has brought the brightness inside and scaled it down to the slow gait of people on the ground rather than to fast glances from speeding metal on the highway. Here the fantasy is savored and walked around in. It's the consumer Garden of Eden in the postwar paradise.

Besides, people come to the malls from towns and suburban tracts as far as fifty miles away. They don't have to know each other—they know what to expect. They will come together in this timeless, placeless space that's always colorful, clean, spacious, comforting, always new, always the same. Good malls make good neighbors, and they are neighbors here, in Never-Never-Land.

Part 2

MALL TREK:
THE MALL AS
THE CITY SUBURBAN

*Rest rubble, sprawling suburbs, jerry-built,
Kerwan's mushroom house, built of breeze.
Shelter from the night.*

—JAMES JOYCE
Ulysses

10

Chicagoland and the Birth of Suburbia

Well, I landed at a shopping center
in an unknown state
Unknown kind of architecture, atmosphere and trait
Unknown brand of labels, unknown market chains
The strangest collection of buildings
upon the fruited plain
And let's go. Let's rock.

—JONATHAN RICHMAN
"Rockin' Shopping Center"

Out on the highway in a rented Grand Prix—the smallest car I could get for this drive—I was passing and being passed by other Americans in their Cutlasses and Corvettes, their Chargers and Colts, Tiempos and Tercels, Horizons and Omegas, Preludes and Ovations, on my way to suburbia.

Beside me was Barbara Lambert, my native guide and guru to the malls of suburban Chicago and, later, to those in and around the Twin Cities of Minneapolis and St. Paul. In her late twenties, Barbara was teaching high-school English and theater in St. Paul, but I first knew her as an effervescent, eighteen-year-old in a yellow jump suit, visiting her older sister, Mary, at college. Mary and I were classmates and friends at Knox College, a small liberal arts college about two hundred miles south and west of Chicago, in Galesburg, Illinois.

When I called Barbara and told her about my mall odyssey, she volunteered to come down from Minnesota to show me the malls she'd known when she was growing up in a Chicago suburb. She and Mary and their mother had shopped at many of them, and as each new one opened they went out to see it. So Barbara not only knew where the more interesting malls were, she knew something of their history. We were going to look at three malls today, and then I would drive her back to Minnesota, to see her new home and meet the man she had just married. And, of course, to see more malls.

I wanted to start this mall trek with the Chicago suburbs because I knew more about them, or at least had more of a feeling for them, than the suburbs of any other major city. I had met my first big-time suburbanites at Knox. Some were from New York, Boston, or Los Angeles, a few more from around Denver and St. Louis, but most of them, like Mary and Barbara, were from what the big radio stations like WLS liked to call Chicagoland. I had classmates from places like Oak Lawn and Oak Park, Northbrook and Elgin, Berwyn and Evanston, Morton Grove and River Grove, Lake Forest and Park Forest and Forest Park. They went to high schools called New Trier and Niles East, Proviso East and Glenbard West—immense schools with college-level courses, actual drama departments, real radio stations, and some even had a *daily* high-school newspaper. This was all new to me, and I was impressed.

On school vacations I visited some of these suburbs, spread out all over the vast flat landscape as far as fifty miles from Chicago itself. The houses and the schools were impressive, but I discovered that my friends were used to staying home a lot. I always wanted to go into the city, but that idea did not seem natural to them. I soon learned why: Besides the suburban reluctance to go to the city, going anywhere meant plenty of time on the road. Trying to get college friends together turned out, often, to be a major task; the highway soaked up a good portion of the evening.

Chicago's suburbs were especially interesting because they were among the most classic, as might be inferred from all the sociological studies of them. The area also tried out a lot of different kinds of malls—Chicagoland represents a kind of shopping-center laboratory for the nation.

      ★   ★   ★

The city of Chicago itself is not really very old as a major urban center. Even with its lake port and its unique system of wood plank roads radiating in all directions, Chicago in the early nineteenth century was just a bustling overgrown village scattered around the remnants of Fort Dearborn.

But the railroad changed that, literally within a single generation. The first train rolled into Chicago in 1848, and soon rail links were established east and west that made Chicago the greatest rail center in the country. Eventually 137 railroads went through Chicago and spawned scores of new businesses: the famous Chicago stockyards, the Pullman Company's rail car manufacturing (relocated from Detroit), and the new entrepreneurs of Montgomery Ward and Sears Roebuck, who sold consumer goods to farmers by mail and delivered them by mail train. Chicago was a terminus and transfer point for passenger trains, which made it a hotel, restaurant, and retail center. Very soon there was a city—enough of one to make a very big fire.

When the city got even bigger, Chicago's wealthy began settling in outlying estates, and then some of the city's middle class moved to nearby suburbs along the rail lines. But the great suburbanization occurred here, as elsewhere, after World War II, when a combination of factors made life outside the city the new ideal.

The formative role of the highway cannot be exaggerated, but there were other more emotional reasons for the swift establishment of suburbia, perhaps more obvious here in the wide land so recently the sole possession of the prairie and cornfields. It was a kind of new beginning for the nation, an attempted return to an original innocence, and a contraction to basic elements of life— home, family, land. The feelings involved were perhaps best described by Don C. Peters, the president of a Pittsburgh construction company, quoted in a 1960 *Time* magazine article called "Suburbia U.S.A.": "The American suburb is the last outpost of democracy," Peters said, "the only level left on which the individual citizen can make his wishes felt, directly and immediately. I think there's something idealistic about the search for a home in the suburbs. Call it a return to the soil. It's something that calls most people sometime in their lives."

Perhaps the dream didn't turn out that way, but the search, the idealism, the call, were all the emotions of the moment. The character of early postwar suburbia comes through clearly in the portraits of Park Forest, Illinois, and Levittown, Pennsylvania, drawn by William Whyte, Jr., in his landmark book *The Organization Man.* Much of suburbia's beginnings seemed to be both a reaction to the war and an assimilation of the changes it made. For example, Whyte's Park Forest had a distinct army-post flavor, in speech and in style. Men's aspirations seemed to be to move up through the ranks of their large corporations, as they had in the army, while insisting on an enlightened, enlisted-man equality that in suburbia came to be called conformism.

But if they conformed, this time it would be for their own visible objectives. Many of these men had left their hometowns and cities once already, during the war. Now they had become used to mobility, and they had learned to get along with strangers. They were familiar with the ways of large organizations through the granddaddy of all bureaucracies, the army. Now they wanted what men alone but overcrowded in alien territory must miss most: a family, a home, and a quiet, symmetrical space with nobody to threaten them. According to contemporary accounts, young women felt the same way; they had often lived together or with parents during the wartime housing shortage, while working in factories and offices. The same fears and the same longings linked them all to the same goals.

Meanwhile, thanks to an industrial capacity unmatched in history in the only major nation physically untouched by the war, this concentration on the basic and immediate was soon given its character by the rampant magic of consumer products. Sociologist David Riesman found that young men in an early 1950s survey were "willing to sacrifice the heights of achievement, though not the plateaus of the luxury economy, in favor of the goals of suburban domesticity and peace."

Clearly implied in all of this was a rejection of the city—even apart from the explicit rejection of what cities were becoming—and perhaps a drawing-back from larger or more abstract goals, such as work as a satisfaction in itself rather than a means to an end. Perhaps it was because early suburbia was largely settled by men and women who had just been through one more war to end all wars, with another conflict on the horizon.

What it meant in practical terms was the location of millions of couples farther and farther from the city in relatively haphazard patterns and densities of population. These couples began having babies at a record rate and in record numbers, beginning the Baby Boom which would carry into the mid-1960s. (Twice as many

Americans got married in 1946 as in 1932; they were marrying younger and having more children sooner. By 1970 the population of the United States had increased by 50 percent.)

At first these new suburbanites lived in tract housing that met their principal demands: single-family privacy and, if possible, a quarter-acre of green land, fast and cheap. Later, subdivisions and tract communities would meet a new need: The big corporations creating the Organization Man were national—executives, managers, and even sales reps were routinely transferred or given the chance to move up in the organization by moving away. Mobility was a necessity, so communities had to be immediately comprehensible. It was better if they were more or less the same, distinguished in levels of affluence by a few key signs, such as the quality and newness of the appliances inside and the car outside, as well as the size and type of home and the size and condition of the lawn.

As they traded their ploughshares for power mowers, suburbanites created an ever-expanding market for consumer products. All of those houses, however clichéd, had their own kitchens and laundries, living rooms and dens, and a bedroom for each child. The suburban dream clearly included refrigerators and ranges, washers and dryers, plus all the detergents, polishes, and other support and maintenance products. And so began the ever-escalating march of items, fed by new technology (such as the synthetic fabrics that made life easier and also made soap obsolete, creating the necessity for presoaks and anti-cling sprays and separate detergents for hot and cold washing) and by the newest and most native American art, advertising.

Suburbia grew so fast and in such a new way that for a while there was a puzzling and embarrassing gap: There were plenty of things to buy and what was available was well known (thanks to television) but there weren't very many places in suburbia to buy them.

Suburbia had another problem that was evident fairly early. All those single-family homes connected by highways lacked centers of informal social activity—places that didn't have a rigidly defined purpose, like schools, and also weren't homes, which required another kind of formality. Housewives were stuck out there twenty-four hours a day. Kids had nowhere to go. Families had no place to go together. Home, family, and the quarter-acre wasn't going to be enough.

★   ★   ★

Our first stop of the day was to be the Oakbrook mall, deep in what Barbara called "the polo part of Illinois." We'd left the thicker bands of development behind and turned off the tollway to an older highway that was dominated by the flat brown fields of a sunny November morning. Oakbrook was both one of the older malls in the Chicago suburbs and the culmination of an era in shopping-center history.

We parked and approached old white stone walls, which surrounded a partially enclosed arcade and a central courtyard with a pond, trees, and flowerbeds, all in the open air. Oakbrook had the usual kinds of stores: big ones like Marshall Field's, Sears, and Lord & Taylor, as well as Walgreen's Drug Store next door to Rogers Jewelers. But there was gently landscaped land between the arcades of stores, and real sky above. Oakbrook was one of the last—and most gracious—of what has become a vanishing breed: the "open" mall.

It was a startling sight; even in my limited mall experience, the lack of total enclosure seemed strange. Barbara led me through it, smiling. Oakbrook was one of her favorites. "I like to come outside when I'm shopping," she said. "There's too much stimulation in the stores. I need the break of coming out."

"Yes," I said, a little dumbstruck. "But what do you do in the winter?"

"We wear coats," Barbara said.

Oakbrook was pretty much the last in a line of shopping centers for which coats were occasionally still necessary. From the beginning, shopping centers were built basically to accommodate the automobile and the pedestrian by separating them—the automobile needed parking space, and people needed walking space. Those needs were created when the automobile became America's choice of transportation, and pioneer shopping centers tried to solve the problems from the very beginning of the auto age. It was, in fact, the Chicago suburb of Lake Forest that has been credited (by the National Register of Historical Places) with the first planned shopping district in the United States, called Market Square, built in 1916.

These districts (the most famous of which is Country Club Plaza, built in 1922 on the then-outskirts of Kansas City) consisted of a group of buildings, developed and managed as a unit, often with a special parking area but always with a street designated for the exclusive use of pedestrians.

Another step in early shopping-center evolution was taken in 1931 at Highland Park Shopping Village in Dallas where, for the first time, storefronts were turned away from the public street and inward around a central area—a special courtyard where cars couldn't go. This turning away from the street was an important change, because it signaled the possibility that the shopping center could create its own special world within itself.

These early and often elegant experiments were temporarily forgotten until after the great suburban surge of the early 1950s. The problem then was very basic: how to move goods and services most efficiently to the growing millions of suburban customers. Supermarkets were early adventures in suburban territory, as were some freestanding chain stores such as Sears. With all that land out there, they could afford to build huge parking lots to lure the car-dependent suburbanites, and soon it became obvious that stringing a few more stores in a small line, then a larger and larger line, would take further advantage of all the asphalt.

But suburbia was becoming more prosperous and sophisticated, and it needed more than hamburger buns and wheelbarrows. At first, urban retailers didn't catch on to the new aversion of suburban women to traveling into the city, now becoming mythologized as unsafe and deteriorating. But gradually the department stores took the chance that suburbanites would prefer to shop in their own new and bright communities. They began cautiously with "twigs" (stores so small they couldn't even be called branches) and then with larger stores and fuller lines of merchandise. When they were finally ready to send out complete stores, some prescient developers were also ready with the idea that the shopping center could be wedded to the big department store.

After the lines of stores got longer and longer at what are now called strip centers, and some developers experimented with doubling them up and forming L- and V-shaped configurations, the concept of creating the interior world was rediscovered. No longer simply separated from the highway by a moat of asphalt, the shopping center turned in on itself, creating enclosure of a kind. With a big department store "anchoring" one end, two parallel rows of stores were joined with a special pedestrian area in the middle. At first these areas were grassy, sometimes with gardens and ponds, fountains and flowers, and except for brief roofs over the sidewalks, open to the sky. They were the open malls, like Old Orchard near Chicago, and Oakbrook.

Oakbrook is perhaps closer to the classic definition of the mall than its newer, fully enclosed counterparts. With its natural green spaces for walking, it is akin to the grassy, shaded fairways used for the game called pall-mall, which was a kind of combination golf and croquet popular until the eighteenth century in England. The word *mall* comes from this game, as do *mallet* (with which it was played), *malleable,* and *maul*—both as a verb familiar to some golfers today, who maul the fairways, and as the name of another kind of mallet, the carpenter's maul (which Ahab used to nail the gold coin to the mast in *Moby Dick*) and the iron- and steelworker's maul (which, to add irony to etymology, became the symbol of the Pittsburgh Maulers, a United States Football League team owned and named by the shopping mall developer Edward DeBartolo).

The fairway where pall-mall was played came to be known as the mall, and after the game itself faded, the *mall* came to mean any shaded walk or promenade, such as London's St. James's Park, or even a grassy open area like the Mall in the Federal Triangle of Washington, D.C.

The word now has a technical definition in the world of architecture—a *mall* means a specially designed pedestrian environment. The shopping mall, then, is more precisely a shopping center with a mall in the middle, inside it. But the older sense of the idea is still preserved in the green courtyards inside the white stone walls of Oakbrook.

Even when Oakbrook was built, in 1962, the open mall was already becoming obsolete and the enclosed mall becoming dominant. Chicagoland continued to experiment with a number of enclosed mall styles, such as the amusement-park theme malls of Evergreen and Old Chicago (which contained a real roller coaster under its glass dome); Ford City, an early attempt at recycling an old city building with public support (and also the first mall to constitute a Catholic parish); Water Tower Place, one of the first urban megastructures with a shopping mall as its major component; and even one of the earliest remodelings of a first-generation shopping mall into an altogether different style, when the amusement park mall of Old Chicago was reincarnated as Mid-America Factory Outlet Mall, one of the largest of its kind in the country.

Our second stop in Chicagoland was one of the newer malls around, Fox Valley Center. Fox Valley was an update of Oakbrook in the sense that it was also the pinnacle of stylishness for its time—

the late 1970s—and was pitched to the most affluent shoppers in the area. Unlike some other fashionable malls catering to the affluent (such as the attractive Northbrook Court near Evanston, Illinois), Fox Valley is linked not so much to a specific community as to the disposable income of anybody who can get to it on the fast ribbons of highway.

But after our peaceful stroll through Oakbrook, a certain eeriness began to accompany our mall tour. Even before we got to Fox Valley, Barbara and I began to notice strange, faceless buildings standing mutely in blank fields. There weren't any houses or even any people visible around them—just these anonymous structures, some solitary, some in groups of two or three identical buildings. Two gray stone and glass rectangular blocks were followed farther on by two identical black-and-white buildings on stilts, with another glassy structure between them, not quite as tall but wider, and presenting the same facadeless face. The buildings on stilts were particularly weird; they reminded me of the vehicles operated by Martian invaders in H. G. Wells's *War of the Worlds,* or perhaps the Imperial Walkers, the war machines of the Empire in the *Star Wars* saga. These inscrutable objects were set down in vast open areas, as if, having landed, they were awaiting orders to link up and begin their conquest.

I learned later that they were office buildings, hotels, and a power plant (though I'm still not sure which was which) and in a sense they were awaiting the restaurants, movie theaters, and other structures that would fill in the space between them and the nearby subdivisions. This was the "Oakbrook concentration," a clustering of new development around a central focal point, sometimes called "metro-nucleation." In this case, as in many others I would see, the focal point was a large shopping mall.

As we got farther from Oakbrook, it was the specter of development itself that began to awe us a little. Once off the interstate and into the countryside, we again began to pass these buildings sitting in quiet isolation amid brown stubble and husks.

This was still mostly farmland, much of it cultivated, with rich black soil between the rows of green and brown. But it was becoming more profitable to plow these crops under and cover them with cement. First the residential subdivisions, then the industrial parks and shopping malls, and now the combined development that was gathering around the malls were driving up land values, making taxes prohibitive and the profit of sale very tempting. We were still a few miles from Fox Valley when we began seeing the signs posted in cultivated cornfields on both sides of the road, offering the fields for development. All this wasn't unique to Illinois. Losing this land was part of the price of the malling of America.

Fox Valley mall itself represented one of those ironies that has become common in America—it was a "rural look" mall built on what was formerly farmland. Inside its very spacious enclosure, Fox Valley used a lot of wood and tan-and-brown bricks and stone to achieve a kind of country gentleman informality. But like many malls I was to visit, it carried out its theme only so far, and could not resist the kind of logic-defying eclecticism that is sometimes so crazy or inspired or just amazing that it constitutes one of the mall's most irresistible and apparently irrepressible qualities. In this case, Fox Valley managed to mix its woodiness and burnt-orange sofas with high-tech appointments and futuristic crisscrossing walkways which altogether added up to a combination of horse country and Flash Gordon, where shoppers might properly be wearing jodhpurs and space helmets.

The mall was bustling, with a cross-section of humanity represented: elderly couples, family groups led by young parents, lots of kids on their own. Barbara remarked that when Fox Valley first opened, she and her mother had walked through it without seeing more than half a dozen people. But no longer.

I asked the assistant security chief where these people were coming from, and he contended that many of them came from pretty far away. In fact he made the somewhat startling assertion that many were escaping the traffic, congestion, and crime, not of the city of Chicago but of other shopping malls, such as Oakbrook and Yorktown, which were closer to the city. His main security problems, on the other hand, were lost children, teenagers fooling around on the ramps, and an occasional stolen hubcap in the parking lot.

In any case Fox Valley is so large and so complete—it has Marshall Field's and Lord & Taylor, but also Sears and J. C. Penney, community conference rooms, and an official U.S. post office—that it is practically autonomous.

As we left, Barbara told me the story of the nearby, sadly named town of Aurora, a story confirmed by professional observers. It was a more severe version of the Greensburg situation, and a story I was to hear again and again. Aurora had been a simple small town until a typical shopping center opened on its periphery, and downtown stores began leaving for it. Downtown soon began to crumble, and the coup de grâce was the massive and magnificent Fox Valley. The sun had gone down on Aurora.

Later, when I was talking to architect Cesar Pelli at Yale, he referred to the vast economic and social consequence of the malls' magnetism, and the power of large malls when they appear outside existing communities. "Towns disappear," he said. It was an awesome phrase. Towns disappear! Move over, Godzilla and H. G. Wells. Who needs atomic breath or a Martian heat ray?

Still, Barbara and I had eaten a pleasant lunch in the large "outdoor" café under the roof of Fox Valley, and our mood was not entirely somber as we drove away under the pale-blue sky of late afternoon. Then, the sunlight hit a stretch of land, more striking in its cold bare beauty than any we'd seen so far: brown sparse fields and black earth, wind-tossed grass, small rolling green hills, and here and there a tree rising out of the horizontal landscape.

We looked at it silently. "This is Illinois," I said finally.

"Yes," Barbara said. "This stretch is real Illinois—what you think of as Illinois. But in a few miles it won't be anymore. They should make this a national park, so people can come through and say, 'This is what Illinois was like.'"

We carefully watched the fields—nothing spectacular, no redwoods or Grand Canyon, just farmlands and hints of prairie grass. Then, as Barbara said it would, the landscape changed, the Illinois fields stopped, and the buildings began.

We were on our way to Woodfield, the biggest mall in the country.

11

The Mother Ship

For all its size and sophisticated design, Fox Valley didn't truly impress me; I could appreciate and analyze it without much emotion. Its size only made me tired. So I wasn't looking forward to Woodfield. Fox Valley was supposed to be nearly as large and I couldn't see how Woodfield was going to be much different. I was impatient to get started on our long drive to Minnesota. One more mall at this point was just wasting time.

But like the observers at Devil's Tower who thought they'd seen it all after the first group of spaceships swooped by in the film *Close Encounters of the Third Kind,* I was in for a big surprise. I was about to see the Mother Ship.

Once inside the upper-level entrance, I was stunned first by the sound. It was the sound of many people. Their talk was like the background roar of ocean surf; their walking sent deep vibrations through the floor, like the hum left over from the birth of the universe. There they were; around and below me, flowing across crisscrossing concourses and down the aisles, from this end of the mall to the blue SEARS sign at the other end, literally in the distance.

Unlike Fox Valley, which segmented its spaces with a varied architecture, Woodfield was so stupendous because its size was so obvious. It was mostly a long rectangular box, a kind of skyscraper on its side. The clear sightlines emphasized the mall's vastness. The decor, too, was basic: hard and bright. The mall felt fast—even the beat of the Muzak seemed quicker. But the people were the most amazing.

We walked downstairs and watched them cascade by—not only the same mix of mostly white middle-class couples, families, elderly, and teenagers I'd been seeing at other lively malls, but a clattering procession of ethnic, racial, and social groups more various than anything I had ever seen except on the streets of New York or San Francisco, and this was all in a single building. There were Indians in saris, Latinos, a Japanese family loaded with cameras and smiles, a trio of beautiful Asiatic young women, giggling like fashion models in a television commercial.

Perhaps most disconcerting were the discernably urban types—the black young man encased in elegant fur; the older woman with smeared makeup, sobbing to herself as she walked; two boys, oblivious to everything else, who bounced a Ping-Pong ball against a blank wall. There were middle-aged matrons in jewels, somber young men in spectacles and suits, a midget, a bum, a whole group of incredibly fat people. I thought this was supposed to be suburbia. *Where did they come from?* What remarkable things were on sale here? Barbara pointed out that comparatively few were carrying packages. *Why are they here?*

I had to stop and calm down. Fortunately, Barbara was familiar with such a strong response to Woodfield. She told me that when her sister, Mary, and Mary's husband, Glenn, came back from their years in the Peace Corps in Thailand, her mother took them to Woodfield, and Glenn went into such shock that he practically had to be carried out. Afterward he railed for hours against the American compulsion to make the biggest of everything.

Woodfield was reputedly the biggest of the malls. Although various developers claim the distinction, and there are different ways of measuring size, it certainly *felt* like the biggest. Glenn was right, of course—Americans seem fatally attracted to the biggest, the brightest, the newest, and mall developers know it. But the sheer magnitude of the Mother Ship did not account for the variety of people there—a variety I'd never seen even on the streets of Chicago. The reason, I found later, had much to do with the character of the suburban communities around Woodfield and how they grew. Altogether, the Mother Ship and its satellites turned out to be an object lesson in the new configurations of places where Americans live and work, and the central role the malls play in their daily life.

Woodfield is in the town of Schaumburg, Illinois, which for more than a hundred years was a tiny community of German farmers. That changed in the mid-1950s, when two of the controllers of postwar patterns of change came to call: the Highway (the northwest tollway was built bordering the town) and the Airport (nearby O'Hare Field was purchased by the city of Chicago and expanded to become the busiest airport in the nation). Schaumburg was incorporated as a village in 1956, when it had corn and soybean fields, a few dairy farm buildings, and 130 citizens. By 1960 it had nearly 1,000 people. By 1970 there were almost 20,000, and by 1978, about 50,000. By the 1990s it may well be the second-largest population center in Illinois.

What the railroad did for Chicago in the mid-nineteenth century, the highway and the airport did for suburban Schaumburg in the mid-twentieth. But this time the expansion was planned and carried out, not in the willy-nilly way of cities but in a systematic application of two organizational forms: the subdivision and the shopping mall.

Local and state government agencies cooperated in careful planning both to accommodate and to manage the residential growth of Schaumburg, which was in the generally booming "golden corridor" of Chicago's northwest suburbs. Schaumburg's boom was also organized around two other events: Motorola established its national headquarters there in the late 1960s, and in the early 1970s Woodfield Mall and its related office complexes were built. Motorola (which has since become one of the most successful and innovative American high-tech manufacturers) brought jobs of an appropriate nature to the suburbs, and its success encouraged other high-tech firms to locate nearby. Then Woodfield became the centerpiece for most of the office development in the main construction period of 1973 to 1975.

Now the entire area—known these days as Greater Woodfield—

is a major rival to Chicago itself. Some half-million people live in the northwest suburbs; there is a labor force of 285,000 within a ten-mile radius of Greater Woodfield, including more than 80,000 potential office workers within five miles. Among the other firms joining Motorola with headquarters there are Data General, Digital Equipment, Western Electric, Nuclear Data, Union Oil, E. R. Squibb, J. C. Penney, the State of Illinois Department of Transportation, and the Big Ten Athletic Conference. The corporate office area is almost four times the size of Chicago's Loop. Chicago's downtown civic center has its famous Picasso sculpture, but Schaumburg even has one of those, too—a thirty-foot Picasso ("The Bather") in front of an eleven-story office tower.

Best of all, Schaumburg has Woodfield, built by the Taubman Company, one of the five largest mall developers in the country. Besides lending its name to the community surrounding it, Woodfield functions as a community center, with frequent musical, theatrical, and cultural events. The Chicago Symphony has played there, and former President Gerald Ford spoke there to an audience of 50,000 people. Woodfield is credited with setting the standard for Greater Woodfield's office campuses and other development with its extensive landscaping and glistening appearance.

Woodfield Mall draws drivers from five states, and buses run from O'Hare to its door. On the day after Thanksgiving, the biggest shopping day of the year, Woodfield regularly draws a quarter of a million people.

There weren't that many people the day Barbara and I were there, but there were plenty. We watched them dance from Sears and J. C. Penney to Lord & Taylor and Marshall Field's, the same four department stores we'd seen in the other two malls on our travels that day. But there were two hundred other shops to check out at Woodfield: On Stage and Just Pants, Tannery West and The Chicken's Lips, Noah's Ark Pet Center and the Yarn Bin, Education Station and the Family Hair Corral, Digital Den and Video Forum, plus Madigan's, Madigan's Juniors, and Madigan's for Men. There were places to eat (Roy Rogers, the Skewer, Vie de France), a post office, and a skating rink. Mothers could rent strollers, and the management provided wheelchairs for those who needed them.

The result of all these factors was the urban mix of people I was surprised to see at Woodfield. Some were probably tourists, perhaps seeing Schaumburg between international plane connections, much as earlier generations had sampled Chicago between trains. Some could have been conventioneers between sessions at the nearby Hyatt convention hotel. Others probably worked there—as technicians, managers, nurses, engineers, secretaries, government workers, retailers—and some lived in the condos that were a new feature of suburbia. Some had probably come from other suburban communities, just to shop. Woodfield was the first of a new phenomenon I would see many times again on my mall trek—the mall as the city suburban.

Our close encounter with the Mother Ship was also a brief one. It was late in the afternoon and Barbara and I had an eight-hour drive before us.

12

The Invention of the Mall: Eureka *in Edina, Minnesota*

By the time we got on the superhighway north, Barbara and I were driving into darkness. I told Barbara about a brief but wide-ranging essay on Chicago-area malls published in *The New Republic*. It was by Neil Harris, professor of history at the University of Chicago. He compared the size and elegance of such malls as Woodfield to the great railway stations of the past. Harris and I had met and talked in Chicago, and he started me thinking that each age has its signature structures which consciously celebrate or unconsciously express what that age values, from the pyramids to the cathedrals and palaces of Europe, to the train stations, movie palaces, and most recently, the skyscrapers of American cities. Places of grandeur—especially in a secular time—also become associated with glamour and romance. I wondered if a mall like Woodfield wasn't fulfilling those functions for this age.

Barbara didn't buy the romance part. "I can't imagine lovers running into each other's arms at Woodfield," she said. I suggested that she just hadn't seen it in the movies yet. She laughed. "Maybe," she said. "But I can't imagine a mall being romantic. Maybe I'm just old-fashioned."

On the other hand, she told me an incredible story of a man who found malls more than romantic. Apparently he found them highly stimulating. The man was called Doctor Dirty, and it was such a fantastic tale that I said she'd have to prove it was true. She said it had all been in the newspapers and vowed to show me the evidence when we got to Minnesota.

A few days later I was looking anxiously out of the Lamberts' picture window at the thickly clouded sky and listening to the weather forecast on the radio. A blizzard was predicted, which in the Twin Cities could mean real trouble. For a moment I considered cutting my visit short and making a dash for the airport. Brian Lambert, Barbara's husband, read my mind. "If you're thinking about making a run for it," he said, "it's too late."

It was midafternoon and we were awaiting Barbara's return from teaching school. I'd already seen several local malls, including Maplewood Mall, where Pat Paulsen was soon scheduled to appear, following Captain Cookie. Today, Barbara and I were supposed to drive out to Edina, a suburb which had the distinction of hosting the first shopping mall in America designed as a fully enclosed, comfort-controlled, two-level mall—and as such, the precise prototype for the majority of malls built since.

But Minnesota snowfalls were legendary, and driving through one, even to see mall history, was maybe more than I was willing to give to my odyssey. When Barbara arrived she reported only a light rain, although the temperature did seem to be dropping. She was all for going. Minnesotans approach their winter weather with a consciously offhand bravado. Even as they talk about how bad it is, they cheerfully stop to help pull one another's cars out of snowbanks and plow one another's driveways. Pretending it's no big deal is a major source of pride, a kind of character-building adventure. I had visions of driving through the dark with snow crashing at the windshield, only to be halted by seven-foot drifts in the middle of the interstate and stranded there until rescued by a grinning Minnesotan on a snowmobile.

We got out on the road as the cold drizzle changed to blowing light snow. The urban-voiced disc jockey on the country music radio station announced a traveler's advisory. "That means they advise you not to travel," he said. But we got to Southdale safely, and as we moved across the windy wilderness of the parking lot, I was grateful for the blank building ahead that promised warmth and protection.

Evidently most people had taken the radio's advice: The mall was almost empty—but not entirely. There was a group of teenagers, in blue-and-white jackets with EAGLES on the back, playing pinball in the Picadilly Circus game room, and here and there an adult couple was shopping.

Although Southdale had expanded a couple of times, adding a new wing in the early 1970s, we had apparently entered the older part, judging from the black-and-white speckled tile floors and the solid, almost weathered look of the construction. The white walls around the center court looked whitewashed, and the wood appointments didn't just look woody, they looked real. Southdale had the feeling of being built, rather than assembled from prefabricated materials and old ideas. Which is only as it should be, since this is where the mall was invented. Although it now seems to be a superior but not unusual mall—with its soaring Garden Court, its Interior Systems furniture shop, B. Dalton Booksellers, Berman Buckskin, Children's Barber, Chrome Concepts, Fanny Farmer, and Eat & Run—in 1956 Southdale represented innovation, creative problem-solving, and aesthetic daring, as well as shopping-center heresy.

When Southdale was being planned, the normal shopping center was a long strip, all on one level, with at best one department store. Gospel was that nobody was going to walk or even ride up to a second level in a drive-in shopping center; if they couldn't reach a store by practically parking in front of it, car-dependent people wouldn't go.

Finally a few daring developers tried a two-level center, and it worked. The Rouse Company did it with the Mondawmin Shopping Center in Baltimore and the Dayton-Hudson Company with Northland in Detroit. A development company formed by the Dayton department-store empire in Minneapolis and the Hudson department stores in Detroit, Dayton-Hudson in the mid-1950s was rapidly becoming a thoughtful pioneer in shopping centers. Their Northland mall was also the first shopping center built as the focus of other development controlled by the same owner: Over the next decade, the 250-acre area around Northland collected apartment and office buildings, a hotel, a hospital, research laboratories, and other businesses. It was the first real experiment in metro-nucleation planned around a shopping mall; later it would happen both spontaneously (as around Oakbrook in Illinois) and with varying degrees of planning and control (as at Woodfield).

At Northland, the two-level open mall proved itself. By a handy coincidence, one chain store had a shop on each level and they did identical business, which seemed to mean that people weren't entirely averse to getting out of their cars and walking around a shopping center, or riding an escalator to see what was going on upstairs. But while others contemplated what exactly this might mean, Northland's designer was hurrying on to the next step, the truly fateful one, at Southdale. His name was Victor Gruen.

Victor Gruen was an Austrian-born architect who had fled the Nazi invasion in 1938 and arrived in the United States with eight dollars in his pocket and some architect's tools. By 1951 he had his own firm, and was becoming known as a brilliant and passionate theoretician and advocate of community planning. He focused on suburban sprawl and the damage he believed the automobile was causing to the social fabric. With his European background, Gruen believed that in order for communities to work they must provide places for people to be together face-to-face, not isolated in cars, housing tracts, and office buildings. He was also concerned with efficient use of land and other resources.

After his triumph at Northland, Gruen was faced with two new challenges in the proposed Southdale mall in Minnesota. At the time, the more important was that Southdale, contrary to shopping-center orthodoxy, was going to be the first mall to have two major department stores. To have two competing department stores in the same center was considered madness. Gruen had to come up with ways of separating them while making them both equal parts of the center, without any disadvantage to either.

While others rubbed their hands waiting to see how Gruen was going to handle this exercise in diplomatic design, he found another problem which may not have seemed as important to the shopping-center business but was the kind of basic, practical problem affecting the ultimate client—the customer—that an architect with good reflexes must consider immediately. That problem, in Edina, Minnesota, was the weather. It not only got very cold and snowy in the winter in Edina, it also got baking hot in the summer. Gruen's answer to the problem turned out to be the most fateful advance made at Southdale.

The solution was, of course, complete enclosure. Gruen saw it immediately and went to the Dayton-Hudson hierarchy with his proposal. He told them about the covered pedestrian arcades in Europe, especially the Galleria Vittorio Emanuele in Milan, Italy, with its arcades rising four stories to a glass barrel vault and a central glass cupola 160 feet high. He argued that economically the additional cost of enclosure would be made up in the lesser cost of the store buildings—being inside, they wouldn't have to be so large or strong. Aesthetically, he told them, enclosure would allow for even more visual order and discipline than already achieved at Northland, avoiding the horrors of jumbled neon outside and permitting a calmer, more unified design inside. Finally, nobody was going to walk around in a big shopping center if they were going to freeze or fry.

Enclosure could also make the central court a much more dramatic place, as became apparent in the planning stages of Southdale. There was something special about spaciousness suddenly come upon inside a building. For the first time a shopping center would have a real vertical dimension, with the central Garden Court soaring to a high ceiling, and the two levels of the mall visible to each other. Also, making the central court a dramatic focal point solved much of Gruen's other problem: There was something for the two department stores to be equidistant from.

Southdale took three years to plan and build. A new heat-pump system was devised to create comfort control, and Gruen was more than proven right about enclosure's economy: It turned out to be cheaper to build such a mall than an unenclosed center of the same size. Both the designers and the developer took special care with the mall's aesthetics, especially in the central court. As often happens, initial innovation bred more innovation. A sculpture was commissioned for the court, to balance and enhance the indoor greenery and appointments—the first known occasion of art being specially created for an American shopping center.

Southdale opened triumphantly in 1956. Its success proved many of Gruen's cherished ideas. He showed that pedestrians and spaces designed for them had not been made obsolete by the automobile, and that this kind of separation of vehicular and human traffic created an appealing and magnetic environment. Like Northland, Southdale was planned as a center for surrounding development, but this time it was only one of a number of such centralizing facilities. Another was a regional health center, which was planned to include a hospital, nurses' home, and laboratories clustered around a park. This was a simple illustration of Gruen's concept of "cellular planning," which he felt would both revive established cities and organize suburban growth into more productive and dynamic patterns.

Gruen most of all conceived of the large shopping mall as an antidote to suburban sprawl. He saw it as a centralizing influence, an organizing principle, as well as an adaptable mechanism for creating community centers where there were none. He saw this effort begin in Northland and Southdale, where formerly dormant civic groups were revived, with the mall as their meeting place. Gruen had foreseen that, despite its basically retail character, the mall could be congenial for cultural activities, including concerts, festivals, and theatrical performances. The secret was to create a venue for human activity that was exciting, comfortable, convenient, and fun. When Southdale did just that, Gruen was vindicated.

But what others in the shopping-center industry saw at Southdale was a little different. They saw that people went there not only to make specific purchases but just to be there. They saw that people stayed and shopped and bought, by the thousands. They saw that two department stores didn't destroy each other with competition; they just brought more people to the mall, which created more business for everyone. The idea of mall synergy—the attraction of numbers of shops and their variety drawing more customers than would the sum of the mall's parts—displaced the fear of competition and became basic to shopping-mall philosophy.

Shopping-center professionals recognized the format's cost-efficiency. They saw that the mall worked. Perhaps they didn't know why, but they knew that an enclosed two-level mall with a central court and comfort control constituted the wave of the future. And they made sure of it, by building just that kind of mall all over the country.

"We discovered that the enclosed mall changed the concept," said Paul E. Leyton, then a vice-president of the May Stores shopping centers. "The idea of having the enclosed mall doesn't relate to weather alone. People go to spend time there—they're equally as interested in eating and browsing as in shopping. So now we build only enclosed malls."

Thus it came to pass that not only Minnesota but Florida and California, where the temperature inside was often the same as it was outside, got enclosed malls. It also came to pass that the Southdale model was stripped down to its basic elements and replicated in thousands of suburbs all over America. Design was standardized, cheaper materials were used, and, mostly, the species was stabilized. And since it was so successful in its suburban niche, it dominated throughout the sixties and seventies.

Success is perhaps too weak a word at that. The shopping center business had been a vague and often dubious proposition in the early 1950s. It had its dreamers and especially its showmen—like Don M. Casto of Columbus, Ohio, known in the trade as Super Don. Casto's enterprises included the Great Western Shopping Center, with replicas of the Seven Wonders of the World built in its parking lot, and the Truman Corners shopping center, which not only was constructed on the land where President Harry Truman's family home had stood, but was officially inaugurated by the former President of the United States, in person.

But for a long time before Southdale, the former grocery store executives, real estate agents, and building contractors who were the first shopping-center developers were floundering around in a business without precedent and without direction. They were mostly trying to persuade stores to invest in this new concept, although the concept itself wasn't clear to anyone. "We were trying to lease a dream," said a young Indianapolis developer named Melvin Simon, who was working out of a two-room office building. "No one had an idea of what a shopping center was."

But after Southdale it was clear. The shopping center was going to be the center of everything for suburbia. Edward J. DeBartolo, a developer based in Youngstown, Ohio, was in his fifties when he roofed over the two parallel strips of one of his centers and created his first mall. His wife asked him why he didn't just sell all his strip centers and retire on the tidy profits. "I can't," he told her. "We're getting into the meat of a new kind of development."

DeBartolo bought an airplane and began selecting suburban mall sites from the sky, scouting likely locations in the Midwest cornfields closest to the junctures of major highways. He built an organization that could handle every facet of mall development, from market research to maintenance, out of his Youngstown head-quarters. DeBartolo built more than forty malls, including some of the biggest, and became one of the richest men in America. His empire came to include banks, office buildings, professional sports teams, condominiums, and cable television, and by the early 1980s was valued in excess of half a billion dollars.

A lot of other fortunes were made in the mall-building business, including some that were spread into other enterprises, like Hollywood moviemaking (Melvin Simon) and the buying (the Taubman Company) and building (the Rouse Company) of entire cities. Of course, some developers also had the kind of Gatsby-esque fun that is an American tradition for the newly rich. One Ohio developer threw a wedding reception for his daughter in one of his malls, reputedly rigging the central-court fountain to flow with champagne.

In the process of the mall march, some monstrosities were created—huge concrete deserts surrounding insolent fortresses filled with the sorriest reduction of glamorous dreams ever perpetrated with a straight face, or even a lopsided smile. Even Albert Sussman, the longtime executive vice-president of the International Council of Shopping Centers admitted that "some centers have abused the landscape, created eyesores, have produced chaotic traffic conditions and even disrupted local community life."

But the malls also created places for people to be, with the kind of peace and comforts, excitement and amenities, and *things* that some communities had never had before. People wanted them. It is simply true that the opening of a mall is in many places the equivalent of a Hollywood premiere. Some malls have become sources of civic pride. The Hickory Ridge Mall in Tennessee was awarded the Memphis City Beautiful Commission Award of Merit, the first enclosed mall in that city to be so honored. Such an event has become more or less commonplace now.

But if the magnates and moguls of the American mall were pleased with how things worked out, Victor Gruen wasn't. He criticized the lack of innovation and community concern, the dependence on pseudoscientific market surveys instead of creativity. And then, in his final years, he practically disowned the mall industry altogether. Gruen went back to Vienna, where he died in 1980.

Although his firm continued to design shopping malls—some of them imbued with his innovative spirit—his successors at Gruen Associates also continued to complain about the state of the business. "Whatever has been done has been motivated by making money," said Edgardo Contini, an architect and Gruen partner in the 1970s. "No shopping center is designed because it should be designed that way. That's a concept alien to this country so far."

"Since Southdale, there have been very few changes," said Cesar Pelli, a Gruen design partner who ended his mall career with a last effort at a true community-centered mall in Columbus, Indiana, before going on to design such other projects as the high-rise addition to the Museum of Modern Art in New York City and the World Financial Center complex at Battery Park City, also in Manhattan. "The same formula has been perfected and fine-tuned," Pelli told me. "But the formula is trite and everyone has learned how to reduce it to the minimum. They know what they can afford not to include. Malls have not become true community centers. At Southdale it was realized that people will come in great numbers with just a few public activities."

There was an undeniably special quality to the Central Garden Court at Southdale, and I felt it as I stood there with Barbara. All of the elements that would be reduced to clichés in other malls still seemed integrated and natural there. The Court and the enclosed-mall concept had other antecedents besides the Galleria in Milan and the arcades in London. Neil Harris mentioned the glass-covered courts of some large department stores, particularly in Europe. (The Galeries Lafayette in Paris are particularly cathedrallike.) Even Gruen later found that the visionary architect Ebenezer Howard had foreseen something like this in his ideas for his Garden City: His ring-shaped enclosed shopping center was called the Crystal Palace.

Southdale was perhaps a somewhat homier version of a Crystal Palace, but the combination of grandeur and simplicity was still affecting. And as pleasing shelter, an interior world to walk through, safe from Minnesota's first winter blizzard, Southdale worked just fine.

As we walked around, I sensed the relaxed relationship that the people we saw seemed to have with the mall. This was simply their place, historic or not, to shop in, to fool around, play games, be bored, be with friends, or do nothing alone comfortably. Maybe even to dream.

I looked into an ice-cream parlor and saw a young couple sitting at a table, completely engrossed in each other. By mall standards this was late at night, almost nine o'clock, on a Wednesday during a storm. But they were there. They were talking about something important, squirming a little, perhaps in pain, but whatever they were discussing, passion was obviously involved.

I turned to Barbara. "See that?" I said. "Tell me that isn't romantic. Those two are doing a scene right out of *Casablanca*. All they need is for Sam to pull a piano out of Northwest Organ and play 'As Time Goes By.'"

Barbara looked. "Maybe," she said.

13

Mallsville, Doctor Dirty, and a Mall of Sundays

Much later in my trek it wasn't unusual for me to visit four shopping malls in one day. But this was still early, I was not yet that seasoned, and even the mall tours of Chicago and Minneapolis had left me dazed and overloaded. So I thought I would take a week off for rest and recreation, and where better to do that but right there in Afton.

Barbara and Brian's house was actually a spacious and comfortable three-room apartment above a garage at the end of a dirt lane, which was off a secondary road, a few minutes from the main highway to Minneapolis. It couldn't have been more peaceful, isolated, and rural. Beyond the picture window was a stand of woods, beginning just a few yards away, and I awoke most mornings to sun and trees and silence.

Afton itself was a reasonably wealthy suburb, populated by 3M executives, and at the time was the official residence of Walter Mondale. (Barbara had seen him there once, buying ice cream.) Afton had very restrictive zoning and had managed to keep most development out. Homesteads were large, up to five acres, and despite the modesty of the surroundings, Afton boasted a racquet club with handball courts and sauna, and fashionable pleasure-boating on nearby Lake St. Croix.

But Barb and Brian were not part of Afton's elite social set, so we sought our entertainment elsewhere. We went into Minneapolis for a play at the Guthrie and a stroll through the Walker Arts Center. Our activities closer to home, I soon noticed—the movies, shopping, food and liquor purchases, even the laundry—invariably took us to shopping centers and malls. Brian was a movie buff like me, so we hit the bargain shows at Har Mar Mall, and I had the experience of seeing *Jaws* on a cold Minnesota night in the unheated theater of Grove Plaza Center. Sharks and ice were an odd combination.

One afternoon Brian and I were eating at a pancake restaurant while the laundry was sloshing around at a laundromat in a white-walled, no-nonsense little enclosed mall. When I told Brian that I was seeing more shopping centers on my time off than when I had been actively looking for them, he agreed that this seemingly rural life was dependent on them. It was even more obvious, he said, in western Minnesota, the true farming area where he had grown up. "Towns there are just gone," he said. "Now they're just a grain elevator, the people that work there, and a store. My family lives a hundred and fifty miles from Minneapolis, but they go once a month to Southdale and do most of their major shopping there."

The highways have made a major difference. "When I was in high school," Brian said, "forty miles was still far to go. Now my younger sister drives forty miles out and forty miles back in a day without thinking about it. The roads are better, straighter, and safer." But it wasn't just the highways. "Malls have become cities in themselves," he said. "They've rearranged population." Even in the silence of the snowy fields and the taciturn towns of rural Minnesota, there were no more Smallvilles: just Mallsville.

Later, back at the Lamberts' house, Brian showed me a copy of his hometown newspaper, the Montevideo *American-News*. Just under the masthead was the proud motto; "Published in West Central Minnesota's Finest Shopping Center."

★   ★   ★

As she'd promised, Barbara took me to a local library to prove that the fantastic story she had told me on the ride up from Chicago was true. In the back room we dug through local newspapers, and sure enough, after a half hour or so of searching, we found it—the whole amazing-but-true tale of the scourge of new mothers and the Twin Cities' shopping centers.

Doctor *Dirty* was the police sobriquet for the man who had victimized some fifty women with an elaborately kinky scam over an entire decade. Every few months Doctor Dirty called up a mother recently discharged from the hospital (the police assumed he got the name from the birth announcement in the newspapers) who was waiting for results of her newborn child's standard blood tests. Using a real doctor's name, he told each mother that tests revealed her baby had a rare disease, unfortunately fatal but, fortunately, easily cured. The antidote to the disease was found in the mother's own milk; all she had to do was breast-feed the infant.

If the woman he was talking to was in fact breast-feeding, Doctor Dirty simply ended the call. But if she wasn't, he continued to weave his insidiously persuasive web. He told her that if she hadn't been nursing her child, there was a problem. As a bottle-feeding mother she was given a drug to dry up her milk, and no other drug could counteract it. But without its mother's milk, he told her, her baby's life was in jeopardy.

Now with the woman in a state of emotional panic, Doctor Dirty quietly proposed his unorthodox solution. He told her that the only way to start her milk flowing again was to jar her system with the shock of extreme embarrassment. If she followed his instructions, he could produce the effect that would save her child.

His prescription was this: The woman was to cut the legs off a pair of panty hose, pull it up over her chest, and cut spaces for her breasts. Then she was to go to a *shopping center*. He told her which one. There, at the appointed hour, in the midst of the unsuspecting throng, she was to whip open her coat and expose herself. Exhibiting her bared, nylon-encircled breasts to shopping-center passersby would stimulate the flow of her milk. At that moment, he said, his nurse would meet her there with an injection to complete the cure. It was a fantastic spiel—but approximately fifty women had shown up at Twin Cities' malls, opened their coats to surprised strangers (as well as one hidden and expectant witness), and waited in vain for the nurse.

The police got their first break in the case when an off-duty

policeman stopped a woman who had just flashed the Hub Shopping Center in the suburb of Richfield, and she explained what had
happened. A full investigation began, a story describing Doctor
Dirty's modus operandi appeared in local newspapers, and some
hospital maternity wards began sending new mothers home with
written warnings about him.

But that didn't stop Doctor Dirty. It wasn't until a woman he
had contacted called the police before going through with her therapy that he was caught. She went as instructed to the Southtown
shopping center in another suburb at the appointed hour. The police were waiting and so was Doctor Dirty, all set to observe the
scene from a phone booth.

The police had enough evidence to persuade Doctor Dirty to
confess to that particular incident, though he admitted none of the
others. But they had never really caught him in the act. He was
sentenced to psychiatric treatment, and police would not reveal his
name. They said only that he was a forty-three-year-old salesman
with a wife and two children in suburbia.

There was a certain perverse logic in Doctor Dirty's scheme. He
selected very vulnerable victims and chose the most authoritative
cover possible, that of a doctor who conceivably held a child's life
in his hands. His prescription combined a crazily appropriate kind
of sympathetic magic—forcing the breasts to spill milk by exposing
them, as if the shock would be applied directly—and a certain rationality in the selection of where this could best happen.

For where else could a woman create more shock, both to herself and to passing strangers, than in the busy shopping center,
when she suddenly opened a trench coat to reveal bare nipples
wreathed in panty hose? Such things just don't happen in the middle-class citadel of the mall. The Doctor might even have tapped a
latent hostility or exhibitionism in some of his victims; perhaps
some enjoyed the idea of shattering the placidity of the mall and the
self-satisfied smugness of its suburban shoppers.

In any case the decade-long rash of female flashers in Twin Cities' shopping centers had evidently come to an end. And Barbara
had succeeded in documenting the most bizarre shopping-center
tale I had yet heard—which seemed to please her very much.

> I remember the surprised faces of some of my clients
> when we drove out to a shopping center on a Sun-
> day and found the courts and malls, the lanes and

promenades, filled with milling crowds dressed in their Sunday best, engaging in an activity believed to be long forgotten, that of leisurely promenading while enjoying the flowers and trees, sculptures and murals, fountains and ponds.

—Victor Gruen
New Forms of Community

I'd read about weddings in shopping malls; one involved two devoted mall employees who had met there, courted there, and figured they might as well get married there. I knew of a shopping center with medical facilities for birth, and one with a funeral home. Many had chapels. While I was in Afton, I learned that another of the Dayton-Hudson Minnesota malls, Rosedale, hosted a religious service every Sunday. So, at the end of my Minnesota stay, Barbara and I went to one.

There was no chapel at Rosedale; the service was held in the basement community room at 11:00 A.M., an hour before the mall opened on Sundays, in the same room where Smokenders and Weight Watchers met. Mall management—as is usually the case—didn't endorse the religious organization, but provided facilities as a community service.

Barbara and I joined a group of about fifty adults and a number of children in the community room. The setting was austere—folding chairs and bare concrete walls painted school-cafeteria green. As the unpretentious service started, I couldn't help thinking of the early Christians, stoically practicing their faith in the depths of the catacombs while Rome cavorted above them.

These weren't stoics, but friendly and modest believers. They carried Bibles, but the main part of the service was a sermon by a young divinity student who encouraged us to develop inner values. The student was black, nearly everyone else was white. It wasn't so much a sermon, really, as an informal lecture, with an overhead projector used to illustrate some of his points. It seemed inappropriate for me to take notes, but later I jotted down two statements I remembered: "I am happy; you are happy," and "Kids have a small data base." The kids were on the other side of a curtain, attending Bible school.

The service ended with everyone smiling and shaking hands. Barbara and I were welcomed as newcomers and invited back. By then the mall was open, and we all headed upstairs.

It was barely noon, and I was surprised at how full the mall was, only a few minutes after opening. Families were walking; gangs of kids were running; and the kind of people I was getting used to seeing in malls, just standing around and watching, were already in place, standing around and watching.

For me, fresh from the spareness of the basement, the mall was a pleasant but slightly jarring sensory explosion. We were suddenly in the land of Shirt Works, Tobaccolane, and Florsheim Shoes, and in the presence of the new "Disney at the 'Dales" exhibit. (The Dayton-Hudson malls surrounding the Twin Cities, including Southdale and Rosedale, are called the 'Dales. Fans of National Public Radio's *Prairie Home Companion,* which is broadcast from St. Paul, are presumably in on the joke when Garrison Keillor, its host, does one of his commercial spoofs for Bertha's Kitty Boutique, located "at the 'Dales: Clydesdale, Teasdale, Chippendale, and Mondale.")

I was leaving Minnesota soon, and feeling a little sentimental. Remembering what Barbara had said about the mall's not being romantic, I thought about hanging back a little as we walked through Rosedale, then running to her with open arms. It seemed contrived, so I thought better of it. Then I did it anyway. I stopped and waited until Barbara saw I wasn't beside her and she turned to look back. She wasn't very far ahead when she noticed, so my run was short and I had to parody slow motion. She laughed, and it was our goodbye.

On our way out to the car we recognized some of our fellow celebrants from the basement. They mixed right in with the main show now, the crowded mall on Sunday afternoon. Some of them were still carrying their Bibles, and they were still smiling.

14

Starting from Reality on Long Island

When a *New Yorker* "Talk of the Town" reporter asked Swedish artist Bjorn Earling Evensen how he felt about his outdoor sculpture in honor of Charles A. Lindbergh being placed in the parking lot of the Roosevelt Field shopping mall on Long Island, which occupies the site of the airstrip from which Lindbergh took off on his famous flight to Paris, Evensen replied, "It was my choice. It is the best place I can imagine, because the shopping center is the reality of today—the traffic, the thousands of people. And it is only starting from reality that the imagination can soar."

Malls have become part of the rural reality and the small town, and in the suburbs they serve a variety of functions. In the suburbs of America's largest city, they may have an ironic role—as cities for the cityless, as a substitute for what the suburbanite rejected and left behind. There, too, malls have been more than welcomed; they have become the capitals of a new reality.

Before I made my way to Long Island and its largest mall at Roosevelt Field, I stopped off in Harrisburg, Pennsylvania, to see some old friends, Michael Krempasky and his wife, Liz. I remembered that Liz (then known as Betty McRedmond) had grown up on Long Island, so I thought I would talk to her about it before I went there. What she told me added up to a portrait of a city family's escape to suburbia in the late 1950s. The shopping malls were also arriving on Long Island at about that time, so I learned what they represented in Liz's life as she was growing up.

Until she was nine years old, Betty McRedmond played in Crotona Park in the South Bronx, with the Irish, Italian, Jewish, black, and Puerto Rican children of the neighborhood. She lived nearby with her parents and her three brothers in a five-story apartment building on Bryant Avenue. It had a marble staircase, fashioned a generation before by immigrant Italian masons using marble from Carrara. There was sunlight in their airy apartment, and Betty remembers the cold tiles in the central hall where she played on rainy days.

The South Bronx was a different place in those days from its media image of today. Betty's father, Jack McRedmond, had been born there, and lived until his marriage in another apartment building nearby; it had a marble foyer, a switchboard operator, and mail delivery to each apartment door, twice a day. It was a stable, urban, largely working-middle-class series of neighborhoods.

The decline of the South Bronx began when Betty was a child. The factors involved included the massive migration of blacks from the rural South and of residents of Puerto Rico when restrictions on immigration from that island were dropped at the same time that the city experienced a postwar housing shortage. The housing situation was exacerbated by urban renewal policies, such as the building of the Cross-Bronx Expressway, which destroyed thousands of apartments and cut neighborhoods apart. Poverty, absentee landlords, abandoned buildings, and fear all began taking their toll.

As the security and quality of their urban life began to crumble, the McRedmonds took advantage of the suburban opportunity. Betty's mother wanted to live in a single-family home anyway, as she had when she was growing up in Queens. Her father wanted a change from his city life, he wanted to live "in the country."

So the McRedmonds became part of the second major wave of

suburbanites, the one that began in the late 1950s and was more specifically responding to the swift decay of the cities.

The McRedmonds' march to Long Island began with Betty's aunt, who went out to Eileen Gardens (a subdivision named for the developer's daughter) in the orchards of Old Bethpage and bought a house that hadn't been built yet. While she was in the developer's office selecting her home design and colors from a book, she heard about a new house, already built, that had just become available in another part of the development. She told her brother, Jack McRedmond, about it; he bought it, and Betty had a new home in suburbia.

A million New Yorkers left the city for its postwar suburbs in the 1950s, and the population of Long Island's Nassau and Suffolk counties grew faster than any other counties in the United States. By the time the McRedmonds got there, Old Bethpage and neighboring Plainview were growing so fast that the residents had to petition to get the township government to put in stop signs.

While Old Bethpage was building new schools and churches and the McRedmonds were settling into suburbia—and getting burned a few times on things that city people don't necessarily know much about, like storm windows and shrubbery—the first shopping centers were appearing. There was one already in Massapequa, with a sidewalk in front and a parking lot in back. The newer one in Plainview had its big lot out front. Then, a couple of years after they moved in, the big vacant lot Betty passed every day on the school bus became their own shopping center.

Jack McRedmond had kept his job as a pharmaceuticals salesman in New York City, so he commuted every day in the family car. Mrs. McRedmond, who had been a nurse, was left with the children in a neighborhood of children: In a block of twenty homes, there were about sixty. Mrs. McRedmond would always remember when the A & P in that new shopping center started staying open on Thursday nights. It meant that she could take the car and do the shopping alone, with her husband watching the kids. "It was her only time alone," Liz said. "She says it kept her sane."

When Betty McRedmond was a little older, she went to the Mid Island shopping center on the highway strip outside Hicksville, the biggest around. It wasn't an enclosed mall (although it became one later) but it had a big store—Gertz—with small shops radiating out from it. Betty could get there and back on a bus.

Later, when she was in high school, the Walt Whitman Mall opened in Huntington Station on the Jericho Turnpike, fifteen minutes away. Walt Whitman was immediately *it* for every teenager who could get there. Some of the kids caused trouble, a favorite prank was dumping detergent into the fountain, which would then overflow with suds and slosh into the doorless shops. But Betty and her friends simply started at one department store—Abraham and Straus, say—and worked their way down to Macy's, visiting the intervening shops to compare prices, styles, and sizes of clothes, earning their wings as junior consumers.

For Betty, new to this array of affluence, it was a fantastic playground—and also educational. She loved trying on the things—high-heeled shoes, coordinated outfits—that populated her fantasy image of herself. But she saw how sometimes the fantasy didn't fit. "Things looked different on a fourteen-year-old than they did on the mannequins in the window," she said.

But learning the thrill of buying wasn't really enough. Betty missed Crotona Park sometimes, and the old men reading Hebrew papers who kept a quiet eye on the children playing there. In Crotona Park she had looked with wistful envy at a Puerto Rican girl with pierced ears, and a black girl's naturally curly hair. But those girls weren't in her Long Island life, and neither was anything like the park.

"You grow up in the suburbs, and it's supposed to be this great place to raise kids, but what they forgot to build were parks and places for kids to go," Billy Joel once told a reporter. He grew up not far from Betty McRedmond, in Levittown, and as a fledgling rock star he played keyboards for a band that headlined in the basement club of a Long Island shopping center.

But for Betty and her friends, the equivalent of going to the city was going to Roosevelt Field Mall. It had opened in 1956, just off the Meadowbrook Parkway. Beginning as an open mall supply depot for bedroom suburbs, it continued to grow, adding department stores and new wings, enclosing in 1967, and including freestanding office buildings and banks, restaurants and services, all spread like crunchy peanut butter on a white slice of suburbia. Soon Roosevelt Field Mall became not just a place to pick up a few things between trips to the city, but an alternative to the city itself.

For the peaceful green lawns were nice, and the whole idea of a yard was novel, but still there was some yearning—especially in those kids Betty's age who remembered their lives in Brooklyn and the Bronx—for something of the pace and scale of the city. Roosevelt Field brought a little more bigness and speed, and a bigger mix of people. It *moved*.

Shopping centers like Walt Whitman became the Main Streets of suburbia just about from the start. They had no real competition. But suburbia was getting bigger. A majority of the manufacturing jobs New York City was losing ended up in its suburbs. It was soon possible for people in communities like Eileen Gardens to avoid going into the city for anything—and many of them did.

For Betty's mother, Roosevelt Field became a little too much like the city; she preferred the more understated Walt Whitman and Sunrise malls. But for others, very large malls like Roosevelt Field came close to being substitute cities, in some surprising ways.

After my visit with the Krempaskys, I got back on the train to New York City. From Manhattan's Penn Station, I took a Long Island Railroad train to the Mineola station, and from there a taxi to Roosevelt Field Mall. I wasn't the only one. The cab driver told me that every morning people came from Manhattan to work at Roosevelt Field. "Reverse commuting" was a fact of life in suburbia.

I met Frieda Stangler, the marketing director for Roosevelt Field, and we talked in her office. The mall was in the midst of a major $7 million renovation, she told me, that would give it a more contemporary and unified look. The renovations included several large new skylights, tile planters containing tropical foliage, natural oak seating, and a fountain and pool. It would be virtually a new mall within the shell of the old; the idea was to change its image from a utilitarian hodgepodge to a stylish Crystal Palace in Garden City, Long Island.

At the moment, though, the first-level area nearest the mall office was a bare concrete warren that looked something like the Penn Station I had just left. The office itself was large and cluttered; it looked like the police precinct headquarters in *Barney Miller*.

Roosevelt Field certainly had some urban dimensions. It covered more than 2 million square feet of leasable area on a total of 110 acres. There was parking for 12,000 cars. Approximately 275,000 people visited it every week, coming from all over Nassau County and eastern Queens. Only Grumman Aircraft, the electric utility company, and the county government employed more people than did the mall itself.

The mall had some 185 stores and services. "The only two

things you can't purchase here," Frieda Stangler said, "are new cars and fresh meat." In terms of gross leasings, Stangler said, Roosevelt Field was the largest shopping center in the country.

The management of so large a mall is even more like a government than it is in other malls. There is more infrastructure to deal with, and at Roosevelt Field the problems can also become positively urban. Security, for example, is taken very seriously. Vandalism is troublesome—when I told Frieda Stangler about Greengate's Christmas decorations, she got a little wistful. Roosevelt Field had to put fences around decorated trees, and made sure that anything that could be torn off was too high to reach. But the mall's security force, primarily made up of retired New York City police officers, is well equipped and trained, and on duty twenty-four hours a day. The equipment includes patrol cars, walkie-talkies, and in a few cases, guns.

"We used to have a group of younger guards," Stangler said. "But now we stress a more mature, authority-figure image. They have to command respect. As someone once said, you get more with a smile and a gun than just a smile.

"But we have just three or four incidents a day," Stangler added, "ranging from wallets being lifted to a stolen car. We have almost fifty thousand shoppers a day, and six thousand employees. You're talking about an average small-sized city. A small city with only three or four incidents of crime is damn good."

A mall must govern not only itself and its customers but also its tenants, and at Roosevelt Field that responsibility is taken seriously. Its ability and resolve to control its tenant mix has twice been tested in court. The mall initiated—and won—both cases. The details differed, but in both situations the mall argued that the businesses involved were detrimental to the mall's image and contrary to its needs, and that it was within its rights to get rid of them.

The mall government also provides the bread and circuses that bring people in for the benefit of its tenant stores. Malls do this more extensively and directly than cities—it's a civic function that malls have refined and expanded. Not only does the mall promote specific merchandise or store buying; it also responds to what the community wants.

Frieda Stangler's own responsibilities fall into this area. She is the marketing director but her job description includes promotions, advertising, public relations, and information—which, of course, was why she was talking to me. What Stangler and her counterparts at other malls do is fairly new in the shopping-center business. "At first nobody even did promotion for their malls," she said. "We were one of the first. It started here in the mid-sixties, when our used-car dealer promoted himself as being in the mall, and that turned out to be a promotion for the mall too. It worked so well that the mall began doing it for itself."

Now promotions are a more sophisticated part of the overall mall government. "We schedule our promotions according to a plan," Stangler said. "There are really two philosophies on how to do that. The first is the 'shoot while the ducks are flying' theory. That means you concentrate heavy promotions at peak times— Back to School, say. The second theory is the 'pull them in and make them change their minds' theory. With this you allow no dead periods, like after the January clearances until Lincoln's Birthday, and you promote all the time. We subscribe to the first theory. We take a good thing and make it better."

Mall promotions can be internally generated, or the mall can take advantage of the various touring mall shows, from the Disney at the 'Dales type of package to the hypnotists, traveling craft shows, petting zoos, and fishing ponds that have made the mall circuit into a latter day vaudeville. Some promotions have direct product tie-ins, and others just try to attract a crowd—although sometimes in a specific way. Roosevelt Field, for example, sponsors events to attract men, who are not the prime mall shoppers.

"If a wife has decided to buy a pair of shoes at the mall," Stangler explained, "but she doesn't want to come alone, and she sees in the paper that there's a car show at Roosevelt Field, she can tell her husband and he might come along. While she shops, he can look at cars and maybe he'll buy something in a store, or he and his wife will eat here or buy ice cream for the kids. The car show not only got him here, it got her here."

But as suburbia and the mall business have changed, more than the mall's appearance has been renovated. There is an increasing interest in learning what the mall's constituency wants, and that means market research.

"Up until the mid-1970s, we were all called promotion directors," Stangler said. "It was just who could put on the biggest show and the best show. Now market research means something."

Roosevelt Field is number one in its market, Stangler said, but part of her job is to gather, analyze, and implement the information that will keep it in first place. "The population of Nassau County is decreasing now," she said. "Any increases in our business will come from getting a bigger portion of the same pie. We aren't dealing with a population boom out here anymore. We have to change our tactics and be more aggressive.

"We're concerned with keeping in touch with our market," she said, and that means making periodic studies of the needs and wants of the mall's constituency. Preferences in products may change according to factors like a troubled economy. "Are we throwing nonessentials at them when what they want is bread and butter?" she said. Also important is simple identification—"Who are our customers?"—and learning what their lives are about.

All this information is used not only to select what merchandise is sold and how, but to guide Stangler in the kind of promotions and community activities she will try to get for the mall. In a curious way, this sets up a direct relationship between the mall government and its citizens—the citizens vote via the market study, and the mall government responds.

Some of the things Roosevelt Field's customers were voting for surprised Frieda Stangler. "I noticed we were getting strong responses to our educational and cultural promotions: museum-type art exhibits, lectures, and so on. We had the cast of a Broadway musical come here to talk and perform. That got a big response. I was surprised, so I looked at our market research again and it showed that a lot of people weren't going to Manhattan very often anymore." So Roosevelt Field had another role to play—as a Lincoln Center for Long Island.

All of this also suggested to Stangler that Roosevelt Field ought to participate more directly in the local community, and be more aggressive in establishing itself as a center for community groups and activities. The mall took one step in this direction when the Roosevelt Field Merchants Association became the first group of shopping-center retailers to sponsor college scholarships for students in its constituency.

And why not? The mall, being malleable, can expand to include nearly everything its customers want, and many malls are doing so, providing urban-style amenities otherwise lacking in the increasingly autonomous suburbs. From the beginning, when the department stores first came to the malls, they've stocked merchandise formerly available only in the city. Now there is more: Besides four department stores, sixteen shoe stores, twenty-one shops specializing in women's wear and eleven in men's, Roosevelt Field had when I visited it seventeen eating places, several banks, a service station, movie theaters, an optician, a tropical aquarium, the Long Island Catholic Supply, an office of the National Leukemia Foundation, Weight Watchers, Van's Car Wash, a hearing aid center, a post office, and the Nassau County headquarters for the Girl Scouts of America.

Malls have become the accidental capitals of suburbia. A mall like Roosevelt Field wasn't part of the original suburban dream, but that dream had flaws that the mall could address—the notorious suburban boredom among them. Everything in suburbia at first was either small or formalized. Liz McRedmond Krempasky remembered that. "Everything for kids was organized—Little League and things like that," she told me. "We rode bikes, hung out at the pool all summer. But basically it was waiting for the driver's license."

But even then, the car eventually had to stop somewhere. After decrying the loneliness and isolation of the suburban way of life in a *Psychology Today* interview, writer and psychiatrist Robert Coles added, "But I guess the nearest thing I've seen in the suburbs to the communal rituals of more traditional communities is the Saturday trip to the shopping center . . . The important thing is the act of going to a particular place where they may know other people or where they may at least recognize others as impersonally like themselves. . . . Some suburbanites may not go next door to meet a person, but suburbanites will come home and discuss at length how they met so-and-so while shopping."

The mall combines urban and suburban elements in a particular way: The idea is to have the urban amenities but within an environment that, like suburbia itself, is controlled. Neither suburbia nor the suburban mall wants to repeat the conditions that drove their residents and customers out of the city in the first place. Suburbia keeps out the poor mostly through the cost of housing, although zoning can play a part. The mall can also segregate by price, and although nobody wants to brag about it, malls can also choose not to include products and styles that might appeal to nonwhite, nonaffluent customers.

The mall is the city suburban, but even with its managed environment it can become too urban for some suburbanites. Soon I would be meeting some of them—suburbanites in revolt against their own creation, the city in their backyard called the mall.

15

Marcia's World:
A Mall Revolt in Washington

WESLEY: There'll be bulldozers crashing through the orchard. There'll be giant steel balls crashing through the walls. There'll be foremen with their sleeves rolled up and blueprints under their arms. There'll be steel girders spanning acres of land. Cement pilings, Prefab walls, Zombie architecture, owned by invisible zombies, built by zombies for the use and convenience of all other zombies. A zombie city! Right here! Right where we're living now.

—SAM SHEPARD
Curse of the Starving Class

I had some friends in Washington, D.C., from my months there editing a weekly paper called *Newsworks,* one of a series of city tabloids geared to a Baby Boom audience that had come and gone in D.C., as elsewhere, since the 1960s. One of these friends was Marcia Mintz, dance critic for the paper and a dancer herself. Marcia had grown up in a Washington suburb and had gone to high school literally in the shadow of what was then the biggest mall in D.C.'s suburbia. Now, another mall—which again would be the largest around—had just opened practically in her parents' front yard, and they were not very happy about it. In fact, some of their neighbors were in active revolt.

Walter Johnson High School—named after the famous pitcher for the Washington Senators—was situated in what was frankly a cow pasture. There were pastures all around it, and cows were in them. The team mascot was "The Mighty Moo." But when Marcia was in ninth grade, the landscape suddenly changed. And so did everything else at Walter Johnson High School.

Because up the hill from the school appeared the Montgomery Mall, a giant two-level shopping enclosure with two major department stores and the full lineup of other shops, services, eating places, and a fountain and everything. It was nothing outrageous as these places went, although it was a little spectacular. But all of a sudden, nobody at Walter Johnson could remember what they did on Saturday afternoon except call one another up at around one o'clock and ask, "Going to the mall?"

So the girls went shopping at Garfinckel's and Hecht's and the shoe stores and ladies' shops, and then the boys would show up at around three and everybody would walk around, checking one another out. Sometimes they'd meet in Bresler's 33 Flavors for ice cream and wisecracks, gossip and giggles, and maybe once in a while to share those transcendent adolescent moments of trying to figure out parents and teachers, God and the future, if any.

It did not take long for Montgomery Mall to become an intimate and almost institutional part of Walter Johnson High School, and therefore of the suburbia it served. Marcia's senior prom and Christmas dance (the Snow Ball) were held there. She spent many of her open-campus free periods there, sharing a chef's salad with a friend or just walking around. The mall management was not unaware of the potency of this relationship. When Montgomery Mall's fountain filled up with the pennies people tossed in for luck, the mall enlisted the school's head cheerleader and its drum majorette to wade into the water in bikinis and sweep up the coins, all for the edification of the cheerfully leering throngs lined around center court—and, of course, for charity.

The nearby city of Washington, D.C., including fashionable Georgetown, was off limits to Marcia until she was sixteen, but even after that she rarely went there. Before Montgomery Mall existed, Marcia and her friends had done their shopping, soda guzzling, and ritual-recreational shoplifting at another shopping center, the Wheaton Plaza. But the major portion of Marcia's suburban *American Graffiti* years took place in the enclosed atmosphere of the mall.

In fact it took only a few years for the mall to become such a part of Marcia's world and the daily experience at Walter Johnson

High School that it was included as a natural and memorable part of
the evening landscape, as seen through melancholy adolescent eyes
in an elegy in the 1970 yearbook:

> It's getting late.
> The sun collapsed behind Montgomery Mall hours ago.
> These halls are empty tunnels interrupted by piles of dust
> left by previous life.

In 1968, Montgomery Mall was the first superregional shopping
center to open in the Washington, D.C., area. Six months later an
even larger mall, Tysons Corner Center, opened nearby. Then
came Landover Mall, Springfield Mall, the Lake Forest Mall in
Gaithersburg, the Fair Oaks Mall in Fairfax . . . and then in 1977
came what one former Washington area mall manager called the
Taj Mahal of the industry: White Flint, the largest of them all.

Washington is ringed by the classic yellow-brick superhighway
to suburbia, the Beltway. Several of its suburbs are even named
after the highway—Green Belt, for instance, and Beltsville. And of
course there's a mall named after it, too: the Beltway Mall. In the
1960s and 1970s, Washington's suburbs grew very fast in area and
population, and generally in prosperity as well. The suburban
malls, especially the superregionals, were quickly accepted. But by
the late 1970s, that growth and prosperity began to cause trouble
for mall developers. Besides the increased competitiveness caused
by the number of malls, there was also the beginning of resistance
from the very people whose lives the malls had transformed.

White Flint opened in an area designated as North Bethesda,
Maryland, but it faces a suburban community called Garrett Park
Estates, which happens to be where Marcia's parents live. They
were among the people who were not happy to see White Flint
arrive as it did.

Marcia's parents live on a quiet, tree-shaded street in this well-
to-do residential community on the outer fringes of suburban development. Their street is at the edge of Garrett Park Estates, sheltered from the highway by thickly wooded hills. Beyond one
gently rising level of trees there used to be a golf course. But visible
now through the thin veil of branches on a crisp, sunny October
afternoon are the tall light-stanchions and the dim bulk of White
Flint Mall.

"They lied to us," said A. Chester Flather, who lives across the street from Marcia's parents and was their representative on the neighborhood council. "I'd like to shut the place down before Christmas. Really sock it to them about the first of December." Chester Flather was a middle-aged man wearing his first pair of designer jeans ("Do you iron these?" he asked Marcia), and, having been apprised of my interest in the White Flint situation, he came bounding across the street as I arrived. The battle with White Fint was clearly the most important fight the neighborhood council had been involved in, and for Flather it was invigorating.

From the first overtures made by the Lerner Corporation, Washingon's major mall developer, Marcia's parents and many of their neighbors were skeptical. They worried about pollution and traffic patterns, the impact of the mall on their landscape, and the relationship of the mall to the place where they owned homes and lived. But, according to Flather, the developer made certain promises: Don't oppose us and we'll put everything in writing—meaning agreements on such matters as lighting, landscaping, sewage disposal. The developer promised to install pedestrian walkways and landscaping.

"There was opposition here at first," Flather told me. "But then people started thinking how it wouldn't be so bad. They liked the idea of having a nice Bloomie's and Lord and Taylor out here, and maybe a few more shops—twenty-five or thirty. The housewives thought they could work there part time." So the Garrett Park Association voted to rezone the proposed site and let the mall in.

But when White Flint opened in March, it was larger than any of Garrett Park's residents had imagined. In fact, it was vast. Many more of the trees that shielded them from the center were cut down than they had expected. The traffic immediately became overwhelming.

Some of Garrett Park's residents were shocked. Formerly sheltered from the highway by woods, distance, and money, they now had huge lights glaring down on them at night and a massive white Taj Mahal drawing a steady stream of cars virtually to their front yards. There were complaints that covenants Lerner had signed promising landscaping and walkways weren't honored. The county government briefly withdrew permits for completion of the mall's interior but reinstated them after Lerner agreed to new covenants. The chairman of the planning board was disgusted with what he said were White Flint's foot-dragging and piecemeal efforts to placate the community. "We feel they have had ample time to provide us with something comprehensive," he told a local newspaper. "I'm loath to deal with it at all on this basis. It's hogwash." There was talk of a consumer boycott of the mall.

Rumors swept through the community, hardening the resentment: unsubstantiated stories of alleged underhanded techniques used to acquire the land and questions about why the mall was permitted despite commercial-development restrictions and a sewer moratorium. "It really bothers me," said Marcia's father, "that a big corporation can come in here and do as they please."

"Our quality of life has eroded," Marcia's mother said. "We moved downtown without having to move."

But even so, there was ambivalence. For all his eagerness in expressing indignation, Flather and the Garrett Park Irregulars weren't really going to call for a boycott, mostly because they didn't believe it would work. The women of Garrett Park were already shopping there. The kids were going there—Flather's own niece worked in a White Flint cinema. It was becoming the new happening place not only for their suburb, but for the entire Washington area. "When I used to tell people that I lived off White Flint Road," Marcia said, "they'd say *where?* and I'd have to spell it. But now White Flint is *it*."

Even Marcia's mother was slightly embarrassed by her complaints—one of which was that the increased automobile pollution was blackening her white lawn furniture. Still, she and her husband had worked a long time to acquire this home in this setting, and as semiretired professionals, they were now spending much of their time at home—something they'd looked forward to for years. But Marcia's mother doesn't dare drive on the highway on Saturday afternoons anymore, and she misses looking up the hill to see the trees. Instead she sees that dimly veiled white colossus. It isn't her world anymore.

I was there on a sparkling Saturday afternoon. Marcia and her boyfriend Larry, who was a graduate student in city planning, drove me through the labyrinth of access roads to White Flint. We parked and walked first into Bloomingdale's, gazing at the big Bloomie's-logo scarves, umbrellas, and handbags, the glass iceballs, automatic teamakers, the yellow infant sleeper suit that says BLOOMIE'S BABY in navy-blue, the natural stone stickpins, Anrel triacetate and nylon fleece designer signature robes, the Death Mask of Tutankhamen 551-piece jigsaw puzzle, and the PUNK sign in blue neon.

Then we moved into the central area of White Flint mall, which was dominated by leather seats and by several levels of plants around the glass elevators going to three floors. At a posh cocktail lounge on the top level, shoppers in wicker chairs could sip decorous drinks and peek below to the Eatery, one of the pioneer suburban fast-food courts offering French, Mexican, and Italian fast food, along with places like "The House of Dill Repute."

Farther on in the mall were Lord & Taylor and I. Magnin and a host of boutiques along the Via Rialto, an ersatz Venice street. White Flint's most original theme area, Georgetown Alley, wasn't yet open; it was to resemble the cobblestone streets of turn-of-the-century Georgetown, that fashionable but city place a few miles away where Marcia wasn't allowed to shop as a teenager. Now she wouldn't have to go there; White Flint brought Georgetown to suburbia.

On our way back to Marcia's parents' house we were lost for ten minutes in the parking lot. Finally finding the exit in the bright sunshine, we were passed by a carload of high-school cheerleaders, on their way in.

White Flint, and malls in general, were still on the minds of Marcia's family later in the day. They talked about this mostly because I was there, but what impressed me was how much they had thought about it already. Amid unflinching evaluations, their ambivalence remained one of the most striking features of their conversation.

Marcia's older sister and brother-in-law joined us for dinner on the patio. Afterward we adjourned to the basement recreation room for coffee and cake—it was Marcia's sister's birthday. Marcia asked her sister about her high-school days, before Montgomery Mall, and what she did. She said she just hadn't gone anywhere much. She had belonged to a church group and a high-school sorority.

Marcia's father seemed anxious to balance his earlier negative statements about White Flint. "Having a mall here is not all bad," he said. "If you live in the suburbs and don't relate to downtown, with a shopping center you have nothing to miss and everything to gain. Out here we had no public space before the malls. We never thought of Bethesda as 'our town.'"

Marcia's brother-in-law traveled extensively in his job and talked about malls elsewhere in the country. He mentioned seeing a chapel in a mall: ". . .a nondenominational non-chapel, totally in-offensive to any religion. It was plastic, indescribable."

Larry, the city-planning student, compared malls to cities. "Cities are a jumble that become organic over time," he said. "They are susceptible to change in unpredictable ways. In cities you are constantly surprised. This breeds a kind of tolerance. But malls are prefab islands with separated functions. They're stable. You could go to a shopping center and never be surprised. A person who encounters life in measured doses and gets everything in her-metically sealed malls is . . . what?"

"Boring," Marcia's father said.

Mall Wars

Garrett Park wasn't the only community in America up in arms over the incursion of a shopping mall in its backyard. In the eighties, the whole question of suburban development and the mall's role in it had become a national issue, and a number of towns, cities, and even suburban areas had begun to oppose the building of malls.

I learned more about this when I attended a shopping-center symposium in Washington sponsored by the Center for Urban Policy Research at Rutgers University and the U.S. Department of Housing and Urban Development. I'd heard about it by chance and arrived unannounced at the L'Enfant Plaza Hotel, where it was being held. When I asked the desk clerk where the mall conference was, she sent me to the basement, where the L'Enfant Plaza had its own mall of shops. It seemed an appropriate place for the conference, but it wasn't really being held there. The clerk had just misunderstood me.

Instead, the conference attendees—consisting of federal and local government administrators, planners, planning consultants, retailers, insurance executives (present, I imagine, because so many malls have been financed by insurance companies), bankers, mall developers, city mayors, reporters, and a couple of geographers—sat in a large, typically mal-furnished hotel function room on a higher floor (if not a higher level), listening to panel-loads of speakers.

They discussed a number of issues, but the hottest topic on the agenda was something called the Community Conservation Guidance, a policy statement issued from no less than the White House during the last months of the Carter administration. This brief statement announced that if development outside cities and towns would (in its words) "demonstrably weaken existing communities, particularly their established business districts," then federal funds would not be granted for programs in support of that development, such as help for new roads and interchanges or sewer and water lines.

Although the Guidance could be used against any kind of development, everybody knew that it was mainly aimed at shopping malls. Robert Embry, the assistant Housing and Urban Affairs secretary who wrote the first draft of the statement, as much as said so when he pointed out that when a big mall is built on the outskirts of a town—usually with the aid of federal money for infrastructure—and the town's business district fades as a consequence, then the towns "come to us with a request for millions of dollars to rebuild themselves and get back to where they were before the shopping center was constructed."

The Community Conservation Guidance received some initial praise in government, city-planning, and press circles. Neal R. Pierce, a Washington-based journalist who specialized in urban and design matters, wrote, "Rather than being too assertive, the problem with a national regional mall policy may be that it's long overdue." (This column ran under the title "Hopes for Control of the Malling of America" in the newspaper where I saw it, so naturally it caught my eye. The title of my article, already published in *New Times,* had apparently entered the language.)

But the mall industry's counterattack was very strong. Albert Sussman, vice-president of the International Council of Shopping Centers and its main policy voice, said that the government was trying "to play God" and "determine by edict where people should live, where they should shop, and what their lifestyles and living patterns ought to be." The ICSC has a substantial war chest for government lobbying and had won impressive victories in the past, notably in getting malls declassified as pollution problems because of the cars that go to them. The organization went into battle once again, and within the first few months of the Reagan administration, the Community Conservation Guidance was canceled, with only a few malls having been temporarily affected by it. "This is a great victory for the industry," Albert Sussman said. "Now we can get back to business."

But that was hardly the end of conflict for the mall industry; it wasn't quite business as usual, as defined in the sixties. The White House statement had been an extraordinary recognition of many conflicts already raging between malls and municipalities and citizens.

During the lunch break at the conference, I talked with Beth Humstone, who was working in Burlington, Vermont, to keep a large suburban mall from being built outside the city. It was a battle that had already been going on for years, and would continue for years to come, eventually involving the state supreme court. Vermont had an unusual legal weapon for anti-mall forces to use: a statute called Act 250 that figured prominently in the mall war between the city of Burlington and a mall developer, the Pyramid Company. Essentially a law that focuses on preventing overdevelopment from causing environmental harm, Act 250 also provides that local government must have the economic ability to pay for services for new development. The proposed mall would at least equal the retail space of downtown Burlington and, opponents contended, would threaten the substantial efforts made for downtown revival.

Both sides hired experts to prepare painstaking studies with elaborate statistics, and lawyers to interpret the Vermont environmental law. The anti-mall warriors even came up with their own fight song, "The Mall That Ate Williston" (Williston being the nearby rural area where the mall would be built). At one point, a district commission on environment ruled against the mall, but the issue went to the Vermont Supreme Court and then back to lower courts, where there would be more battles.

What I found in talking to Beth Humstone, and later to others who had been involved in similar confrontations, was that for all the legal wrangling and statistical convolutions, there were often strong feelings involved, with both sides certain theirs was the fight for right. These were *wars*—some with epic-sounding titles like *Ithaca* v. *Pyramid,* or *Appleton, Wisconsin* v. *General Growth.*

I found a ground-level account of one of these wars in *Mother Jones,* written by Jay Neugeboren, a writer and 1960s activist who was living in Hadley, Massachusetts, when the Pyramid Company proposed a new mall just outside of town. He became a leader of the opposition, which contended that traffic through town would inevitably change the main street from the town's center to, in the words of another of the anti-mallers, "a retail black-topped strip for the benefit of people 30 miles away." Other issues raised at one point or another were the mall's impact on schools, crime, water treatment, and the character of the town, plus the possible destruction of the two smaller malls already in the area.

Pyramid struck an early alliance with the town's officials, promising them some $300,000 in taxes from the mall, so mall opponents (unlike those in Burlington, which had town government backing) were on their own. Pyramid also guaranteed itself some local business support by forming a new company to build the mall with local partners, thereby cutting them in on the profits.

The developer launched its initial blitzkrieg with a team of executives and an elaborate slide show for town officials and citizens depicting an opulent, landscaped modern mall that would contain trees, a running brook, and a waterfall, creating a "rural atmosphere" inside the building, which would sit on more than twenty-five acres of former farmland.

The town's officials quickly approved the plan—too quickly, as it turned out. They violated the town's own regulations by not allowing the required time for public response, and the anti-mall forces called them on it. A court decreed the mall must stop, and Pyramid, which had begun bulldozing the site within hours after the officials voted, was temporarily halted in its tracks.

The issue was then left to a town meeting of citizens to settle. While opposition and controversy grew in Hadley, Pyramid (according to Neugeboren) launched a public relations campaign that included telephone calls and letters to key citizens, the courting of senior-citizen groups with free dinners, and on the night of the town meeting, Pyramid allegedly bought all the drinks at Hadley's two biggest bars. Their efforts worked. In an unusually large and contentious meeting, Pyramid won by a three-to-one margin.

But the war wasn't quite over. The Massachusetts courts entered the fray with an injunction preventing further construction until a hearing could be held on the merits of an alleged zoning law violation. The mallers then escalated their own efforts. Pyramid petitioned the Hadley government to rescind the very zoning law that was at issue in the courts. A subsequent town meeting did rescind it, and since the law the court was considering didn't exist anymore, the case was declared moot. Pyramid had won unconditional victory. They built the mall.

Although Hadley did not thereupon instantly die, Neugeboren asserted that much of what the anti-mallers had predicted eventually did come true: Traffic increased, as did automobile accidents and crime; taxes were raised to pay for road widening, repairs to the sewage treatment plant, and expansion of the town dump. Meanwhile, the business of the two existing malls, as well as of the neighboring towns of Amherst and Northampton, was bled by the new mall. It did so well, in fact, that Pyramid thought about expanding it.

Some local papers that had favored the mall were less enthusiastic about the new traffic tie-ups. But they also reported the response of the first shoppers at the new mall: "It's beautiful; it's just like Disney World."

Although some mall wars involve disputes over effects on the natural environment, most focus on the damage a mall might do to an existing central business district, or CBD. Such damage had apparently been done often enough that local governments were increasingly worried; they'd seen enough other towns disappear. And they didn't have to be small towns anymore. A city the size of New Haven, Connecticut, felt threatened by a major new mall planned nearby. "Will North Haven's Big Mall Be New Haven's Death Knell?" asked a *New York Times* story, and its answer was: quite possibly. A HUD study reached the same conclusion, prompting an "Editorial Notebook" comment in the *Times* favoring the withholding of government help for the project, and this was after the Community Conservation Guidance was history.

For those fighting malls on this issue, the chief problem has been lack of appropriate legal weapons; they sometimes resort to whatever weapons are at hand, like environmental laws. The anti-mallers of Appleton, Wisconsin, tried that. They claimed that the developers in identical bright-green jackets from General Growth Companies could not build their mall on land crossed by Mud

Creek, because environmental law forbade construction that inter-
upted the flow of a navigable waterway. Mud Creek, in fact, had
been navigated exactly once, when anti-mallers paddled their ca-
noes a few hundred yards during the spring thaw. General Growth
called the environmental issue a phony, but Appleton claimed the
right to use any weapon to defend itself against a company that had
marched over local opposition in other towns. General Growth—
obeying the injunction of its own name—had malls all over America: in Bettendorf, Iowa; Leesburg, Florida; and San Juan, Puerto
Rico, for example. Appleton anti-mallers felt that General Growth
therefore had no special interest in the integrity of downtown Appleton.

Even though the Mud Creek stratagem didn't work, it helped
arouse sentiment in Wisconsin toward changing state policy or law
to reflect the concerns of town centers threatened by malls. Each
such mall war establishes precedents, and there are similar move-
ments in other states to change laws at least to allow the CBD
issues to be confronted directly.

A lot of mall wars fought on this issue, however, seemed to end
in the way we are used to wars ending these days—in an odd sort
of accommodation. The compromise is usually annexation: The
city government simply takes over the land where the mall wants
to locate. This way the city gets tax money and some control over
the mall through zoning laws; the mall developer is happy because
the mall gets built.

The irony is that annexation does not solve the basic problem of
damage to the CBD. Yet few cities pass up the opportunity. "There
is no question that when a city can annex a shopping mall, that
indeed takes place," said Thomas Muller, an economic analyst and
mall wars expert for the Urban Institute. "From a fiscal perspective,
annexation helps the city a lot. But it doesn't do much for the
downtown."

The other common accommodation in recent mall wars is perhaps even more ironic. It is the malling of the CBD itself. This is
more or less what happened in one of the early mall wars that pitted
Ithaca, New York, against the Pyramid Company.

Ithaca is an almost perfect example of the small growth market
of the future. Its largest employer is Cornell University, and its
economy is otherwise based on electronics and other industries requiring an educated work force. Ithaca is an old town in a beautiful
setting. But this same combination of factors that make it attractive

to the mall also make for a citizenry that values its old and established downtown. So when Pyramid swept through to build their mall on the periphery, Ithaca rose up to meet the invaders.

But even their substantial organized opposition could not win the day. After the smoke had cleared, a somewhat shell-shocked Mayor Edward Conley told an audience in Amherst, Massachusetts, gearing up for their own mall war: "It's naïve to think you can co-exist with those people. . . . The mall people work twenty-four hours a day to eat you alive."

Yet with a careful town revival, which included the Ithaca Commons—a city-run, car-free shopping and community center—and Center Ithaca, a downtown multi-use mall, Ithaca survived the opening of the suburban mall. Citizens could go downtown to watch blacksmithing exhibitions, listen to the Glacier Memory Sextet and Ithaca A-Capella, attend lectures on dog obedience and grooming, as well as chamber orchestra performances, poetry readings, senior-citizen square dancing, children's plays and church choir concerts. Ithaca survived by fighting mall with mall.

There are other issues involved in a more general opposition to rampant malling, the principal ones being concern over suburban sprawl and the loss of open spaces and agricultural land. By 1981, experts were estimating that America was losing 3 million acres of prime farmland a year, and that if development continued at that rate—together with soil erosion and water shortages—there could be an indigenous food crisis by the end of the century.

The farm problem evoked special emotions in a country that was for much of its history a nation of farmers. But like the Illinois cornfields we passed on the way to Fox Valley mall, the best farmland is usually flat, and flatland is ideal for houses, roads, and shopping centers. So the value of farmland tripled and in some areas quadrupled in the 1970s, which made for prices only developers could afford. Farmers sold out, for reasons not always economic (who wants to farm next door to a shopping center?) and developers bought up the land, sometimes holding it in reserve for years. Some efforts were made (notably in Suffolk County, Long Island) to make it easier for farmland to remain either farmed or open land, but the embattled farmers of America have rarely stopped a shopping center for long.

For their part, the mall developers were convinced that their side was right—and convinced enough in some cases to endure years of court battles and enmity. They could even get indignant, as

I learned from their speeches at the L'Enfant Plaza Hotel. "Did malls cause the growth of the suburbs?" one speaker asked himself, and answered, "Only an idiot would think so." Some mall advocates went on to argue—as Victor Gruen once did—that malls actually combat sprawl by organizing development around them.

Other speakers said the idea that America was running out of agricultural land and space in general was sheer nonsense. Some acknowledged that CBDs were getting hurt, but they felt that government interference was un-American because people wanted the malls—their market studies proved it.

They also asserted their right as American businesses to go where the profits are, and in many cases those places were the so-called "middle markets," the smaller cities (like Burlington and Ithaca) with a growing population of educated and affluent citizens employed in such growth industries as electronics and recreation. One market research firm found that retail sales were likely to increase 54 percent by 1990 in such smaller places, against some 37 percent in larger markets. So these wars were worth fighting.

In fact, there may have been a harbinger of things to come in the Battle of Battle Creek, Michigan, as reported by National Public Radio's *All Things Considered*. The city of Battle Creek, predominantly black and poor, had a showdown with the suburban township of Battle Creek, predominantly white and prosperous, over a proposed suburban mall that the township wanted but the city, fearful for its downtown, didn't want. This battle was ended by a unique third-party "Big Power" intervention: The Kellogg Company, colossus of both Battle Creeks, said that it would not build its new corporate headquarters in the area unless the city and the township merged so that the mall could be approved and built. Kellogg wanted the mall because it would have the kind of classy amenities that would satisfy upper-middle-class executives and white-collar workers. Under the economic gun, the cereal-dependent voters in both city and township agreed to Kellogg's terms: They merged and approved the mall.

Do anti-mallers ever win? Once in a while—like the community groups in State College, Pennsylvania (home of Penn State University), who organized an aroused and educated citizenry for two years of skirmishes until the Oxford Development Company withdrew its plan for a mall outside of town.

Perhaps such a victory inspires those who continue to fight mall wars all over America. Back in Greensburg I read about a neighborhood in Pittsburgh fighting against the proposed Parkway Mall (another mall named after a highway) and particularly against the use of federal funds to build it. "Don't take my money to kill me," one small retailer told a reporter. Residents in another Pittsburgh suburb fought another proposed mall because they feared its size, and they worried that some of them would be forced off their land to make way for it. "We're not trying to stop progress," one resident said into a television news minicam. "We're just trying to save our homes." In eastern Pennsylvania, mall opponents in the Lehigh Valley printed bumper stickers that said. DON'T MALL US!

There was an interesting coda to the mall war phenomenon, when Bette Davis starred in a made-for-television movie called *Family Reunion*. She portrayed the embattled matriarch of the fragmented founding family of a picture-postcard New England town who fights to save the ancestral homestead from a conspiracy to seize it, in order to build on it a shopping mall.

The shopping mall as villain, supplanting other impersonal and unfeeling representatives of mindless and heartless progress—from the evil landlord to the mortgage bank, the government, and the massive and polluting corporation—is something new and intriguing in popular fiction. It is particularly interesting in this case because the plot of *Family Reunion* was reportedly based on a magazine series that surveyed hundreds of American families concerning recent societal changes that have most affected family life.

Apparently those who responded thought the mall represented one of those factors, and the makers of the movie thought the mall was enough of a common enemy to provide a mass television audience with an inspirational battle they could instantly understand. So there must be more A. Chester Flathers out there in the Garrett Parks and Ithacas of America, waiting to do battle.

17

D.C. Panoply—
and the First Black Mall

Most of the boomtown publicity of recent years has gone to places like Houston and Phoenix, while New York City and Boston still retain their images as the nation's centers of wealth and culture. Even the suburbs of Chicago have been studied more than those of Washington. But the facts show that Greater Washington is the richest metropolitan area in the country, that it has been growing in wealth and population through thick and thin, especially since the 1960s, and that much of this growth has occurred in a wide swath of suburbia.

Washington also has the highest education level in the nation, the highest percentage of heads of household between the ages of twenty-five and thirty-four, and of women in the work force, and the lowest percentage of the population over age sixty-five. Most of the money is out in the suburbs, which, except for Prince George's

County, are virtually all white. (The city of Washington has a majority black population.) Five of the twenty most affluent suburbs in the nation are in the Washington metro area.

So it should hardly be surprising that in the late 1960s and early 1970s, suburban Washington experienced a boom of major shopping-mall construction. Developers fought one another for potentially lucrative properties, and the sheer number of malls and their greater and greater opulence as the years have passed made mall-to-mall competition probably the fiercest in America. This is another kind of mall war, pitting developer against developer for the rights to mall empires.

Jean Callahan, another friend from *Newsworks* days, took me out to the first truly major mall in the area, Tysons Corner Center. It opened in 1968, just as that part of suburbia in Fairfax County, Virginia, was beginning to boom. Before the mall, there was nothing at Tysons Corner except what you would expect had you happened on its name on a map of the South—a gas station, a general store, and a fruit and vegetable stand. But it was exactly the kind of corner for a shopping mall: the intersection of three major highways, including the Capital Beltway.

In fact, two developers wanted to build on this site: the Lerner Corporation, a local outfit, and the Rouse Company, from not far away in Maryland. Both developers submitted proposals to the Fairfax County Planning Commission, which recommended the Rouse plan. But then there was a tumultuous ten-hour meeting of the County Board of Supervisors, featuring expert witnesses for both sides armed with drawings and plans, charts and studies. Whether the actual meeting was where the decisive action took place or not, by the end of it the supervisors had voted, 4–2, to go against the Planning Commission and award the mall rights to Lerner.

It was a fateful decision. These were the early days of the mall boom, and the meeting influenced more malls than this one. With this foothold, Lerner became the master mall builder of metro Washington, and the Rouse Company looked elsewhere for its spheres of influence.

According to contemporary accounts, Tysons Corner mall was a revelation to suburban Washington. Overnight it created a mall sensibility—an appreciation, if not a hunger, for comfort-controlled, plushly appointed and richly stored, bejeweled and begardened enclosures. It was immediately perceived as the perfect expression of suburban affluence and the appropriate symbol of suburban prestige. If your suburb was going to be anywhere, you had to have a major mall. Otherwise, nowheresville. Without a mall you were a *rube*.

By the time I visited Tysons Corner, however, there were many newer malls, and in areas of high competition, newness counts. All the same, Tysons looked to be a community center still; perhaps less of a spectacle than before but nonetheless the place for a significant population to shop and eat and hang out, and to call its own. In fact, one of its problems had become urban-sized traffic jams around the parking lot.

Nothing much interesting happened to us as Jean and I walked around Tysons, except that during lunch in the Magic Pan Crêperie our waitress flubbed one of her programmed lines ("I'll take your check when you're ready," she said as she handed me my change) and realizing her error she almost fell apart, like those movie computers that start to spew smoke and nonsense when they make a mistake.

I learned more about the place from an excellent piece in the *Washingtonian* magazine, written by Lynn Darling. Darling interviewed old people at the mall (some of them purposely sitting where they could watch children's pictures being taken with the Easter Bunny) and teenagers ("Why would I go to another shopping center? I wouldn't know anybody there. Here, if I wait around long enough, I can see just about everybody I know") and mall store employees (one of whom repeated the line I was to hear often: "You work here long enough, you find out this center is a regular Peyton Place," but when the teller is pressed for details, the stories turn out to be pretty tame, quite familiar, and of decidedly local interest).

Darling also got a middle-aged shopper to come close to admitting what is otherwise implied: "We come here because it has everything we want and nothing we don't want. There aren't any problems with parking, or crowds, or crime, or . . . well, we don't have to say what the other problems are."

The other problems that white suburbia perceives are black people, and Washington's racial situation was going to figure in the future of the next mall Jean and I went to, Landover Mall.

At the time we visited it, Landover intrigued me for another reason—its head-to-head competition, via very pointed media advertising, with another mall. In the short time I'd been back in

Washington, I'd noticed television ads for Springfield Mall, accompanied by the slogan, "Springfield Mall—it's something else!" spoken in a bubbly voice. Television ads for malls outside the holiday seasons were rare then, but not really strange. What did catch my eye—and ear—was a television spot for Landover Mall. It featured an innocuous video montage of mall scenes but with a sizzling sound track: a woman's voice proclaiming in the semihysterical tones of a rabid game-show contestant, "I used to have the Springfield habit, but now I go to Landover Mall—it's *more fun!*" Her voice then collapsed into deep throaty giggles, accompanied by the clinking of glasses and assenting male laughter.

Aside from the fact that nobody said anything about shopping in these ads, or prices, or even stores; aside from referring to regular mall-going in the language of drug addiction; aside from the idea that malls were selling themselves as being "something else" and "more fun," there was the startling tactic of naming the competitor, at the time pretty daring in advertising.

That, and the sexual implications of the ad piqued my interest, so I got Jean to drive out to Landover Mall to see what might attract bored suburban housewives and men of leisure for afternoons of wild abandon.

What we found was a slightly down-at-heel mall, dark and severe, with a polluted pond as a centerpiece, its picturesque wishing-well pennies lying among cigarette butts, plastic forks, and foam under an oily slick. Apart from the Tropica plant store and two beauty salons, I couldn't imagine what would entice a suburban woman. The ads, it seemed, were all competitive hype.

By then it was Happy Hour at the Porch on the Mall, and our tour was therefore over for the day. As we got into our half-price drinks, we chanced to overhear a man and woman at the next table arranging an extramarital tryst. So maybe there was something to this sexy image-making after all. "Maybe their spouses are at Springfield Mall," I suggested to Jean.

Then Jean told me about a story she had just done on single women in Washington. It turned out that the women she interviewed were meeting men not so much at bars and parties, as she expected. Most of them were meeting men at shopping malls.

There was an even more interesting twist to the Landover Mall story which developed after my visit. It seems that I had seen Landover when it was coming close to its all-time low point. The mall had opened in 1972 with high hopes of joining the other big malls as a citadel of affluence, with its own market sphere, catering to the ever-expanding and ever wealthier white middle class. Market projections showed that Prince George's County would grow to a million mostly monied inhabitants. But as the 1970s went on, that's not what happened.

Fewer people moved to the county than expected, and many of those who did were black. Instead of the unbroken march of single-family houses on neat white streets, there were apartments and low-income housing as well. The upper-middle-class whites headed for other suburbs, and those who lived in the Landover area soon began shopping at the newer malls elsewhere.

So Landover, a huge mall with four major department stores and, at its height, more shops than Tysons Corner, was that rarity in malldom, a suburban mall on the skids. Predictably, mall management and mall stores were at each other's throats, as nighttime vandalism in the parking lot spread and beer cans were strewn along the mall courts. Landover sank into a Muzak-glazed depression.

Then, gradually, Landover's merchants began to accept the fact that black people made up 70 percent of their customers instead of 35 percent when the mall opened. They began to treat them as a clientele by adding merchandise that appealed to them, and soon found that there was enough of a market to revive the mall's business. One store reported that 80 percent of its sales were from the "high fashion young black trade." Mall management was inspired to clean things up and restore the fountain and pond with sparkling fresh water. Another ad campaign was started, this one more realistic. Landover Mall experienced a rebirth, as possibly the first successful black shopping mall in suburbia.

Later on this trip, I visited two of the newest shopping-mall expressions of Washington's recent affluence. I'd already seen White Flint, the grandest so far, but there were others, closer to the city of Washington itself. They were also "specialty malls," which began coming into vogue in the late seventies. Technically a specialty mall has mostly high-fashion shops and a greater variety of eating places, anchored either by the most fashionable department stores or by no department store at all. But essentially what a specialty mall specializes in is rich people, or people who spend money as if they were rich. In the retail euphemisms of the day, these are the "upscale" customers or, even more obnoxiously, the "high end" market.

Washington was a prime place for these centers, for no matter what community functions malls fulfill (Tysons Corner hosts the Vienna Society of Artists show each year; Lakeforest Mall in Gaithersburg had its own Shakespearian festival, complete with "sonnet readings and Shakespearian proclamation in the Penney's court area"), the major function of a Washington mall is usually to express the affluence of its customers.

Affluent Washington is pretty much a nouveau riche city, having grown very fast in the last generation, and it is still looking for legitimacy among the urban centers of America. One of its bids for both prestige and urban efficiency was the Metro subway system. The major Metro stations are strange and wondrous: spacious enclosures out of which shoot long escalators, climbing at some stations so steeply that, going up, you seem to be riding directly into the sky. The stations themselves, resembling the bare shells of Victorian-era terminals brought underground, add a sci-fi ambience with electronic fare-card machines and circles of light inlaid along the tracks that silently blink when a train approaches.

Especially when the system was new and pristine, when the blink of the lights in the eerie quiet of the station was followed by the efficient hum of the train, one felt a quality of a clean but quaintly adventurous future already under way. Somewhat in this spirit, down the tracks (which were already down the rabbit hole) lay a brand-new mall, a kind of logical extension of the Metro.

Out past the Pentagon and Pentagon City stops was Crystal City and, attached to its station, the specialty mall called Crystal City Underground. The same brick floor that covered the station led gently into the mall, where the decor dropped the Metro's austere efficiency and assumed a more fanciful air, with gingerbread-house motifs and cute shops like Larimer's wine and cheese store, which proclaimed, "Established, though not on this spot, 1894." Welcome to Wonderland.

Crystal City Underground was something of a theme mall, designed by a Santa Monica, California, architect to resemble the turn-of-the-century streets of (for some reason) New York City. But the basic themes of the mall were money and newness. For just as it bore no resemblance to the chaos of shops and kiosks in New York or Boston subway stations, the mall did not serve subway patrons only. Even though it was underground, it had other entrances connecting it to the fifty thousand people living in high-priced condominiums just above it, and in a series of eight hotels stretching to the nearby National Airport. Altogether, this is the lucrative market it was designed to serve.

As I walked through Crystal City Underground for the first time, I came upon a wine and cheese party celebrating the opening of a new shop, the Bed 'n Bath. Though this was perfectly appropriate for a contemporary Wonderland, it was a good deal fancier than the Mad Hatter's tea party.

I chatted with a laconically polite woman in an expensive pants suit who said she was a friend of the owner. (The Underground began with many locally owned shops, but eventually shifted to specialty chain outlets, like Casual Corner and Crabtree & Evelyn.) At one point I mentioned Tysons Corner mall. "It's all right, I suppose," she said, "but it smells like hot dogs." So much for the erstwhile capital of suburban splendor in Washington. The king is dead; long live the Underground.

The last new specialty mall on my tour was the Mazza Gallerie, developed by the Neiman-Marcus department store, which was also its anchor. Although in a business sense Neiman's may have overextended itself here, psychologically the Texas-Washington connection makes perfect sense. The unquestioning clear-eyed worship of wealth I found most prominently displayed in two places in my travels: Washington and Houston. But that may have been because I didn't get to Dallas, where Neiman-Marcus is headquartered.

So perhaps the most expressive of Washington's mix of mall fantasies is this Mazza Gallerie, a severe structure of white Italian marble, not unlike what a Washington presidential monument might look like if it, too, were anchored by a Neiman-Marcus store.

The Gallerie opened with a typical Washington social event, the black-tie celebrity gala, with charity as the usual pretext for Washingtonians to dress up and mingle with power. In this instance they had the additional thrill of having the huge Neiman-Marcus store all to themselves for an evening's worth of private pawing of pavéed-diamond watches, cabochon rubies, mulberry silk dinner dresses, nylon storm coats, brown velvet evening suits, silk crepe de chine tunics, and lambskin patch-pocket blazers.

The Gallerie eventually got forty-five posh stores, including

Ted Lapidus and other designer outlets based on Rodeo Drive in Beverly Hills, but as this opening gala was being prepared, only Neiman-Marcus was opening. The store's management office was awhirl. "Get me Pearl Bailey again," someone shouted to a secretary. A copy of *The Social List of Washington* sat on one desk amid sandwich remains and ad proofs. Press kits were being prepared, complete with photographs of Richard Marcus and the manager of the Washington store, plus fact sheets on them that included the first names of their wives.

Meanwhile, in the store itself, salesgirls were sorting out shoe boxes on a woven beige rug that looked like an enormous sweater. A black fashion model was being photographed while a high-powered young woman was giving her sales staff a pep talk, emphasizing the goal of getting the *very best* clientele in Washington. Since then, that goal has had to be broadened somewhat and the Gallerie changed, but ambience still matches these aspirations.

Before I left, I peeked into the still embryonic mall, the shops mere outlines drawn in slightly surreal, Thurber-esque wobbles on plasterboard walls. But soon it would be a mall, and for all its glitter and all the high-fashion charge Washington would get from it, there were things that would always be part of it—inescapable, intrinsic to the mall environment—no matter how far above the hot dogs of an aging suburbia Washington and its new malls might aspire. One of them was represented by a panel truck parked outside. It was from Muzak.

A few days later, just before I left Washington, I had lunch with Marcia and Larry, and reported to them my final mall activities. I'd finally made it out to the Beltway Plaza mall on Greenbelt Road at Exit 28 of the Beltway. There was something primal about all those names—here was a mall that was on the highway and bragged about it, offered obeisance to it with its own name. It was enclosed and air-conditioned; it had more than eighty stores and room for five thousand cars to park. There was no pretense.

Next I would be turning my attention west, to the newest parts of America. There, migration had occurred not only in past centuries but again and in great numbers after World War II, both in the West and in areas of the South—which together have become known as the Sun Belt. This last great migratory wave had splashed back new cultural ideas and fashions upon the whole country. The centers of the Sun Belt, in particular, had taken the shopping mall to their literal hearts. No story of the mall would be complete without the West and South, just as no account of the Sun Belt can neglect the mall, its social and cultural role, and its style.

As I talked to Marcia and Larry about my western plans, I remembered a moment in White Flint Mall when the three of us were standing together. While my eyes were scanning the mall, Marcia's were darting to the various products on display, and Larry had looked at both of us and laughed. "If you're not a consumer here," he said to me, "you must feel like an agnostic touring the cathedrals of Europe. Most people here are worshipers."

It was true. What I was doing was counter to the mall's nature and purpose, and certainly different from what everyone else was doing in the mall. I did shop in malls, I roamed around them thinking of nothing, I ate and drank there, I watched people, and I enjoyed myself, pretty much like everybody else. But the main business of my mall odyssey was to be empathetic and objective, observant and receptive, a listener and an analyzer, alien and human.

Now I would be leaving the more familiar East and Midwest, where I had friends and guides to help me and accompany me, and going off to places I had never been, and where I would be largely on my own. As we concluded lunch in Washington, I mentioned some of these thoughts. I must have been pretty poignant about it, because suddenly Marcia looked a little concerned.

I laughed. "Aw, shucks, Marcia, don't worry," I said. "It's a lonely job, but somebody's got to do it."

Alice Moulton-Ely

Market Square, Lake Forest, Illinois: first planned shopping center in the United States (1916).

The Rouse Company

Faneuil Hall Marketplace, Boston, Massachusetts: first attempt to rehabilitate an historic urban area.

William Severini Kowinski

Galleria, Milan, Italy: prototype for American
shopping malls.

William Severini Kowinski

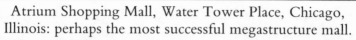

Atrium Shopping Mall, Water Tower Place, Chicago,
Illinois: perhaps the most successful megastructure mall.

Tom Cramer

Gruen Associates

Fox Hills Mall, Los Angeles, California: stylish example of
urban redevelopment.

Harborplace, Baltimore, Maryland: proved that marketplace
malls could be successful in an urban area.

The Rouse Company

Gruen Associates

The Commons and Courthouse Center, Columbus,
Indiana: architecturally important attempt to combine public
and private spaces.

Greengate Mall, Westmoreland Mall, Greensburg,
Pennsylvania: examples of how a mall can change a
community's social patterns.

Metrocenter, Phoenix, Arizona: an example of malls as a
center of growth in the West.

Trump Tower, New York City: suburban shopping set in
urban elegance.

Southdale Center, Edina, Minnesota: first fully enclosed
shopping mall in the country.

Suzanne Opton

Monroeville Mall, Monroeville, Pennsylvania: adding a
contemporary look to a small town.

Suzanne Opton

Westmoreland Mall, Greensburg, Pennsylvania: a good
example of a large, controlled, and well-managed space.

Part 3

PARADISE ENCLOSED: THE ODYSSEY CONTINUES

Across the sands of all the world, followed by the sun's flaming sword, to the west, trekking to evening lands.

—JAMES JOYCE
Ulysses

18

From the Prairie to the Plains: Sex, Drugs, and Rock & Roll at Gateway Mall

Anyone whose ideas about the heartland come from media stereotypes would be surprised by Lincoln, Nebraska. I know I was. Lincoln has a progressive city government and its school system has won national recognition for excellence. There is an intelligent openness reflected in its university and general citizenry. It is all-American football crazy where the Nebraska Cornhuskers are concerned, but in Lincoln I also heard a reggae band from Jamaica. It is the city where the midwestern prairie meets the western plains—the true gateway to the West. But it also has many of the same new problems usually associated with bigger, more coastal cities.

While I was there I would be visiting Barbara Cottral Bean, a classmate at Knox College, and her husband, John Bean. Since I arrived on Amtrak's San Francisco Zephyr at five in the morning, I had booked a room at the Clayton House, a hotel on the main downtown artery of O Street. After a few hours' sleep and a phone call to Barbara—whom, I learned, everyone was still calling Barbie—I looked out my hotel window onto O Street and found myself gazing directly at a huge white sign plastered over a mammoth building: GOING OUT OF BUSINESS, it said.

After a shower and coffee, I walked over to investigate. The building was the Brandeis department store, as large inside as it looked from across the street. Already it had been stripped to its bare walls. As I learned later, Brandeis had been a Lincoln landmark for decades—the young Henry Fonda had been employed there once as a window dresser. Now, most of the floors were already closed off, and all that was left were a few long tables of sorry-looking merchandise, the last dregs of strange clothes in bizarre colors and irregular sizes, and some tawdry Nebraska Cornhusker souvenirs. (However, there was a red Cornhusker tasseled cap in my size, so I bought that.)

Lincoln had its suburban malls—two of them—that were drawing off business from downtown. The central district had made some changes—it had recycled older buildings (like Barrymore's, the backstage of a monumental old theater now become a college bar) but its main new attraction was a contemporary downtown mall fortress on O Street called the Centrum.

The Centrum was right next to Brandeis—connected to it, in fact, by an elevated walkway. When Barbie came to meet me, we ate lunch there. We walked through the gleaming interior street of shops and fast-food outlets (right at the entrance was a Charlie Chan's, which already disturbed my preconception of Nebraska) to a large, sumptuous Mexican restaurant, with waitresses in wine-colored cocktail dresses slit to the thigh. I was glad I wasn't wearing my Cornhusker cap.

By now, what outlying malls can do to downtown districts was no longer a surprise, and Lincoln's mayor was alert to the problem. She was Helen Boosalis, who at the time of my visit was also serving as president of the United States Conference of Mayors, which represented some 840 cities. She was the first woman elected mayor in an American city of more than 100,000 population. I got an opportunity to talk to her about how her city was coping with its malling, and the first thing I asked about was the closing of the Brandeis store.

"That was a shock to everyone," Helen Boosalis said. "After the skywalk opened connecting the Centrum to Brandeis, their sales went up, but their parent corporation decided to close the store anyway. We've had proposals by others for that building, but not for a department store. From what I read, the days of big department stores downtown are over."

For years, Lincoln had a comprehensive plan for development which included its suburbs. Nebraska grants broad annexation powers, and Lincoln was quick to annex Gateway, the first suburban mall. But the plan called for radial development, with downtown as the true center. "I've always said," Mayor Boosalis told me, "what do you think of first when you think about your hometown? Downtown."

When Gateway mall began cutting into their business, downtown merchants were complacent at first—they felt they had a captive audience because the central business district is sandwiched between the Nebraska state capital buildings and the huge University of Nebraska campus. But in the mid-1970s, the city council received proposals for three major suburban shopping centers, on sites set aside for them in the comprehensive plan, and that scared the downtown merchants. The council eventually turned down the malls but warned the merchants that if they continued to let downtown slide, the applications would be reconsidered.

So the merchants came up with the Centrum, originally planned as a huge enclosed colossus until the city government objected. "It was so large that it would have blocked out our Nebraska sky," said the mayor. "We also wanted windows—some relationship to the street. We got it scaled down, but we lost on the windows. They wanted people to come inside and walk there."

At first the Centrum provided the shot in the arm that downtown needed. One of the department stores that had first come to Lincoln at Gateway mall even opened up a second store in the new enclosure. "I think it may be the first case in the Midwest of a store in an outlying shopping center putting a new store downtown," the mayor said.

But now the closing of Brandeis had cast some doubt on the downtown's future. Mayor Boosalis said those suburban mall proposals could still be revived, but in a general sense she was pleased with how Lincoln had coped so far. "We've paid attention and kept up," she said. "Omaha has the same zoning powers as we do but they didn't use them in the same way. They went with shopping centers everywhere, and now they're spending millions of dollars to save their downtown."

★   ★   ★

Once I moved over to Barbie and John's house and met their two young sons, David and Jeffrey, I told Barbie about the visit to our old college I'd made on my way to Lincoln. Knox College is in Galesburg, Illinois, about an hour's drive from the Mississippi River. Galesburg had two major claims to fame as a quintessential heartland-of-America place: Carl Sandburg was born there and Knox College had been the site of one of the Lincoln-Douglas debates. But even without these distinctions, Galesburg looked like the mythical midwestern town, with wide flat streets lined with leafy trees and large, wood-frame Victorian Gothic homes. It was this aspect that affected the young Ronald Reagan, who spent a few years of his childhood in Galesburg; it was where he learned to read. "I was deeply impressed with the big green trees and the dark red brick streets," he wrote in his autobiography. "They fitted into a picture of bright-colored peace, the way some primitive lithographs do."

I hadn't been back to Galesburg in a decade or so, and neither had Barbie, so she was interested in hearing about my visit. My first and most startling impression of our old campus was that it was empty. I walked across the grounds and through the buildings and saw hardly anyone; if I hadn't known better I would have guessed it was spring break.

That's not how I remembered Knox. The town may have been that peaceful in the mid-to-late 1960s, but the campus wasn't. Barbie and I had been part of the largest class in Knox history, but our numbers were superseded the very next year, and again the next, as the rest of the Baby Boom thundered into higher education. So the student union and the campus coffee shop we knew had been a constant panoply of chatter, laughter, coffee, and smoke, and the dining halls had been noisy and full, with winter coats overflowing the coatracks and heaped on the floor in characteristic intimacy.

Now the Baby Boom had been and gone, and Knox enrollment was something like half of what it was in the peak years. So the coffee shop was silent. The students were quieter, too.

Things were again different when I went into town, and that brought into the conversation with Barbie the saga of Jay Matson. When Barbie and I had known him, Jay was the tall, bearded poet, who strode our campus in mysterious silence and wrote a small number of short, intense poems. He was from Galesburg, and seemed very much in the tradition of other writers and artists of a peculiarly midwestern weirdness who had lived there at one time or another, including Edgar Lee Masters, author of _The Spoon River Anthology;_ Eugene Field, author of strange and famous children's poems; Dorothea Tanning, the theoretically unlikeliest painter to be born in Galesburg in that she was the only woman and only American to be part of the original surrealist group in Paris; and Jack Finney, best known for the two film versions of his story "Invasion of the Body Snatchers," but who also wrote an equally creepy story about how this town's past had occasionally risen up to take vengence on its attempts to change, called "I Love Galesburg in the Springtime."

The last time I'd seen Jay Matson was in the winter of 1969, when he was living in a farmhouse on the outskirts of Galesburg. A radiator pipe had broken, so he had no heat and there was water everywhere. Several rooms of the house were like skating rinks.

But in the 1970s, Matson's life changed. Galesburg had just gotten its suburban mall—called, predictably, the Carl Sandburg Mall—and downtown business was hit hard. At one point some thirty stores were vacant. Matson decided to open a restaurant, but downtown merchants resisted him. So instead he bought an old meat-processing plant outside the central district, refurbished it, and opened The Packinghouse, a restaurant that became an enormous success. Matson went on to do the same thing with several more old buildings, and suddenly the town caught on to the idea of selling itself as a historical place. With the help of outside guidance and funds, Galesburg began preserving buildings and installing decorative hitching posts on Main Street. Meanwhile, Matson was presumably laughing all the way to the bank.

I lunched in one of his restaurants, which had introduced Galesburg to such items as cream cheese and lox, filet mignon, and snails in puff pastry. There was a salad bar on an old Railway Express wagon, and several kinds of quiche on the menu. But what truly astonished me about the place was how crowded it was. There were young men and women in business suits streaming in; I'd never seen such clothes and coifs in such numbers in Galesburg before. The reason for it was obvious: These were the grown-up Baby Boomers, now the lawyers, accountants and bureaucrats of town. The college dining hall had moved off-campus.

It was an object lesson in the continued cultural power of the Boomers. There was a connection here as well between the fact that

a high percentage of Boomers went to college, and that they pa-
tronized a place like The Packinghouse. The connection was in the
sophistication of the menu, and in history-as-style. But it was also
perhaps in the resemblance between the enclosed college campus
and this consciously created environment—for this wasn't just a
restaurant; it was an artfully designed experience, accomplished by
a poet turned entrepreneur.

Many of the Boomers eating in The Packinghouse had also been
exposed in their youth to the enclosed mall, so they were used to this
themed ambience. For those of us at the beginning of the Boom,
malls may not have been part of our lives right away. It was that way
with Barbie: She hadn't really become aware of malls until she'd
become a mother. We talked about her experience at the mall in Iowa
City, where she and John had been living when David, their first
child, was born. Since Barbie was an active writer of fiction as well
as a mother, former teacher, and journalist, she later expanded on
our conversation in a letter. This is some of what she wrote:

> The mall in Iowa City was called, simply, the
> Mall, and I could get to it in five minutes in the car.
> It was just a long, one-level brick enclosure, not too
> big, just right. Walgreen's at one end, Sears at the
> other, Killean's [a branch of a Cedar Rapids depart-
> ment store] in the middle with a nice fountain (in-
> door of course) in front of it.
>   It's hard now for me to remember what was so
> momentous about my first trip out of the house
> alone with David. But he was just out of the womb
> and I had this need to explain everything to him, to
> ease his bewilderment, to protect him from smells
> and colors and the noise of the car, to apologize for
> all jolts and sudden changes. The first place we went
> was the mall and I was incredibly proud of being
> able to manage it. At first I didn't have an Um-
> broller (one of those little fold-up strollers) so I car-
> ried his car seat inside the mall (in that big easy free
> parking lot I had no trouble parking near an en-
> trance) and carefully put it in a Walgreen's shopping

cart which they blessedly provided and which everyone drove all up and down the Mall.

So inside the mall, we were safe and free. Safe from the weather, which is a double menace when you have a tiny baby, safe from noisy trucks and dirt and wind, safe from curbs and alleys and sudden bumps. If he fell asleep in the cart, I could browse in Waldenbooks as long as I liked, or for baby clothes at the ABC Kiddee Shop. Once or twice I even nursed him in a dressing room.

When he got bigger and could sit up in the cart, the Mall was our treat, our secret indulgence, and we went almost every day. David liked the fountain and the Coloring Book toy store and we both liked Waldenbooks and the record store. Sometimes we would eat at the A&W, which was exactly the same as a drive-in A&W, except you could just push your Walgreen's cart loaded with baby and packages into it, get your food, and sit at one of the tables. Nothing could be easier.

And when he got big enough to walk, the Mall was a space big enough for him to run in during the winter and empty enough on a weekday for him not to cause a disturbance. I usually saw someone I knew, since I knew mostly young mothers then and that's where we all went. Mothers would gather around the fountain and watch their children play as though by a pond in the park. And yes, David saw his first movie at that Mall, in Cinema I.

But a young-mother mall has to be uncomplicated, not too big, and above all *flat,* so our mall days were over when we got to Lincoln. You can't do Gateway or the Centrum in an Umbroller. It was a big readjustment—maybe it wasn't Iowa City I missed so much as the Mall.

She added some ideas about how malls fulfill some of the needs and fantasies of a young mother.

There is no need like the need of a mother alone in the house with a small child, her first small child, for public space. I used to fantasize the ideal spaces—large rooms full of play equipment with comfortable chairs for mothers to sit and socialize, like nannies in the park. But you can't go to parks in the winter, and even in summer you aren't likely to see anyone you know. Malls—flat, controlled malls—come very close to fulfilling what is probably a vestigial need.

Barbara closed her letter with a final fantasy:

For those of us who tried to re-create our own child-hoods in a changed world, who tried to do what our mothers did but without grandparents a few blocks away or in the house, without other mothers home all day in the neighborhood, the mall was a surro-gate grandmother's house. (The modern little Red Riding Hood, instead of being sent to Granny's house, would be sent to the mall, and the wolf would be an eighteen-year-old with long hair and a Ted Nugent T-shirt in a Mustang convertible, who would appear disguised as a benign clerk in the rec-ord store.)

If Barbie and I had come upon the mall relatively recently, clearly it was part of the lives of another generation literally from the beginning. I was later to hear still more stories that confirmed this. For example, a television camera operator in Pittsburgh told me that whenever he and his wife dressed their two-year-old daughter to go out, she would immediately begin chanting, "Mall! Mall!"

The mall was part of the life cycle of Lincoln, Nebraska, as well. Before the Centrum, there had been Gateway, a classic open center of the 1950s which had since been partially enclosed, but still had the wider courts and the floors sloping slightly toward the cen-ter (for drainage) that are sure signs of formerly open malls. Gateway was very much the community bread-and-butter mall, with Ward's, Kresge, Sears, and a freestanding edition of the Bran-deis department store—only this one wouldn't be closing.

Not far away—in fact, virtually at the end of the Gateway parking lot—was another, smaller mall called East Park Plaza. It was
newer, with narrower courts and a darker, lower ceiling than
Gateway's. It was also obviously more upscale. Its slightly varied
floor levels were decorated in patterns of deep-brown, with lots of
greenery, in contrast to Gateway's flatness and its plain white walls
and ceilings. East Park even smelled different; unlike Gateway,
which smelled of cement and brick, East Park smelled, not unpleas-
antly, of plastic. The customers were also different. In Gateway,
families flowed through the wide white courts, with children stopping to watch the mechanical toys lurching out of Thingsville. In
East Park, the customers were more often lone sleek women gliding through the semidarkness into small specialized shops, like
Asian Gifts.

These are the environments the children of Lincoln know well. I
spoke with a junior-high schoolteacher, Marilyn Hoagland, who
agreed to ask her students to write a few paragraphs about their
malls. Several of them did.

Eileen Hatfield's response was brief and pointed: She made a
case for the Centrum's greater popularity with junior-high kids
than Gateway, because it's easier to get to on the bus, and "you can
eat somewhere other than a tearoom, like the hot dog place or
McDonald's. Also, kids go to the Centrum and then go to a movie.
At Gateway I think there's more senior high kids because more kids
go to the game room."

But the longer essay and argument for the mall was by Todd
White, who began with the proposition: "The Freaks (Smokers,
Drinkers, etc.) have their corners to hang out on. But they keep
their corners to themselves. So we 'straight' people need somewhere else to get together. So why not shopping malls?"

According to Todd, you can go to the mall alone and still find a
friend there. "In a mall you can do all kinds of fun stuff, without
your parents' watchful eye, that's pretty fun to do! Like play
Ditch-'em and hide n go seek. All of the games and things are
harmless—don't hurt anybody—but still receive scorn from shoppers."

The mall presents other scornful adversaries, too, like store
owners who assume the kids are stealing. "They can really make
you feel uncomfortable. Even if you are not screwing around, you
can catch hell from one, for going through and looking. One

bawled me out for playing with his Slinky. If it wasn't supposed to be touched, what did he have it sitting out for?

"And the old people. God! What prejudices can be found in old people. . . . If I told them all *their* faults, it'd take an hour. I don't call them all bums and winos, so I wish they wouldn't call me a 'perverted pot smoker.'"

Todd wrote that policemen were hardly ever problems, though "usually, when you get in trouble with one of them, you deserve it. Like throwing a hamster off the third floor of the Centrum.

"But all-in-all, shopping centers are fun," Todd concluded. "Not harmful fun, like spray painting a window, but fun fun, like getting together with friends, shopping around, and sneaking in R-rated movies."

The kids of Lincoln were not only experiencing the same kind of malls as the rest of the country—they were experiencing it all. Barbie's babysitter and friend was Mary Samson, a sixteen-year-old who lived next door. Mary got a group of her senior-high friends together to talk to me about what life and the malls are like for teenagers after junior high.

When I started asking them about some of the phenomena associated with teenagers in the parts of the country that get more media attention, Mary laughed and looked at her friend Nora. "We knew that was coming!" Mary cried. "When Nora said to me, what do you think he'll ask about, I said, what do you *think* he'll ask about?" And Mary and Nora chanted the answer in unison: "Sex, drugs, and rock and roll!"

In all three categories, Lincoln was pretty competitive with the rest of the country. Early sex was a matter of concern but not uncommon; high-school students' getting pregnant was mostly considered just dumb, but neither the school system nor the students ostracized those who decided to have their babies. Drugs in junior high were so common that heavy experimentation was considered an almost embarrassing indicator of youth; by Mary's age, students were expected to be through with that phase and to know how to handle recreational substances. As for rock & roll, Lincoln had its own New Wave bands at the same time as New York and L.A.— Beebe Runyan and the Furniture, for example, and Jim Jacobi's Crap Detectors.

Lincoln also had divorce—so much of it that in one school, located in an area of abandoned Air Force housing that had become a virtual ghetto of divorced mothers because of its cheaper rents, over half the children were from broken homes. The stresses of divorce and the changes resulting from it—like coming home to the empty house of a working single parent, and the increased emotional and practical responsibilities—were keenly felt by Lincoln teenagers, including a couple in the group Mary had assembled.

Although Mary and her friends talked in a refreshing way about their career aspirations—they spoke, for example, of such things as meaning, achievement, worthwhile goals, and helping others—they also felt under enormous pressure to compete.

They were feeling the pressure from teachers, from parents, from everything around them. "It makes me *crazy*," Nora said. "Right now I just want to worry about growing up slowly, taking everything evenly, and having fun, but I'm afraid that when it's time to make my decisions about what I want to do, there isn't going to be enough time left, because I'm not going to be prepared, or there isn't going to be a place for me in what I want to do."

"I feel I have to make adult decisions," Mary said. "But something inside me says, *Hey, why do I have to do that? I'm only sixteen.*"

So even in Lincoln, and even for them, there is a need for escape, for a different, slower world. It was when Mary and her friends talked about the mall that they laughed the most.

They had hung out at Gateway when they were younger, often going at noon on Saturday and staying until the mall closed. The mall, too, seemed to be a junior-high rite of passage. "Before you get your driver's license, the only place you can go to get away from parents and get wild is the mall," Mary explained. Parents would drive them there because "they'd rather we were at the mall than out driving around at night with older kids, or hanging out at the park or someplace," Mary added. Nora agreed. "It's safer. They know where we are, they can find us, and they feel better that there are other adults around."

Not all the adults were happy with them, though. "We were pretty rowdy," Nora laughed. "Stores didn't like us 'cause they thought we were ripping them off." But what they mostly did was meet, watch, and walk. "We must have walked that mall a million times."

Now that they were in senior high, they laughed about the younger kids who hung out in the skywalk at the Centrum smoking cigarettes and trying to look cool. They don't go as often now themselves, but they do go together on shopping trips and sometimes they'll head for the mall just to be in its contained world of movement and color.

"You notice people more in the mall," Mary said. "On the street I feel like I have to get to where I'm going right away. But when you're walking through the mall you're not rushing. In the mall there's so much to look at that you relax."

So by senior high, when the pressures intensify—PSATS! SATS! College applications! Achievement tests! Scholarships! Majors! Careers!—already the kids of Lincoln are looking for a place to relax, to shed the burdens of home and school, to walk around in a world that's there to look at, and maybe a place where they can still be sixteen.

19

From the Plains to the Bay: How Malled Is My Silicon Valley

The concept of satiation has very little standing in economics. It is neither useful nor scientific to speculate on the comparative cravings of the stomach and the mind.

—JOHN KENNETH GALBRAITH
The Affluent Society

My journey through the West and South was a single continuous trek, and my means of travel between metropolitan areas was generally the train. The typical way for a writer to travel is, I suppose, to outfit a car or a van or truck, give it a name, and set out on the great American highway. I decided to take the train instead, for a number of reasons. I like trains. (That's the main reason.) I like traveling on them because they combine the best aspects of other modes of transport. They travel at ground level so there are things to see and there is time to see them. You are not inserted in an airliner seat and popped out at your destination like a cassette. Neither do you have to divide your attention between the road, the hieroglyphic road signs, and the demonstrably insane actions of other drivers on the highway.

There are people to talk to on the train—all kinds of people, not just those rich enough to fly or so poor they must take the bus. Because of the fare structure there are lots of families on the train, and there are groups and couples, and people traveling alone who are not necessarily carrying attaché cases. Some people are traveling short distances, some are on their own marathon voyages. But you don't have to talk to any of them if you don't want to; you can read, listen to music (if, like me, you bring a Walkman-type cassette player—mine was an Aiwa in a dark-blue case); you can eat, drink, and watch an America through the windows that you often cannot see except from the train. If you want company (or if someone is boring you), you can leave your seat or compartment and go to the club car or the observation lounge. The train gives you options.

I found that the trains also became a refreshing and useful contrast to the malls I was traveling to visit. Instead of walking around a static and sometimes claustrophobic internal world, I was in another kind of self-sustaining enclosure hurtling through an immense landscape of nature and human evidence.

I started my westward trip by train from Chicago on the *San Francisco Zephyr,* Amtrak's longest run. (Later I would travel on the train that passes through the most states—the *Crescent*—and I would ride over the highest point in the Amtrak system, in Wyoming, and the lowest, in the California desert.) From Chicago to Galesburg, the *Zephyr* rolls along the same route that the covered wagons took; before that it was an Indian trail, and before that a path hewn into the prairie by buffalo herds. After my stops in Galesburg and Lincoln, I got on the *San Francisco Zephyr* again for the last time. I was taking it to the end of its run, to the city by the bay.

Sometimes the conversations on the train were directly relevant to my mall trek. A young woman from Wyoming, for example, told me about Cheyenne's new mall—its first. "It's Frontier Mall, of course," she said. "Everything there is Frontier something. It's a big hit. Everybody goes there, especially the kids. Something for people to do, finally."

Many people I met were interested in what the malls mean to America. Sometimes I raised the issue, but sometimes they did. The train seemed just the place for extended and even philosophical discussion. I had one such conversation with Tom Schellens, a graduate student in architecture from Ogden, Utah, who was on his way to San Francisco for his brother's wedding. He told me about Trolley Square in Salt Lake City, which had reassembled actual old mansions within its monumental spaces. We talked about how malls handled the past, which was becoming an issue in more and more places. I told him about Barrymore's, the bar made out of a theater backstage in Lincoln, and how sad I felt being there in a place that had known years of reifying magic and now was background decor for young drinkers.

"Everything's being turned into a bar," he said. "It kind of says something about the times. There's a chain of them now, O'Hoolihans, that's buying up all the hexagonal tile and stained glass in the country for their bars. It's chain nostalgia, instant warmth."

But in talking about what had happened to Oneonta, a small town in New York State, he put in a good word for recycling old buildings, whatever their uses. "The town is between Albany and Binghamton," Schellens said. "They had a small shopping center, then a small mall, and then a big mall came in close to town. The city was behind it, but it drove down the old shopping centers, and downtown too. The city decided to go to urban renewal. They tore down half the town before they were stopped. The way people fought it was by renovating old buildings and showing they could be put to profitable uses. One guy took over an old Victorian house and built a bar on the first floor, with a small movie theater on the second floor. . . . It's better that it's a bar than for it to be torn down."

The trip from Lincoln to San Francisco took about thirty hours, so besides talking to people, I overheard parts of quite a few conversations. One subject that came up repeatedly was fear: People were afraid of crime, of cities, of chemical pollution, of government cutbacks that either affected them directly or that they feared would create tension and trouble and would harm the environment that everyone shared. An elderly woman from Los Angeles, for example, talked about how relaxing it was to be on the train and traveling, because at home she didn't feel safe going past her front door because of crime and smog. She found many sympathetic listeners.

These comments, too, had some bearing on my mall trek, as did some of the sights outside the window—for instance, the many times the landscape was broken by the graveyards of automobiles.

There was a series of them just before Greeley, Colorado, including one tableau of six or so cars on the banks of a stream, pointed nose-down into the water like a pack of pastel animals taking a drink. I was at lunch when I saw this, and a man at my table observed, "Those cars are a real mystery. There don't seem to be any roads around here. There must be more junkyards in America than anywhere in the world."

But the real value of these long train rides to my mall odyssey, I believe, was the experience of the landscape and the sheer expanse of American spaces. I watched it happen for a day and a half from the *Zephyr,* through the plains and the contour-plowed, serpentine grass fields reaching to a horizon of startled mountains and the dominion of huge clouds watching over them. Then miles and hours of bright sun on dark earth. Then rumbling through Denver, past cattle pens and shopping centers, the Rockies in the misted distance, snow peaks blending with cumulus.

I was in the lounge car when we made slow turns through the Snowy Range, and we were in the true West. The crowded lounge car was locked in awe. We bounced through the hanging clouds, past the broken fences, the rotted cars lying on their sides in a ditch: gleaming piles of metallic refuse like rainpools. Then the red-and-green wide land zoomed past, trailing telephone poles.

Alone in my compartment I saw antelope feeding near a glimmering stream. I saw Medicine Bow and the Virginia Hotel, and a boy standing alone in a parking lot, watching the train go by. I saw a lone horse gallop in a long green field, and cows nuzzling a power tower. I saw clouds unlike any I'd seen before—island mountains in the air, levitated and luminous—and great chunks of dirt rising from the scrub between Laramie and Rawlins, Wyoming. I stayed up in the darkness of the empty lounge car with a few new friends, sipping Jack Daniel's; we were the last ones awake, waiting to see the Great Salt Lake.

I awoke to the first brown hills of California, then the mountains near Donner Lake, where we slowly curved through snow and fir trees, with deep, bright valleys below us. By afternoon we neared San Francisco. We were coming into it by train, the way the second wave of settlers did, after those who came by wagon or the sea, but before those who settled the West with the highway. We had passed through some of the natural extremes of the land humans tried to conquer. Now I would be going inside the worlds humans were making for themselves.

★   ★   ★

Most of my time in San Francisco was spent on malls in the city itself, a subject of later chapters. After a few days in the city, I rented a car and headed south to the Silicon Valley. But along the highway to San Jose I encountered two malls in contrasting contexts.

I found Serramonte Center in the darkness off a highway just south of San Francisco. I wasn't looking for it specifically, but I *was* looking for a shopping center because there was something I wanted to buy. At first I pulled into the parking lot of what turned out to be either a high school or a community college. Then I found the mall, huge, flat, and completely undistinguished.

Inside, its one level was brash—there were lots of bright colors in the store logos, lots of space in the wide courts, lots of noise of people in the high, wide halls. Unlike most malls these days, this one had a large grocery store, where I found what I was looking for. But then the mall itself began to grab me. There were flowers and plants spilling over blank cement spaces, and an obvious difference between the very dim lighting of the courts and the very bright fluorescence of the stores—not very subtle in its use of mall psychology, I thought. Nothing at all in this mall was remotely subtle. The general run of merchandise seemed characterized by the large Montgomery Ward store.

What struck me was that this mall was so full of life. It was teeming with people of all ages, races, and the nationalities that characterize the Bay area: Latinos, blacks, Orientals of various countries, as well as the California beach blonds and other white ethnic groups. It was clear, moreover, that none of these people were tourists. Serramonte was not something anyone would come just to look at.

What also caught my eye was the bulletin board of upcoming activities for the mall's patrons, in what apparently was Daly City and vicinity. This week there was a special Salute to Dance: on successive days, appearances by Grite Sorenson from the Daly City Studio of Dance, Jix O'Keefe teaching Fun with Exercises, Mrs. Marie Brizuela demonstrating ballet. . . . Later would come Polynesian dancers, Polish dancers, the Women's International Folk Ensemble, and the Philippine Martial Arts Society. Cinco de Mayo, the Latino holiday, was being celebrated, climaxed by the Miss Daly City Pageant at the mall.

It was only later that I realized what Daly City was: one of the most flagrant examples of dehumanized tract housing in America, visually depicted in Richard Lester's film *Petulia,* with its symmetrical lines of ghostly-white identical houses winding up the hillsides into infinity; and most memorably preserved in music by Malvina Reynolds's famous song which, while applicable to a lot of suburbia, was actually about Daly City and its little boxes made out of ticky-tacky all look just the same.

But for all the uniformity of Daly City's low-income housing tracts, and even the aircraft hangar ambience of Serramonte Center, here was a mall that worked, both as a mall and as the community center. It was efficient and energetic, and it was also where Daly City was allowed to happen. The activities scheduled for Serramonte Center probably wouldn't otherwise take place in Daly City at all. Also in May there would be the Wonderful World of Whittling, the Summer in the City Fashion Show presented by the Skyline merchandising department, and finally a program sponsored by the Daly City History, Arts and Science Commission called Salute to the Artists of Tomorrow.

Some miles farther south, in Palo Alto, I encountered the Stanford Mall in Palo Alto in the afternoon. This mall was built on Stanford University property by a private developer, but the university retained approval rights over the design. What they got was also a one-level, somewhat sprawling mall. But this had a much more architecturalized exterior, done in the manner of Stanford's Spanish-arched university buildings. The materials, the design, the ambience were all much more expensively stylish.

There were shaded courts and lots of wood and stone. With its cafés, bike racks, and the largest bookstore I've ever encountered in a mall, this was obviously catering to an academic clientele. But its shops and its style were tastefully affluent; Palo Alto is mostly a very affluent community. It was as if the upscale people of Palo Alto sighed and said, You know we're going to get a mall sooner or later, so let's make it a good one. Stanford mall is serene and conservative; its colors, patterns, and textures work well with the topography, and the open areas use the blue Peninsula sky to good effect.

The Stanford Mall was a satisfactory mall for the satisfied. Serramonte Center seemed much more vibrant and stimulating. Still, as different as Palo Alto and Daly City are, their communities were both served by different styles of the same malleable form, the shopping mall.

★   ★   ★

Palo Alto is the northern edge of what is known as the Silicon Valley; the southern border takes in the city of San Jose. Silicon Valley is not a name on the map; neither is it a topological or chemical description. It does not refer to a valley made of a nonmetallic element having both an amorphous and a crystalline allotrope, with an atomic weight of 28.086, a boiling point of 2,600 degrees Centigrade, and a valence of 4. Silicon Valley is instead an economic and social phenomenon, comprising a twenty-five-mile-long corridor of businesses and residences whose presence here is chiefly due to electronic industries that depend on the semiconductor, the silicon chip. Until the 1970s, these industries didn't exist, and neither did Silicon Valley.

San Jose used to be a sleepy little market town surrounded by a vast flat expanse of orchards and grapevines: the pruneyards. Then the highways came, and the San Jose government began encouraging the development of stucco housing tracts and industrial parks. Jobs at nearby aircraft plants helped create an early suburban *The Life of Riley,* similar to the milieu depicted on that William Bendix sitcom of the fifties. Then the high-technology companies came to the valley, more than a thousand strong by 1980. The population of San Jose doubled three times in thirty-five years. At the end of World War II, only eighty thousand people lived in San Jose. Now it is bigger than Boston. In the 1970s, it was the fastest-growing population center in America.

I stayed in a motel in west San Jose. I put on my running stuff and jogged the long straight avenues, past the level reaches of Spanish-style homes, their lawns as green and trimmed as Astroturf. As I ran, my thoughts turned to constipation. An awful lot of pruneyards in some of the richest soil on earth were ripped out and replaced by something like 2,500 subdivisions, crammed together with no center and no interstices. They "interface" with traffic, impersonal streets, chemicals, and smog. They are, however, still overwhelmed by sun and sky. The soft-shaped brown hills are still up there. The sea is still somewhere nearby.

Part of the old city survives, but it seemed only to be a source of worry. I read a story in one of the local newspapers, the San Jose *Mercury,* that began, "Clergy and lay members of downtown San Jose churches were bluntly told Saturday to begin to prepare for the worst, that the urban social problems they have had to deal with to date are only a harbinger of what is yet to be." In east San Jose there was a barrio of some 200,000 Mexican-Americans, many of them poor. The city's schools suffer from racial segregation. Other stories in local newspapers called San Jose "a city of concrete and sprawl," and discussed what to do about the lack of unity and identity in Silicon Valley. A headline said, boldly and forlornly: SAN JOSE IS NOT A "COMMUNITY" YET—SOME SAY THERE'S HOPE.

But the old downtown is not the city's true center. As close as you can get to a common ground, or so a lot of people in San Jose will tell you, is Eastridge, the oldest, largest, and most comprehensive of the many malls of the Silicon Valley.

A young man working at a bookstore in San Francisco was a child in San Jose when he went to Eastridge just after it opened. "It was like going to a circus," he told me. When I went there a decade later, it still was.

There were some 150 stores in this huge, exuberant mall, from the balanced and comprehensive lineup of department stores—Sears, Penney's, Macy's, and the Emporium (is this the same Emporium Ozzie and Harriet were always talking about?)—to the minutely specialized shops that the old *Saturday Night Live* show satirized so effectively with their Scotch-tape store. Eastridge didn't have one of those, but it did have Shaver's World. Everything from electronics to candlesticks were sold in the mall, and the range went from such no-nonsense services as car repair to ego-enhancing products like the fashion blouses in Above the Belt, sold under its prominently displayed motto, FLATTER YOURSELF.

As if to compensate for the wide spaces San Jose has filled with buildings and highways, the areas allowed for walking and gathering were unusually large in Eastridge mall. Walkways skirted both floors, zigzagging from the first to the second so that in some places people could walk on any of three levels. The mall was dominated by an expansive center court, emphasized by the recessed corridors of stores around it, with the ceiling as a single all-embracing canopy, a kind of starship Big Top.

Eastridge was solid, big, and secure. It was also bright, dazzling, and a little eccentric. In center court was one of those anomalous areas that I always find so baffling and fascinating and somehow moving; for me, they both define and humanize the mall. Here it was comprised of a high, spindly metal sculpture in back of a large pool of water that rolled gently down three brief levels. The pool was bordered by a low wall of smooth stone in an excessively multisided geometrical design. Also bordering part of the pool was a recessed open area where the floor was covered by a bright-red carpet. On the other side of the carpet was a long section of sofalike seating.

The clash of effects was what made this so mallish: It was as if the pool of an outdoor park were set down in a sunken conversation nook and then stuck in front of an airport gate waiting area. The juxtaposition was giddy enough, but what made it even more characteristic of malls was that beyond the visual impudence, the area *worked* for the people who came here. I saw kids crawling all over the stone walls while their parents sat resting in the sofa seats, perhaps dreaming of airplanes to nowhere.

But the real gathering went on at the immense food court on the second level, called the World's Fare Restaurant. This was the most elaborate food court I'd seen so far, and the most successful. An attractive scattering of tables tinted in violets and blues was surrounded on three sides by neon-titled outlets selling Mexican, Chinese, Italian, German, and English-style fast food. The place was as close to a European city square as I'd experienced in a mall, although there were no cathedrals in sight—just the blue neon of the Top Half and the yellow of Wicks 'n Sticks. Still, a Kate Hepburn carrying cannoli from San Remo's Italian might catch the eye of a Rossano Brazzi, looking up over his Giant Burger from Kathy's Broiler. Who's to say?

Certainly it seemed possible, with all the mixing going on. Groups of uniformed employees taking coffee breaks from the Donut House mingled with solitary women shoppers carrying takeout from Chinese Food, near a dad watching his kids while nursing a beer from the Hofbrau, and a Chinese family dividing a pizza. Mostly there were the young: muscular males in SURFING IN MAUI T-shirts, more dressed-up boys with razor-cut hair pretending not to see (could it be possible they weren't seeing?) an amazing number and variety of young women dressed in a riveting range of outfits, from short shorts and platform shoes to stylish and demure summer dresses, slinky and assertive with unbuttoned blouses, or in tight, dry-cleaned jeans and low-cut jerseys, or shiny tight silver running pants with their equally shiny hair pulled back from round, Jane Pauley faces. At one point I saw six of them—six hues of bare-backed skin in jeans, shorts, and pants; six pairs of bare shoulders;

and all that long, rich American hair in shades from blond to black—all lined up together at Picadilly Fish 'n Pies.

Eastridge has the status of a downtown for another reason: Some of the affluent white middle class is reluctant to go there. The Silicon Valley that developed in the 1970s and 1980s is psychologically and stylistically expressed elsewhere. For a while at least, its mall of choice was The PruneYard.

It's all there below you, from high atop one of the two office towers that are part of the PruneYard complex. All that you survey from Sebastian's bar is the Silicon Valley of plenty.

At four o'clock in the afternoon I joined the white-collar bunch from the towers and nearby—from Four Star Travel Service, Title Insurance and Trust, the Bank of the West—who would rather watch the traffic for a while than go down there and fight it. About 675,000 people live in San Jose, but they own over a million cars. The cars have been streaming out of Atari, Dynabyte, Apple, and Acurex for hours already on a carefully staggered schedule. Some left at 2:00, some at 2:15, and 2:30 . . . and all through the afternoon they process, at 4:15, 4:30, 4:45—from GenRad, GE, BASF, Exar, Intersil: Silicon Valley's poetry in motion.

The new industries here are different in more than name and product from most others in America. They may have Friday afternoon beer blasts where managers and employees of all departments mix and swill; they throw corporate Christmas parties in posh San Francisco hotels that cost a quarter of a million dollars. They have flex-time and employee-participation schemes more often associated with Japanese and European companies. They also keep a close eye on the equipment, because San Jose is a den of high-tech spies and thieves.

As in the Gold Rush days in the North and the Land Rush in the South, people can get rich quick in this green valley, and the evidence is all around. There's no experience like stopping at a light in your subcompact rented car and looking up—and I do mean *up*—to see a blonde in a Rolls offering you a cool glance from on high. This is no longer just a characteristic Southern California scene— the Mercedeses and the Silver Shadows are common sights in San Jose. Besides the silicon entrepreneurs and their lawyers and bankers, a really good high-level engineer (high tech or genetic) writes his own ticket here. But then there are the legions of other engi-

neers, assembly workers, office and service employees who have to
do a lot of squirming to make the payments on those expensive
pink and cream gingerbread houses. For them, too, it is those
glimpses of wealth and the image of young men and women with
careers ascending like smart rockets and their casually charming and
confident spouses that set the style, down there, in the valley.

Which may all mean that some of the shopping malls here are
playing to a hopeful, ambitious, and insecure constituency. So what
they would want from a shopping mall is fun, fashion, and forget-
fulness. Some of the malls know this, and they know they are the
only places these people will get what they want in San Jose—the
only places they'll probably look for it. There's no alternative.

So they compete for the image of "The Right Mall." When I
visited San Jose, it was The PruneYard. Some people said later that
a new mall, Vallco Fashion Park, inherited the mantle of The Right
Mall—these things change and can even change back. Besides, The
PruneYard didn't get to be The Right Mall by accident, and there
are still plenty of its kind of people for more than one such mall to
prosper. When I found The PruneYard's management offices elsewhere in these towers, I also found a person who defined for me
this new kind of mall for a new kind of place in the present—and
probably the future—landscape of America.

She was Carmen Rutlen, The PruneYard's public relations and
marketing director. She appeared to be in her late twenties; she was
attractive, and well-dressed, with a feisty intelligence. At first she
launched into a standard but nevertheless precise description of
what The PruneYard was all about: "The PruneYard is a specialty
center. We have no major department stores. Instead we have seventeen restaurants that cumulatively operate as our 'major.' We
were one of the first to do that," she said.

Then, without drawing an extra breath, she went into a sort of
sociological description of PruneYard customers, with an easy pop-
psychology emphasis. "We will attract people at that time of day
that they feel good about themselves," she said flatly. "I think I'm
typical of our shoppers—people who feel they deserve to live rich,
full lives, who have money, or feel they should. That's typical of
this area—it's the Me Society. The woman who goes out with
curlers in her hair or wants to be anonymous doesn't shop here.

"We play up our image with classy catalogues and our slogan,
'Treat Yourself to The PruneYard,'" Carmen Rutlen continued.

"But The PruneYard isn't expensive. There's lots of people here like me—poor, but who think rich. The PruneYard is not a practical place. It's illusionary. We're very aesthetic, very frivolous. We change our flowers six times a year so our flower beds always have color spots. We have these frogs in our fountain that spit water—kids love it. We have a stage in the courtyard for performances, but we keep it up all the time, and it's interesting to see people react to it. Some walk around it but some like to walk right across it, depending on how they feel. Women in heels have to avoid the cobblestones in the walks. Sometimes they get lost—again, it's all frivolity."

I asked her about marketing surveys. "Yeah, I've done some of those," she sniffed. "Mostly with our merchants, to find out who shops here and why. The shopping trend is northward. People will drive from the South up. I guess they still associate class and culture with San Francisco. Freeways can be a natural boundary—some people won't cross a freeway even if a place is closer in miles than where they eventually go." The PruneYard was within five miles of well over half a million people.

But then Carmen Rutlen got a little testy. "People make a mystery of marketing. Dealing with the public is like dealing with the psychology of a person multiplied many times. We're trying to fulfill the needs of people in this time and place. I looked *marketing* up in the dictionary—and it isn't there. It's not magic! It's sensitivity. It's common sense, and the guts to try something different."

The PruneYard itself was low and compact, with a curved tile roof and narrow corridors of dark wood opening onto a central courtyard. It was bordered rather than completely enclosed, and true to Rutlen's words, it was illusionary—the layout, the ambience, suggested nothing more than a Hollywood set adaptable to scenes of the Old West, Mexican border towns, and, in a pinch, Tahitian villages. The flowered courtyard could have been where Marlon Brando and Karl Malden had their last shootout in *One-Eyed Jacks*.

Within the rough-wood labyrinth under the Spanish tiles were some sixty-five shops like Eleganza, Lady & Sir J., Con Liquori, the Chocolate Soup, and Movies To Go, as well as the seventeen restaurants, including El Burro, The Garrett I and II, and the New Bumbleberry.

There were well-kempt women browsing over Pearls of Majorca in Jardin de Parfum, choosing a Classic Catalina swimsuit in Beyond the Reef, and fingering the seashell-shaped soaps in Beth's Bath Boutique. This was indeed shopping as candy for the senses and the imagination, the act of shopping as show—frivolous, illusionary, aesthetic.

The PruneYard sponsored more formal shows with that same ambience of frivolous but basically complacent imagination. During the month of April, for example, there was Professor Plum's Jazz ("It's time for the toe-tapping, knee-slapping sounds of the South," said the publicity sheet); a panel of professional graphologists from the American Handwriting Analysis Association to read the character of customers through their handwriting; and Easter goodies distributed by Peter Pruneyard; plus informal fashion shows at noontime, three days a week. In May there was a "60's Nostalgia" show with Beggar's Opera, followed by 50's nostalgia with Gregg Andrade and the Perspirations. In June the Razzano Dancers would perform, and of course there would be the annual pipe-smoking contest.

But for all this, The PruneYard didn't glitter or gleam. It was all very low-key. The shops were almost hidden in the Frontierland architecture. It was very much in the prevailing style of the workplaces of Silicon Valley's high-tech firms, with their little wooden bridges and Oriental-delicate trellises. There was nothing space-age about the place; perhaps it tried to hark back to some half-remembered past, some hazy vision of a slower, smaller San Jose, compact and peaceful, when these truly were pruneyards.

Although people gathered in many of its restaurants, and the kids stopped off at Mrs. Field's Chocolate Chippery after school, there was this aspect of seeking refuge in quiet time which seemed centered in the café and bookstore, the Upstart Crow—the kind of chain store that could start only in California. The good-sized bookstore inside The PruneYard was complemented by an indoor area of picnic tables, where I saw students doing their homework while sipping fruit juice. There was also a large outdoor café that—one must hasten to add when speaking of malls—was actually outdoors. Trees shaded many of the tables, leaves fell on them, and birds boldly danced for the crumbs of croissants and pâté.

I sat at an outdoor table, for hours, as it turned out. As I lunched in the sunshine, two attractive women, probably in their twenties, were discussing over salads the latest men they had met.

The blonde, wearing a purple blouse and shoes in several shades of violet suede, and with violet nail polish on her toes and a slightly brighter shade on her fingers, approved of her companion's latest find. But she—brown hair, a bare-shouldered white blouse, and swirly, light-brown spring skirt—just shrugged. "But he's so *preppie,*" she said.

"Clones" is how Carmen Rutlen put it, with disconcerting directness. But not everyone here conformed to the stereotype of either high-tech preppie or specialty-store-ensembled woman. At another table nearby was a group of five young men and women, all wearing jeans and T-shirts. One of the T-shirts was imprinted with the information UPPITY WORKERS COMMITTEE LOCAL 535. Their conversation seemed to be about land-grabbing and mineral exploitation.

After they all left—the glossy women, the uppity workers—I stayed on, seduced by silence and sun. One of the tables near the hedge that bordered the sidewalk was soon occupied by a well-dressed woman, in her forties perhaps, with a deep tan. She came out of the bookstore with a copy of *Jonathan Livingston Seagull* and sat down in the sun, where she read, sipped red wine, and smoked cigarettes, glancing somewhat anxiously at the parking lot every few minutes. Eventually a man of about the same age but not as well-dressed, wearing a short-sleeved shirt and slacks, hurried to her table. His nervous expression was met by her broad smile. He sat down and they ordered more wine.

The scene appeared to need privacy, so I went inside the bookstore to look around. After a few minutes of wandering the quiet aisles, looking at titles through my own wine-and-sunshine haze, a soft but peculiar sound emerged from the general hum. It was coming from the cashier's station in the middle of the bookstore. There, a middle-aged woman stood, a book in her hands, reading aloud in a quiet voice to the young man behind the counter. The words were inaudible from where I was. He was listening to her, his eyes blinking a bit rapidly and his face rigid with control and concern. For as the woman was reading, she was softly crying.

I knew that I should be leaving, but I sat outside again and ordered coffee. It was already late afternoon and shadows crossed the tables at the far end of the café. There, two elderly women sat down, all abuzz, soon to be joined by two more, and their four voices joined in cascades of words and laughter.

In the speedy desert of highways and heat, broken by inscrutable buildings like pyramids, some people needed only a simple place, a garden, an oasis where the complexities of their lives could be expressed as well as forgotten, and the pressure of reality lessened. Some needed good bread, wine, and sunshine, a place to talk about politics or lovers, or meet one. Others might require the dance through giddy colors and the splash of products, the newness that stylish clothes can bring to the self.

The place to find those things, and more, in San Jose is the mall. As San Jose grew, the mall was firmly established as the form that would meet people's needs for shopping, entertainment, and community. There was no fight about it; that's what happened, and what had to happen. Town centers are hard to establish quickly—certainly not fast enough to keep up with the growth of Silicon Valley—and they are costly and cumbersome, with such arcane requirements as elections and taxes. Better to let private enterprise subsidize community facilities directly and to take advantage of the incentive of the profit motive to make them good ones. Of course, malls weren't building schools and sewage systems—at least, not exactly; not yet.

The importance of the mall as community center is underscored here because it was at The PruneYard that a conflict over the right to petition in a mall resulted in a Supreme Court decision. Based on an interpretation of the California state constitution, those rights were upheld; the petitioners won a landmark case, and the mall lost.

I asked Carmen Rutlen about the decision, and although she referred me to The PruneYard's lawyers for an official response, she allowed as how if the mall was to be treated as a public place for the purposes of free speech and petition, perhaps the public ought to be paying taxes for The PruneYard's twenty-four-hour-a-day security force and the maintenance of its buildings and grounds.

I also spoke with a local activist who tried to petition in San Jose malls (on behalf of a proposition on the California ballot requiring no-smoking sections in public places) after the PruneYard decision was supposedly implemented.

"In many instances, the reception was very unfriendly," he said. "We were harassed, intimidated, and discouraged. The malls all got a letter from the California Secretary of State advising them of the new guidelines, but the mall managements found ways to use the

rules against us. The guidelines said petitioners can't obstruct traffic, so the manager says we are—and we say we aren't. Each mall
has its own rules, too. Some will let you set up a table but you have
to stay right there."

These conflicts are far from over. The essence of the mall is
control; it is what in many ways makes them work. But, curiously,
The PruneYard itself made a case for an opposite, or at least miti-
gating view. For it was the serendipity of the place, its unpredictability, that humanized it. Of course, conflict would change it. It
would no longer be a haven of quiet and fantasy.

My coffee done, I was alone with the stillness and the birds. But
I could pause under these peaceful trees no longer on this now very
late afternoon. I had more malls to go before I slept.

Just a few miles away from The PruneYard was Westgate Mall.
Westgate was not frivolous, aesthetic, or illusionary. The green
plastic chairs in its main court didn't match. There was the pervasive smell of chlorine, a "Y" swimming pool smell. The clientele
was obviously different, too, leaning toward the white lower middle class. Fully enclosed, suburban-standard issue, Westgate Mall
was the very model of a bread-and-butter mall. Sears, Penney, and
Montgomery Ward were the anchors. It also seemed to be an older
mall, with wide courts and low, corrugated-style ceilings, and
floors resembling speckled concrete.

Westgate also had virtues of practicality. It had a Family Dental
Center and the Westgate Beauty Academy. In the early evening
there were young people about. This mall (Carmen Rutlen told me)
doesn't encourage teenagers to hang out there, but they were there
anyway. I saw a junior-high boy open the ladies' room door, then
elaborately pretend it was a mistake. The junior-high girls inside
kept their cool. They seemed to know the joke already.

There wasn't much of any interest in Westgate Mall, but it
wasn't depressing there. It was just a place where women could
shop with curlers in their hair.

Next I stopped—very briefly, as it turned out—at an "entertainment mall" called The Factory. It was another western-style
wooden warren of storefronts, with a disturbing number of dead
ends—especially disturbing because it was early evening on a Friday and the place was deserted. It was the closest I saw to a ghost-
town mall. At the end of one blind alley was a club, and the dress

code posted at its entrance included the admonition "No Chains." That's not my idea of entertainment, so I got out of this mall before sundown.

The drive to my last mall of the day took me along various highways and byways deeper into the mountains, to a theme mall called The Old Mill. When I finally arrived there I was encouraged by the signs of life in the parking lot and at the entrance. It was prime time now, on a hot Friday night.

I went inside and took a quick walk around. The Old Mill was completely enclosed, but small and dark. It had two levels of tight corridors and a kind of Disney-esque toy-village motif, complete with painted second stories on a row of quaint first-level shops called the French Quarter. This was the fast-food court, with outlets offering crêpes, Italian sausages, fish & chips, borscht, moussaka plate, and, perhaps inevitably, something called a French Quarter Pounder.

The New Orleans theme was carried on in the Bourbon Street Restaurant, Disco and Lounge, but all this was a sideshow to the main theme in the main court, the center ring. There, running the length of the court, was an actual, though artificial, old millstream. And there, rising above it, was a turning waterwheel—the old mill itself, I presumed. What the two themes—New Orleans and the mill—had to do with each other was not immediately apparent.

Maybe it was the end of a long day, but this place took the cake for artificiality. The whole mall seemed halfhearted, an example of failed wit. I also felt a wave of claustrophobia envelop me. But there were plenty of people around, obviously up for a good time. It was a happening place.

The life-size waterwheel and stream were surrounded by separate outdoor café areas (this time definitely indoors), one of which belonged to yet another edition of the Upstart Crow. So, since I was too tired to drive back so soon, I got a French coffee and sat down at a table overlooking the stream to nurse my growing grudges.

That stream bothered me a lot. It felt sinister and deeply perverse. It wasn't a stream, even if it looked like one. It had no delicate and complex ecosystem giving it life, and no raw power or element of unpredictability or danger. It had no natural reason for being, no source, and no outlet.

To believe a real stream is like this one is a potentially dangerous mistake, especially if that perception affects attitudes and actions toward real streams. Likewise, that waterwheel. It didn't grind grain or contribute to the making of food, although it had a hand in selling it. It didn't make power; it used power. These things weren't real.

What happens, I thought, when the chief community centers of our time are such willfully artificial distortions of reality? Don't they then have the power to derange our sense of the world, and of ourselves? We navigate by still points in the turning human landscape, but the mall is among those institutions with the power to destroy those still points, not only physically (by building on top of a stream and smothering it) but by distorting the very idea of what they are—by faking the only stream some of these people are likely to see on a regular basis. More than that, if people learn this false idea here, they may not understand the real streams they may see.

The mall is in many cases a celebration of falseness, but as it turned out The Old Mill's offensive phoniness wasn't the only strong impression I felt that night. As I sipped my coffee and tried to relax, I noticed two girls in their late teens sitting nearby.

They were dressed up—that was obvious. They were both pretty, classically and quietly, and dressed up in a quietly eager way. One wore a turquoise blouse that set off her eyes, and a neatly pressed skirt. Her companion wore a light-brown shirt dress with red stripes and a red belt, and her neatly folded soft red sweater was tied across her back. Both had long, shiny brown hair.

They sat at a table, talking, waiting. Waiting for what? The magic, I supposed. The magic that might come along some Friday night. Here they were, living amid all the gleaming office towers, the blank factories and freeways, the garish chaos of the highway strips, the stilted subdivisions, the beehive condo complexes, the feverishly neutral airports, bland hotels, and chain everythings—all of which I had seen on my drive here through brown hills and green mountains, and all of which I had been seeing for days.

I remembered the last part of my conversation with Carmen Rutlen at The PruneYard, after we'd finished with official business. She had talked about life in the Silicon Valley. Like most people there, she was from somewhere else. She was born in South Dakota, but as an army brat, the daughter of a military officer, she had grown up in Europe and South America.

"People don't know each other here," she said. "Everyone can be very friendly, but when it comes to asking for a favor—that's something else. They have walls around everything—their houses, and themselves."

So I looked around at The Old Mill with new eyes. I saw tiny bright lights in a controlled darkness. Instead of the sound of engines, I heard the lapping and splash of water. I watched the big wheel turning and turning. I saw a young woman sitting alone on a step, gazing into the stream. There were small tables all around me, each with a small candle. The coffee was good. People moved softly beyond. Something could happen here tonight. In any case, it was a clean, well-lighted place.

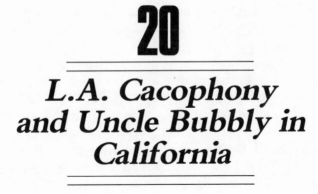

20

L.A. Cacophony
and Uncle Bubbly in
California

Although it was called the *Pacific Coast Starlight,* the train from San Jose to Los Angeles traveled in the daytime. I took it on Mother's Day, so a lot of mothers and grandmothers were getting on and off at intermediate stops on their way to family or on their way back. Most of them wore flowers. Passing through the land, some of them recalled when it was all open, or filled with orchards.

There were still vast wide fields, which gave way to narrow passages in lush green hills, opening to fields again. Later in the day we passed through marshes, where long-necked migratory birds were feeding and lifting to the sky. A young horse stood alone in a field, oblivious to the noise of the train. A column of low clouds seemed to be marching quickly northward beside us.

In the lounge car I noticed a blond young woman reading *Cosmopolitan* next to a blond young man, who was peering over her shoulder at the magazine. They were attractive enough to be models of the California beach-blond way of life, and as it turned out, that's just what they were. Soon a crew began setting up reflector umbrellas and posing these two for still shots set against the moving landscape. They were shooting pictures for a surfing magazine; the subject of the article was "surfing by train." We were definitely heading into Southern California.

Los Angeles was the original unfinished city of the Sun Belt, sending out tendrils of freeways which sprouted shopping malls. Like L.A., the malls are artificial environments that seem to be natural, and they help their denizens forget about the fragile underpinnings of this seemingly natural way of life in Southern California. Bodies bared to the nurture of consistent sun and warm skies form the daily reality, but Los Angeles lives with great vulnerabilities. Its water comes from afar, as does its gasoline. L.A. is dependent on complex systems it can't always control. Besides the effects of possible economic and social upheavals, which seep into consciousness here through the survivalist and apocalyptic cults, there are the yearly reminders of vulnerability to nature in fires and floods and the endemic earthquakes. L.A.'s apparently permanent state of change means that the transience some experts associate with high levels of urban crime is a given condition of life here. All these factors add up to an underlying insecurity, contained within L.A.'s contradictions. Yet there is great creative energy, also born out of all these conditions.

So if L.A.'s malls are bolder and crazier than those elsewhere, it's only because they express everything that the city is. From the severe poshness of the Beverly Center and the Rodeo Collection malls in Beverly Hills to the rococo silliness of the Olde Towne mall (where the Olde Towne band plays in the enclosed amusement park square) and Topanga Plaza, the mall is part of L.A.'s laid-back adventurousness and the fantasies it devises to oppose its fears.

For example . . .

Just off the Ventura Freeway, I found Topanga Plaza, a typical Southern California complex with theaters, an amusement park, a huge supermarket, four department stores, and a mall full of shops. The walls at the entrance were yellow, the banisters orange. There were dark-orange columns with purple stripes, and a central court of gaudy tile and lots of midway-style lights. Down the midway poured legions of teenaged girls, themselves poured into tight jeans and tops.

Farther along, the motif changed slightly, to multishaded blue. While I was walking around there, excerpts from an operetta were being performed by a group from the University of Southern California; they stood on the violet and midnight-blue tiles just below Montgomery Ward, in front of the Sunset House Gadget Tree.

Here, as in other L.A. malls, a lot of energy and effort was expended to maintain an internal environment much like what the external one would be if it didn't have all those cars. The temperature, inside and out, was about the same, but the mall was fully enclosed.

Not a quarter of a mile down Topanga Canyon Road was a companion: the Promenade Mall, a slightly more upscale center with three department stores and eighty shops, plus restaurants and services, from the Isle of Wigs to Kimo's Polynesian Restaurant and the Bank of America.

The decor inside was more subdued than at Topanga Plaza, all browns and off-white. Even more teenaged girls were here, however, in roving bands of six or eight, also wearing tight pants and T-shirts that said things like PRINCESS and SPOILED ROTTEN.

Closer to the more clustered region of Los Angeles proper, I visited Fox Hills Mall, a huge, architecturally unique center in West Los Angeles which opened in 1975 as the hub of an urban redevelopment project. It was the first three-level mall in California.

As Southern California grew massively around the fringes of old and neglected town centers, urban renewal meant the eradication of those old centers. They were typically replaced with shopping centers and malls. (Almost every native Californian I met, north and south, had stories about the "renewal" of his or her hometown.) This went on even as formerly empty suburban areas were getting their malls. As Albert Sussman of the International Council of Shopping Centers noted, "Before, we were building shopping centers to fill a vacuum. Now we're plugging up the holes." In California particularly, shopping centers were seen as the wave of the future for every kind of place—and they were very profitable. "If used properly, there is something in redevelopment for everyone," as a California redevelopment official named Bud Pichetto told a gathering of shopping-center executives.

Fox Hills was a little different; here, there had been an attempt to fit the mall into the existing community, as well as a huge mall could fit. There were approximately 130 shops there, with crisply bright neon logos in an impressive variety of calligraphy. But the mall's strangest and most attractive feature was a large orange metal-and-glass jungle-gym-styled tower that rose from the first level to the third in the central court. There were stairs on it that led to all three floors of the mall, but also to the glass-walled cubicles of the structure itself where children could sit and look down. There was also a large seating area near the top of it, where teenagers gazed out on the ant farm of a mall below them, and did their homework.

As I stood atop this giant orange Tinkertoy, I was surrounded by two young Asian children playing, two teenaged girls in the yellow blouses and gray skirts of their school uniform, and a black couple sitting and holding hands as they talked. It was a scenic overlook, a park bench, a meeting place, a playpen, and a sculpture to be experienced from inside as well as out.

There were so many schoolchildren around because it was four o'clock on a weekday, and this mall was a bus transfer point. While the kids waited for the next bus or for their parents, they lined up for a slice and a soft drink from Lord Byron's Pizza, cruised through Casual Corner and Mickey Fine and the Polka Dot Shop, dropped some quarters at the Sega Center game room, visited boyfriends who clerked in mall stores, or just leaned on the curved surface of the wall, spacing out. I even saw three girls in a circle in the corner of a court, tossing around a lemon. And they love their mall. "It's great," one teenaged girl told me. "There was nothing here before. Just an itty-bitty shopping center."

Even such a carefully designed mall as Fox Hills had one of those strange, eccentric areas of no apparent purpose that is even more characteristic of Southern California malls than those in other places. Here, it was a multilevel brick terrace that surrounded a kind of sacred putting green—a patch of Astroturf that seemed to have no reason for being there except perhaps to be worshiped.

Another such area was a feature of Fashion Island, farther south, in Newport Beach. It had a brown wooden miniature footbridge that rose from the ground, arched over nothing, and sloped to the same level again. There was no reason for that footbridge. There was apparently no reason either for my favorite inexplicable mall icon, located in the Del Amo Fashion Square before it was mated with the Del Amo Center to create the largest mall in California. It was a circular purple rug about four feet in diameter, surrounded by eight globe lights on tall black stands, sitting on a side court like a shrine. What could this mysterious rug be in homage to? The gods of carpeting? The patron saint of retail sales?

Or, could it be . . . *mallness itself?*

Fox Hills was another mall designed by Gruen Associates, the firm founded by Victor Gruen which had remained on the cutting edge of mall architecture since Gruen invented the first enclosed mall at Southdale in 1956. The firm's main office is in Los Angeles, so I went there to learn more about mall design and about Victor Gruen.

There I met William H. Dahl, a partner in the firm who was associated with Gruen as far back as Southdale and has continued to design malls since. But the Gruen firm works on more than just malls. They are architects, planners, and engineers for projects around the world, including comprehensive regional and city plans and development programs. Their client list included Citibank, General Electric, Amtrak, the U.S. Army Corps of Engineers, Sea World, and the University of the West Indies. Their architects themselves come from all over the world, an outgrowth of Victor Gruen's policy of never turning away a trained architect from an oppressed nation. Gruen never forgot his own beginnings in America as a refugee from the Nazis in Vienna.

I asked Dahl about Victor Gruen, who retired from the firm in 1968 before returning to Vienna, where he died twelve years later. I'd gotten the impression from Gruen's writings that the highlight of his career was the heady period of Northland and Southdale malls, when he got to put many of his ideas into practice on a large scale with a minimum of compromise. He did something then that no one had seen before. But for Gruen, these mall designs were only first steps. He went on to devise a master plan for the restructuring of the entire city of Forth Worth, Texas, for example. His Fort Worth plan was celebrated for both accommodating the automobile and providing human-scale spaces within urban-efficient concentrations, yet with countryside to spare. But for all the praise and study this plan received, it was never fully realized.

Still, Gruen continued to express his ideas through his writings and in smaller-scale projects, and he built a major design firm. As Dahl described him, Gruen remained a man of great energy and unabated creativity, even though the shopping-center industry ultimately disappointed him.

"Victor was a very dynamic man," Bill Dahl said. "He was totally committed and tenacious. He would develop a concept and never give up. Everything was oriented towards his work. He was a controversial man. Many developers were not particularly appreciative of some of the things he did and said. He embarrassed them from time to time. Towards the end of his career he really wasn't as concerned with how these people felt, but about his ideas. I guess in that way he was a great man."

What Dahl remembered best was the delight of working with Victor Gruen. "It was very exciting around here when he was in town. He used to keep two secretaries busy—he was a prolific writer. He surrounded himself with energetic young people with ideas, and he was able to convert young people to his energetic ways. He was a great teacher—he taught all of us a lot. But he was also able to elicit ideas from people. It was like intellectual popcorn—ideas were popping around all the time. He could focus on the good ones and make them work. He could participate, as well as offering his own ideas.

"He was an easy man—you never felt tension around him," Dahl continued, breaking into a smile. "There are endless stories of the practical jokes. Once, Victor came back from a trip and the company's name had been removed from the door. When he came in, people pretended not to recognize him. When he went to his office there was somebody else sitting at his desk—an office boy, who asked him what he wanted. . . . He was fun-loving. We called him Uncle Bubbly."

Since Victor Gruen's retirement, the design of shopping malls has become an even bigger, costlier, and much more complicated business. Bill Dahl invited me to accompany him to the nearby site of a mall in progress. Along the way he described what the design process is like these days.

"It starts when a developer somehow ties up a piece of property that he thinks has shopping-center possibilities. Then, through market research or intuition or a combination of both, he establishes that there's potential for a four-or five-department-store center, with two or three hundred thousand square feet of tenant space, or whatever. Once that program is established, we come in. We get together information such as topography, property line definitions, subsoil conditions—because they all will frequently impact on what you do. Then we begin the process of evolving a design."

"Where do the department stores come in?" I asked him. "I've heard other designers complain about how much influence they have—more than they used to."

"Department stores have a tremendous influence on the final outcome," Dahl said. "They play this game of location. Will they be at this end of the center or another? They establish standards— the width of the malls, the size of the courts—and while they don't control design, they certainly have the influence on what happens in the design. They may say, We don't want certain art forms, certain landscaping—or they want certain materials, certain colors, a certain ambience in the mall. One in particular, which shall remain nameless—we have a theory that you always show them what you don't want, because they'll come back and show you what you do want, but if you give them what you want in the beginning, they'll come back with something terrible.

"It's all a slow process of evolution that today takes several years before you settle on plans," Dahl continued. "You have the governmental agencies that impact on it, department stores that influence it, and the economy is playing a greater role in what's happening because the department stores are like yo-yos: When the cash registers are ringing there's no tomorrow, but as soon as the economy slows up and the profit picture changes, they tie the purse strings and that's it—you sit back and wait for something to happen."

Dahl didn't look old enough to have been around since the pioneering days of mall design. He was tanned and fit, with lots of hair and a quick smile. He drove a sports car and piloted his own airplane. "I do that for therapy more than anything else," he said. "It really doesn't make much sense otherwise." But perhaps this just emphasizes how young the shopping-center industry is.

Still, Dahl is a veteran in a rapidly changing and complex business—which he made clear when I asked him about the influence of market and motivation studies on the design process. "We do lots of studies," he said, "but I've been working in shopping centers for almost thirty years, so it's kind of an intuitive thing—understanding why people will go from one place to another. There are no set rules. If you have the perfect cornfield site, which is sixty to seventy acres and has a nice square shape, you just go in and put that shopping center down. That's very simple. But today the perfect site doesn't exist. Now you're dealing with a lot of other influences that require judgment.

"We have a site in Mexico, for example. It's thirty-five acres and we built about a million and a half square feet. It was on a site that had sixty feet of lava, and it had a ninety-foot slope. . . . We have a project in Hawaii where we have to go around a cemetery. In Oregon, we have a light-rail system running through the site. So it's those judgments you have to make that are based on experience much more than on research."

We arrived at the future location of the proposed Montebello mall, a 1-million-square-foot enclosed shopping center.

"This site is probably one of the most difficult I've ever dealt with—sites are getting more and more difficult," Dahl said as we got out of his car and climbed into a pickup truck. Between conferences with the on-site engineer, Dahl detailed some of the problems as we rumbled over the vast tract of land already opened and contoured by the small army of machinery moving around us. The area's rolling hills had had to be graded to a number of flat levels. There were problems with power utilities below- and aboveground. Twenty electrical towers had to be uprooted and moved, which involved closing the nearby freeway to traffic while the lines were dropped. Then, temporary towers were built and put into place. Sewage lines crossed a corner of the site, and a cement bridge had to be constructed over the culvert to support the eighty feet of fill that would be going on top of it. New gas lines had to be installed underground. Altogether, site improvement alone was going to cost some $26 million.

Even before the mall was built, it had altered the boundaries of the two cities it straddled, so that the muncipality that had been left out would get the sales tax from one of the department stores.

Back in the Gruen offices, Dahl had talked about the energy conservation designs he had developed, and about the latest theoretical innovations the Gruen firm was trying to persuade developers to try: the principle of the "spine," which basically meant a kind of linear pedestrian street that would run through a number of clustered buildings offering a variety of elements, including office, hotel, cultural, and entertainment as well as retail facilities, thus avoiding duplicated parking and a no-human's-land of cars separating a multistructure project. Once again the Gruen emphasis was on the pedestrian environment.

"We always try to stretch their imagination a little bit," Dahl said, talking about developers. "We've been working on this concept of the spine since 1970. We don't take giant steps, but we head them beyond what conventional wisdom suggests that you do."

But out in the field, with dust swirling around three giant Caterpillar land movers rolling side by side, with two more right behind them, Bill Dahl's immediate task was to innovate a solution to the problem of what to do with a lot of rocks. The excavation had run into more rock than expected, and there was no place to put all of it. The landfill site they'd been using wouldn't accept any more. Dahl had to decide what to do, but he didn't seem to mind.

"Look at all the machinery!" he said with a grin. "This is the part I like. . . . I love it!"

21

Lord Wedgwood and the Valley Girls: This Is the Last Place

Were this world an endless plain, and by sailing eastward we could for ever reach new distances, and discover sights more sweet and strange than any Cyclades or Islands of King Solomon, then there was promise in the voyage. But in pursuit of those far mysteries we dream of, or in tormented chase of that demon phantom that, some time or other, swims before all human hearts; while chasing such over his round globe, they either lead us on in barren mazes or midway leave us whelmed.

—HERMAN MELVILLE
Moby Dick

There are so many malls on the freeway into Orange County, California, and they are so close to its edges that they practically leap out at you and yank you in. There is one at nearly every exit. At some points, shopping centers have pushed up against the freeway behind mesh fences on both sides, threatening to swallow it whole. Meanwhile the car radio spits out a rapid-fire onslaught of mall advertising: "*The Big Ben Shopping Center!*—Come on out and have a good time! Lots of bargains! And see our forty-foot-high Big Ben Tower!" . . . "Hey, come on out to *The Mall of Orange*! Great stores, great prices, great place!" (Followed by the chorused jingle): "The Mall of Orange! The Mall of Orange! Our mall is your mall! Our mall is your mall! The Mall of Orange!"

For all the hype, many of these malls are really something to see. In Orange County, even the run-of-the-mill mall is fascinating—that is, if you're hooked on mallkatecture. Then it's as if you're a cathedral worshiper in Europe.

San Jose had begun my California education in the variety of mall design—the possibilities for exuberance, expressiveness, boldness, and even silliness inherent in the simplicities of the mall form. The malls of the East could be large and internally elegant—those that went beyond the usual seemed to key on some romanticized inspiration from New York City—using steel and glass, internal light, and sophisticated design and merchandise in an approximately unified style. Or they simply tried to surprise with size.

In the Midwest, horizontal spread and size were definitely the biggest ideas in the more ambitious malls: internalizing the prairie and the plains but humanizing them with wide streets and adding to them the glitter of midwestern dreams—the otherworldly, intense, gleaming brightness, dreamt perhaps on long midwestern winter nights. There was an eclectic quality in some, natural to the land of Galesburg's and Lincoln's eccentric frame houses, with their turrets and cupolas and clashes of style. The best embodied a kind of shopping-mall classicism, a cleanliness of form.

But for all their elements of surprise and variety, the malls of the East and the Midwest were likely to seem Calvinist and careful next to the malls of California.

It was on the freeway to Orange County that I discovered a taste I'd acquired on my mall odyssey for a specific aspect of mall architecture: the central court. This was not a subtle choice, since the central court is often the purposeful focus of a mall's design. But for that very reason, it can be the most pleasing of mallkatectural experiences. And now it is becoming something of a lost art.

I had seen some interesting examples, in Illinois and Minnesota in particular, of the large, dominating central court. But it wasn't until I took an impulsive turn off the freeway that I found one that took my breath away.

Westminster Mall was a classic California cathedral with a white stone exterior. Inside, the mall was gleaming and futuristic, with brightly lit logos over the shops and a complex of crisscrossing walkways even more elaborate than those of Eastridge in San Jose. Despite its size, however, the mall seemed user-friendly and even modest. Then it opened up into a soaring central court, and all modesty evaporated.

The court covered an enormous area, both horizontally and vertically. High above was the orange ceiling dome, layered with white. From it hung a huge net sculpture, in appearance part fishnet, part computer grid. According to the plaque below, it was called "Belay On," and its creator was Jock De Swart.

Between the ceiling and the top store level were a series of small windows, like transparent teeth, to ring the rim with sun or starlight. Below, the two levels of the mall bisected the court with a complex of ascending and descending walkways; a third level was built between them, but in the center court only. A matched pair of abstract sculptures stood in the spacious middle area, near red-orange striped sofas on a 1950s' car-interior-upholstery carpet. Tucked into the first level of the court was a large café. Altogether this court combined intimate spaces with monumental scale and audacious effects. It was the collision of a hot-air balloon, a flying saucer, and a living room. I was awestruck.

Westminster Mall was built by Homart, the mall development arm of Sears Roebuck, the world's largest retailer. Later I told a young Homart executive about my admiration for Westminster's central court, and such monumental courts in general. He knew about Westminster Mall and said that there were Homart malls elsewhere with even larger and more elaborate courts in the same basic style. But now they were built much less frequently, and hardly at all by Homart.

In fact, he said, Westminster Mall had been one of the last of its kind. It opened in 1974, a recession year, and after that Homart eliminated the big central courts for economic reasons. They wasted energy, the department stores denigrated them as "unproductive space," and some people felt the courts were too cold and too grand. So malls built in the late 1970s and after tended to have smaller central courts, with more emphasis on the side courts in front of the major department stores.

Westminster's cathedrallike court was, therefore, a relic, and it's too bad. For one thing, the big courts are often the best expression of something unique about mallkatecture: the dextrous balancing of incongruous elements in a collage of effects that produces a beautiful lunacy.

The grand courts also fulfill the social function of monumental spaces missing from most other contemporary buildings; they supply that element of showy majesty that other architecture neglects, especially in suburbia. In the past, size and splendor—whether elegant or vulgar or the likely combination of both—was present not only in many public buildings; there also used to be at least a few grand residences in every American town and certainly in the cities. Now these are harder to find. In many places, only the mall is left for, in the cities, the megastructures with mall components to supply the great staircases, the fountains, skylights, gardens, atriums, and aviaries once found in both private and public buildings.

Now, with shrunken homes and even smaller apartments, modernist severity and drive-in everythings, apparently there is still a need for the personal and social experience of grandeau. Malls are sometimes called cathedrals of consumption, meaning that they are the monuments to a new faith, the consumer religion, which has largely replaced the old. But the metaphor can be extended beyond that, or even beyond the comparative size of malls and cathedrals. In past ages, when religion dominated even civic life, the churches were often the most sensually satisfying social gathering places in the community—which may be one reason people went there. They not only saw their friends and promenaded in their Sunday best, but where else could they get elaborate architectural effects, stained glass, candles, incense, costumes, oratory, and singing, save in Westminster Cathedral? Now it's more likely to be Westminster Mall.

Farther down the freeway is the area's greatest monument to the consumer culture, the complex collected under the name of South Coast: the South Coast Town Center, South Coast Village, and the mall generating the highest dollar volume in Orange County, South Coast Plaza.

The complex includes several clusters of office buildings, hotels, restaurants, and entertainment and retail establishments. (Much of it was planned and has been overseen for the past decade by Gruen Associates.) But South Coast Plaza mall itself has a longer history, which makes it of interest not only to mallkatecture buffs but also to those conversant in one of the possible academic-growth fields of the future (especially in California): archaeomallogy, or the archaeology of shopping centers.

South Coast Plaza opened in 1967 as a standard bread-and-butter suburban mall. Then, through the 1970s, Orange County got richer and richer. Instead of letting a new fashion-oriented mall come in nearby, South Coast Plaza simply expanded to include upscale shops and decor. When this phase of expansion was finally completed, South Coast Plaza had 6 major department stores, upward of 175 shops, and over 2 million square feet under one roof.

How it was done is especially interesting, for the expansion was accomplished vertically as well as horizontally. Now there were two strata representing different eras of merchandising, one on top of the other. And you don't have to be a scientist to notice the difference.

Down on the old, proletarian first floor there are shops like Woolworth, Singer, and Kinney Shoes, their brashly lit logos lined up around Sears. The Sears court has speckled, restroom-style floors and old-timey decorative touches like hand-carved wooden horses originally made in 1855 (or so the historical marker says) for a carrousel in Butler, Pennsylvania. But the truly fascinating aspect was that the customers walking across this court so clearly belonged to it. They were wearing double-knits, polyester stretch pants, and logo T-shirts.

Up on the second floor it was a different story. Under low false ceilings and among off-white, apartment-chic walls with tasteful track lighting and skylights above, Courrèges, Halston, the Polo Store, and the London Shop were discreetly placed in procession next to I. Magnin and Saks Fifth Avenue, their store logos lit in subdued tones or not lit at all.

The customers likewise fit into the effect of Palm Beach Under Glass—they floated by in Gucci loafers and designer clothes, and many of the young women appeared to be on safari in long khaki *bwana* shorts. The two groups of stores, and the two groups of people, were a short escalator ride apart; the higher classes could even watch the lower below, and those on the first floor with rising expectations could gaze upward to see them embodied. When South Coast Plaza is buried in the mud of centuries, archaeomallogists will be able to dig down into two levels of Orange County history as precisely as if one city had been built on top of another.

South Coast is becoming a major urban center for this part of California, and South Coast Plaza is its highly profitable capital. Even Lord Wedgwood of England was obliged to recognize its primacy and power. While I was in the vicinity, Piers Anthony Weymouth, the sixth Lord Wedgwood, appeared at South Coast Plaza as part of a United States tour promoting Wedgwood bone China. There, in the mall court, for the first time anywhere, he demonstrated the strength of his china by balancing a one-and-a-half-ton Silver Spirit Rolls-Royce on Wedgwood demitasse cups, one under each tire.

At South Coast Plaza, I was confronted with something else that emanated from Southern California but which generally didn't amuse me: the theme restaurant. Even the more original themes found there failed to seduce me, like the Back Bay Rowing and Running Club at South Coast, with waitresses in handsome green-and-blue striped rowing shirts and dark-blue shorts. But then I saw one that hit me where my fantasies lived. It was called the 20th Century Limited.

The 20th Century Limited Dining Car Restaurant and Station Saloon did to me what all theme restaurants, parks, and rides are supposed to do—it overwhelmed me with the fantasy. It did so with modesty, accuracy, and taste. It was partly the theme itself that got to me, of course—the high days of American train travel. But even when a subject is close to one's heart, it is the execution that counts. In fact, that's when it becomes all the more important. That's where Barrymore's in Lincoln failed for me; it desecrated the theater.

Beyond the Station Saloon was a small but convincing train platform. I peeked inside the two elegant train cars and they fulfilled my expectations of what the real things must have been like, with upholstered lamps and carved tables. As I looked in one, an older couple, perhaps even old enough to have ridden on the real *20th Century,* went aboard for dinner. I think the fact that dining was also the original purpose of what this car purported to be en- couraged my willing suspension of disbelief. Altogether, it was enough to make me admit that a theme really could be done well, that it really could be magic.

In my Southern California mall trek, I did not make it to the Galleria in Sherman Oaks, partly because nobody had heard of it then. "Valley Girl," the hit song chanted by Moon Zappa, had not yet made it famous. But I did visit Fashion Island in Newport Beach, where the local equivalent of Valley Girls and Boys hung out, and I talked to Vicky Carey, the recreation director for one of the planned villages in the huge planned town of Irvine, of which Newport Beach is a part. She wasn't very happy about the kids and the mall.

Vicky Carey was herself only twenty-eight, and she'd come to California a few years before from Lincoln, Nebraska. She saw all the problems—broken homes, latchkey kids, drugs, drinking, boredom, selfishness, and mindless materialism—hit California first. She felt a lot of sympathy for the problems these kids had, and said that despite the affluence and the great natural surroundings of beaches and mountains, "This is one of the toughest places for teens to grow up." But they sometimes made it hard for her to do her job, and sometimes she just lost patience.

Like the time she organized a dance on a Friday night, with a good live rock band. It was well publicized and admission was only a dollar. All of four kids came. She got angry, and went looking for where the kids were. She found them, hanging out at the mall. Most of them were drunk or stoned or both, she said. She tried to persuade them to give the dance a chance, but they weren't interested. It was grody to the max. But the mall was like . . . awesome. Totally.

That's when Vicky Carey became a little nostalgic about Lincoln. But then, she hadn't been back there for a while.

Toward the end of my stay in California I drove westward along Route 27, the winding, two-lane Topanga Drive, through the heavily wooded narrow canyon, past a community theater mounting Shakespeare on Sunday, and past—even here—the Topanga Canyon Shopping Center. I stopped for a cold drink and a look around. It was a modest community strip center stuck down off the road with a couple of shops, the community law offices, a posh restaurant, and an unposh bar that was packed with men in lumber shirts, some playing pool and some watching TV, and a young woman writing poetry at a damp table.

A shopping center out in the woods seemed incongruous, I thought, but everything in it fit. Maybe that was part of the genius of the form. I'd seen a similarly modest shopping center on a quiet road between Ipswich and Gloucester in Massachusetts. It contained the Ipswich Video Barn, the Essex Antique Coop, Flowers by the Sea, The Body Shop (an exercise emporium), and The Apple Orchard Restaurant. A visitor from another planet who landed there wanting to know what this area of Massachusetts was like would not have to go anywhere else.

From the Topanga Canyon Shopping Center, I drove on until I reached the Pacific Coast Highway. There was a sign saying that this was the end of California Route 27; you had to turn right or left, north or south. But the sign was hardly necessary. Straight ahead, the sunlight was glancing off the surface of the broad Pacific.

It was there that I remembered a poetry reading I had attended in Berkeley in 1969, and a poem I heard read there by a tall and theatrically handsome San Francisco poet named Lew Welch. A few years after that reading, he simply disappeared.

As I remembered it, the poem began with the image of standing on Mount Tamalpais, the Northern California mountain that native Americans and Bay Area poets consider sacred, looking toward the sea. This was where the frontier ended, the poem said, where the West reached the limit of its definition; where America stopped. There was a repeated line that expressed this, which I imperfectly remembered as: "This is the last place./There is no place left to go."

On this trip I had been observing the ecology of shopping malls—not an activity I would have predicted for myself in 1969. But it seemed to me that California's malls also said something about the American frontier. America had flung itself headlong to its natural and national borders, and now it was rapidly filling in the territory it had more lightly overrun. The frontier had always represented an escape and a hope—the hope that the mistakes and tyrannies of the past were left behind, that the new land would be better, and that something better could be built there.

But now there are no more external frontiers. Now even the physical frontier was internal; the new worlds had to be created, one way or another. Some of those worlds were being conceived and controlled, managed and protected, in the separated, self-sustaining enclosures of the mall. For America now, it seemed, the mall was a new frontier. There was no other Eden to be found here. This is the last place. There is no place left to go. If there was to be paradise, it would have to be paradise enclosed.

22

Fear and Malling in Las Vegas

From Union Station in Los Angeles, a beautifully surviving art deco masterpiece, I took the *Desert Wind* to Las Vegas. Hot air, of course, is a lot of what Las Vegas is about, and appropriately enough I was on my way there to attend a convention, of the International Council of Shopping Centers.

On the way, shopping centers again became a topic of conversation. I lunched with Keith and Melissa, a young couple who'd flown to Los Angeles from Denver to investigate a job offer Keith had and to evaluate the city as a place to live. They were taking the train back just for fun.

Keith and Melissa had pretty much decided to stay in Denver. It wasn't that they didn't like L.A.—they would have access to the mountains and rustic recreation, as they did in Colorado—but even with the new job's raise in salary, they still couldn't afford the same standard of living they had in Denver. So they were thinking about the pleasures of home more than ever.

But those pleasures were being threatened by a mini mall war in their neighborhood. A developer wanted to build a big multi-use center on land that had been donated to the city for recreation. The development would mean that some cul-de-sac streets would be converted for through traffic. It would change where they lived, Keith said, "from a nice suburban neighborhood to—the whole thing."

Between the fast lanes of Los Angeles and Las Vegas is something called the desert, and the experience of it from the train window was just what I needed to put all this mall business in perspective. It began with mesas on both sides of us, so close that the grain in the rock invited touch. Evening was beginning, and the sun was behind us. The play of light and shadow in the desert was fascinating and mystifying. Under a cloudless sky I saw shadows on the ground and across the face of a hill without being able to see what was making the shadow, what was interceding with the sun.

There were moments as we moved through the silent desert that timelessness leaped from the landscape. It was my first view of a terrain like this, which seemed to embody abstractions. Watching the sun through the rocks was like seeing sacredness.

We were forty-five minutes from Las Vegas before the first signs of humans appeared: a dirt road, a solitary house, and two boys at a crossing who, instead of waving, gleefully mooned the train.

The sun was setting behind the hills and the land lost its abstractness; for the moments before darkness it became the rocky surface of an inviting but solitary and dangerous planet. Then came the final approach to Vegas, in the desert air paved with power lines.

Aesthetically, and in a few other well-known ways, Las Vegas is the neon trailer park of the Western world. It was first settled in 1855 by Mormons, who promptly abandoned it in 1857. For the better part of a century, it seemed the Mormons had made the definitive statement. Then casino gambling was legalized in 1931, and the boom was on.

When my train arrived, the neon fan dance of Las Vegas was there, right outside the station. But fresh from my limited transcendence in the desert, I noticed first the bright full moon. When I pointed it out to my cab driver, he said he'd been too busy to look up. There hadn't been many busy weekends lately—the conventions had been small. So he was glad to have a big one coming in now. Conventions are the lifeblood of the city these days, and all that matters is that conventioneers are moving around town spending money. Anything that impedes them or distracts from this activity is righteously shunned. So Las Vegas is a desert city where people hate to see it rain.

I was part of this convention crowd now. The International Council of Shopping Centers had roughly ten thousand members, most of them shopping-center owners, developers, and management people. It brings anywhere from three thousand to five thousand people to Las Vegas each year.

"It's an unusual organization because they manage to hold this large group of entrepreneurs together," Bill Dahl of Gruen Associates had told me in Los Angeles. "They exchange every imaginable kind of information—like sales numbers, maintenance, security, leasing arrangements for department stores and tenants—just a tremendous amount of information."

I shared a cab from my hotel to the convention with a developer who said pretty much the same thing. "I don't know any other business like it," he said. "Very successful people who started this industry have been openly telling other people how to be very successful. If you ask a developer how much his center is making, he'll tell you. It's kind of amazing when you think about it." The ICSC also holds regional conventions, sponsors awards, lobbies Washington on the industry's behalf, publishes a monthly newspaper in addition to the standard texts on mall development, public relations, and security (as well as others like "Snow Removal: Strategy and Tactics"), and it runs a yearly educational session called the University of Shopping Centers. The ICSC, founded right at the beginning of the enclosed mall revolution in 1957, has been instrumental in making the industry a comprehensive and efficient success, and probably also in creating a national sameness.

The ICSC convention had several elements. First there were the usual meetings where a lot of people wearing name tags sat on straight-back chairs and listened to a group of experts lined up on either side of a dais discussing topics of concern, from the major issues affecting everyone to the more specific problems of small shopping-center financing, roof repair, and security. Developers discussed mixed-use projects and new methods of financing; de-

signers, new energy-saving innovations; and everyone wondered
how to appeal to working women and what to do about the coming of shopping by home computer.

Then there was the Trade Mall, a huge exhibition center full of
a circus of shopping-mall stuff, where companies like Audio Image,
Ltd., the Atlas Door Corporation, Federal Sign, Gardco Lighting,
Metropolitan Ceramics, and Verd-A-Ray Corp. displayed products
of interest in the mall world, such as Electra-Matic Carpet Main-
tainers (with twenty-five-gallon solution tanks feeding a solid brass,
three-nozzle thrusterjet directly into mall carpet fibers), Luxalon architectural ceiling systems, Pedigrid recessed tread mats for mall
entrances from Decogard, the Roll-o-matic sliding closures for
storefront security, and the latest in mall floor-care products, interior visual information displays and control terminals, trash recep-
tacles and ash urns.

The Trade Mall was educational. Mall people learned how to
respond to the boom in market segmentation studies from the new
demographic data suppliers and analyzers, or how to choose a logo
design that has feminine appeal (a must), or how to select the right
style of mall jingle, from country-flavored tunes for the bread-and-
butter malls to symphonic backgrounds and seagull sounds for
high-fashion malls.

The third element of the convention was the hospitality suites,
which were set up in the big Las Vegas hotels, mostly by developers. There, conventioneers could relax, cop a free drink and a
snack, and engage in one of the favorite pastimes of the ICSC convention, Deal Making, which means exactly what it says—the
making of deals between retailers and developers looking for tenants in a new or expanded mall, or between developers looking for
financing and those in a position to supply it.

Besides all this, there were also the usual Las Vegas convention
attractions: casino shows in the evenings, gambling just outside the
door of a session on Creative Financing in a Changing Market, and
the demure prostitutes who floated through the hospitality suites,
mixing in disconcertingly well with the wives. But behind the so-
ciability and the amenities, the deal making is ferocious and continuous. I found that shopping-center people who at first greeted me
effusively soon made polite excuses and backed off when they realized I only wanted to talk and ask questions, not make a deal.

                          ★   ★   ★

In *Larceny, Inc.*, a movie released in 1942, Edward G. Robinson plays a bank robber who buys a luggage store next door to a bank, to make tunneling into the vaults more convenient. But the store becomes an inadvertent success, so he decides to give up crime and become a businessman. He has a vision: to open a "shopping center—like a big department store, with each store a unit." "Jeez," says his dumb sidekick, played by Broderick Crawford. "We'll be typhoons!"

Forty years later, the big typhoons who blew into Las Vegas were increasingly dominating the shopping-center business. They were the ones with the choice hospitality suites in Caesar's Palace, the Desert Inn, and the Hilton. The economic rigors of the early 1980s had shaken out many smaller developers and the increased sophistication of the mall business meant that only the strongest were going to survive.

One of the biggest—Ernest Hahn of California—spelled it out (in an interview published in *The Real Estate People*): "There are probably about fifteen developers throughout the country who are readily accepted by the chains, and the fifteen of us develop about 90% of all regional shopping center space in the United States. Basically, each one has a sphere of influence, a particular geographic area. Of course, that doesn't mean that my firm won't build anywhere in the United States and other developers won't come into our area. There's nothing cut and dried about it. We have gradually grown out of our original spheres of influence and started leapfrogging around the country."

Hahn is his own best example. Beginning in an office located in the corner of a used-furniture store in Hawthorne, California, Hahn eventually became the most powerful mall developer in the western United States. Now he had major malls in Memphis, Dallas, San Diego, and Los Angeles (he was the developer of Fox Hills) and was considered one of the most forward-looking developers in the country. "The role of the developer is really now that of a sort of small city builder," he told a shopping-center forum. "He's no longer just creating stores and being the landlord."

In a perhaps unguarded moment, an official of the ICSC wondered aloud what I was doing at their convention. "Most of these guys are really ordinary," he said. "They wear polyester leisure suits, they are concerned with the details of retail and real estate, and they aren't very bright. The only interesting developers in this business right now are Rouse and Hahn."

It was an intriguing choice of names, for besides their reputations as innovators (Rouse in the East, Hahn in the West) they had something else in common: They'd both recently come under the financial umbrella of a Canadian outfit called Trizec. Trizec bought a considerable chunk of stock in the publicly owned Rouse Company, and through a U.S. subsidiary Trizec bought the Hahn companies outright. Rouse and Hahn had already been involved in one joint project (Santa Monica Place in California) and a Rouse Company official told me he expected that these two giants would eventually merge. So it seemed the mall business, like so many others, was going to be concentrated in still fewer companies and conglomerates.

Besides Ernest Hahn, a tanned, kind, and quietly intelligent man who favored suits in modest, classic cuts and light colors that blended in with the western ambience, there were other mall industry stars moving about this ICSC convention. There was affable Ernest Homer, head of Homart, the developing arm of Sears—the largest retailer and biggest advertiser in the country—who handed out a business card that was also bigger than anyone else's. Melvin Simon was there, patient behind his aviator glasses as he took considerable ribbing from the dais for his Hollywood moviemaking activities (he produced *Porky's,* among other films), but in his own rapid-fire presentation he showed a firm practical grasp of the latest twists and turns in the shopping-center business. (Then he promptly changed into casual traveling clothes, strode to the head of the line waiting for taxis in front of the Hilton, pressed a bill into the right hands, and was gone.)

And, as always, quiet, modest Albert Sussman was there—the executive vice-president of the ICSC since it began, and its chief organizer, conciliator, facilitator, and the personification of its continuity. He was everywhere at the convention, keeping everyone happy, and still enthusiastic about the shopping-center business and all its burgeoning activities. But he wasn't the only example of continuity; except for James Rouse (who had recently retired), nearly all the major pioneers of the mall industry—its Edisons and Carnegies, its Fords and Selznicks—were present and active.

By and large, it indeed was a homogeneous group of white middle-aged males with a polyester point of view that made up the bulk of the conventioneers, just as I'd been warned. Although there were a few black mall managers and other minorities, and a scattering of women mall managers—along with a great many women public relations and marketing directors—there weren't very many women participating at the executive level in the convention. Most of the women who showed up for the cocktail parties and official get-togethers were wives. Since their husbands were usually too busy deal-making to talk to them or to me, we talked to one another. The ironies were obvious: While these men were trying to figure out how to appeal to mall customers who are mostly women, and especially how to adapt to the needs and desires of working women, their wives were left to play slot machines and order from room service.

One woman I met at a large noisy cocktail party sponsored by a large company with a great many shoe stores in malls, had just moved to a small southern city with her husband because his company had transferred him there from Chicago. In Chicago she had been a bank executive; in her new home she was expected to take tea with the ladies in the afternoon, she said, and that was about all. "I don't know how much longer I can take it," she said, looking lost. Her expression didn't change when her husband happened by, said hello, thrust a business card in my hand, and went off again.

Between the sessions, breakfasts, lunches, receptions, and interviews, the only actual shopping mall I visited in Las Vegas was the new and glitzy Hahn mall called The Fashion Show. It was pretty much geared to catch the eye and dollars of high-rolling tourists, and especially these bored spouses of conventioneers. The mall eschewed the garish neon that surrounded it and attempted to bring some low-keyed class to the Vegas strip. But it also indulged in some show business; one of its features was the Promenade of the Stars sidewalk, made up of concrete squares bearing the signatures and handprints of Las Vegas entertainers.

That The Fashion Show deliberately differentiated itself from the style of the strip was perhaps partly an acknowledgment that an actual shopping mall can't compete directly with the casino enclosures, which use some of the mall techniques to concentrate attention on their interior world. But the casinos have more insistent merchandise to offer. They are malls of money, sex, booze, and the most ineffable and irresistable merchandise of all, luck.

Near where I stayed in a small new hotel at a far end of the strip, there was a shopping center like none I'd see before, but it seemed appropriate to Las Vegas: All it had was a convenience grocery store and an adult bookstore, anchored by a topless bar. It was therefore, in more than one sense, a strip center.

After the convention was over, I flew out of Las Vegas at night. There was no direct train to my next destination, but this time I was glad to be flying. After five days of it, this was one place I wanted to leave quickly and be somewhere else. We took off, and for a moment the city was a blaze of intensely bright color below. Then, in an instant there was nothing but blackness, and it was gone.

23

The Inside of Paradise in Phoenix Rising

It was not long before out of the desert blackness below the plane there emerged another flat canvas of lights over a vast distance. If it had been daytime I would have seen hundreds of miles of brown desert speckled with sage, and suddenly a huge pool table of greenness, as lush and continuous as felt. That's what my airplane companion told me. She was only in her twenties but she could remember when the country between Phoenix and Tucson, where she grew up, was still occupied mostly by farms on irrigated land. Phoenix was one of America's cotton growing centers, and sugarcane was a significant cash crop.

But then the cities grew and claimed the land already once reclaimed from the desert, and the people in those cities needed the water that had once gone to the farms. The area grew so rapidly, my seat companion said, that after she went away to college she would fly home for vacations and see a new city below her, every year.

The western can-do propensity for creating a desired environment regardless of natural limitations is certainly demonstrated in Arizona. Making the desert bloom with indomitable stretches of green was only the first step. Arizona began to experience the unforseen side effects of artificial change, the environmental ironies that other ages might see as the inevitable trappings of tragedy. Beginning in the 1930s, people were going to Arizona for their health, especially those with allergies and lung problems who might find relief in the dry, clean desert air. But people brought their cars, and when industry followed them to Phoenix, the formerly pure city jumped into the top ten of the national polluted-air hit parade. Meanwhile, the hay fever sufferers who flocked to Tucson because it was free of pollen had planted so much of the pollen-producing foliage they remembered from eastern homes that Tucson now had twice the incidence of asthma and hay fever as the national average.

But in Arizona even the absence of the sea can be overcome: Tempe, near Phoenix, has Big Surf, an indoor environment featuring a machine that creates a giant (and perfect) wave every ninety seconds, all for the pleasure of desert surfers. "It has all the advantages of the ocean and none of the disadvantages," boasted the manager of the facility, interviewed on a local television program I watched one morning in my Phoenix motel room.

Still, the desert cannot be completely ignored. Car doors and motel-room doorknobs are hot to the touch; air conditioning is a necessity everywhere. So it is only logical that the enclosed mall should be a vital part of the new Arizona landscape.

Like many Sun Belt locations that have outgrown their original centers, Phoenix has severe problems with its old areas. The newspapers carried daily stories and letters about the notorious downtown and its atmosphere of decay and alcoholism. Meanwhile, the new Phoenix was rising over three hundred square miles, and sixteen big shopping malls were scattered through it. On television, I also saw a store manager in one of the Phoenix malls tell NBC News that these malls were simply "a better downtown that the marketplace invented."

I visited about a half-dozen of these better downtowns there, including a couple of the oldest (the Collonade, formerly an open mall with the telltale inward-slanting floors and with a set of rugged stone stairs obviously made for the outdoors next to a comparatively fragile-looking escalator in the new enclosure; and the Town and Country shopping center, Arizona's original open mall, spread over some twenty-two acres) and some of the newest (including Scottsdale Fashion Square, which had an outdoor central court featuring palm trees).

Unfortunately, I was a little early for the opening of the Borgota, also in affluent Scottsdale. It represented one more step beyond other historical-theme specialty malls, and perhaps right into the Twilight Zone. It was a malled village of expensive shops in the desert, designed to replicate a thirteenth-century walled village in Italy. The illusion was carried out with such dedication that the mall's bricks were brought from Rome and the shop signs and menus were printed in Italian. According to reports, the Borgota's inaugural festivities included the launching of a flock of white doves from its imitation Italian bell tower into the Arizona sky.

But the most indicative of the malls of Phoenix lies out on Black Canyon Highway and is called, appropriately, the Metrocenter. Because I was driving madly from mall to mall in unfamiliar territory and had no idea of how long it would take me to get from one to another, I rarely made appointments to meet mall officials. So it was with a good deal of surprise that, dropping in on the marketing director of Metrocenter, I found myself greeted like an old friend.

Emma Louise Philabaum was older than most marketing directors I'd met, and she instantly exhibited a combination of warmth, intelligence, and efficiency that cannot be artificially contrived, though many try. She took me into her office and began briskly and cheerfully to tell the story of Metrocenter.

Phoenix was growing fast in the late 1960s—the population would be a third larger by 1980—and projections showed that it was growing most toward the northwest. A forty-year-old real estate developer named Russ "Rusty" Lyon, who with partners had just formed his own company called Westcor, bought a huge parcel of land and began planning a major commercial complex, which eventually became a co-venture with Homart: the Metrocenter.

"All this was farmland and freeway then," Philabaum said. "But Rusty had no trouble getting the department stores to come in. Metrocenter was the first mall in the world to have five department stores. It opened with empty space, and it was two years before we filled it all, but from the beginning it became a magnet—a central focus for a new community."

In fact it became the literal center of expanding rings of development, beginning with motels, banks, and restaurants, then a medical office complex, a family recreation center, and finally several apartment complexes. By the mid-1970s, Metrocenter was the hole in the donut of a community that had not existed before. Moreover, as Arizona's first multilevel enclosed mall, it was drawing business from nearly the entire state. It was the first on a new frontier for the shopping malls of the West.

Metrocenter was huge. In one of those comparisons publicity writers love to put in their brochures, it was bigger than thirty-five football fields, which means that the entire National Football League could practice in it with room to spare. It was boldly designed. Metrocenter was shaped like a "Z," with iconic forms and bold lines in solid stone outside, and an interior full of curves and color, with an ambience and symbology influenced by the American Indian architecture of the Southwest. In particular, Metrocenter's courts combined space-age contours with totem pole sculptures and the ancient texture of stone floors and walls. It was all the more striking because this was the work of four different architects, each responsible for specific areas of the mall. The responsibility was divided for reasons of efficiency as well as creative effect—the mall is that large.

Inside on a spring afternoon, sunlight splashed across the swirled gray-and-white speckled tile near the ice-skating rink. (Outside, Philabaum said, there was the usual spring crime wave of stolen sprinkler heads from the mall grounds.) A large mall does not always harbor real novelty but it is more likely to than a small one, and Metrocenter had its share of strangeness, like a shop called Funny Shirts and another called Sherry's Plaster Palatium. It also had Champagne Nails, where ladies had their nails done while sipping free coffee; and one of those totems of contemporary America, the shop devoted to fashions for the bathroom. Here it was Bathtique; it carried personalized soap (Norm, Pam, Pedro, Peggy, Sid, and Stan), all-over body paints for lovers, and Vinyl Seat Designs of red, yellow, green, and blue, as well as a lime-green "T-Shirt for Toilet Lid" with the legend THE END IS IN SIGHT in black.

Metrocenter was not only the focus for a new community but was large enough to serve people through an entire life cycle: There was Kids' Stuff for infant clothes and Young World for children's (WE HAVE FIRST COMMUNION VEILS AND GOWNS, a sign in its window said) and Toy World, followed by Susie's Casuals and

Fashion Conspiracy for Juniors, Foxmoor Casuals for young women, Alrow and Nobby for career women, and Women's World for the "fuller figure of later years." Boys' clothes were available at County Seat, young men's at Chess King; there was the Bank Store for style-conscious careerists, and Richman for the traditionally minded. Fashion Center Bridal will outfit the bride, Gingiss Formal Wear the groom, and Expectations Shops and Motherhood Maternity sell "everything for the expectant mother."

Metrocenter had three chain bookstores and a public library, eighteen women's clothing stores, eight for men, and ten or twelve for both, not counting the department stores. There were five craft stores, nine financial institutions, Winona Market Research, one figure salon, and a branch of Arizona State University. There were three bakeries, some thirty places to eat out, fourteen card and gift shops, eight home decorating stores, nine home entertainment shops, seventeen jewelers, three plant stores, one pet store, three movie theaters, and twenty-four shoe stores. Among the special events in Metrocenter was the periodic appearance of Magic Carpet Ride, a group that simply told stories aloud, a community function that has not been part of the life cycle in many parts of America for quite some time.

Before I had ventured out to the mall to inspect all of this, Emma Louise Philabaum hurried to tell me about what Rusty Lyon did for an encore. In this relatively virginal landscape, Lyon also scouted new locations from his own airplane, harking back to the glory days of DeBartolo in the Midwest. "When he saw that Metrocenter was such a magnet for new development, he went out and bought a lot of land in Paradise Valley," Philabaum said, "and he put together Paradise Village, the first planned urban village in Arizona. The idea was to create a small community where you could be born, work, and live and die and never have to leave. It was a big project. The land had to be made usable—it was on a flood plain. Then we had the largest private road-building project in the state at that time. Land was donated for parks and school sites." At the middle of it was, of course, the Paradise Valley Mall.

After giving me directions to Paradise Valley, Emma Louise Philabaum excused herself. It was the end of the day and there was an orchestra performance that night. "I have to go home and iron my husband's trousers," she explained.

*   *   *

I drove on down the highway. The gingerbread-brown hills were already strewn with gingerbread subdivisions bearing names like Cresta de Oro and Sierra Grande. Beyond a stretch of gingerbread desert along Cactus Road and within sight of some serious mountains in the distance, I came to Paradise.

Paradise Village in the last light of evening managed to look like a quiet, modest housing development with cul-de-sac streets (some with calm names like Willow, others of more "new town" style, like Emile Zola and Joan of Arc) but this complex was planned to include an industrial park, office complex, a two-hundred-bed hospital, the Phoenix Mountain Nursing Home, parks, bike and hiking trails, an elementary school, and a golf course. Housing will include apartments and condo townhouses in addition to single-family homes.

Paradise Valley Mall was the center of a retail and recreation complex that will include two (and possibly three) other shopping centers. The mall itself—a smaller, more intimate, and even more strikingly iconic version of Metrocenter—was designed to be an actual kind of paradise: "a state of perfection beyond the reach of ordinary terms," as Westcor's brochure put it. To that end it included an extensive collection of Edenic flora and fauna: palm and olive, eucalyptus, Aleppo pine and weeping elm, evergreen pear, Arizona ash and jacaranda trees outside, while interior gardens nurtured dracaenas, queen and Kentia palms, bamboo palms, and ivy.

Most of the people I saw in Paradise that evening were teenagers, hanging out in the Patio (the food court, with an overhanging motto of FOOD, FUN, FROLIC), staring at one another in the midst of the Great Hot Dog Experience, Sloppy Joe Shack, and Pizza D'Amore. The whining and whirring and riveting stutter coming out of the Superfun arcade met the swirling sound of people, and from somewhere came the strains of Bob Seger singing "On Main Street."

Meanwhile the Hudson Institute has predicted another doubling of the population of Greater Phoenix in the next thirty years. But there's a growing concern over sprawl that could mean a more carefully planned expansion. According to Philabaum, the city's Citizens Committee recommended that future development be organized in the urban village form. So if Metrocenter represents the Phoenix of today, Paradise Valley may be the Phoenix rising in the future.

★   ★   ★

That possibility was on my mind when I took a drive out to another future-oriented project, the experimental community devised by the visionary architect Paolo Soleri, called Arcosanti.

For years I'd been hauling around, from residence to residence, a book published by MIT Press that contained Soleri's plans for his "arcology," an energy-conserving community partly inspired by the cosmological writings of Teilhard de Chardin. And I do mean hauling: The book measures two feet by one foot, with 122 pages of theory, description, and drawings. This elaborate attempt to work with the environment to create a community form that would reunite humans with the intimate earth, I thought would bear watching.

But about seventy-five miles outside of Phoenix, at the end of a rutted dirt road in a remote and arid landscape, the visible evidence of arcology consisted of a kind of tiny agricultural commune centered around a few buildings that looked like the remnants of an abandoned amusement park. After more than a decade, the envisioned Arcosanti was still an elaborate Plexiglas model on display inside the reception building.

Soleri has continued to raise money for his dream from his lectures and books, from tourists who come here, and from the sales of his haunting and delicate wind chimes. But even to begin to finance this experiment in America, he probably would have to graduate from the status of minor cult figure to true celebrity. His forays into that realm have not been all that successful—the major moment in a television interview with Dick Cavett came when Cavett remarked that Arcosanti sounded like living in a shopping center, and Soleri admitted the concepts were similar. Still, not even the revered Buckminster Fuller realized any of his really major designs. So far, what Soleri had in actual concrete at Arcosanti was a very nice home for himself and a very good coffee shop for tourists.

Arcosanti might be ready in another decade, but meanwhile this part of Arizona was developing so fast that horse ranches faced new subdivisions on the other side of the same road. At this stage, Arcosanti was supposed to be primarily an educational center, according to our tour guide. "We're creating an environment for man," she said, "but first we must create the man to fit into this." But less than a hundred miles away there was Paradise Village, another planned community of the future that in fact already exists, with real people who don't need to be created to live in it. They were mostly white middle-class people, it seemed to me, but then, that's another question about the inside of paradise.

24

Tucson: When Worlds Collide

Before I drove from Phoenix to Tucson, I phoned ahead for a motel room from the same chain as my motel in Phoenix. It had been pleasant, inexpensive, and centrally located, with a coffee shop for pre-malling breakfasts. I thought the Tucson branch would be a good bet. When I hit the edge of Tucson, driving on the main highway where this motel was supposed to be, I started looking for its sign. There were lots of motels there, but none of them was mine. I drove past a numbing series of exits until I found myself on the edge of the desert—and there it was: the last outpost.

This motel, however, had no coffee shop, although there was a truck stop next door where I could eat among truck drivers wearing huge cowboy hats with strange arrays of feathers stuck in them. In fact, this motel was itself a truck stop, and demanded payment in advance because of all the fly-by-night truckers who stayed there.

It was a spooky place, on the edge of nowhere, yet almost part of a fast-growing city. After passing the afternoon in the motel pool, which was practically like swimming in the desert, I thought I would drive back toward civilization and find a real restaurant for dinner.

It was easier thought than done. The city of Tucson, if it existed, was apparently found by choosing the right highway exit into the maze, without any clues. I tried several that seemed to lead to bright lights but I didn't find anything I wanted to get out of the car for. The bright lights belonged to subsidiary strips of fast food and service stations.

Finally I found what looked like a central area. At first it was fairly scary outside my air-conditioned rental car. Desperados roamed the streets of rotting wood saloons and fast-food outlets. It was like a frontier Dodge City overlayed with neon.

A few minutes of driving later, I was actually grateful for the appearance of large blank-faced stone buildings that announced a hotel and office fortress. I parked and walked through a small mixed-use mall to get to it. The mall was Las Placitas, with offices, shops, and residences that seemed brand-new but mostly unoccupied. The semienclosed square of Las Placitas was also empty, as were the surrounding streets. I located the hotel and an entrance to its dining room just below street level: With some relief, I went in.

I found myself virtually alone in its fancy expanse. I had been virtually alone since I hit Arizona, and in my current motel I wasn't even comfortable. But my waitress talked to me, and she turned out to be a writing student at the University of Arizona.

She told me that Las Placitas was a city-sponsored project that was failing. She didn't like malls much herself. "I go through them as quickly as I can," she said. "They upset me for some reason." She began to look upset. "Unfortunately, most bookstores are in them, so I have to go." But then she had to admit that after three years in Bolivia, when she saw a Denny's Restaurant in Mexico City, she cried.

She told me about an event going on right then down the hall in a bar in the lower level of this immensely quiet hotel: a jam session sponsored by the Tucson Jazz Society. I thanked her, and after my dinner, I went.

I opened the door to the bar like Alice walking through the looking-glass. It was an amazing change. The bar was large and filled with sound, color, and mostly young people listening to an enthusiastic and reasonably good ensemble. People were friendly, and there was even a newsletter with jazz poems and interviews. I spent the rest of the evening there, listening to music and hearing about real life in Tucson. There was life in Tucson after all, if you could find it—and in the habitual heat of this city, smaller than Phoenix but seemingly just as spread out, life was inside something.

At the Las Vegas convention I had briefly met Roy Drachman, a pioneer shopping-center developer whose offices were in Tucson. He was beginning his summer in Palm Springs now, but I had called his son, Manny Drachman, and the next day I went to see him.

I left early for my appointment and took all my belongings with me. After locating Drachman's office, I looked for another motel, and I found a handsome Rodeway Inn virtually next door. The woman at the desk was friendly; she wondered if I didn't want to ask for the commercial rate. So I did, and she gave me a wonderful room with glass doors that opened onto the patio and pool. It was a welcome haven, since Memorial Day weekend was a day away and I intended to take some time off.

Manny Drachman was a big man sitting behind a big desk and smoking a little cigar. He told me about Tucson's growth—beginning with those who came during World War II to work in the big aircraft plant that sparked further industrial growth. Then IBM came to town, starting the parade of other high-tech firms. New residents were also drawn by word of Tucson's climate.

Drachman's father had gotten into shopping centers shortly after the war, beginning with small neighborhood centers. He hadn't developed regional malls—Tucson had only two, with probably two more on the way. Tucson's growth had inspired a great many small shopping centers—too many for the market, Drachman said. What was needed now was organized multi-use development, and that's what the Drachman firm was getting into. (In this way, I thought later, Tucson might be like some newly developing countries that skip intermediate steps in technology and go right to the state of the art. In this case, they were skipping the proliferating regional-mall stage and going right into the latest mall form, the mixed-use center.)

Drachman talked about their latest project, a twenty-one-acre mixed-use center, not quite finished, called El Mercado. It included shops, services, restaurants, offices, and a motel.

"Where is it?" I asked. "El Mercado?"

"Here," he said. "You're sitting in it."

I was also, it turned out, staying in it. After the interview was over I returned to the Rodeway Inn and didn't leave El Mercado for the next three days. I stayed in my air-conditioned room with color television and radio and did some writing; I browsed through the shops and used my "charge privilege card" at the Good Earth Restaurant (which transferred my check to my motel bill), gorging myself on healthy food—salads, hearty breads, inventive entrees, and a nice selection of healthy wines.

But most of my time was spent in or around the Rodeway pool, in the sunny brightness of day and, half-immersed in a warm whirlpool with a cognac in one hand and my Aiwa cassette player plugged into my ears, under the bright stars at night.

I eventually visited both of Tucson's malls, where I also remained plugged into my cassette earphones, letting the strains of "The Planets" accompany me past the old people watching soap operas in Video Concepts at Park Mall, and listening to Eric Satie's orchestral music while strolling through the huge courthouse-rotunda-style El Con. El Con had a curious section of somewhat seedy shops with logo signs hanging out over the mall, more like a real city street of the 1950s than anything I'd ever seen in this kind of mall. I liked El Con for its funky-monumental style and for some of its zany-looking fast-food places. Park Mall was more upscale, with a more stylish design, but both malls had a lively mix of ages and races. Park Mall and El Con aren't very far from each other, and they seemed mored like the city downtown than its old downtown did.

My major epiphany in Tucson came as that Memorial Day weekend ended; before moving on, I headed out on the highway for one necessary task—the laundry. I found a laundromat on the East Broadway strip, and while my clothes sloshed and spun, I drank a beer sitting crosslegged on the hood of my rented Pinto, and looked out at the end of the day.

I looked at the evening, the startling hanging blue clouds, the paler-blue sky, one white star already out, and some white and tangerine still at the horizon. There were mountains on three sides of me, everywhere but at my back, and they might have been there, too, except for this shopping center where the laundromat was.

The mountains to the east were already fading into night. To the west, rimmed in the last eggshell tints of dusk, and straight

ahead to the north they loomed, silhouetted in deep blue against the
lighter clouds and, still lighter, the blue sky.

As all the colors began fading into the same deepening blue and
then into darkness, I remembered a movie I saw when I was still in
grade school. *When Worlds Collide* is now something of a cult classic, since it was produced by one of the masters of the 1950s science-fiction film, George Pal. At the end of the movie, pilgrims
from Earth (which was crushed to cinders by a passing star) arrive
on a new planet to begin human history all over again. All we see
of this planet is an absurdly perfect horizon of blazing-pink mountains and turquoise sky—the new Eden. It is so obviously a painting that when I saw it again with a hip contemporary adult
audience, they laughed. Still, those mountains were supposed to
represent the wonders of a completely new world, and at least
when I first saw it, they had that effect on me.

Now I wondered if the first settlers here saw these mountains
and this desert as just that wondrous. They were to me now. Another few sips of my Lowenbrau, and I lowered my gaze below the
now nearly invisible mountains to the K MART sign. Then I looked
at the red and blue, green and white Hi-Val gas station and convenience store next door to my laundromat. I tried to tell myself that
these belonged here with the mountains. They are just the part of
this world that humans have built, and festooned with bright color.

The built environment is not just a way of satisfying human
needs and of expressing human possibilities. It is also a separation
from the rest of the world, an escape from its terrors. In the process
of our overanxious overkill, it also seals us off from the world's
wonders, and leaves us with ourselves and our creations. The built
environment—and all the colors, sounds, moods, tastes, occupations, diversions, conflicts, and releases we have filled it with—absorbs us. It changes our internal sense of time and cycle and pace; it
literally changes what we see and hear and smell and otherwise
sense, out of what there is in the world we are capable of sensing.

This is the built world of which the mall is in many ways the
logical conclusion. We bring what bits and facsimiles of wonders
we can inside, and gradually we forget the real ones. We are building new rules and new perceptions along with new environments.
Now the only paradise that is likely to satisfy us is paradise enclosed.

Maybe this wasn't an unusual sort of thought or observation,
but it hit me with straight emotional force, and I knew it was be-

cause of Tucson: In the spring the days were blazing but the nights were cool and the evening full of air, blowing softly, and there was still the palpable presence of the desert. It is out there, and it is stronger.

But here, under the canopies at Hi-Val, it was Norman Rockwell time. A kid in his baseball uniform was filling up the family car, watched by a blond girl in a black Danskins top and jeans pumping gas into her VW bug, and a family waiting in their pickup truck for dad to pay for the gas, and maybe pick up a quart of milk and some Twinkies. The station had two additional signs in green and white: SNACK SHOP and SELF REPAIR.

Deep in the Heart of Mallness: Four Days in the Houston Galleria

The distance between Tucson and Houston was immense and empty. From the train window there was a day and a half of vast land, of rock, scrub, and stone broken by a small ranch, a small town, and a few animals in the long solitude. So every object in that continuous landscape became a discrete and memorable picture: horses in a field of brush and old tires, a sun-tanned girl standing at a crossing to watch us clatter by, four cows huddled around a tiny windmill, a man watering the infield of a small baseball diamond. Meanwhile the clouds were discernably hanging in space, not pasted against the firmament; the sky was not only wider out there, it was somehow taller.

As the mountains of Arizona receded and we headed into New Mexico, the railbed became sandy, and between the sand and the mountains there was either water or the illusion of water. Hours later we crossed the Rio Grande into Texas. Across the border in Mexico there were cramped houses dotting the hillside above a big sign that said RIO GRANDE MALL IN JUAREZ. It was the most definite border I'd ever seen, the closest to my childhood belief that borders, even between states, were magical lines and what was on one side would be completely different from what was on the other. Here it was actually true. On the Texas side were factories and freeways. On the Mexican side were houses tumbled on the hillsides. But then, the Rio Grande Mall was not in sight.

I met a young woman who spoke in the tones of the deep South. She was a sophomore at Mississippi Southern College in Hattiesburg, majoring in history. "I just *love* history," she said. She remembered that the thing to do in high school in Hattiesburg was to drive around the shopping mall. "I don't know *why,* but it just was the thing to do."

In the evening the landscape flattened and for long stretches it turned green—the cultivated fields became as lush as those in Illinois. By morning the land was still flat and green. Houston was coming on slowly. There were only the freeway signs to warn of what was ahead.

For a while in the late 1970s and early 1980s, Houston was hyped as the Sun Belt city of the future and its Galleria as the last word in shopping malls. Since the Galleria included two hotels, one at each end of the shopping mall, I decided to stay there for a few days. I checked into the Galleria Plaza and went out to explore what would be my shopping-mall living-room for the next ninety-six hours.

Houston has a downtown, which has been completely transformed since 1970 into an area of monumental office towers and hotels connected by a network of underground passages. The Galleria, however, is located west of downtown in the Post Oaks area, and its development sparked a kind of second glass-towered urban center, without much in the way of streets—just freeways and boulevards for cars. All of these tall environments are internal, fed by the air-conditioned, rolling environments of automobiles.

My first impression of the Galleria mall was that it could no longer be considered new or amazing. Perhaps due to the rigors of humidity, it had a worn look and feel that would be premature in other places. Physically it wasn't nearly as impressive as at least half a dozen other malls I'd seen so far on my odyssey.

It was Friday at lunchtime, and I walked the length of it looking at the people. Some were clearly comfortable here; they were having a good time, and it made me happy to look at them. Three teenaged girls in summer scants were walking barefoot on the white tile. At the famous skating rink (no longer as unusual for a mall as it once was) there was a line of little girls winding out onto the ice to the piped-in sound of "Angel of the Morning."

There were plenty of stores, of course. The Galleria was known for its Neiman-Marcus, Lord & Taylor, Marshall Field's, and its very expensive small shops, although the Galleria also hedged its bets, shopping mall-style: Across from Cartier is the Swiss Colony. Both have their logos nicely mounted on the Galleria's mirrored silver facades; one sells diamonds, the other bologna.

But for me the character of a mall is also in its common areas, its public courts. The closest thing the Galleria had to a central court was the lobby area in its center which opened vertically to the soaring distance of the Galleria towers, offices, and condominiums above. Around the glass elevator were small white pods, spaced apart like tree stumps, where individuals could sit and gaze. Many were doing just that as I walked through. The Galleria attracted a lot of tourists, from the United States and Mexico and the world, and since it was a weekday lunch hour, there were Houston business people and shoppers there too. The people pausing in the lobby looked solitary, even when obviously in family groups. They sat apart and looked around, and none of them was smiling. I think it may have been because what they were looking at was money.

The money was mostly implied; it was in the price of products in the stores more than in the mall itself, but these soaring towers were enough of a suggestion. The sense of stratification was palpable, powerful here. Houston was supposed to be a city of quick wealth, and the Galleria was its palace. So what must it be like to sit here on little white stumps and think about money? A middle-class family may have worked its way up to a Marshall Field level, but there was still Neiman-Marcus to conquer. Then there still would be the little shops they would probably never be rich enough to enter with confidence. For all the hype, not much that was special was available to the walking public. But maybe it was different a little higher up the scale—maybe that's where the glamour started. The luxury had to be somewhere. Even that jogging track on the roof of the Galleria—which usually figures prominently in stories about it—was inaccessible to anyone but those who paid their yearly dues to the University Club. Without money, without Houston's megabucks, you might be simply one of the lost ones sitting on the little white stumps, looking up.

On Saturday afternoon, the Galleria was packed. In Neiman-Marcus a Japanese tourist stood still and gaped openly at a tall blond young man in gym shorts and a T-shirt cut low on his not particularly attractive breastbone who pulled out a fat billfold from his shorts and bought something at the perfume counter. Farther along the mall a blond woman in a red Lacoste shirt and Levis bought a paperback of *Princess Daisy* in Waldenbooks and spotted a twenty-cent error in her change. She let everybody know about it. Father's Day was coming up and one store had a sign in the window: WE HAVE THE PERFECT GIFT FOR YOUR DADDY—AND SOMETHING FOR YOUR FATHER TOO.

Going up to the third level on an escalator, a little blond girl was perched on her father's shoulder. She looked at me and pointed to the lights over the skating rink. At the top of the escalator she was put down, and spotting something else she liked, she immediately ran off in the opposite direction from her parents. They caught her heading toward Neiman-Marcus, crying out—much too much like the little blond boy to the flying saucers in *Close Encounters of the Third Kind* —"Toys!"

Meanwhile, people were standing in line at the Magic Pan Crêperie, watching a bored-looking Mexican woman make crêpes. She sat before a wheel of frying pans rotating around a pile of crêpes. She took one frying pan off, deposited the finished crêpe on the pile, dipped the pan in batter, and put it back on the wheel, and then did it again. The people watching weren't peeking into the kitchen—this was the floor show.

By early evening the skating rink was mobbed by junior-high and high-school kids, and Texas pom-pom girls of all ages. I had a quiet dinner at Delmonico's, where a pianist played "As Time Goes By." My waitress said she was going to write a book, too—it was going to be on 101 ways to cook popcorn. The bartender was from Atlanta and he didn't like Houston because there was nothing to do but go to bars.

Back at the Plaza there was a convention party for Chevy dealers. A big sign said HOWDY PARDNER and everyone within sight was wearing a cowboy hat. I took the elevator straight up to Annabelle's, a bar and restaurant at the top of the building, to look at

Houston in the dusk. I was amazed at how many trees there were—
as far as I could see there were groves of trees interspersed with
groves of office towers. I decided to see what the view was from
the bar at the top of the other hotel, the Houston Oaks, at the other
end of the Galleria.

On the way through the hotel I passed a number of artificially
dressed-up high-school couples; it was prom night at the Houston
Oaks. By the time I got to the top it was already dark outside.
Now Houston was visibly a continuous city—a city united by
light.

I shared the elevator back down with a blond young woman in
a red jersey who was talking into a radio. A male voice at the other
end informed her that there was a group of kids causing a disturbance on the tenth floor. "What are they doing?" she asked.
"Drinking beer," came the scratchy answer. "What kind?" she
asked. "Come again?" the puzzled voice responded. "Never mind,"
she said. "Where are they?" "On the floor, near the elevator."

She punched the tenth-floor button. "How boring," she said to
me. "Why couldn't they be drinking Amaretto?"

"Are you the heat?" I asked.

"Yes," she said. "The head heat."

"I am tempted to break the law," I said.

"Thank you," she said.

There was not much happening at the Galleria on Sunday. In
the afternoon I returned to Annabelle's for another look at the
Houston landscape below. It fascinated me. It looked like a huge
arboretum that grew occasional clumps of hothouse skyscrapers.
Whenever I'd ventured outside the Galleria, and even inside it, I felt
a terrible tension—of unfulfilled expectations and disappointment
rubbing up against hype and complacency, all in the invisible atmosphere of the money everybody believed was here and here alone. It
came from cab drivers and clerks, from traveling businessmen who
were wondering whether they were missing something by not
moving here. As I looked down at the Houston landscape I had the
sudden thought that it was tailor-made for guerrilla warfare—the
forest enclaves, the high-ground towers, the underground warrens
downtown.

Monday, I had an appointment with Karen Pulley, the Galleria's
manager. I had met her briefly at the ICSC convention in Las Vegas
and she'd impressed me with her incisiveness and bold speculation.

She'd made a comment about the artificiality of the mall's internal world and the possibly dangerous unreality of an environment of sealed-up glitter. So I thought she'd have an interesting point of view.

But in her office it was a different story. She was alert and charming, but she was obviously apprehensive. She talked about the glamour and excitement of the Galleria, about its wealthy international clientele, including entire families of rich Mexicans who crossed the border on a Friday with empty suitcases and went home on Sunday, luggage filled with Galleria treasures. "Sometimes I can walk down this mall and never hear English," she said.

She kept glancing at her watch and thinking of other people on higher and lower levels I could talk to about the Galleria and its builder, Gerald Hines, who was responsible for much of the development in this and other parts of Houston. Instead, I asked her about herself. Karen Pulley had been the marketing director and then the manager of a small mall in Virginia before she was hired to manage the Galleria. "I used to have to defend where I worked," she said, "but here it's sink or swim. We aim to be as perfect as we possibly can, and maintain high standards. The Galleria is a very special place, and all our management here is constantly in a fishbowl.

"But the added pressure tends to make us perform better," she quickly continued. "We have a lot of fun—we're under a lot of pressure so we need to have fun. And we have pride." She stopped and smiled and waited. I suddenly felt very weary. I'd failed to get her to say anything that didn't sound preprogrammed by the paperback heirs of Norman Vincent Peale or the head coach of the Houston Oilers or—most likely—Gerald Hines. So I thanked her and left. The interview had taken a painful fifteen minutes.

I wanted to get out to Westwood Mall anyway before the day was over. This was the mall, I'd learned in Las Vegas, that was arming its security guards for the first time this week. So I got a cab for Westwood, in farther suburbia.

On the ride over I looked at Houston's always choking freeways and thought about a newspaper account of the controversy surrounding an article written by Larry McMurtry about Texas writers. McMurtry, the Texas-born novelist (most famous, I suppose, for *The Last Picture Show* and *Terms of Endearment,* but most famous to me for one of my favorite novels, *All My Friends Are Going to Be Strangers*), contended that despite their tendency toward self-congratulation, Texan fiction writers hadn't yet produced the rigorous, high-quality work they should be producing, especially in the ferment of the newly urbanizing population centers—and McMurtry included his own novels in this criticism. He attacked Texas writers for intellectual laziness and complacency, and wrote, "There are yet no solid achievements in Texas letters."

Other Texas writers did not take kindly to this evaluation at first, although eventually some came to agree, the newspaper article said. The editor of the publication that had printed the essay, the *Texas Observer,* commented that McMurtry had applied "universal literary standards in a province that's currently mired in mutual admiration."

I had the same feeling about Houston and its Galleria. It was time to apply some universal standards to them, too. As a city, Houston was already being faced with the realities of an overburdened infrastructure, traffic, pollution, poverty in the midst of plenty, crime, and simple unhappiness—Houston had the highest divorce rate in the country. The city was beginning to respond, with a new mayor and some new attitudes. The response toward pollution in Houston used to be a joke: That's not pollution, the saying went, that's the smell of money. Now Houston was beginning to recognize that pollution is the smell of decay.

Similarly, the Galleria was being forced to face its own realities. Its huge expansion was postponed, and when the Mexican peso was devalued, some of its shops lost more than half their business. Hype isn't enough. The Galleria would have to face the fact that even in the world of malls, it just wasn't that great.

26

The Captain of Westwood

Among the more interesting working sessions I attended at the ICSC convention in Las Vegas was a small round-table discussion on security. One of the participants was Kenneth Oswald of the Centers Company, the mall management concern that had spun off from the Dayton-Hudson company, developer of Southdale, when it divested itself of its malls. Partly because of crime problems their Detroit malls had experienced, earlier than did most suburban malls in the country, the Centers Company had emerged as a leader in mall security.

Oswald told us that all Center Company malls, for the first time, would now be arming their security guards. He said he didn't like it much but it was necessary. Others at the table were also worried. This was a new admission of vulnerability for malls. Safety had always been a prime psychological appeal, but it had never had to be enforced like this before. Then, too, guns in the mall presented very practical dangers.

Another participant was Joel Blaisdell, who had recently come from a mall in Rochester, Minnesota, to manage the Boulevard Mall in Las Vegas. "In Rochester, security was all public relations," he said. "Here, the guards have guns and they scare the hell out of me. But one of my first days here I saw a man striding through my mall with a gun on each hip. He wasn't security. He was a customer."

That got Herbert Grimshaw, a developer from Schenectady, New York, talking about the differences in the East. In many eastern states, he said, by law, guards can't carry guns, and mall security guards have no real police powers. But those gun laws also make it less likely that a customer will have a six-shooter on his hip.

Oswald said that guards must be rigorously trained to draw their guns only in life-threatening situations. Blaisdell agreed, and added that he'd seen a gun drawn only once, and then drawn in anger by a security guard who couldn't get a delivery truck to move from an entrance it was blocking. "The gun wasn't fired, thank God," Blaisdell said, "but the guard was."

Oswald had mentioned that one of his malls in Houston—Westwood Mall—would be arming their guards for the first time the following week. Since I was going to be in Houston then, I decided I would visit Westwood.

I'd called ahead only minutes before I got into a cab to go from the Galleria to Westwood, but since my purpose was to get information from the management on security matters, I wanted to make sure someone there would talk to me. After my edgy interview with Karen Pulley, I was a little edgy myself. So I certainly wasn't prepared for the next few hours at Westwood, where I was welcomed with old-fashioned southern charm and hospitality, and given a major taste of a mall manager's life.

I was greeted at the management office door by a young woman with a stuffed animal in her arms. She was Debra Lowe, the assistant manager and promotions director. The stuffed animal was for a mall employee's daughter who was in the hospital recovering from minor surgery.

In her office Debra Lowe told me about Westwood's history and the incredible growth of the nearby suburbs that made up its market. Westwood was out in the Houston hinterlands, where malls were often the centers of otherwise chaotic growth. In the suburbs immediately surrounding Westwood, the population had doubled between 1975 and 1979, the first four years the mall was open. In the nearby tract where Debra lived, the population had gone from two thousand to twenty thousand in the same period. The idea wasn't so much that Westwood had caused these people to move close to it, but that it was their community center from the beginning. It also brought people together from various suburbs, near and far, who came because they happened to like Westwood Mall.

Westwood had a lot of competition from the many malls in the area, Lowe said, but it had established its own socioeconomic as well as loosely geographic market. It wasn't at all the same market as the Galleria's. "Our jewelry store did eleven thousand dollars' worth of business on Mother's Day," Debra said. "We thought that was pretty good. But some guy walked into the Galleria and bought one twenty-thousand-dollar ring." She laughed. "But that doesn't happen every day, even at the Galleria. We do better consistently."

I asked her about the security furor, and she said it was true that Westwood had experienced problems. Several stores had been broken into and one night a security guard was tied up during a robbery. Since then the mall had gotten its own security force (the hog-tied guard was a rent-a-cop) and outfitted them with uniforms and a parking-lot patrol van with police-style party-hat light on top.

The idea was visibility: "We don't necessarily want to catch the shoplifter," Lowe said. "We want him to see us, and think twice." But my information about Westwood's guns turned out to be not quite correct. Although the security staff was trained and ready to go, the licenses hadn't come through yet, so no guns were being worn.

Debra Lowe asked me if I wanted to meet R. L. Thomas, the mall's manager. I was reluctant, since I had the information I had come for, but as a courtesy I agreed. And then I sat spellbound for the next couple of hours at R. L. Thomas's desk, frantically taking notes as he spun his stories about his life as the Captain of Westwood.

Thomas was a friendly man in his late sixties who talked seriously but with only slightly abashed enthusiasm about a job he clearly liked. He began by responding to my questions about the gun situation. "My own thinking on that has changed," he said. "Time was, the idea of a gun on a security guard's hip would have scared me to death. But now I see the need for it here. We've got a lot of social change going on in Houston. The cost of living is high and there are a lot of people coming here expecting a lot. They get disappointed and sometimes they get desperate.

"All of our security people have been trained on the firing range," Thomas said. "We have three-fifty-seven Magnums with thirty-eight-caliber shells. But the idea is that the pistol in the holster is a sign of authority. Those guns will never leave the center, and our guards aren't allowed to be in uniform out of the center, either."

Thomas talked in detail about other security arrangements (which included guard dogs roaming the mall at night) and then just started talking about himself and his job. In contrast to most of the younger mall people I'd been seeing, he hadn't been trained in mall management or even in retail. His only previous job was a quarter-century hitch as an officer in the United States Navy. He earned his pilot's wings in 1943 and worked behind a desk on twelve different aircraft carriers through 1969, when he retired.

Thomas got his first job as a mall manager by the simple, if unlikely, procedure of answering an ad in the newspaper— WANTED: Manager for Southland Mall in Memphis, Tennessee. He was hired by Monumental Properties to replace another navy man who was becoming a district manager.

Monumental, it turned out, liked to have retired military officers running their malls. "If you've been a lifer in the military," Thomas told me, "you don't really know where you fit in as a civilian. The world could have passed you by all those years. But if you've got management experience, if you're used to working with people, you're a natural for this job. If you can manage a division, you can manage a mall."

Thomas spent two and a half years managing the mall in Memphis before he thought it was time to retire. "I moved down to Corpus Christi because my children and grandchildren were there, but I got bored. So I called Monumental up and told them I'd caught my share of fish and hit more than enough golf balls, so if they had a center open and they wanted me, I was ready."

Monumental took back the veteran volunteer and posted him to Houston. When the Centers Company took over Westwood Mall, they kept Thomas on. Coming out of retirement was a decision he never regretted. "There's never been a light day, and never a day like the one before," he said. "I have a great team here. I'm having fun."

As manager, his duties included all the usual rule-making and enforcing at Westwood, but Thomas saw his job more as a matter of communication, diplomacy, and paying a lot of attention.

"I try to help out with problems my tenants may be having," he said. "Like a woman who has a small shop here—she was being charged extra by a freight hauling company because she had no back door and her stuff had to be carried around to the front. The problem was that they were charging her more for hauling her freight from our loading dock to her store than she was paying to have it shipped from California to Houston. We resolved that through the Centers Company. I called them in Minneapolis and they said they'd had trouble before with this particular carrier. So we got her a better deal."

Thomas also keeps an eye out for potential trouble. "If I see deterioration in merchandise that's really serious, I have to speak to that tenant. And if I don't get a good answer about it, or if after a while there isn't any improvement, I can put them in default of their lease and they have to leave. I had a case like that not long ago, but before I did anything, I talked to some other mall managers who had this same chain in their malls. One told me these people had pulled a 'midnight move-out' on him. Another told me they'd been a problem at his mall and he'd put them on a month-to-month basis. So, being tipped off, I told them to be out by July. I can deal with basic honesty—if a tenant tells me, We're having problems but here's how we're going to deal with them and we expect to have them controlled by such and such a date, well, then I'm willing to give them the benefit of the doubt. But somebody who's keeping too quiet or lies to me . . . I don't have any patience with them."

According to Thomas, there's a lot of day-to-day communication as well as competition in Houston's mall world. "We all know each other around Houston," he said. "We all know everything about each other's center. Everybody gets kidded a lot. But communication is useful, and not just about problems like that tenant I had to get rid of. If I have a tenant here who's doing real well and wants to expand, I check with other malls—how's the tenant doing there? Is this a good move or might the business be overextending itself?"

Thomas also scouts other malls for ideas, for possible new tenants, and just to see how the competition is doing. "I'm expected to
spend one field day a week out of this mall. I can't always do it, but
once every two weeks or so I'll take one of our girls and the maintenance guy and we'll hit two or three malls in one day. I'll be
looking for types of tenants I'm interested in for here. I needed a
bath boutique; now I need a panty-hose/leotard-type place. My
leasing guy is in better contact with this, but once in a while I'll
stumble onto something. Like Video Concepts: I was having a
cocktail with Gary—he's our leasing guy—and I said, 'How about
a Video Concepts?' He said, 'Goddamn, I forgot all about that. I'll
get one.'

"Meanwhile, when we're out at other malls, my maintenance
guy is looking at the floors, the lights that are lit or the bulbs out,
comparing his performance to theirs. I'm looking for watermarks
on the ceiling, and I'm looking at stores. I make notes on a tape
recorder and our secretary transcribes it. We all talk about it later."

Thomas laughed. "The other day, I wanted to meet the new
manager of Baybrook Mall. I went over there and the first thing I
saw was their new lighted directory. Our directories aren't lighted
but we're getting new ones that are, so I was inspecting his at Baybrook to see how it's done. I was looking all around it, down on
my knees to look underneath at the wiring. Later on, when I met
the manager, he said, 'So that's who you are. I was wondering
when I saw you out front, practically taking my directory apart. I
knew you had to be in the business.'"

Besides scouting other people's malls, Thomas does some informal market research in his own. "I present my card to a customer
and ask them questions like What do you feel is lacking in this
center? And they tell me: a mature woman's store. A family restaurant. Meanwhile, I'm finding out who my customers are—a
woman, thirty-five, married to a doctor, lives nearby—and what
she likes here or doesn't like. . . . Several women told me that it
was tough to get waited on in a certain department at Joske's. So I
went and tried to buy something there, and it was true, so I told the
store manager about it."

Thomas tries to minimize the potential for problems right from
the beginning. "When a guy comes in here with a business, we
listen, we get his financial statement, and we go into detail about
the lease, and if we're interested, we bring him back. We're at
ninety-eight percent occupancy, but full occupancy isn't always the

most important thing. I work closely with our store managers. I feel we're a family. We have to work together to make the whole thing work. If the mall itself isn't working, the stores can't make it. And if the stores don't make it, we're not doing our job. We can't guarantee they'll make it, but we try to make sure they've got a good chance to begin with. I don't want a new guy coming in here and failing. It could be a disaster. I've seen marriages break up over it. I've seen guys lose their home and car. A new shopping center often brings in tenants just to make numbers and fill up the black holes. But you don't establish credibility with stores whose doors are closed."

After my interview with the Captain of Westwood, I went out to inspect his mall. It was certainly shipshape, and it indeed had a lively tenant mix—from Sears to Frederick's of Hollywood, Joske's to the Nut Hut—and a clientele of matching variety: sleek career women gliding out of Margo La Monde and being stared at by men leaving National Shirts; well-tanned teenagers carrying giant Miss Piggy cards from the Hallmark Starship Shop and comparing the slack in the behinds of their jeans in front of Chic-fil-a; an old man eating a vanilla ice-cream cone; a young black woman in a straw cowboy hat holding the baby of a young white mother who was sitting on a bench, exhausted.

In the cab back to the Galleria I thought: Karen Pulley probably makes more money than R. L. Thomas, or she eventually will. She was a smart, attractive young woman with a future. But R. L. Thomas was a happy man.

27

The Logical Conclusion of Atlanta: Rocking Shopping Center

From Houston I had taken the *Sunset Limited* to New Orleans, and after a few days there I caught the *Crescent* to Atlanta. The train progressed through landscapes gradually more familiar to me—the shapes of the trees and the contours of the hills were recognizably those of the eastern United States.

Early in the trip I met Phaedra, a bright and verbal sixth grader who quickly elicited from me the purpose of my journey and told me that for the lowdown on kids in malls I should interview her. I agreed, if only to avoid the feeling that I was being interviewed. "Okay," I said. "What do kids do in malls?"

"They play with toys," Phaedra said, "without buying them. My favorite is Chinese yo-yos. Kids hate clothing stores. I used to, until a couple of months ago. Now I love them. I guess that's one of the changes of adolescence."

Phaedra went on to tell a couple of jokes about boys and puberty, mostly having to do with their voices changing, until her parents came to collect her. I'd noticed them earlier, reading aloud to each other from a biography of Beethoven.

Later I met Lisa, a young woman with an appealingly southern, Elizabeth Ashley voice. She was from an old New Orleans family; when they spoke of losing their fortune in the war, she said, they meant the Civil War. "I've read all of Tennessee Williams' plays and I've seen all the movies," Lisa added, "because my family is just like that."

We were well into Georgia by then. "Living in these small towns is not as idyllic as some people think," Lisa said. "I know people who moved to them because it's a good place to raise children. A good place to raise children? Sure, so they can become imbeciles just like the people who are born there and are taught to do nothing but go the way of their parents, get a job in the local plant, and stay there all their lives like they're supposed to. So they take bright children and put them in a place with absolutely no intellectual stimulation—what sense does that make? All because they're afraid of the city and crime and traffic in the streets.

"I live in a suburb of Atlanta, right by the Air Force base," Lisa continued. "There is an 'X' on my roof so the jets know to put down their landing gear. They come over all the time. The noise you wouldn't believe. Thank God my lease is up soon. There are malls all over the suburbs and you can usually tell what kind of a suburb it is by the mall. If you're thinking about moving into an area and you want to know what the people are like there, you just go to their mall. If you see a lot of young mothers with kids, you know what the houses are going to be like and the income level isn't high."

We were coming into the suburbs then. There was strong late-afternoon sunlight on the Full Serve pumps and the Sweetwater Inn, the red earth rising beside the train, a blur of trees, and flashes of sunlight on both sides. With whistle blowing, we were careening down into Atlanta.

Atlanta is the apotheosis of suburban malldom. It is a growing Sun Belt area, but there is a discernable city and an actual downtown, and the suburbs are distinct from it. But in Atlanta's growth there has been a tug of war between the new suburbs and the new downtown to see which would be dominant as the center of Atlanta's identity—and for a while the suburbs were clearly winning. They were doing so largely because of the malls.

Atlanta's suburbs were malled quickly and thoroughly. The downtown retained shopper loyalty for a time after the suburban population boom began in the 1960s, but by 1977 the Atlanta suburbs had more than four hundred shopping centers and discount stores, including ten major shopping malls with two or more department stores each, and several others with one. Development slowed down some then, but the suburbs still added half a dozen more large malls and major multi-use developments with mall shopping components in the early 1980s. Meanwhile a lot of Atlanta, in body and spirit, was becoming located in suburban malldom.

One of the prettiest malls I saw on my odyssey was Phipps Plaza in the new silk-stocking district of suburban Atlanta along Peachtree Road. It was a high-fashion mall anchored by a handsome Saks Fifth Avenue and by Lord & Taylor. Its shops included Tiffany, Gucci, and the Executive Image, as well as an office of Dean Witter Reynolds discreetly tucked in back of Rainbow's End Toys.

Phipps Plaza made use of contrasting high and low ceilings, and skylights that alternated with artificial lighting. It had some striking storefronts—the deep-wine art deco doorway of Jonni L. Walker's Panache, for example. Even the browns of the floor tiles were of pleasing shades, and a red-orange rug outside Saks caught squares of sunlight that formed spontaneous and soothing tints and textures.

The ambience was carried out in the central-court area and in the eating place there, called the Park, where customers went through a cafeteria line to buy simple, inexpensive, but very good sandwiches, as well as fresh-baked desserts and cinnamon coffee. Its tables faced the elegant open court, and already on the tables were real cloth napkins. The court plaza was sunny and decorated with plants.

All of these may have been small touches, but they accumulated to create a soft, modest atmosphere of tranquillity and grace, suggesting perhaps an updated southern mansion. I imagined that tradition-minded Georgians, whose families perhaps lost their fortunes in the War, might enjoy coming here just for that atmosphere of quiet quality, where they could glide down the spiral staircase with the polished wood banisters in Saks, and become old southerners again in a cool island of old southern calm, apart from a world of traffic and change. Phipps Plaza is a mall that recalls the myth of southern gentility.

But such antebellum dreamers, if they exist anymore, don't represent the overwhelming reality of the new Atlanta. As the new assistant manager of Waldenbooks at Phipps Plaza told me: "People get upset because we don't have a drugstore, or a stamp machine. They expect a mall to have everything." Possibly because, just across Peachtree Road, there was a mall that did have everything.

Lenox Square, a sprawling complex that opened in 1959 and expanded several times, was always Atlanta's major mall. It contained one entire level, called The Market, of fast-food outlets and fresh fruit and vegetable stands; another level, The Plaza, was also devoted to eating places, including four restaurants, specialty food shops, and a sidewalk café. More than one hundred retail stores, from Achilles Ltd. and Athletic Attic to Yoroubian Tailoring and Zachry, were on the Garden Mall and Skylight Mall levels, with three department stores, including the second Neiman-Marcus store ever to be located outside of Texas.

Such upscale stores as Courrèges and Ciro of Bond Street followed Neiman's lead. For all its sprawling energy, with a somewhat more fashionable mix than most malls its size, Lenox combined style and completeness, not only in its stores but in its appearance. (The Neiman-Marcus court also featured one of those decorative mall marvels: a pile of large, brightly colored cubes, pyramids, and spheres surrounded by live greenery, like a scoop of geometry in a bed of lettuce.)

Lenox Square is so identified with Atlanta that it has an Atlanta Visitor's Center. Mid-America Research also has an office there, and its people continually prowl the mall conducting interviews with their video minicams. "This is the place conventioneers and other visitors are likely to come to, as well as people from Atlanta," one of Mid-America's interviewers told me. "It's got the best cross section of people."

According to Berma Brown of Lenox Square's management, 40 percent to 60 percent of its business comes from tourists. "Ed Noble—the man who started this—had a terrible time convincing the city fathers that it was needed," she said. "The suburbs here were like separate little towns then."

Now, however, the mall had recently been praised by Atlanta's Mayor Andrew Young. "We see what Lenox Square and other shopping centers have done for our area," he said. "Lenox Square has just about created a new downtown."

Whether Lenox Square functions as a community center for Atlanta's black population I'm not qualified to say, but Berma Brown did bristle a bit when I brought up the question. "Our malls don't think in racial pattern terms," she said. But I'd only asked because I hadn't seen many blacks there.

The rest of the suburban shopping centers I saw around Atlanta I took in on a single afternoon and evening in the company of my cousin Shirley Severini, who was living and working in Atlanta and was soon to be married there. She was buying last-minute items for the wedding and for a new apartment, and she was going from mall to mall to find them. Although she'd been in Atlanta for just a few years and worked downtown, she knew which stores in which malls were likely to have exactly what she wanted: the Sears at Cumberland Mall for shower rods and housewares, for example, and the bridal shop at Perimeter Mall.

So among the centers where we stopped were these two major malls. Cumberland Mall was, in terms of leasable space, even bigger than Lenox Square. It had 4 anchors (Rich's, Davison's, Sears, and Penney's) and around 125 shops. There was a big central court, suspiciously reminiscent of the hanging-garden and layers-of-lake look below a soaring glass elevator that Atlanta's John Portman made into a dominant style for his downtown hotel lobbies; this was somewhat miniaturized, suburbanized Portman. There was also a cylindrical sculpture with wooden benches on top, a little like the orange scaffold at Fox Hills in Los Angeles.

By now my malling hours were numbered, and with Shirley off attending to business, I had taken to strapping on my Aiwa and walking through the mall courts with my own sound-track music supplanting the mall Muzak. With Willie Nelson singing "Heartbreak Hotel" I strode through Cumberland's western theme section: a brick alley with a hot dog stand, a café, a stamp and coin shop, and High Country clothes. While professor Longhair sang "Who's Been Foolin' You?" I passed El Chico Restaurant and the local egg-roll outlet, Gingiss Formalwear, First Atlanta Bank, and Good Grief!—a store "devoted to Snoopiness of all kinds": dolls, overnight bags, pennants and pins, cups and Frisbees.

Among the high-school girls and couples on shopping dates, I saw a lot of young women shoppers in their twenties in house-wifely jeans and shirts, some with small children. I thought about what Lisa had said on the train, and sure enough, Shirley told me that the area around . umberland had a lot of apartments and con-dos and office parks. There was more expensive housing just com-ing in, but it was mostly a young-marrieds, relatively modest income area.

Perimeter Mall was next, in the northeast market area; it was slightly smaller than Cumberland but had nearly as many stores, and the same sense of comprehensiveness. Again I turned on my cassette player to walk around while Shirley went off to do the serious shopping; it was 8:30 P.M. now, so the teenagers were out in force. Since this was going to be the last mall of my suburban Sun Belt odyssey, I had brought along my rare and treasured tape by Jonathan Richman and the Modern Lovers. I slipped it into the Aiwa, focused the earphones, and strode off to the tune of "Rockin' Shopping Center."

> A one-two, one-two: bassman . . .
> Well, I landed at a shopping center
> in an unknown state
> Unknown kind of architecture, atmosphere and trait
> Unknown brand of labels, unknown market chains
> The strangest collection of buildings
> upon the fruited plain
> And let's go. Let's rock.

Past Pearl Vision to Bathtique, Motherhood Maternity, and The Gap to the Penney court and the gazebo staircase, the ceiling sky-lights surrounded by marquee bulbs glowing white.

Chess King and Thom McAn. Long-haired junior-high girls sit-ting outside on white planters stop spooning ice cream to jump down, turn around, and head for ⅓ OFF TOPS at the Airport, a sale on harem pants at Sweden, and a Casual Corner T-Shirt Clearance.

> All right
> You see the different labels and the different brands

until they're reaching across the land
the different colors and the different states
and the different labels—let's tell about based on
all the different states for all the different traits
and of this date I hate no state
let's rock
let's go
all right

Outside of McDonald's a pause at the patio table to look up past the umbrella to the skylight stained in diagonals of magenta, pink, and pale-orange in a sea of purple. A mother fusses with little brothers, and two old friends share a mall bench quietly. How terribly strange to be seventy.

Well I walked through the mall and I walked up and down
I done got tired so I done sat down
I watched the people for a while, you always learn a little
do doody doody doik doik doik doik diddle

Kids swarming for cookies at the Bake Shop, cheesecake at Happenpappen, carob maltballs and peanut colada at the Grove. A Georgia bulldog and a Georgia peach hold hands and promenade through the outdoor court by the pizzeria, the travel agency, and the barber shop. There's a bus shelter under the big mall logo, a "P" that looks very much like half a highway cloverleaf.

Yeah. All right.
Well the giant sign says Montmartre Plaza
these centers, I don't know, it has a
weird insignia they put on all the bags
wrote it on the walls, even made a flag
if I were a shopping center I'd sure be embarrassed
I know I'd never get a date with some cute little building
like from Paris
let's rock
let's go

Then I met Shirley and her fiancé, Dan Flathers, and we were off for some fine down-home Georgia cuisine at a place called the

Boston Sea Party. Perimeter Mall had been the far perimeter of my suburban and Sun Belt mall trek, but not the end of my odyssey in Atlanta. For Atlanta not only represented the logical conclusion of the mall as the city suburban, but it also played an early and formative part in the coming of the mall into the American city—the latest and perhaps most surprising phenomenon in the malling of America.

Part 4

THE CITY AS MALL

Cityful passing away, other cityful coming, passing away too: other coming on, passing on. . . . Pyramids in sand.

—JAMES JOYCE
Ulysses

28

From Fortress Atlanta to the Hotel California: Suburbia's Revenge

You must ask two questions. First, what is the real nature of synthesis? And then: what is the real nature of control?

—THOMAS PYNCHON
Gravity's Rainbow

Of course, they aren't always *called* shopping malls. They are "festival marketplaces," or atrium shops or arcades, or enclosed urban shopping experiences. After all, this is the *city*. Shopping malls are those hulks on the highway, suburban nests of tackiness where women in polyester stretch pants cruise the fluorescent aisles of mass-market department stores searching for last year's designer knock-offs before wolfing down a Stuft Potato and flouncing through little cardboard shops with absurd names like *Slipper World* or *House of Nose Jobs,* stopping occasionally to beat up one of their yammering kids.

It's true that some of the stores are different (though many are not) and the architecture is more vertical or urban-inflected, and they're surrounded by other city buildings instead of just concrete and cars, and maybe they're part of massive megastructures or are housed in restored old buildings, but in fact the basic deal—the organization, the approach, the delivery system—is the same. There may be no cachet at all in saying so, but they are shopping malls, essentially the same as their suburban progenitors. And they're right here, in the big American city.

But what a pill for the cities to swallow! After Levittown changed the image of the suburbs from sanctuaries for the rich to the province of factory workers with funny last names and Organization Men with homebound wives who did nothing but shop and polish furniture, anything suburban was good for a laugh. Then the malls came along and they were perfect—ugly, vulgar, pallid, and pretentious; as uniform as the subdivisions that supplied them with customers and gave them their endlessly replicable form, they were founded on blithe tastelessness and full of plastics. They were, in a word, *suburban*.

By that time, however, the laughter was getting a little hollow. Jobs, and now retail and entertainment, had joined the white middle class in what was becoming a self-sufficient suburbia, and cities were in danger of becoming irrelevant. Meanwhile the city centers themselves were dying. They acquired an unshakable reputation as tense and dangerous places of crime and fear, with their dark and dirty streets of dehumanized speed and impersonal gloom cringing between massive cold buildings. Nobody wanted to come to the city anymore, and even the people who lived there were afraid to walk the streets at night.

Something had to be done to turn this blight and emptiness back into life and gold. But surely not *this*—not these strange visitors from another plenitude, representing the awful new emphases of the American way which, unfortunately, were able to leap tall buildings with a single bound.

Well, yes. It didn't happen overnight, but eventually the shopping mall came to town, a little secretively maybe, and definitely in urban guises. So now millions of urbanites who wouldn't be caught dead at the Pathmark Supercenter were at Trump Tower, scampering from Buccellati (with its painted cherubs on the ceiling) to the Bath Shop, glorying in the entowered magnificence—the indoor waterfall, the theatrically uniformed guards, the tuxedoed pianist playing flower-petal music in the foyer, all in the rich warm embrace of peach and rose-colored marble walls.

Elsewhere in Manhattan, they were sipping cappuccino on the raised platform in the center of The Market at Citicorp Center, an outdoor café on an indoor stage, listening to a cellist playing Haydn as the sunlight poured down through the skylight, with a background hum of others heading for the surrounding shops and restaurants, including Les Tournebroches, Richoux of London, and Alfredo the Original of Rome. At the South Street Seaport, they dodged an American youth-hostel group in luminous orange flak jackets wheeling their bicycles past suburban junior-high schoolgirls in miniskirts carrying balloon sculptures, Israeli tourists wielding Nikon Super Zoom movie cameras, and a young boy in a Michael Jackson band-jacket clutching a Cabbage Patch Kids doll, to buy spring sweaters at Laura Ashley and stand on the weathered brick gazing at the water as a bagpiper played "Amazing Grace" in front of Gourmet Treats.

In Chicago, they find themselves accepting a rose and a card from a young woman inviting them to a free exercise session at Casual Corner in Water Tower Place, performed by a blonde in a metallic baby-blue chemically treated astronaut fire-resistant race-drive disco jumpsuit with jogger's flap who praises it by saying, "It seals in sweat, so dancing in it is a trip." They might then see a young man wearing a black eyepatch sitting on a bench on the top shop floor between two young women, surveying the still brightly lit and dazzling stores hours after they've closed. "I never come here when the shops are open," he informs his companions.

In Los Angeles, they shop at Century City Shopping Centre, where they might see a sexy young woman walk past Country Club Fashions with her shoulders slung back, her chin high, and her breasts thrust forward, then another young woman walking in the opposite direction who passes her, apparently oblivious, until she suddenly breaks into a perfect parody of the first woman's walk, for the benefit of no one in particular.

In Pittsburgh, they stop for a drink and live jazz on a weeknight at One Oxford Centre, a soaring silver cylinder that feels a little like the inside of a flashlight. Or they walk across the cool tiles of the Freight House (which adjoins the refurbished neobaroque train station and, together with it, makes up the center now called Station Square) to shop for fine chocolate, unfinished wood furniture, carpets, and silk; they stop at the Patisserie, where the wife of a former steelworker pauses over the unfamiliar breads while her husband sips French coffee and samples his first brioche. "I like to try something different," he explains.

In New Orleans, they sit with *café au lait* and hot *beignets,* in

Café du Monde in the French Market, now reconstituted as a shopping center, and listen as their waiter, a stocky young man in regulation white cap, complains about his day. "Everybody's in a hurry and giving me a hard time. They've been driving me crazy—and in *this* place. This is a place to have coffee, read the paper, watch the women, have a cigarette—take it *easy*."

They are something new in America's cities—a new kind of place where people are gathering again, easily and confidently, as perhaps they haven't gathered in central cities for years. That, in a sense, is what is so extraordinary about the scenes in these urban snapshots: They are so ordinary and yet so recently rare. City malls have also sparked a revival in urban retail and influenced the organization of other urban structures, such as (in New York City alone) the Manhattan Art and Antiques Center (three levels of shops and galleries), the new Carnegie Hall complex, and the remodeled Port Authority Bus Terminal ("We are aiming at a shopping mall atmosphere," an official confessed to a reporter). New office towers and residential high-rises everywhere show their influence, with enclosed atrium shops and restaurants.

From the Renaissance Center in Detroit to Harborplace in Baltimore, urban malls have been built for the express purpose of reviving a troubled city center. That's a far cry from the not-too-distant past when cities snubbed the shopping mall.

If I had been a mall in those days I think I would have been a little offended. In many ways the mall was an urban-derived form, with suggestions of city plazas, hotel lobbies, and railroad stations, and direct roots in big-city department store courts and the arcades and atriums of downtown buildings. But at the time, these elements were being eliminated from cities; they didn't fit into the new orthodoxy of city architecture and organization, as defined most prominently by New York City's master builder of the 1930s into the 1960s, Robert Moses. The Moses version of the modernist Radiant City made wonderful theoretical sense. The city would be a place of shining, unornamented, one-function towers. City people would live in one gleaming tower and go to work in another; meanwhile, those who slept in suburbia had clean, fast highways to the city, where they would work and play. Everybody could go to the green ribbons of parkland and the pristine white beaches.

But it didn't work as planned. The highways turned into one-way expressways to suburbia, while the human-scaled environment of the city—the streets of small shops mixed in with single-family homes, duplexes, and apartment buildings, as well as small parks and the drugstores and other informal gathering places—were being replaced by anonymous towers of cement and steel. These International Style skyscrapers were free of supposedly wasteful ornamentation, from gargoyles to Art Nouveau to the kitsch that spoiled the clean lines of pure design. But people, less perfect than straight lines and not as cold, had to live and work in these buildings and these cities. As art critic Robert Hughes points out in his book on modernism, *The Shock of the New*, when people themselves had any control, the pure design often went out the window: In a housing project in France designed by modernist factotum Le Corbusier, the residents filled their severe apartments with ornate fake period furniture and the plastic chandeliers they liked.

Meanwhile, out in the suburbs, the malls had already blended the blank exteriors of the International Style's lowest common denominator with interior environments rife with the clash of color and kitsch. They enclosed their enactments of scenes that had traditionally given people pleasure: peaceful but active streets, splashing water, trees and plants. People flocked to them. The mall was in some sense an expression of the same postwar desire for the modern style of newness, efficiency, and control as governed the city's attempted transformation, but the malls were retail environments, and they ultimately could not afford to be beholden to aesthetic theories or planners' visions. They had to make people happy or else nobody would come in and buy things.

The malls responded with what the city no longer had: clean, safe, human-scaled environments where people could walk and see other people along the tree-lined internal streets. They didn't lock out the kitsch and kin of human tastes and interaction; they enclosed them in a protective embrace. They didn't embody visions of the ideal; they fulfilled pedestrian fantasies.

What the cities had done to themselves was pretty clear by 1970. New York and other big cities had already made their mistakes, but some cities still had the opportunity to look at all this before they leaped. Atlanta was growing at a tremendous rate but most of the activity was in the suburbs. When the city fathers finally decided to rebuild the downtown, they turned to an Atlanta architect who had learned these lessons. He was John Portman, and in his own way he became as important to the American city of the seventies and

The Malling of America

eighties and beyond as Robert Moses had been to the urban ideas of the fifties and sixties.

"Our whole philosophy has been related to trying to understand the human reaction to his environment and how we can elevate and enhance the human experience," John Portman told a reporter. It's a statement that could have been made by Victor Gruen or James Rouse about their suburban malls. Portman was rejecting the modernist approach, which tended to be prescriptive; he used the same approach the malls had been profitably practicing, which was to give the people what they wanted and would enjoy—and then some.

Portman's designs for the city of Atlanta had much in common with what the malls did in Atlanta's suburbs. His celebrated hotel lobbies enclosed lush fantasy environments. With their soaring, light-filled spaces, their hanging gardens and bodies of water actually inside a building, they turned the city outside-in. If the streets had become blank and dangerous, Portman created a Babylonian dream-utopia inside and protected it with walls and comfort control.

Portman's monumental lobbies are his trademark, but other elements of his buildings that are part of the new look of American cities have much in common with the suburban mall approach. From his first Atlanta projects—the Hyatt Regency Hotel, the Peachtree Center, and its Peachtree Plaza Hotel—Portman did not build structures that did only one thing: His hotels were more than hotels, and in Peachtree Center the various buildings—office towers, hotels, merchandise mart—were designed to relate closely to one another. They are all examples of the new urban planning doctrine of multi-use, which says that a variety of different activities going on all the time is a key to making an urban area safe, pleasant, and economically alive. Malls had more or less been doing this in suburbia already, and Portman's designs took another tip from malls: He put all of these activities under one roof, or at least in clustered and connected structures designed and sometimes managed as a unit. Enclosure could protect and control a variety of components and enact a number of fantasies in the city as well as the suburbs.

This first kind of urban mall mated the vertical skyscraper with the horizontal street of the mall and came up with the megastructure. Sometimes the mall is itself the main event of a mixed-use megastructure, as in Water Tower Place in Chicago, a seventy-four-story complex with four underground parking levels, corporate and professional offices, seventeen floors of the Ritz-Carlton Hotel, and forty floors of luxury condominium apartments. But its primary focus, its most obvious showplace, is the eight-level atrium mall, with two department stores, shops, services, restaurants, cinemas, and the Drury Lane legitimate stage. It is a quintessentially urban megastructure, where you can live at the Ritz and eat at McDonald's.

Other megastructures emphasize something else—offices or hotel—but they always include a mall of shops. Many are physically linked to or are near other planned and controlled enclosed environments, such as convention centers and domed stadiums. They generally are designed to attract all the elements of the new urban constituency: people who live and work in the city, people who live in the suburbs and come into the city to work or for shopping and entertainment, and people from far away who come to the city as tourists, business travelers, and conventioneers. The traveler has become especially important as cities try to shed their forbidding images and compete for this growing market. Traditionally peripatetic Americans are traveling again, for business and fun and both. This presents the perfect opportunity for cities— where else but Fun City are these people going to go? Fun Suburbia?

Megastructures are often criticized, both for being the same in every city and for being cut off from the city street. That's also been a criticism of suburban malls, but once again, replicability and the inward-looking environment turns out to be attractive in a fast-moving and mobile society. Particularly for travelers to cities, perhaps still wary of crime and traffic and the city's size, the replicated megastructures inspire confidence just as the chain outlets and suburban malls have: The National Hometown becomes the National Big City Experience. The megastructure promises reliably comfortable accommodations and a safe good time; the convenience and security of having so much of the city's benefits under one roof or under connected roofs: from meeting rooms and convention halls to shopping and shows.

The criticism that the megastructures isolate themselves from the city has a number of intriguing aspects. First of all, not every urban megastructure is so isolated. The I.D.S. Center in Minneapolis had become a prototype for other city malls, with glass walls and roofs and pedestrian traffic that flows through from the street,

so that there is ample access to both street and sky. The Eaton
Centre is integrated into the life and infrastructure of Toronto, and
has become an example for truly urban malls in the United States.
But part of the function of the megastructure plainly is to create an
inner-directed environment, protected from the city outside. Suburban malls have learned that there are many benefits to being a
large, controlled, and privately managed entity, which can maintain
the image of newness and safety that is absolutely essential to the
success of urban downtowns. Then, too, this formula of enclosed,
protected, and controlled space means that the necessary mixture of
uses can be delivered in one blow. Although the criticism may accurately reflect the megastructure's weaknesses, they also define the
reasons for its success.

In *The New York Times,* architecture critic Ada Louise Huxtable
wrote approvingly of Portman's Atlanta projects in 1974: "He is
making downtown Atlanta an object lesson in people-spaces and
people pleasures." As Portman imitations and new megastructures
designed by Portman himself have sprung up in other cities, other
critics have offered less positive appraisals. Their basic objection is
summed up in the words of Michael Sorkin, writing in *The Wall
Street Journal:* "Whatever their formal achievements, Mr. Portman's
buildings are like giant spaceships, offering close encounters with
the city, but not too close. The buildings are always adamant about
their alien status. . . . The longing expressed in Mr. Portman's architecture is for magical worlds apart, for 'people' places removed
from the hurlyburly. But the reality is otherwise."

But is the reality otherwise?

Peachtree Plaza, Portman's last Atlanta *tour de force,* is a slim
seventy-three-story cylinder covered with reflective glass. Inside,
there are eleven hundred hotel rooms, two huge ballrooms, several
restaurants, cafés, bars, a nightclub, and the Lobby Court Lounge.
There are shops within the hotel, and it is connected to a shopping
mall and a major department store. At one end of a transparent
skyway is the Atlanta Mart convention and exhibition hall. Surrounding the hotel is the Peachtree Center complex of offices and
condominiums. And, of course, it has the patented John Portman-
designed lobby, a seven-story hanging gardens of Babylon containing a half-acre lake.

The lobby is pure amenity, which the dictionary defines as an
attractive feature or convenience, and which, in city-planning and
shopping-mall jargon, generally means an attractive feature that has

no other purpose than to be attractive. For this lobby is not where people check into the hotel or pick up messages. It is not the first thing a prospective guest will see.

The actual entrance to the hotel is not from the street in front of it at all (that's where the shops are) but from the driveway and parking garage behind it. The check-in counters are on the basement level, a floor below where the lobby starts. Once the car keys are handed over to the valet and the credit card passed back and forth at the "front" desk, the guest steps onto an escalator and is wafted up into Amenityland.

I was a guest there for my stay in Atlanta. After I checked in, I contemplated the wonders of the atrium, its interplay of mysterious cement, tumbling greenery, artificial light, and the shafts of illumination on still waters—and wondered how deep they ran (but not enough to ask anyone). After doing most of this contemplation while munching on hors d'oeuvre-sized pretzels while being served drinks by smart-suited waitresses in the semicircle sofas of the Lobby Court Bar—a kind of parlor-by-the-lake—I began my hotel exploration with dinner in the Terrace Room, also on Level 5 (along with Café Express and Lakeside Breakfast). I was going about this systematically, for I had plenty of time. I was staying in the Peachtree Plaza for three days.

The Terrace Room was a reasonably opulent restaurant with its own artificial waterfall, one hundred feet wide. The food was good, the service accomplished by sleek waiters. At a nearby table a middle-aged man in checked jacket and sports shirt and his pants-suited wife were obviously enjoying the classiness, and except for the presence of her parents, so was their well-tailored teenaged daughter. Outside, I considered, were the streets of Atlanta, which looked hot and bleak from my rented car, and which some people said were not safe at night. Certainly there was no waterfall out there to eat beside.

On the next level up was The Inner Circle, which featured the latest in ersatz Las Vegas entertainment, very high on flashy tight costumes for both male and female performers, many costume changes, and no more than a few representative bars of any one song. It was alarmingly like a television commercial for a show being performed somewhere else.

The Peachtree Plaza was, of course, topped by a revolving restaurant and bar, but since my room was on an upper floor I didn't have to go that far to get the essential experience of this hotel complex: the elevator. It was cylindrical and transparent, mimicking the style of the building itself, and it moved gradually but quickly up over the city, which seemed to exist at that moment only to increase the sensual pleasure of this erection. Below, the city seemed a collection of vertical shafts juxtaposed with low, circular structures. After a few days in this inner-directed enclave populated by businesspeople and businesses, the hotel itself could be characterized as a phallic fortress of commerce and commercial sensation. In fact, one may go to the swimming pool on Level 10, where the building narrows into its shaft that rises for another sixty floors, lie at poolside in near nakedness, and look through the transparent roof to contemplate the building violating the clouds. The skyscraper's libidinous assertion, its twentieth-century cockiness, has not been lost in the new urban megastructure; it had just been made more accessible to us all.

There was more to this unreal reality. Within a short walk of the Peachtree Plaza was the Omni International megastructure; 14 stories and 500,000 square feet of office space, a 472-room luxury hotel surrounding 5 levels of shopping-mall retail and entertainment, and connected to the Georgia World Congress convention and exhibition center. There are similar Omni Internationals in Miami, Florida, and Norfolk, Virginia, all these developed by the Alpert Corporation, which built hotels, office complexes, and shopping malls separately in several southern states before combining them in urban locations.

Omni's mall interior was dominated by a professional-size skating rink and a general feeling of cool darkness, in contrast to the hot, bright Atlanta streets. The contrast was so sharp, in fact, that neither the streets nor the interior world of Omni seemed any more real than the other, and neither seemed very real at all.

From the outside, Omni was a forbidding structure, and even the interior was more efficient than warm, but it was still where things are in this downtown, and the blank streets were where things are not. Inside were terraces and hanging ivy, six movie theaters, a post office, the First Atlanta Bank, as well as Murdick's Fudge, Shirt Shack, The Great Wall, the Electronic America game center, Givenchy, McDonald's, Delta Airlines, Spectrum International, the French Restaurant, and The Land of Green Ice. There was a city police headquarters inside as well, so not only was Omni self-contained, it had its own army to defend it.

But if such megastructures don't interact well with the streets they are meant to rescue, they do interlock with each other. Not far from Peachtree Plaza and Omni International, there's Portman's original Hyatt Regency (with its lobby hollowed out of the entire 22-story height of the hotel) and Portman's more recent Marriott Marquis, a 1,700-room luxury tower. They can also interact with other kinds of comprehensive structures, such as the Memorial Arts Center, with its theaters, symphony hall, and art museum; or the Fernbank Science Center, which includes a planetarium, botanical gardens, and the 65-acre Fernbank Forest (this, however, is outdoors).

The megastructures and their pals bear a stylistic as well as practical relationship to the Atlanta International Airport, which brings in the tourists, conventioneers, and business travelers to populate the downtown environments. The new Atlanta International is one of the recent hothouse varieties of airport that have been crossbred with theme parks and malls. I made a special visit just to see it, even though I wasn't flying anywhere. It was a space age place, with high-technology decor and functions, but it also had a Visitor's Center (just like Lenox Mall), a currency exchange, and Interfaith Chaplaincy. In the *Star Wars* light metallic-gray halls of the Transportation Mall, a disembodied voice with the sweet neutral tone of HAL (from *2001: A Space Odyssey*) crossed with the voice on the special band picked up by your car radio which instructs you to remember that you're parking in the Goofy row of the Donald Duck lot at Disney World here reads you your options for getting from gate to plane: the train system, the moving sidewalk, or the pedestrian walkway. With its banks of television screens monitoring flights, as well as the rest of its technology, the Transportation Mall looked as if it could itself lift off at any moment.

The rest of the airport hosted a kind of aviation theme shopping center, with stores, lounges, and game rooms. There were waiting rooms for general use, with tiny television sets attached to seats, and special airline waiting rooms. Eastern Airlines offered a choice of themes in theirs: a high-tech Ionosphere Room, and a clichés-of-the-Old South room with ceiling fans rotating at a stately antebellum pace. Together they summed up nicely the new Atlanta city identity.

From the airport to Omni, the new Atlanta could be seen as a linked succession of magical worlds apart, making up the urban reality that matters. The space ships have taken over: They aren't part of the city. They are the city.

John Portman's designs have become centers of the downtown revivals of other cities, including Detroit, Los Angeles, and San Francisco. Finally, New York City itself succumbed to the outsider and entrusted him with the transformation of one of its major points of identity—Times Square—by commissioning the hotel megastructure known from the beginning as the Portman Project. So, the city that sponsored the first postwar urban revolution was seeking to be rescued from its excesses by the progenitor of the second. His response was a 50-story megastructure with a 48-story lobby, containing a hotel, a 1,500-seat legitimate theater, and a number of lounges and restaurants, including the first rooftop revolving restaurant in Manhattan.

Not just Portman's buildings but megastructures of all kinds flooded into American cities. Polydras Plaza is a hotel and mall complex at the end of a ramp from the New Orleans Superdome. Horton Plaza in downtown San Diego includes a performing arts center and senior citizen high-rise in addition to a hotel and shopping mall; and the California Plaza in downtown Los Angeles is scheduled to open in 1989 with three office towers, hotel, condominiums, restaurants, retail stores, a dozen movie theaters, and a new contemporary arts museum. It will be, in the words of its developer, "a city within a city, from high-rise to commercial, from arts and sciences to residential, you name it, it'll have it."

Other cities may have less grandiose multi-use centers but they may also have several of them. St. Louis is either studying or has begun building five that incorporate major mall components, and Des Moines, Iowa, is planning to open three by 1990. Washington, D.C., will have a big specialty shopping center at National Place, a large mixed-use project in Metropolitan Center, and several smaller malls downtown, including one built around an existing department store. Meanwhile, all this shopping-mall activity downtown has inspired cities such as Providence and Dayton to reclaim their old arcades and turn them into contemporary mixed-use and shopping mall facilities. Atriums, arcades and sumptuous lobbies have become the urban rage.

But the megastructure is not the only new kind of urban mall container. There is another, which might seem to belong to an entirely different urban ethic, and yet it fits in quite well with the multi-use centers. The city that was the early indicator of both this new variant's potential and its compatibility with other recent urban forms, such as the megastructure, is San Francisco.

29

Having a Mall, Wish You Were Here: What's in the Heart of San Francisco?

According to a 1983 study financed by the Urban Investment and Development Company (the developers of Water Tower Place in Chicago), San Francisco's was the city center that had improved the most since 1970, which also happened to be the year I'd last been there. When I arrived this time, I did indeed see many changes in the heart of San Francisco. It had been malled.

I got off the relatively new BART subway at the Embarcadero stop on the edge of downtown. It was a brief and relatively seamless walk from the subway car through the high-tech tunnel and into the Hyatt Regency San Francisco Hotel—a John Portman design that was even more futuristic than Peachtree Plaza in Atlanta.

Inside the Hyatt I walked among young tourists in costly gauzy dresses who caught the eye of young Japanese men in designer sweaters as they photographed brunchers in the central cafés. The cafés nudged the carefully carelessly-placed leather toadstool ottomans and the circles of sofas with reading lights, in the hotel lobby component of this inner courtyard/atrium/arcade. Around the check-in counters there was a momentary illusion of ordinariness, until the gaze drifted upward to the warren of rooms and windows facing inward to the scooped-out interior and its seventeen stories of ivy, concrete, and glitter. Around the corner from the registration desks were the elevators, in front of which was a sign: ELEVATOR SECURITY PROVIDED FOR YOUR PROTECTION. PLEASE SHOW YOUR HOTEL PASSPORT.

Being without a passport, I strolled through as much of the rest of the Embarcadero Center complex as I could on a Sunday. It included well over a hundred shops, boutiques, restaurants, and cafés in three buildings; another office building completed the project and linked it all directly to the Hyatt lobby. The whole interconnected series of complexes covered five city blocks.

According to its management, many of the Center's weekday customers work in the other skyscrapers of this area's new high-rise heaven—people with the income and desire to shop for shoes from Pappagallo, imported custom-tailored suits from Filian's European Clothing, Italian knitwear from Benetton, clothes and accessories from Joseph Magnin, Mark Fenwich, Maro, Le Beau Monde, On Drumm Street, and Jean René Lingerie; to lunch at Sprouts or Salmagundi, Enzo's Ristorante or Vanity Fair Bookseller and Coffeehouse. Which doesn't mean they can't also nip into Radio Shack for a new tweeter, or grab a sponge at Bathtique.

Elevated walkways also linked the complex, connecting open-air plazas floating above courtyards of landscaped greenery; but from ground level, the density of packed high towers of stone and glass formed the dominant impression. Within and among these buildings were condominium apartments, and many of the high-rises had a ground floor of shops that ranged from fashionable clothing to functional services like groceries and dry cleaners. In the midst of it all, at Drumm and Clay streets, was a strange expanse of gardenlike park where the local high-rise dwellers brought their dogs. The most remarkable feature, besides the green peace and flowery comfort in the shadows of massive buildings, was a unique contribution to the decor: a highway ramp, rising out of the ground as if from some subterranean suburb of hell, a relic of the pre-Portman, pre-megastructure era of urban planning.

I walked farther through the new forest of high-rises and parks, away from the Embarcadero. When I looked back at the new heart of San Francisco from the vicinity of North Beach, the extent of the central city's transformation became clearer. It was like the unbroken series of office towers of many other cities—the Manhattanized skyline—but somehow it seemed bizarre in this, the most eccentric of old American cities. Perhaps it was the motif of earthtoned stone instead of New York City steel holding up the glass that made this city's megastructures so iconic, like an Aztec or Inca imperial capital, an imagined Mayan metropolis. Or perhaps it was the influence of the Transamerica Building, its pyramid shape rising like an obscene gesture—a totem pole that seemed less intent on reaching for heaven than in giving it the finger. It was still in many ways a unique and wonderful city. But this was no longer just the province of the quaint, the New World city with Old World charm.

But on another side of San Francisco that old image was upheld, a little forcibly, and partly by a bit of mall history. For that downtown series of stone monuments embedded in silent green parks gave way to strenuous San Francisco hills, to the color of North Beach, and then down the last steep streets to the sea, to Fisherman's Wharf, where a new urban mall species first appeared on shore. There, Ghirardelli Square and The Cannery were the first to show that a collection of shops, selected and managed by a single developer, could survive in the city without being inside a mammoth structure but in rehabilitated older buildings once used for something else.

Some say the idea got its first test in San Francisco's Spaghetti Factory, which actually was a spaghetti factory before being reclaimed as a restaurant. But the first large-scale experiment was probably Ghirardelli Square, where in 1964 a set of shops opened in the buildings erected in 1893 for the purpose of manufacturing chocolate.

Both before Ghirardelli Square opened, and in many cities long afterward, old buildings that had outlived their uses in the city generally met one of three fates: They sat empty, idle, and deteriorating; they were torn down to make way for Progress in the form of newer and usually larger buildings; or in a few rare cases they were "saved" by historical preservation committees, and perhaps turned into sparsely attended museums. But Ghirardelli Square introduced what has now become a series of urban clichés: It "reclaimed" old buildings by fixing them up but retaining at least some of their historical qualities, and it "recycled" them by turning them to other uses, sometimes as offices or condos but usually as shops or eating places. Bigger buildings—like Ghirardelli Square—could be converted into specialty malls. The potential of this idea was confirmed by the nearby Cannery, which opened its shops in 1967 in the renovated buildings of the abandoned Del Monte cannery.

By the time I saw Ghirardelli Square on my mall odyssey (I'd been unaware of it on previous visits to San Francisco) I had already seen several urban malls, including newer and more famous ones modeled on its idea. But I was more charmed by it and by The Cannery than any others. Perhaps it was the San Francisco spring weather; certainly in Ghirardelli's case it was its location—it sits on a hill with a clear view of the bay. But I think the appeal of these two had something to do with their pioneering; by all accounts they've both gotten slicker than when they started, but in the beginning they were improvising. They didn't start out knowing how to overdo a good thing, so they didn't. The buildings weren't over-renovated to a Disney finish, and they still don't trumpet their historical character. They just looked like good, old buildings.

There was also an air of informality and a sense of space, an easy flow from surrounding streets and yet the promise of special spaces within, and a number of other qualities that may owe as much to San Francisco as to the taste of their developers. For even while these places function as necessary counterpoints to the starkly modern downtown towers, especially in preserving the image of old San Francisco vital to one of the city's prime industries, tourism, they are also havens for the real characteristics of this extraordinary city.

I had lunch outdoors in the Cannery courtyard, under the canopy of the Ristorante La Strada, sunshine leaching through the red-white-and-green Italian flags onto the edge of the red-and-white checkered tablecloths. Not only was the setting delightfully clichéd—so was the scene. Beautiful young women sat alone sipping wine at nearby tables, just like in the commercials, and at another an older woman was complaining loudly to her companions that no one at this restaurant spoke Italian. She was, of course, complaining in Italian.

Just beyond the restaurant, under the trees, there were picnic tables with birds hovering about, and a young man played airs on an autoharp. There were couples, families of all the racial combinations of San Francisco, and people of all ages, including a couple of kids in sandals sitting upside down on a bench.

The Cannery's retailing was low-key; a series of sunny courtyards, shops, and coffeehouses in buildings that had the look of a Spanish mission. Later that afternoon, a man in a white apron emerged from Crivello's Oyster Bar, stood in an acoustically and theatrically favorable spot in the courtyard, and began singing arias. He held his arms up to the women on the landing above him, along the high dusty yellow-orange walls. Then he smiled, bowed, and went back to work.

As I approached Ghirardelli Square, a little higher on the hill, I caught the rousing finish to Professor Gizmo's one-man band performance of "The Stars and Stripes Forever" on washboard, harmonica, horns, bass drum, whistle, high hat, and tambourine, with an American flag popping out of a pistol barrel as his finale. The crowd applauded and started to disperse, but some dropped money in his till. "Thank you," Professor Gizmo said in a loud, clear voice, "especially to those of you who realize I am in business for myself. I am not paid by any government agency, even though I display their logo."

Many of the people walking up the steps to the shops were from San Francisco suburbs ("the freeway crowd" I heard one vendor call them with ill-disguised contempt) and out-of-town tourists. Among them was a family of four in front of me, obviously from New York, walking in two sections—father and daughter, mother and young son. The mother hit the son. The father glanced back. "You knocked the kid down," he said. "I know," she said. "And I'm glad."

In the square itself, tourists mingled with kids on bicycles in the village-square-size courtyard leading off to various levels of shops and restaurants—to the Chair House, Maui Jewelry, Almond Plaza ("everything under the sun in almonds"), Scan Trends (Scandinavian furniture), Bebe Pierrot (baby chic), Foxx Fire, and East of Java. There was a billboard listing scheduled entertainment: the Juggling Mizmos and Tommy, the Roller Skating Accordionist; Danny Daniels, world's worst juggler; and Gary Schnell, Dog Day Afternoon puppeteer.

I stayed on until after the white sails in the bay stretched homeward and sunset had fallen across the water and gone behind the hills. The nip in the air sent the last shoppers home and brought out the first diners, to the Blue Whale, or the West Coast edition of

New York's Maxwell's Plum. The lights around the mermaids in the old fountain went on, as did the big lights above on the huge Ghirardelli sign, the same sign that ships could see when they passed through the Golden Gate from the 1920s until it was darkened during invasion fears in World War II, not to be lit again until Ghirardelli Square became a mall.

Ghirardelli Square and The Cannery had done so well in attracting tourists in this tourist city that an imitator appeared on Fisherman's Wharf itself. It opened in 1978 as Pier 39, a theme mall that, lacking an actual historical building to renovate, constructed one from scratch to look more or less historic, or at least old. It was built mostly out of what appeared to be weathered New England clapboard; it covered forty-five acres and was the largest development on the city's northern waterfront.

Its developer was Walter Simmons, a San Francisco native and ex-Pan Am pilot, who got a lot of mostly unwelcome local press for allegedly shady dealings in the four-year process of obtaining all the permits needed from the city for his mall. By 1981, Pier 39 was in financial trouble and was eventually sold to another developer.

Still, there were plenty of people around when I was there, and Simmons's flamboyant touch was still evident, especially in the many chatty little plaques explaining Pier 39 that were scattered through the winding two levels, along the wood staircases and alternating tunnels and plazas of the project. One plaque explained that due to a new steel and concrete pier built around the old one, Pier 39 was now one of the safest places to be in the event of a major earthquake—not an idle comment in San Francisco. But, the sign goes on: "There's only one slight problem. The Embarcadero Roadway in front of Pier 39 is built on loosely packed landfill, which would liquefy just like quicksand in a giant quake, and turn Pier 39 into an island. But thanks to the many fine restaurants and bars, you could have a great time here, even after the BIG ONE, while you're waiting for a rowboat to take you back home."

Since Pier 39 depends heavily on tourists, Sunday is a banner day, as it is elsewhere on Fisherman's Wharf. A French tour and a group from Japan were marching and gliding in bunches along the crowded stairs and wooden walkways, past Barbary Coast Dolls and Daisy Hill Puppy Farm (where all the puppies are toys), All-American T-Shirt and North Beach Leather, Boudin Sourdough French Bread bakery and What's A Churro? (it's Mexican pastry),

Camera Cabin, On Edge Too (braids, trims, and notions), Brass International, and Joyce's Dancing Dragon. Girls in floppy hats and slit skirts examined orange-crate-label art at California Collectibles; kids were trying to talk parents into attending the UFO Exhibit, while the grown-ups would rather be in the cool darkness of the California Wineries Tasting Center.

For the truly guilty, there was Let's Get Organized, organized into organizers for Workroom, Desk-Den, Kitchen (bags marked WINE), Car, and Children (GOIN' TO GRANDMA's totebags). Also on the lower level, amid Behind the Wheel (car- and truck-related items), Left Hand World (gifts for left-handed people), and Mouse Stuff (Disney toys), there was the kind of carnival entertainment that went on all over the Wharf area, although perhaps with a little more sideshow emphasis here than elsewhere—a man juggling hatchets, for example, on a unicycle.

Pier 39 has itself been roundly criticized for its tackiness and for being "not San Francisco" by city residents. But although this is still a city of strong neighborhoods with long-standing indigenous shops and services ("Most people do their regular shopping in the neighborhoods," the manager of the Upstart Crow Bookstore in The Cannery told me, "but they come here for something special"), the shopping-mall form, in its various guises, is well on the way to becoming a newly indigenous part of San Francisco's city land-scape. Each represents a different style of the same mall delivery system, geared to the urban market as it is perceived in the 1980s.

"You have to realize that shopping is one of the favorite forms of entertainment, and urban dwellers now do it better," James Bronkema, manager of the Embarcadero Center told a reporter. "There are more adults who demand quality and special merchandise and have the money to pay for it, too." Add the tourists and suburbanites, and you have the constituencies for all types of urban malls.

The clear trend is toward the urban mall in this old, traditional yet anticonventional city, from the massive Ferry Building complex to a garage converted into a mall of shoplets in the booming Castro neighborhood. It also represents the very mallish movement toward what a San Francisco marketing counselor called "the con-cept of merchandising as theater."

The city of San Francisco has changed, partly because of its quiet integration of various forms of urban malls. But the new kind of city mall it spawned became—in slightly different, refined, and augmented forms—the phenomenon that truly opened the gates of cities everywhere to malls. In the resulting frenzy of development, malls would be hailed as the salvation of cities, and of the mall industry as well.

But that didn't happen in San Francisco. Although there were other precedents, such as Trolley Square in Salt Lake City and Chattanooga's Choo-Choo, the urban sea-change occurred in one of the oldest cities of the East, where an old marketplace became a bigger tourist attraction than Disney World and galvanized the revival of an entire central city, inflaming the imagination of developers, bankers, and city officials all across America. It happened, fittingly or strangely (depending on your point of view) during the American Bicentennial celebration, on the waterfront where the American Revolution began.

30

Faneuil Hall Marketplace: The Mall Heard 'Round the World

The goal of the city is to make man happy and safe.
—ARISTOTLE

There hadn't been a sunny Sunday in Boston for two months, but on the late October afternoon when I first visited Faneuil Hall Marketplace the year after it opened, the day was bright and brisk and people were out in frenzied droves. They were shoulder to shoulder inside Quincy Market and along its flanking courts, sampling croissants from Au Bon Pain, fried bread, souvlaki sandwiches, prosciutto on bulkie rolls, scallops at the raw bar, ice-cream sundaes with "real whipped cream," and opulent salads from the Produce House.

They were buying fresh meat and vegetables in the steamy central corridor, BOSTON'S THE BEST T-shirts in the below-street-level shops, and novelties from pushcart vendors. They watched the jugglers and clowns do tricks for them in the courtyard. They climbed stairs to the refurbished rotunda inner dome, past the restored old signs on the brick walls and the black wrought-iron tables leading to the Magic Pan Crêperie restaurant. On several levels of the South Building they browsed through shops that displayed the latest tweeds and twills, gleaming glassware, and jewelry in hushed velvet cases. Soon they would be able to shop in the North Building, which would complete the original plan for the Marketplace.

I had lived in Cambridge and worked in Boston for most of the first half of the 1970s, and what I was seeing on this visit was all but inconceivable then, particularly so near to Boston Harbor. When I followed a few people carrying their salads and sandwiches and bottles of wine from the Marketplace to the new Waterfront Park, I remembered a day in the first summer I had spent in Boston, when I was downtown with a companion and suddenly got the overwelming urge to find the sea. I didn't know in which direction to walk, and I don't know if I caught a salt breeze to guide me unconsciously, but I marched us straight to the waterfront. When I found the water it was murky and rancid; the wharfs and piers were rotten, the warehouses black, the area desolate. What had begun with euphoric purpose ended in numbed sadness.

Later, when I had lived in Cambridge for a few years, I would sometimes take visiting friends on one of the tour boats that cruised Boston Harbor. On one such ride we heard the disembodied voice of an unseen guide naming through a tinny microphone an unending series of invisible relics of Boston's past—places in the harbor area where something significant had been, but after more than a century of decline, was no longer.

"That was the Boston Navy Yard," the voice intoned toward the end of the tour. "It was saved by President Kennedy, but"—and the bitterness in the voice was undisguised—"closed by Nixon. Massachusetts was the only state that voted against Nixon in 1972." The history lessons were well taken, but the peaceful hour of thrumming through water, wind, and sunshine had been ruined. On subsequent trips I learned to avoid boats that had guides.

Now, things were changing on Boston's waterfront and back toward Faneuil Hall. Boston was making something new out of something old. I walked back from the waterfront, passing near the border of the North End, a genuine and still self-sustaining Italian area, where the tourists and students drinking cappuccino in Cafe Pompei were still likely to be outnumbered by neighborhood residents until late at night. An elevated freeway ramp had formed a

barrier to the North End, but now that the Marketplace was bringing so many visitors, the city gave the freeway's cement base a coat
of bright paint and inscribed an equally bright sign above the single
portal to the North End to identify it for tourists—thereby turning
it into a self-managed Italian theme park.

As I wandered along the periphery of the Marketplace, I saw a
few people stopping at Faneuil Hall itself. Faneuil Hall is not really
part of the project that bears its name; it is wholly owned by the
city and has been in more or less continuous use since before Daniel
Webster spoke there. The American Revolution was debated in
Faneuil Hall for a decade before Lexington; abolitionists spoke there
for thirty years before the Civil War; and in the 1970s it hosted
debates on Vietnam and nuclear power, taped for a Public Broadcasting television series called *The Advocates,* which usually featured
a young man named Michael Dukakis, later to become governor of
Massachusetts. But no one except small bands of tourists had ventured into the area around Faneuil Hall for years—until now. Now,
from the Cradle of Liberty, it was just a short walk to the Proud
Popover.

The old Haymarket vegetable stands were still operating
nearby, but there was no doubt that the main action was at the new
Marketplace. One of its bars—called Cityside—had already become
the new "in" spot for the city's singles on weekends, and travelers
who got into cabs at the airport and asked to be taken someplace
interesting for a couple of hours between planes were routinely deposited at the Marketplace. Tourists with and without native guides
were already heading there before tramping on to the Old North
Church or Beacon Hill.

Back in the Quincy Market courtyard, a scattering of mostly
young people was braving the late afternoon chill to stand in the
sunlight and the open spaces. They were peculiarly well-dressed,
and some seemed to be posing. Some looked like models of the
new urban life-style; some just looked like models. A young man in
Icelandic fur coat, pressed jeans, and new Frye boots was splitting a
loaf of French bread and a bottle of Perrier with a young woman in
expensive casual clothes. Silently he rotated 360 degrees on his
heels, looking at the market buildings, the stone courtyards, the
benches, and small trees that at nightfall would glow with tiny
white lights. "I can't believe it," he said to his companion. "It's
another world."

In retrospect, it seemed a perfect other world for Boston, and its identity as a historic city. The mix of shops and eating places catered to Boston characteristics: the low-cal cosmopolitanism and casual consumption of its high-income, highly educated classes. It was an enclosed Paris of Yesterday inside the shell of Boston's feisty past.

That this marketplace would be so successful wasn't always so obvious; in fact, the whole idea of it was heresy not so very long ago. The project involved some creative leaps, major gambles, and years of effort on the part of the unlikely combination of people it brought together. For this was something new in the American city. Ghirardelli Square and The Cannery in San Francisco had simply been new business ideas carried out by individual entrepreneurs, but the Marketplace was an intentional attempt to revive the center of a major city—and the city itself—by means of this new kind of urban shopping mall. As such, Faneuil Hall Marketplace was the first of its kind, the first recycling of historical buildings developed into a major urban mall through close private and governmental cooperation and planning.

The makers of this other world of the Marketplace were several, and it is difficult to sort out the exact contribution of each. The City of Boston was deeply involved, especially its mayor, Kevin White, and its redevelopment director, Robert Ryan. Under the leadership of James Rouse, the Rouse Company developed and managed the project. But it all began with one man in Boston: Benjamin Thompson, an architect, teacher, entrepreneur, and urban theorist who became the project's designer.

Some Rouse Company people intimated that Ben Thompson tended to exaggerate his role in the final design, whereas Thompson said that the merchandising plans were pretty much in place when Rouse was called in, and some participants in Boston's City Hall suggested that both Thompson and Rouse were simply instruments of their wishes. But on one point all involved agreed: It was Ben Thompson who had the first vision of a revived Quincy Market, and it was he who first set about making it a reality.

On another autumn afternoon, Ben Thompson shambled into his Cambridge office, his eyes still filled with the faraway sights of Venice, which he likes to visit and from which he had just returned. Across a brick alley from his office was the Design Research building, a striking structure of gleaming glass, the main outlet of the prosperous business Thompson started after leaving the chairmanship of the architecture department at Harvard's Graduate School of Design. According to some, it had made him rich. Thompson's shirt and trousers were both striped, but the stripes were faded like the colors of a Renaissance painting. His shirt had a button missing and was held closed with a safety pin.

I had bargained with his wife and colleague, Jane Thompson, for an hour's interview; but it lasted more than four, though Thompson talked for only a small fraction of that time. Instead, he searched out copies of old speeches and articles, dusted off scale models, and ran his many multi-image and musically accompanied slide shows.

The story all of this helped to tell began in the mid-1960s, when Thompson had begun poking around the deteriorating old market buildings near Faneuil Hall, taking pictures of rotting window frames and knolls of trash. By then he was already disenchanted with both the effects of new development going on in the cities and the ways in which the little that was left of the past was being preserved. Boston's major step in downtown redevelopment had been Government Center, designed by modernist architect I. M. Pei. But Thompson didn't think much of this expanse of brick plaza linking the new City Hall and the federal building. "It was built and managed as a monument," he told me. "The plaza ices up in winter. The whole space is overscaled. The only thing it's really good for is a riot." In fact, it had served that purpose several times.

At first Boston planned to do the conventional thing with the Quincy Market buildings: It was going to tear them down and erect skyscrapers. "There was a period in the sixties," Thompson said, "when new was great. People believed everything new was going to be glorious." At Harvard, Thompson had caused considerable controversy by simply restoring one old university building. Donors were miffed—they wanted their names on a new one.

But some people were beginning to sense that all this newness wasn't necessarily working, and City Hall began to feel some heat for destroying more of what Boston was famous for: its history. So Thompson was asked to look at the Quincy Market buildings. He agreed they should be preserved, but he thought they should also be used; they should help revive the life of the city as well as represent some of its history. This was almost as heretical as not tearing them down.

"The only model of historical preservation in the sixties was Williamsburg," Thompson explained, "the exact restoration to one period." But Thompson saw old buildings in the context of the living city. He admitted that he was influenced by urban theorist Jane Jacobs and her contention that healthy city streets need a mix of people and uses, and both old and new buildings to help achieve that mix. Old buildings didn't have to be turned into museums to be useful.

Thompson was also among those who did not agree with the efforts to create entirely new cities within the boundaries of the old, to make them instantly into breathtaking utopias of gleaming efficiency and rationality, amazing machines for the future, so clearly superior to ticky-tacky suburbia with its pathetic backwardness, its sad wallowing in dinette sets and lawn care while the jet age was moving forward at supersonic speed. But neither did he agree with the other conventional view of cities as doomed dens of overcrowding, crime, and craziness, destined for obsolescence, with the suburbs the only hope for the future. "I felt that suburbia was ultimately going to be too stratified and boring," Thompson said.

By the late 1960s, the situation for the cities was becoming desperate. Many downtowns had become deserts of concrete, impersonal by day and desolate and dangerous at night. The highway ramps were not the graceful geometries they appeared to be in the drawings, but ungainly monsters cutting through city blocks that were now more the province of motorized vehicles than of hapless humans with no place to walk and nowhere to walk to anyway. Entire organically and efficiently functioning neighborhoods had been destroyed by bulldozers and dynamite. Thousands of people were imprisoned in acres of uniformly substandard high-rise projects, which they rapidly tore to pieces. For some central cities, the riots in the mid-sixties and again after the assassination of Dr. Martin Luther King, Jr., in 1968 were the final blow. The destruction started by the bulldozer was finished by the torch.

It was under the pressure of these events—as well as the street warfare over the issue of Vietnam at the 1968 Democratic National Convention in Chicago, and the aftermath of Senator Robert Kennedy's assassination—that Thompson's ideas for the future of the city coalesced. It was then that he presented them in an impassioned speech to the students of Wayne State University. Thompson claimed that the participants on all sides of these struggles were battling a common enemy: "an oppression so huge and monolithic that few residents of the Establishment have identified it at all." It was "the disintegrating quality of modern environment." Environment affects all, Thompson claimed—psychologically, biologically, spiritually. The city, in particular, was not only antiblack and antipoor, it was antihuman.

Thompson's prescription basically stated that buildings and cities should be designed as environments with the needs and wants of people in mind, no matter what their uses: "private dwellings, commercial centers, housing developments or industrial 'parks.' Each bears a responsibility for affecting people—inside and outside. Each piece of construction must counter the current massive assault on human sensibility from overscale, monotony, chaos and personal isolation. If we are going to reverse those trends, everything we build must inject the affirmative values human beings need as much as food—the pleasure of tactile and visual things, assurance of physical security and freedom, variety of stimulating impressions and experience. Above all, there must be some kind of contact with the changing seasons, with nature and natural light."

Thompson looked to the cities of Europe for his models, to the street markets of Lausanne, the squares of London, the Tivoli Gardens of Copenhagen, the river walks of Paris, and to "Venice, for the layers of intriguing movement . . . in a day and night pageant of color and action."

European cities were a particularly valuable lesson because a mix of periods still existed in them. "Those societies," Thompson said, "have moved less quickly to destroy the values that have made them civilized after centuries of human effort." In practical terms, Europe proved that an old building didn't have to be a museum, that it could be useful if its architecture was allowed to emerge but its function was oriented to the needs and wants of people in the present.

"When I talked to those students, I was asking, 'why should a city be such a miserable place? Can a city be a fair?'" Thompson said to me. "But it's not enough just to see what's wrong with it. In architecture, you have to do something about it."

Thompson bit off that last phrase with the insouciance and fatalism of Humphrey Bogart in *The Maltese Falcon* asserting that if somebody killed your partner you were supposed to do something about it. In Boston, Thompson was about to get the chance.

The City Hall office of Boston redevelopment director Bob Ryan overlooked the Marketplace during its transformation, as did the office of Mayor Kevin White. "The mayor watched it all happening," Ryan told me as we looked out his office window. "And they knew he was watching. That area was in really bad shape then. I live in the waterfront area—and I have since 1970. I couldn't bring a guest back to my apartment then—nobody wanted to go near there. There was traffic right in front of Faneuil Hall, and the rest of the area was dark. The Quincy Market buildings caught on fire several times. The only people down there were winos."

By then, it had already dawned on city officials that like other American cities, Boston had real problems and had brought some of them on itself. All Bob Ryan had to do was glance out his office window to see one of the problems, maybe the source of many others: that eyesore of the Southeast expressway ramping its way through downtown, cutting Boston off from the sea, and its people from each other. The postwar lords of the city thought they could win the war against traffic and urban blight all at once, by churning out those immense ribbons of concrete linking cities and suburbia in a stately and convenient flow—so many highways so fast that it was like a war production assembly line. But it turned out that laying concrete was like sowing dragon's teeth: Up would pop armed men in the form of Chryslers and Chevrolets, and they were heading out of the city and not into it.

To begin with, the system devised to manage traffic rationally had somehow irrationally worsened it. These highways, which were—as Robert Caro wrote in his Pulitzer Prize-winning biography of Robert Moses, *The Power Broker*—"of dimensions literally unknown in history, could be opened one month—and be filled to absolute capacity the next," and "expressways opened in 1952 were by 1955 carrying the traffic load that had been forecast for 1985." It was as if expressways were elongated Petri dishes for breeding cars: Like the offspring of fruitful fruit flies left in the lab overnight, they would just be there in the morning, buzzing bumper to bumper on what had been a beautiful, modern, wide emptiness of level new concrete.

That was just the beginning of the auto infestation. This business of planning around highways and cars had gotten out of hand. Boston decision makers were starting to listen to people like Lewis Mumford, the urban scholar, when he said, "Forget the damn motor car, and build cities for lovers and friends." Cities had been fighting the idea of people getting together on the urban landscape. Sidewalk cafés were not only unheard of in American cities, in many they were illegal; they were classified as traffic obstructions.

The new urban theorists were saying that the city should not be fighting its own nature as a place where there are a lot of people, but should be using that fact to the city's advantage and for the people's pleasure. People-oriented places not only could bring a little excitement and fun back downtown, but—these theorists said—lots of active people at all times of the day would make the downtown safer. "Life attracts life," as Jane Jacobs wrote.

Like other cities, Boston had experienced severe economic dislocations as well as planning problems. By 1975 there were only half the manufacturing jobs in Boston that had existed thirty years before. The long-term loss of textile and shoe manufacturing throughout New England was virtually complete. Moreover, the city continued to lose population, and the percentage of the old and poor grew.

But by the 1970s, analysts and planners in Boston's Redevelopment Authority and Economic Development Industrial Corporation were beginning to piece together a way out of the mess. For one thing, the loss of manufacturing that had looked like disaster was beginning to seem like a beneficial purge, for thanks to Boston's many universities, textile mills were largely replaced by high-technology companies in the near suburbs. These were highly productive industries with a future, and with a different kind of worker—educated and interested in the cultural and entertainment opportunities a city could provide.

Meanwhile the universities and cultural institutions had not abandoned the city, and the service sector—particularly in the growing fields of medicine and government—was getting larger. Cambridge was still full of architects and lawyers, and there seemed to be less of a tendency for the young to leave the city as soon as they graduated. Some were moving into industrial lofts and into areas adjacent to the city where rents were cheaper and sound old houses were available to be bought and fixed up. Firms locating in the new office buildings downtown were also employing more people.

All of this pointed to the need for a stronger downtown. The Redevelopment Authority already had plans to create a residential area on the waterfront, along with the landscaped Waterfront Park. But between Government Center and the waterfront were the old Quincy Market buildings. Something was needed to link these two areas.

Benjamin Thompson finally convinced the city that what they

needed was a rehabilitated Quincy Market, with shops, food, enter-tainment—a permanent city fair. "What was missing," said Ryan, "was something to support the residences and offices. We needed this area to be economically and culturally diversified and lively, where mixed and multiple uses could convene."

There was also the historical significance of the area to consider. Faneuil Hall was the natal place of the city of Boston. In fact, the Quincy Market buildings were standing on what in colonial times had been the sea; beginning in the mid-seventeenth century, ships had discharged their cargoes at precisely the spot where Faneuil Hall would be built as a market and meeting place in 1742. The port area grew at such a pace that six acres of landfill were poured in front of Faneuil Hall to support a series of market buildings, the last being the three Greek Revival structures built in 1826 during the administration of Mayor Josiah Quincy. For the rest of the nineteenth century and part of the twentieth, they were the center of a chaos of farm wagons full of produce and barrels of beef, and cargoes unloaded from ships in the first major harbor of the New World.

Now those Quincy Market buildings, as decayed as they were, offered a particular opportunity. For at last the city realized it had something the suburbs didn't: its history. And as the American Bicentennial came closer, historical matters were much on the minds of Boston officials.

There were still plenty of problems. At first, Ben Thompson worked with a company that restored buildings, and with a number of individual entrepreneurs who would open shops. But legal problems arose and the city wanted a new developer to take charge of the whole project. When the shopping-mall developer James Rouse was approached, and agreed, new history was made for the American city and the shopping-mall industry.

Rouse had an abiding interest in cities, and his analysis of their problems and the proper solutions was similar to Thompson's, although Rouse thought on an even larger scale. Like Victor Gruen, Rouse talked about the decay of American cities and the deleterious effects of suburban sprawl. He tried to make his malls centers of community and organized development, and he actually built a city in the suburbs—the planned town of Columbia, Maryland, which also serves as the Rouse Company headquarters. Rouse had plans for more city-building, including a community for 300,000 on

Staten Island, but he couldn't find the financing. Instead he turned to the urban mall as a way of rebuilding existing cities.

Rouse built Columbia in the early 1960s during the administration of President John F. Kennedy—the thousand days of "Camelot"—and he had the Kennedy-era characteristic of pragmatism at the service of idealism, and an attitude of always moving forward. "He works in a competitive business, a tough environment," Ben Thompson said of Rouse, "so he can be very tough. But he has a very optimistic view on life. He's got that quality of a child in him. He's able to dream."

The Rouse Company had one successful urban mall not far away, the Gallery in Philadelphia, but it was much closer to the suburban mall model than the Marketplace would be. Still, Rouse would bring his infectious enthusiasm and his company's expertise in creating human-scale, adaptable environments that were also efficient retail selling machines. As a plus, he brought some clout with financial backers, based on his company's past successes in suburbia.

The process of putting together a financial package was drawn out and difficult. Perhaps the first and most significant innovation of the Marketplace project was, in fact, its financing, for it involved unprecedented public participation in a privately owned retail project.

Before Rouse came in, Boston had already obtained a federal Housing and Urban Development grant to restore and structurally renovate the market buildings. The city and state contributed more funds and gave a ninety-nine-year lease on the land to the Rouse Company for $1. After completion, the city would receive a portion of the profits and the state would receive sales tax—if there was going to be any.

Not many financial institutions believed there would be. Even after this deal was made, Boston banks refused to finance construction. Pouring more than $40 million into fixing up some low-rise old hunks of granite in the literal center of Boston, on potentially very valuable land, and fitting them out with little shops and cafés, did not seem like anything more than a well-intentioned but inevitably disastrous idea to a lot of people.

But funding was found, from outside Boston, and construction began. Through recession and cost overruns, and watched over by a nervous mayor, James Rouse kept it going. It was already 1976,

about a decade after Ben Thompson had snapped those first pictures
of the old market. But the timing turned out to be perfect.

On August 25, the night before it opened, Mayor Kevin White
had dinner with Benjamin Thompson and James Rouse in one of
the Marketplace restaurants. As they put the restaurant staff
through their paces in a kind of shakedown dinner, White gently
cautioned Thompson and Rouse that "Bostonians are conservative.
They may not come around here for a few months."

The next day, on the 150th anniversary of the dedication of the
original Quincy Market, conservative Bostonians showed up
100,000 strong. So it was that embattled Boston stood and fired
another shot heard 'round the world.

"It really opened at just the right time," Robert Ryan said. "It
was 1976, the Bicentennial, and already that summer we'd had the
Tall Ships come in and the waterfront was jammed with people to
watch them. The Queen of England's visit, too. People saw all of
that on television and they said—Hey, Boston has changed."

As for the Rouse Company, they watched the Tall Shops come
in that summer, too. The Marketplace, immediately profitable,
opened the eyes of mall developers across America by doubling the
take per square foot of leasable space realized by the better suburban
malls. And in the comparison that has since become the proudest
boast any urban mall can make, the Marketplace drew more people
yearly than did Disney World.

For the city of Boston, the Marketplace provided the desired
link from downtown to the sea, and so excited the office workers in
the area (who deserted Government Square and streamed down to
it for lunch) that the New England Telephone Company emptied
its waterfront building of switching equipment and turned it into
offices at the behest of its white-collar workers who wanted to be
where the action was.

More than this, Faneuil Hall Marketplace sparked a downtown
revival, the dimensions of which no one had imagined or foreseen.
It spurred more waterfront high-rise housing and the construction
of the Bostonian, a new hotel opposite the Marketplace in something of the same period style. But it also inspired development
elsewhere in the central city—so much that city government was
able to weigh carefully the merits of each project instead of taking
all comers. One of the largest new developments was the Copley
Place project, developed by the creators of Water Tower Place in

Chicago; it included two hotels, a shopping gallery, a Neiman-Marcus store, offices, residences, restaurants, and entertainment facilities. One of its first major successes was hosting the huge international convention of Shriners. The old downtown was prodded to improve itself, too. Jordan Marsh, Boston's premier department store, began a $220 million redevelopment of Lafayette Square.

Meanwhile, Faneuil Hall became a new downtown focus for the entire metropolitan area—so that while the New England beauty pageant held its preliminary rounds at the Hanover Mall, Liberty Tree Mall, and Framingham Shoppers World in the suburbs, the finals were held in Quincy Market's courtyard.

Because of the runaway success of the Marketplace, the city government made historical renovation and recycling an official policy, and it went on at a fever pitch: All five of the huge granite warehouses as well as smaller buildings on the waterfront were turned into apartments, condos, offices, restaurants, and shops. Part of the old City Hall was redone as a restaurant, an old fire station became a theater, and the Prince Spaghetti factory converted to condominiums.

It wasn't only the economic success of the Marketplace that caused Boston's new awakening. It was, Robert Ryan said, a dose of "urban magic." Cities had become forbidding places, but for centuries this port-side excitement had been found only in cities and was traditionally among their major attractions. The truly enduring symbol of the city isn't the loom or the coin: It is light.

The idea spread quickly, as historical restorations and renovated waterfronts became the passion of developers, city officials, and entrepreneurs all over America. "It's like *Star Wars*," Bob Ryan said. "Everybody wants to copy it. Cities all over the world want to replicate Faneuil Hall Marketplace."

"What amazes me," said an aide to Ryan, "is how many people now claim they'd had the vision to see how this would succeed. They got it about twenty-four hours after it opened."

Ryan was looking down at the Marketplace from his window. "A lot of that area had been torn up to replace city sewers, so that some of it could be channeled away from the harbor," he said. "As work went on, tides came in and the whole place became a swamp . . . but now look at it. You can go down there to the Marketplace and buy a slice of pizza, listen to the Boston Symphony, or buy a seven-hundred-dollar suit. Or you can just sit and watch people."

"Mayor White's joke," said the aide, "is that if people complain about being bitten by the merchants down there, that's all right. A few years ago, they would have only been bitten by rats."

Although the Rouse Company's success with the Marketplace electrified the mall industry, at first there was still some caution expressed: Boston might be a special case. But with its very next try, in Baltimore, the Rouse Company demonstrated this success could be replicated, and a new era in American cities and the mall industry really began.

31

Our Mission in the City: Mall Technology and the Yuppies

On a bright summer morning in 1980, a few days shy of Independence Day, Mayor William Donald Schaefer stood on the deck of the *Pride of Baltimore,* brushing away his tears. The *Pride,* a sailing replica of the classic clipper ships, was leading a flotilla of fifty-seven vessels into Baltimore's Inner Harbor, where the original clippers had been built and berthed. Just beyond the new moorings of the restored eighteenth-century frigate *Constellation,* the first commissioned American warship, was the flotilla's destination: the two compact, green-canopied pavilions of Harborplace, a covered garden of shops, restaurants, cafés, and markets, reflecting the sunlight like the sea itself. For years there had been nothing on this historic spot but derelict buildings. Even a few months earlier, it had been an open patch of dead grass. But today the pavilions and the tiered terraces between them were awash with 150,000 cheering people.

On board the *Pride of Baltimore,* along with the mayor, were the other principals responsible for Harborplace: James Rouse, Mathias J. DeVito, the Rouse Company's new chief executive, and Benjamin Thompson, who had designed Harborplace and was already at work on the plans for the South Street Seaport in New York City. The flotilla advanced and Rouse was beaming; DeVito (as Schaefer said later) was walking about the boat on a carpet of air. Ben Thompson was at the bow, snapping the pictures he would later assemble into a sequence of slides. Each shot came a little closer to the dock: first the pavilions in the distance and the bright flags flying over them, with the mass of humanity below. Then the people themselves, figures and colors set against the brightness behind them, their hands extended in waves, their mouths open in shouts. Then, finally, the faces at the dock, welcoming the visitors with broad smiles.

The crowds had begun arriving very early in the morning, and the entire Baltimore police traffic division was there to guide them. When the *Pride of Baltimore* docked at noon, thousands of balloons were launched, cannons roared, and a tenor stepped forward to sing the theme from *Camelot.* For the thousands who stayed until after dark, when the Baltimore Symphony assembled on the plaza to play the "1812 Overture," the cannons boomed again and fireworks spread across the water and the doubled harbor sky.

In its first week, more than a million people walked through Harborplace. Its inaugural was timed to coincide with the city's annual Maritime Heritage Festival, so also on hand were chantey singers, bagpipers, dance bands, folk singers, face painters, clowns, storytellers, jugglers, and puppet shows. In the mall itself that week, Anna's Fried Dough sold more than 20,000 pieces. Just Burgers sold 15,000 hamburgers; Southern Style Barbeque used 2,000 pounds of ribs, 1,500 pounds of minced barbecue, and 600 pounds of chicken. Dianna's Carribean Cooking used 500 pounds of goat, 180 pounds of duck, and 125 pounds of rabbit. Trishaw Express sold about 500 egg rolls a day. Italian Village sold 1,200 cannoli. Hats in the Belfry averaged 500 hats a day sold. Touch of Brass sold 75 brass crabs in the first four hours they were open. Children's Bookstore reordered their entire stock at the end of the week.

"Perhaps never in Baltimore's history has there been such a felicitous blend of mercantilism, public pride, pageantry and, let us face it, simple curiosity," observed the *Baltimore Evening Sun*. "This week's grand welcome of the twin pavilions at the Inner Harbor has become much more than another opening of another mall." "With the opening of Harborplace," added the *Sun* in a cascade of editorial alliteration, "Baltimore will mark a turning point in a revival that rivals its remarkable recovery from the 1904 fire."

By the end of the first five weeks, Harborplace had played host to 10 million people. The population of Baltimore is just over 2 million. All summer, pleasure boats docked there and women and men in swimsuits disembarked to mix with the men and women in business suits coming over for lunch from the World Trade Center. By fall, a radio spot was heard one Sunday morning, sponsored by a Baltimore church. "On your way to Harborplace," a voice suggested, "why not stop in for Mass?"

The first major urban mall since Faneuil Hall Marketplace—not a restoration this time but brand-new buildings in a historic waterfront location—was a major success. For Mayor Schaefer it represented vindication and more than relief. Even months after it opened, when I spoke with him in an ornate receiving room in Baltimore's City Hall, he was still emotional. There had been substantial opposition to the plan, culminating in a city-wide referendum in which 40 percent of the voters voted against it. Schaefer himself had postponed development of the cherished Inner Harbor spot, until he met James Rouse and saw what he'd done in Boston.

Like Boston's Marketplace, Harborplace turned out to be both the unifying element for redevelopment already accomplished and a powerful catalyst for more. It linked the rest of the harbor area, from the Science Center to the Convention Center to the World Trade Center. It would attract and serve visitors to the spectacular new National Aquarium, and it would double the number of downtown restaurants in one swoop.

"Harborplace has already accomplished its goals," Schaefer told me. "First, it's known all over the U.S.—all over the world. Second, its brought in a tremendous number of people from outside the city, outside the region. Third, our own people like it. When they go there they feel good, and they feel good about their city."

But for the Rouse Company it was an even sweeter victory. The company knew that it had to prove that Faneuil Hall wasn't just a fluke or a product of a Boston mystique; it needed Harborplace to demonstrate that the ideas behind Faneuil Hall Marketplace were exportable. When Harborplace did just that, a whole new frontier opened up to mall developers, just when they sorely needed it.

For as the 1980s began, the suburbs seemed saturated with malls and other development, especially in the East and Midwest. High construction costs and interest rates, growing zoning and environmental restrictions, and the suburban mall wars added to the woes of developers. But suddenly the Rouse Company had become the prophet of potential profits in an area written off for decades. The city! Who would have guessed?

Suddenly the city made sense for the shopping-mall industry. Rouse's vice-president for public relations, Scott Ditch, rationalized it this way: "The suburban shopping center was an attempt to bring out to the suburbs a little piece of the city. . . . Downtown has always been the place retailing worked best."

But what a difference from even a few years before. In 1975, just months before Quincy Market opened, a city planning consultant and futures analyst who, with Herman Kahn, co-wrote *Things to Come,* B. Bruce Briggs told a receptive International Council of Shopping Centers symposium that cities were "a relic of the past. We may keep some alive as museums."

Museums—or malls? Suddenly cities and developers everywhere were jumping into urban mall development. Waterfront developments ranged from the transformation of the Jackson Brewery in New Orleans into a six-level mall with a one-hundred-foot-high atrium—the first mall in history constructed to have its opening coincide with a World's Fair—to a concrete shopping mall in the shape of a ship at Myrtle Beach, South Carolina. Philadelphia opened Penn Landing; Salem, Massachusetts, christened Pickering Wharf; Seattle unveiled Pike's Place; and new city mall projects— on the waterfront, in historical buildings, or in downtown multiuse centers—were announced for Chicago and Hoboken; Athens, Georgia, and Troy, New York; Cincinnati, Ohio, and Richmond, Virginia; Portland, Oregon, and Portland, Maine; Pittsburgh and Louisville; New York City and Boise, Idaho.

Meanwhile the experts, both in and outside the mall industry, were falling all over one another trying to explain the changes. The new city market was the talk of the shopping-center gathering I attended in Washington. Tourists were showing up in cities instead of just in national parks, one speaker commented, and conventions weren't being outmoded by communications technology, as some people feared, but becoming more popular because of easier and cheaper transportation.

Peter Leibowits, president of Cadillac-Fairview shopping centers, cited social changes: more women working, more singles and childless couples, later marriages and childbirth, and corresponding changes in the American Dream for people who would rather walk to work and see good theater than maintain a half-acre in the suburbs. Another mall official called it part of "the cycle of revolt"—first, cities were rejected for suburbia, and now the fashion was going the other way. "When I was growing up, cities were something that were going to be replaced by something else," said Frank Spink, Jr., a veteran mall developer and shopping-center expert. "But now we're looking to them for opportunities."

In economic terms, the opportunities were being created by growth in white-collar and service sector jobs, finally replacing manufacturing jobs the cities had lost. In 1947 there were more factory workers than office workers in Manhattan's central business district by a margin of 20 percent. By 1977, office jobs were almost double the number of factory jobs. This also held true for cities with a less skyscraper-oriented image than New York. In Baltimore, three out of five adults were white-collar workers by 1980, and even in Pittsburgh—the Steel City—the largest single employer was no longer the Jones and Laughlin steel mill, but the University of Pittsburgh.

A 1977 study by the Department of Housing and Urban Development showed that service and office jobs were growing in more than two thirds of the downtowns surveyed, and that 30 percent to 80 percent of the white-collar jobs were focused in 2 percent or less of the city—in the downtowns. The study concluded that "growth in downtown office space over the past 10 to 15 years has probably been the most radical change experienced by our sample downtowns."

But there was also a growing number of downtown residents, particularly among the young urban professionals of the Baby Boom and after, a category that thanks to the Democratic primary campaign in 1984, became known as the Yuppies.

The Yuppies had a lot to do with the renovation and recycling trend, particularly when they flooded into marginal neighborhoods with cheap but basically sound housing and rehabilitated them in the process known as gentrification. Their dreams had changed from the ones that motivated their parents to create suburbia. What the Yuppies yearned for, according to James Rouse, was "a house in the city, a pair of skis, and baking bread in the oven."

Some saw these signs and became euphoric. "The ambience of the city itself will change in the next few years," according to Herbert Bienstock, an urban analyst at New York City's Queens College. "I think we will begin moving into what I call the Elegant Eighties." There were cautionary voices as well. The population flow was still greater in the direction of suburbia. Some studies showed that more cities were still falling apart than were reviving, and that the deteriorating areas of cities were getting worse at a faster rate than the reviving sections were getting better.

Still, there was a constituency for the right mall in the right place in many cities, and so a technology for the urban mall quickly developed, just as it had for the suburbs. Although other mall executives agreed with his major points, Matt DeVito of the Rouse Company spoke on these matters with a special authority—the authority of success.

In the Rouse Company headquarters at Columbia, Maryland, Matt DeVito was newly ensconced in the chief executive's spacious but homey office, with its endless desk discreetly to the side of a friendly couch-and-coffee-table nook, overlooking a patio that overlooked a man-made lake. James Rouse had retired shortly before Harborplace opened—a somewhat unwilling victim, some thought, of one of his own idealistic pronouncements: that at age sixty-five a person had given enough time to work and should be free to try something else. So, at sixty-five, James Rouse left the Rouse Company—and promptly founded a new one, involved in inner-city rehabilitation, including a couple of familiar-looking waterfront projects in Norfolk, Virginia, and Chicago.

A Rouse Company employee once told me that from the beginning, James Rouse was the visionary who believed that if you met real needs and did things right, you would make money as a consequence. But it was his brother, Willard Rouse, who had been the one to make his visions and ideas work. After Bill Rouse died in 1970, others in the company took on his role.

Matt DeVito seemed dedicated to the ideas of James Rouse, as did the others in the Rouse Company—much as Disney's people were to Walt's. But as we talked, I got the impression that DeVito had more of the practical orientation attributed to Bill Rouse. De-

Vito's style was nuts and bolts, and that's what he talked about in regard to the mall in the city.

The mall is not the salvation of every city, he warned. "There is some kind of retail opportunity in almost every American city," he said, "but many see the success of what we've done and they have overgrandiose ideas."

The first element necessary to a major mall project, where there is a market to support it, is an active and capable city government. Usually, the city government has already exerted leadership in sponsoring and encouraging neighborhood rehabilitation and new white-collar jobs downtown, for these new people in the city are the core of the mall's market. The suburbanites and tourists come later. (Life attracts life.) Large urban malls are also immensely complicated and costly. Government funding and exemptions are deemed crucial at all levels, and city government has to clear the way.

"It is Mayor White who made Faneuil Hall. It is Mayor Schaefer who made Harborplace," DeVito said. "And it is Mayor Koch who will make the Seaport. A suburban mall next to one of these things is a piece of cake."

Then there are the elements of change that developers look for: new office buildings and multi-use centers (especially containing residences), new hotels, a strong commitment to convention trade and tourism. In siting urban malls, the location of such places is crucial, as are cultural and entertainment facilities, particularly large, controlled, mall-compatible enclosures like multipurpose cultural centers and sports arenas. All of this not only creates a constituency but also sets up an atmosphere of activity and glamour in which, as DeVito said, "the city is beginning to look romantic again."

The urban mall responds with a special merchandising mix geared to new urban expectations. Although some city malls contain department stores, many do not. According to Edward Lawrence, researcher for Urban Investment and Development Company, "People won't buy refrigerators downtown anymore, but office workers will buy suits and shoes." So the role of the urban mall is basically as a specialty center, with shops providing service and variety.

Most of all, they must be fun. In explaining the success of Harborplace, Michael Hirten, a Baltimore columnist wrote, "The concept feeds on the simple premise that Americans now consider shopping their favorite leisure pastime."

This was already true in suburbia, and in fact Matt DeVito chose to emphasize not so much how urban malls are different but how they are outgrowths of the suburban experience. "We learned in our suburban malls to prize the individual merchant who could do things with excitement and real flair," he said. "There is a yearning for small, special places, to be 'like the old days.' We also learned that people love to eat—that they would come to a mall just for an eating experience. We were already moving in this direction in the suburban mall."

But in city or suburb, the key is the mall's basic form—what DeVito called "the technology we developed in the suburbs." "The suburban mall is perceived as attractive, safe, comfortable, and dependable, with lots of greenery, lots of light and entertainment. These things work," DeVito said. "They work because a mall has one management that controls the environment, one mall manager who understands that people have to be comfortable. . . . Our mission is to do downtown what has been done in the suburbs."

32

New Illusions: What the Mall Doesn't Do to Save the City

Any city, however small, is in fact divided into two, one the city of the poor, the other of the rich; they are at war with one another.

— PLATO

Within several months in 1980, *New York* magazine went on the stands with two dramatic, and dramatically different covers. INFO CITY! the first proclaimed in yellow letters splashed over a dark-blue computer grid: BEEP! NEW YORK BEEP! IS NOW THE INFORMATION CAPITAL OF THE WORLD."

WOUNDED CITY, the second cover said, in blood-red slashed onto a gray subway wall, its subtitle in graffiti style: WHAT'S HAPPENED TO OUR LIFE HERE?

The first story, by Desmond Smith, proclaimed: "What is now unfolding is the most massive restructuring of the city's economy since the Industrial Revolution." This new economy would be centered in Manhattan, where computerized information-processing systems and telecommunications would lead the way to a postindustrial society of white-collar, high-technology prosperity generating a secondary economy of skilled and unskilled service employment in, for example, the hotel industry.

The second story, by Nicholas Pileggi, began: "Despite an extraordinary midtown building boom, unprecedented tourist growth, 120,000 new private-sector jobs, and a balanced municipal budget, there is a pervasive feeling among New Yorkers today that their city is falling apart." The story cited increased vagrancy, crime, middle-class lawlessness and basic incivility, and the advanced deterioration of the city's infrastructure: public transit, roads, bridges, sewers, and water systems, which made basic survival possible.

New York dramatizes this situation of coexisting extremes and of change going in opposite directions, but the condition is not unique to New York. The contemporary American city is schizophrenic. New Orleans booms with offshore oil and downtown reconstruction, but its streets crumble, its houses deteriorate, the water and transportation systems are antiquated, and the crime rate is high. Boston was indeed successful in transforming its central city and adding thousands of new high-tech jobs, but a 1982 Brookings Institution study found Boston to be among the nine American cities in most serious decline.

On the other hand, cities with much worse reputations show the kind of countersigns that have been Boston's recent glory. Detroit, gripped by economic decline and victim of massive white flight, has been rehabilitating neighborhoods, rebuilding the downtown, and increasing its tourist and convention business. Buffalo, New York, lost 9 percent of its population in the 1970s, but has been filling its downtown waterfront with chic condos and restaurants, including a $177 million complex called Waterfront Village, which features a new yacht marina. Cleveland's near-bankruptcy got national headlines and it was forced to send its schools into receivership, but Cleveland also began a downtown building boom and expanded employment in medical technologies and services. BOOM AND BUST OVERLAP IN CLEVELAND said a *New York Times* headline, but the same applied to other American cities.

"It's a two-city phenomenon," George Sternlieb, director of the Center for Urban Policy Research at Rutgers University, told an ICSC convention audience. "The city of Manhattan, of Society Hill, of upper Michigan Avenue—and the rest of the place. The rest of the place is dying."

The rest of the place is generally nonwhite, non-Info City,

and non-malled. Unemployment among blacks and Latinos was extremely high through the early 1980s and income was low (median income for Puerto Rican families was half the U.S. median). "Historically, New York has had an exploited underclass," Sternlieb told another audience. "Now it has a redundant underclass. There's no role for them."

The urban mall is usually not looking for its markets in this part of the city. "Revitalization is for people who aren't poor," Philadelphia architect Richard Huffman told a reporter.

It is, however, hard to see what the urban mall can do about this. It can employ more people in construction, and in service jobs when it opens, and it can make systematic efforts to employ minorities and help them become entrepreneurs and managers, as Harborplace in Baltimore has done. It can try to attract a wider community with its merchandising. But in its first several years, few blacks were seen at Faneuil Hall Marketplace (possibly because of active discouragement by whites from nearby Charlestown) and even the Gallery in Philadelphia, which is located near a black area, attracts a constituency that is 70 percent white and substantially suburban.

Malls could go into minority areas, and some have been relatively successful. But as an article in *Shopping Centers Today* said, under the apt title MINORITY CENTERS: TOUGH BUT NOT IMPOSSIBLE: "For an industry with bywords like 'disposable income,' minority areas often don't hold great promise."

It was partly for this reason that there has been criticism of public funding participation in urban malls that are essentially private enterprise. Unless mall developers take greater risks, government funding will be necessary for centers in low-income areas, and if the funds—and the attention—are absorbed by the more glittery projects in booming downtowns, such centers will get short shrift. That was precisely the charge made by blacks in North Philadelphia when they criticized the amount of federal funding channeled into the Gallery II project downtown versus the much smaller increment of public funds spent on a modest mall in a black neighborhood, run by the National Business League.

When Benjamin Thompson issued his manifesto to the Wayne State University students, he blamed the environment for problems that were on the face of them at least substantially political and social. But "making the city a fair" doesn't address problems that require political solutions.

There is a danger that the downtown malls and their success gleam so brightly in the eyes of city officials and business people that they are blinded to the problems not only of deteriorating areas but of the basic public infrastructure of the entire city. When that happens, the mall is in danger of becoming a participant in a white, upper-middle-class Info City enclave, a "city within a city," to borrow another phrase from George Sternlieb, as well as from the developee of a Los Angeles downtown complex.

There is evidence that this is beginning to worry the cities. Although Mayor Schaefer of Baltimore easily won reelection, his opponent in the party primary, William Murphy, a black former city judge, made the downtown projects such as Harborplace a major campaign issue in 1983. Murphy claimed that they were part of city policies that ignored the poor and the majority black population, which Schaefer, generally credited with greatly improving Baltimore's neighborhoods, hotly denied. In Boston, after his administration was clouded by scandals involving aides who benefited from property deals on the waterfront, and he was criticized for the overwhelming proportion of his campaign contributions that came from city employees, private contractors who did work for the city, real estate developers, and commercial property owners, Mayor White declined to run again in 1983. The two ultimate mayoral contenders—one of them black—strongly stressed the need to concentrate more on improving housing and business in the city's neighborhoods than on further big downtown projects.

But the urban malls themselves have their own problems. In some ways they are very malleable to external needs and conditions, but they cannot violate their natures as unified, planned, and controlled entities, and that is why they alone can't save the city.

The mall's preplanned, all-at-once development is one of its most valued attributes in planned urban revival. When a mall is placed, its impact is immediate and powerful. Real estate activity booms nearby, and developers of other big projects—hotels, condominiums, arenas—who may have had some doubts, have fewer. All of this seems to prove the aptness of a quotation from nineteenth-century planner Daniel Burnham which James Rouse practically turned into a company motto, and which he repeated at the Great Cities of the World Conference in Boston, an international gathering of officials and scholars: "Make no little plans," Burnham said. "They have no magic to stir men's blood and probably themselves will not be realized. Make big plans. . . ."

But at that conference, Jane Jacobs had a reply. Although she praised Quincy Market and other Rouse city projects, she had a warning: "Big plans can make big mistakes. . . . Even this market, if it becomes the recognized, dogmatic answer to what you do to give people a good time in cities, what you do with old buildings that need recycling . . . it will turn out to be a smotherer, a routinizer. . . . And we'll be sorry if we don't have alternatives.

"If we make these big plans which have to be rigid plans," Jacobs continued, "both in time and scale, we are then in no position to adjust to the effects of our own plans. We're in no position to even acknowledge the effects. We're too committed to what we are doing. And for this reason, I think that all big plans are inevitably big mistakes. That's the way life is. Life is an *ad hoc* affair."

For Jacobs, the city in particular is an *ad hoc* affair. It thrives on unpredictable diversity and on openness to change. In *The Death and Life of Great American Cities,* she stresses the role of old buildings as well as new in the urban mix: "The district must mingle buildings that vary in age and condition including a good proportion of old ones so that they vary in the economic yield they must produce." The reason is simple: Space in old buildings is cheaper to rent, and can be afforded by risky, marginal, maybe innovative or off-the-wall businesses, or even places that make no money at all but add to the life of the community and the liveliness of the street.

The irony of expensively renovated malls is that rehabilitated buildings are no longer old, or cheap. They can cost quite a bit to rehabilitate and still may be more costly to maintain than new buildings. Add this cost to the mall's way of operating, with base rent, overage rent, plus common-area and other mandatory charges that each tenant pays, and businesses aren't going to survive on a shoestring. And the mall, in city as well as suburb, chooses its tenants and decides what they will be allowed to sell, how and where, and for how long.

This affects the very qualities of "specialness" and individual creativity that is supposed to characterize the urban marketplace. I talked to the owner and originator of a business that went into Faneuil Hall in the beginning. "When we started, everybody was excited," she said. "It was a bunch of people who hadn't done anything before, and they were starting their own businesses and really believed in them. We all went in like Mr. Rouse did and took a chance, but now we're getting the shaft and they're making money. A lot of small businesses folded, and the ones who are staying are real tough business people—they've expanded into the spaces of people who left, and they've moved on to other malls, too. But the small businesses that made this place what it is, the original ones on the plaque on the mayor's wall, are getting the shaft."

She talked about lease problems ("We're on a one-year lease now—how can you borrow on that?"), about lack of storage space and frequency of crime, about unfair expenses and demands by management, but mostly she felt tied down by mall rules and their inflexibility. "They're not allowing me to make a living, but we're paying for redesigning their offices. They don't compromise. It's all numbers. This business that I love—I can't do what I want to save it. I can't change design, lighting, hours. I can't change what I sell. I can't even go in there at night without permission. And I can't sell my own business, because it's against the rules."

Faneuil Hall Marketplace had a very high turnover of businesses, mostly because it was so expensive to be there. "When a tenant leaves, it's the fault of two parties—ours and the tenant's," James McLean, manager of the Marketplace, told me. "There's always going to be unhappy people. But businesses here have to do better than even in suburban malls. We don't have big department stores or chains to pick up the slack. The shops have to do it all. This ain't for amateurs. It's for pros."

A normal city street can be for amateurs as well as pros, at least theoretically. In buildings of varying ages and rents, a used-book store, a day-care center, a political storefront, or a store specializing in roasted palm fronds can exist on whatever revenue it can generate or borrow or beg until its owners decide to quit trying. Then a video editing room or a studio for a new dance company can try its luck. Low-profit but needed services are also possible on this kind of street: a shoemaker who is slow but does good work, a grocer who stocks what his customers want without total obeisance to profitability. When an area becomes gentrified and severely fashionable, rents rise and anything not so high-powered fades away. Even in the urban mall, low- or no-profit isn't possible unless the management plans it that way.

Apart from economics, the mall as a rule tries to control everything that goes on within its domain. At Faneuil Hall Marketplace, even the entertainers in the courtyard playing their violins with their cases open for contributions are selected by management and restricted in what they do and for how long. The only kind of diversity a mall can deal with is the diversity it plans and controls.

The urban mall developer may look for originality but usually gets "unique" ideas that collect small items with fast turnover at a stiff price—like stores that sell nothing but banks (antique, new, big, little, piggy) or objects shaped like hearts. When Quincy Market discovered that something called the fruit kabob (sliced fruit on a stick) sold like crazy, many of its food markets started selling similar items. One of the most profitable products in the Marketplace is the chocolate chip cookie.

By the mid-1980s, many cities find themselves awash in "cute-ification." Whether the city can be saved, economically or aesthetically, by the chocolate chip cookie is a question for the future. For the present, however, the urban mall's concentration on such matters and its high rents make the appearance of small but needed services in the mall, or even in the vicinity of the mall, very difficult to find.

Ben Thompson, Faneuil Hall Marketplace's architect, understood some of these problems. He could hardly be unaware of them—Jane Thompson, his wife and colleague, wrote an article for *Urban Design International* magazine which spelled out four basic dilemmas the Marketplace might have to face: proliferation (shops either expanding to other cities, or chains that come in from other urban malls, creating "more of a mass-produced, coast-to-coast image of a shopping mall, and less like Boston's unique place"); homogenization ("Whatever anybody makes money at, everyone else will want to make money at"); physical and aesthetic deterioration; and the deleterious effects of tourism ("Everywhere in America the continued proliferation of T-shirts threatens to build the image of an underwear factory").

Sure enough, all four problems appeared at the Marketplace. It shared shops and chains with Harborplace and other city malls, it went through the fruit kabob panic, tenants have complained about leaky roofs and icy floors, and at least for a while the Marketplace was beset by what one waitress there dubbed "tackola."

Tourism presented a particular danger. The Marketplace originally expected that about 12 percent of its business would come from tourists, but a few years later a conservative estimate put it at one third. This can be dangerous for an urban mall because tourism may be seasonal, and undependable in bad economic times. The low quality of the merchandise can speed deterioration in the mall, which is more or less what happened at the Atlanta Underground, an urban mall that used actual old Atlanta streets, unearthed from beneath an underpass, below the level of present streets. It eventually closed down. That's one difference high-risk urban malls must pay attention to, for while large suburban malls almost never fail, city ones can.

Ben Thompson talked to me about some of these problems between slide shows in his Cambridge office. "We've succeeded somewhat. We'll probably get better as time goes on. We work within limits. We don't always have freedom of choice," he said. "Sometimes it comes down to your ability to convince people—but maybe that day you're tired."

Thompson was following his own thoughts, yet was anxious, it seemed, to take me into the process of his thinking. He wasn't exactly defending himself; he was sharing his problems.

"It took a lot of doing to talk people into having a bread shop at Faneuil Hall," he said. "A sidewalk café in Boston? Well, they're all over Europe. They're nothing to get frightened about.

"The American tradition is not to do these things in the city. People said, 'Who will take care of the flowers? Vandals will smash out the lights.' But the fact is that vandalism is very low at Faneuil Hall. Disney discovered that if maintenance is high, it sets standards of acceptable behavior, so people don't litter much.

"We haven't got the variety we want," he admitted. "They need variety of common services—places to get a key made, buy an aspirin. But that can come later. The reason that a town like Hyannis survives is that it has the post office, telephone company, the dentists. If every place is a gift shop, it won't work."

Then Thompson ran some slides of the Quincy Market buildings, before and after their rehabilitation. He pulled out a tray of the opening of Harborplace in Baltimore, with the balloons and the fireworks over the harbor. "One of the happiest parts of looking at that—I haven't looked at it in three weeks—is the looks on people's faces," he said. "You spend a lot of time dealing with leaky roofs. But the responsiveness is what all this is for."

Then he talked about Venice. "There are cafés in San Marco

Square that have been there for hundreds of years. Venice was created by artists, common people, musicians—not city planners and developers."

Thompson pulled out one more tray of slides, of Venice. "Before we leave today," he said to me, "let's look at these, and dream."

33

Let Us Dream: Venice, the Quixote People, New York's Seaport, and the Malling of Time

In the center of Fedora, that gray stone metropolis, stands a metal building with a crystal globe in every room. Looking into each globe, you see a blue city, the model of a different Fedora. These are the forms the city could have taken if, for one reason or another, it had not become what we see today. In every age someone, looking at Fedora as it was, imagined a way of making it the ideal city, but while he constructed his miniature model, Fedora was already no longer the same as before, and what had been until yesterday a possible future became only a toy in a glass globe.

—ITALO CALVINO
Invisible Cities

In the early afternoon a smattering of sun fell on the tourists marching and meandering across the Piazza San Marco. There was the chatter of several languages and the flapping of pigeon wings, and a small ensemble of instruments played "New York, New York." The waiters at the café tables were hurrying, watching the approaching clouds. Then the rain came, and the crowds put on their translucent rain wraps, tinted pink and green, and scattered to the surrounding arcades, where they filled the restaurants, the sheltered café tables, and the shops, and circulated in a plastic parade behind their tour leaders.

Suddenly the square was empty, and the imagination could freely wander across its silent expanse, to try to feel the inconceivable centuries of solemnity and blood, beauty and plague, and the moments of those different worlds enacted here on these stones. When the rain stopped and the people returned, it became clear that it is not only the cathedral and the palace that gives the Piazza San Marco its endurance, but also the yellow chairs of the cafés.

Ben Thompson was right: To dream about American cities and their malls is to dream about Europe—its cafés and restaurants, its arcades and squares, and now, its shopping malls too.

Can an American city—or a city mall—aspire to the condition of Venice? I went there and to a few other European cities after my American mall trek had pretty well been completed, and looked around with that question in mind.

Venice, of course, is not itself a mall, nor does it have one, exactly. But it does have certain features that would make it interesting to mall designers and analysts. First of all, like the mall it is a carless environment, which deeply benefits the atmosphere of Venice. When you walk through narrow streets and across wide squares, part of the magic lies in fully experiencing the sights and sounds before you while, at the same time, you anticipate what wonders might be around the next corner: perhaps a palace, or a vendor of ices; the silent tributary of a canal, or an orator beside an artist's easel. The intense quiet in some places quickens that anticipation, as well as sharpening your ability to respond to the bursts of language and music and color.

All of this is much different from the ambience of Florence, another Italian city known for art and history, which I visited immediately after Venice. The constant clamor of traffic noise and the need to jump out of the way of kamikaze cars and motorbikes on the narrow twelfth-century streets of Florence—which is jarring enough for a first-time visitor to any Italian city—was, after Venice, shocking to the marrow.

Still, Venice had become a tourist attraction, and responded with obvious changes. Each small, narrow street, or *calle,* around the Piazza San Marco was now jammed with posh shops for visitors armed with American Express, Visa, and Eurocard. The shops were arrayed along the calles in a configuration very much in vogue among American mall designers. Like the narrow, twisting streets of the Latin Quarter of Paris, the Place de Clichy and the Boulevard

St.-Michel, the crowded riot of colorful, small-scaled shops in the compressed area of these calles has become a mall model.

But there was still the enduring, ancient magnificence that has survived all this neon and tourism, if only barely. High above the shops and shoppers rose the upper floors of beautiful buildings, displaying their astounding age and resilience simply by being there. The effects of aging were clearly visible but added to the beauty of these buildings, like the old weathered faces looking out impassively from the high windows.

Shopping has achieved in Venice, as in tourist attractions everywhere, its own *raison d'être*. The Venice merchandise seemed no different from that in Paris, and most of it could be found in New York. Shopping has simply become the sport of middle-class travelers, their movable feast. There is no escaping the feeling that it could overrun and even destroy Venice; at the same time, tourist interest seems crucial in keeping the city's ancient treasures from melting away.

Venice has many problems, beyond its embrace of tourism: Its population has declined precipitously (from about 200,000 a generation ago to around 85,000), industrial pollution has accelerated the decay of statues and palaces, while poverty and complacency have allowed the deterioration of other buildings to go unchecked. Still, some preservation goes on—aided in part by the characteristically American can-do spirit of such groups as the Friends of Venice in Dallas and the America-Italy Society of Philadelphia. Venice also retains a loyal core of permanent citizens, some by birth and others by conversion to the city's beauty and way of life.

At times, and to many travelers, Venice seems only a museum hosting a tourist amusement park (but one not so clean, efficient or amusing as Disneyland) and therefore not much different in kind from American city malls. But these calles and canals, these piazzas and cathedrals have seen more than a thousand years of history—not only of wars, empires, and epoch-making innovations in science, art, commerce, and politics, but of the constant daily activities of people living in a continuity of culture. San Marco is not simply the name of a cathedral and a square where strangers sip soft drinks and buy tour maps, but—as every citizen knows—San Marco is the city's patron saint, the battle cry of Venetian soldiers in the Battle of Agnadello in 1509 and of the peasants who fought against Napoleon's invasion almost three hundred years later. Most of us visiting Venice know little of this and understand less. The population of Venice at any given moment is now composed of tourists who will be here for an average of eighteen hours, and of residents whose families have been walking these steps and crossing these squares for more than ten centuries. That gives this city its strange vitality, and makes it so haunting.

The dilemma of Venice may simply be that it is not adding to its history. Yet it does have an indigenous life separate from its imperial past and its tourist present. For the Piazza San Marco is not the only square in Venice. I spent a Sunday morning in another; it was simply a wide paved expanse around a fountain, with a few cafés with seats jutting out into the square. Church bells rang all morning and tourists crossed the square with packages, but the people who lived around it came out in the sun to stop for a moment by the fountain; while children played, a mother grabbed their soccer ball and kicked it soundly against an ancient wall, to the children's amazement. The modern world—television, feminism, rock music, tourism—has changed daily life in Italy and in cities and villages across Europe. But the traditional society of the piazzas very often has absorbed the changes and endured. The communal life of the square, or the public gardens in Milan, the plaza in a Spanish town, has never been completely lost, so it doesn't need to be artificially recovered. It doesn't necessarily prevent change; it absorbs it and itself changes without losing its character. It is a still point in a turning world. It is, in short, a place—a visible place in the invisible city.

Milan, a large and bustling city, is not high on the list of tourist destinations in Italy. But on this malling holiday it was a must, for it contains one of the great shopping-center shrines: the Galleria Vittorio Emanuele. When Victor Gruen designed Southdale, the first enclosed mall in America, he pointed to this Galleria as its antecedent. But the Galleria is more than history; it is a lesson for the present, especially for malls in the American city.

The Galleria, designed by architect Giuseppe Mengoni, began construction in 1865 and was completed in 1877. It combines the cool and quiet arcades that can still be seen in central Milan—far back from the street in green and quiet exclusivity under domes and arches—with the city's monumental architecture, its central train station, the huge marble and stone bank buildings, and other structures dating from the nineteenth century, as well as the ancient monuments: La Scala, the center of Italian opera, and the Duomo, the great cathedral that lies just beyond the Galleria and which was itself only completed in 1858, although it was begun almost five hundred years earlier.

So the Galleria was an appropriate part of this city from the beginning. "The new Galleria is truly a beautiful thing," composer Giuseppe Verdi wrote to a friend: "In our country still there is the sense of the *Great* united to the *Beautiful*."

To contemporary eyes as well, the Galleria is of operatic scale. It is literally an indoor street, with immense, solid, weather-worthy walls rising to meet semitransparent arched ceilings and a central glass dome. These are buildings with an architecture of external stone turned inward, with real windows and balconies facing in. The Galleria radiates from the central dome with two long spokes connecting a major street with the Piazza del Duomo and two shorter spokes perpendicular to the main ones leading to other streets. Like a cathedral, it is in the shape of a cross, and its frescoes and other decorations as well as its size make it a commercial companion to the cathedral just beyond its portals.

Under its stone arches are shops; Flograna has the best in women's clothes, Barbisso da Rossi has hats, Duroni Ottica sells eyeglasses, and Gadgets sells gadgets. There are department stores, restaurants, and cafés with tables on the covered street (and the largest café, Motta, has some outside as well). People pass through it constantly, a mixture of city citizens and visitors: a man with his jacket draped over his shoulders (a happy movie cliché), a girl in an I LOVE NY T-shirt, a stringy young man with long beard and faded jeans, uniformed soldiers of several nations, kids on bikes, women with packages, a man walking his bulldog.

The Galleria is a literal crossroads for this city, and not only for visitors to the nearby Duomo and La Scala and the tourists who come specifically to see it; it is said that in the normal course of a business day, most of the people in central Milan pass through the Galleria. This is cause for major envy on the part of American urban mall designers. The Galleria lies at what planners call a 100 percent location—a place where everybody is bound to pass and there is activity around the clock. Such locations in American cities have been largely lost, especially in the postwar period of suburbanization.

European cities like Milan and Paris also have major suburbs, but the urban core has always retained its centrality, especially for the more affluent and city-bred who were not about to leave behind a cultural life that has taken centuries to build. It is the less affluent and the immigrants from villages and other countries who live in suburban housing that is no less tacky than the worst American tracts.

American cities, untouched by the devastation of war, were instead devastated by social change and their own actions. "You have to face this fact," urban expert George Sternlieb told a luncheon audience at an ICSC convention: "The one hundred percent locations are not in the cities anymore. The one hundred percent locations are where the freeways meet." That, of course, is where the malls went, so perhaps it is fitting that the first American Galleria was in the suburbs. Now in American cities the urban malls cannot rely on the existence of 100 percent locations; they have to create them.

Even in European cities there are places that have been irrevocably changed by the effects of technology and the march of time. As in America, one such former 100 percent location was the central market, but for very large cities a single market where meat, produce, and other goods had to be trucked in through traffic (partly caused by all the customers who had to get to the same market at the same time) no longer made practical sense. In London and Paris, for example, the central markets were deteriorating and finally abandoned. In both cases, they have recently been replaced by variations on the shopping mall.

Covent Garden in London is the more modest example. In its appearance it resembles Faneuil Hall Marketplace in Boston, although it seems to be larger. It has a familiar mix of small shops and restaurants in the refurbished buildings—called, in standard mall terseness, the Market—and a sparse but attractive architecture that does not suffer from overrestoration to a high polish. Near the Covent Garden Market when I visited it was a kind of pushcart flea market, much larger and a good deal less organized than the Faneuil Hall attempt. There were performers in the courtyard, too, and even a few apparently authentic soapbox orators.

A more dramatic change was apparent in the old market area of Paris at Les Halles. The cycle of destruction and construction that has completely transformed this huge site began in the 1970s and continues in the 1980s. First, the old market buildings were demolished and the entire area excavated for the Paris Metro and underground parking garages. Then new landscaping and building began, climaxing (if not ending) in the Forum Les Halles, an enclosed mall containing some two hundred shops, at least sixteen restaurants, and other facilities.

The Forum had shopping-mall elements most Americans would recognize: the fake street signs inside, the electric directory of mall shops, and many of the shops themselves—Ted Lapidus, Charles Jourdan, Bally, as well as such familiar types as Video Club, Durotennis, Atomic City (youth fashions), and Game's, and fast-food outlets like Taites & Galettes and La Pizza.

Forum Les Halles was linked by a pedestrian-only area to that controversial shopping mall of the arts, the Centre Georges Pompidou. The entire area became the most active and booming part of Paris, a gathering place for tourists and Parisians, and revived surrounding streets with new shops and restaurants. This success confounded many of its critics. But Forum Les Halles works for the reasons malls are supposed to—it's a controlled, managed, pedestrian fantasyland. It works better than an enclosed mall here might be expected to, partly because it has aesthetic flair. It mixes contemporary and traditional styles and materials—Plexiglas and stone, marble and neon—in symphonic combination. It also succeeds partly because the Parisian culture is strong enough to adapt and to make its new institutions adapt to it, even if they look like airports.

This may be a mall, but inside it sells fresh meat the way Parisians are used to buying it, and its cafés and courtyards are nothing new to the students drifting over from the Louvre and the Pompidou. When I was there, young people sprawled against an impressive outdoor sculpture to read in the sun, while shoppers sat at café tables nearby, reading newspapers. The wide plazas do not alienate or confuse Europeans as they sometimes do urban Americans; these spaces are simply used, for promenades and for children to run in and ride their tricycles. I even saw one child rolling a hoop, and immediately recalled the same image in a painting by Giorgio de Chirico of a town plaza and the surrealism of everyday life.

Maybe it was mostly my own romanticism about Europe that made these places seem successful. But I think it also had something to do with the sense of credibility that seems to be at the heart of European culture. Richard Eder, reporter for *The New York Times,* once wrote about a Parisian restaurant where "precision is at the heart of the warmth and cheerfulness." Then, expanding his examination to Paris in general, he asked himself, "Why is there such gleaming order—glasses, linen, fresh flowers—in the humblest restaurant at the start of the lunch hour?" Later in the piece, Eder answered: "What is worth doing is worth doing well is more or less the idea. . . . Their talent is to come between bombshells, attentively reconstruct the civilized detail of nonheroic times, and believe that this, if it does not endure, will at any rate recur."

This does not seem to be a major tenet of faith in the much younger America. It also isn't very modern. Credibility of this kind doesn't seem to impress the American consumer; it is only the response to the momentary impulse, the persuasive novelty, that is convincing.

A firestorm of expensive development around it could still ruin the Forum Les Halles area. When I was there, a good part of its charm was in contrasts: the corner where the Rue St.-Denis crosses Rue Rambuteau, for example. I sat there at a sidewalk table and watched a steady flow of all kinds of people: blue-collar and white-collar workers, students, middle-class visitors from other parts of France, tourists from other countries, all mingling in a very colorful and somewhat seedy area of cut-rate clothing racks, sex shops (LIFE SHOW—SWEET GILRS, said the marquee of one) and fast food, but not far from such elegant old cafés as Aux Deux Saules. The atmosphere here was quietly electric—everyone looked at everyone else. It was not bawdy, not intellectual, not fashionable, not earthy or hungry or coy. It was all of these things. It was sexy.

More recent visitors to the area have observed that while new businesses opened in wider area, there was still a mix of the inexpensive and casual and even lunatic along with the posh and pricey. If so, perhaps it is due also to the wider variation that Europeans seem to bring to the whole matter of rehabilitating and restoring old buildings. I was impressed by the sense of appropriateness in the restorations I saw. For example, in Paris I stayed part of the time in a Holiday Inn—but it was no normal Holiday Inn. It was a huge Belle Époque building dating from 1866, with magnificent courtyards and appointments that were appropriately restored to splendor. It was in the center of the Place de la République, and it fit perfectly in style and scale with the surrounding buildings.

From there, I walked one evening to dinner at the Restaurant Chartier in what used to be a library. This building had probably never been magnificent; it had simply been old and useful. Now it was a restaurant, and there was no attempt either to disguise the fact that it had been a library or to make it a decorative theme. It was in fact an unreasonably cheap restaurant frequented by students

and others looking for a budget meal. Everyone sat at large tables
and the turnover was rapid. I sat next to a French student who
knew enough English (since my French was so bad) that we could
communicate with the aid of words we wrote and diagrams we
drew on our paper tablecloth, but no sooner had we finished dessert
than the tablecloth was whisked away and a new one slapped down
for the next seating.

There's little doubt what might be done with such an eating
place in America. It would become a glossy theme restaurant with
menus printed on scrolls or fake books, and waitresses wearing
phony glasses and visors. It must be fun the first time. But food
would be more expensive, and not nearly as good. It is true, as Ben
Thompson said, that Europe proves that old buildings don't have
to be museums. But Europe also proved to me that old buildings
don't have to be malls.

> It does seem to me, that herein we see the rare virtue
> of a strong individual vitality, and the rare virtue of
> thick walls, and the rare virtue of interior spa-
> ciousness. O, man! admire and model thyself after
> the whale! Do thou, too, remain warm among ice.
> Do thou, too, live in this world without being of it.
> Be cool at the equator; keep thy blood fluid at the
> Pole. Like the great dome at St. Peter's, and like the
> great whale, retain, O man! in all seasons a tem-
> perature of thine own.
> —HERMAN MELVILLE
> *Moby Dick*

There now is your insular city of Manhattan, belted round by
wharves as Indian isles by coral reefs; commerce surrounds it with
her surf. Right and left, the streets take you waterward. In the extreme downtown is the South Street Seaport, the birthplace of this
city and an old public marketplace, more recently an official historical district and, as of the summer of 1983, host to the most ambitious urban mall project developed by the Rouse Company.

In a four-block area, this mix of rehabilitated nineteenth-century
buildings and new structures housing shops, offices, and apartments, as well as the reconstructed Seaport Museum, was inaugurated by the governor of New York and the mayor of New York

City. Opening-night notices from the *New York Times* architecture critic Paul Goldberger were good. While acknowledging that the recent raffishness of the area was totally gone, he called the Seaport "as elaborate an evocation of the New York of the nineteenth century as we are ever likely to see . . . an evocation done, for the most part, with neither the literalness of Colonial Williamsburg nor the cuteness of Disneyland." It comes closer, he wrote, "to containing the real energy of a city than any other such project anywhere else" and proclaimed that it "manages to have a lot of life to it for a place that is planned down to the last square inch."

Soon after this grand opening, the tour buses came, and people shopped at Ann Taylor and Pineapple Primitives, Burger Boys of Brooklyn and Gaylord's Saffron, Laura Ashley and Zaro's Bread Basket. Much more of the Seaport project would open the next year, leading the commercial revival of New York City's waterfronts. Eight major riverside projects were planned for the other side of the city alone. "Someday the river between Manhattan and Queens will be like Venice," said developer Tino Scarpa, who was born in Milan and immigrated to New York in 1961. "Boats will flow back and forth at all times of the night and day."

The Seaport project was controversial for several years before it was built. The eleven-block historical district is operated by the South Street Seaport Museum, a nonprofit educational corporation chartered by the state of New York in 1967, and charged with the responsibility of preserving the area, as well as the last sailing ships and other artifacts of its three centuries of glory, which lasted into the early 1900s. This was the last substantial area of buildings from the nineteenth century and earlier that was left in Manhattan.

But when the commercial project at South Street Seaport was first discussed, the issue wasn't whether or not to preserve historical buildings (that had been decided), or how best to revive this area of the city (although the skyscrapers pressing upon its borders demanded some decision on that). The main issue was how the nature as well as the existence of the Seaport would be best preserved.

That issue hadn't been raised to quite such an extent in previous urban projects, and this time it was raised almost as much in response to those projects as it was to the special situation of the Seaport itself. The first president of the South Street Seaport Museum, Peter Stanford, opposed a single major commercial development, which he called "a superfunded superblitz." But he was succeeded as president by John Hightower, formerly the director of

New York's Museum of Modern Art and party to the decision to use the Modern's air rights to build a commercial high-rise above its old midtown structure as a way to guarantee its long-term financial security. That project involved an architect and architectural firm (Victor Gruen Associates) with experience in mall design.

Hightower supported a single large development done by a single large developer for the Seaport. "With major development, we at the museum can achieve in five years what it might have taken twenty-five," Hightower said. In his view, the income derived from the Seaport Museum's share of the commercial development's profits, as well as the four-block restoration itself, was necessary to support the work that had to be done on the remaining seven blocks of quickly deteriorating buildings. It would fund the work necessary to focus on the historic character of the area, which was the museum's educational mission. It would also bring a lot of people to see it.

In the face of uncertain government and private philanthropic support, the partnership between private enterprise and a nonprofit institution was, in this view, simply facing reality. According to Hightower, "The fact is that shopping is the chief cultural activity in the United States." Those who continued to ignore this perhaps unpleasant fact were, in the somewhat petulant words of another museum official, "the Quixote people."

One of the Quixote people tilting at the Seaport mall was Paul Goldberger's predecessor as architecture critic at the *Times,* Ada Louise Huxtable. Once the Rouse project was announced with the enthusiastic backing of Mayor Edward Koch, Huxtable wrote of her own deep ambivalence: "I have very mixed feelings for the Seaport. I guess that what I'm really doing is saying goodbye. Because what will surely be lost is the spirit and identity of the area as it existed over centuries—something that may only be important to those who have loved the small shabby streets and buildings redolent of time and fish, or shared the cold sunlight of a quiet winter Sunday morning on the waterfront with the Fulton Market cats, when the 19th century still seemed very much alive."

There was already a collection of shops and eating places in the old Fulton Market building (since torn down and replaced) when I visited the Seaport several months before the Rouse construction began. The food area was particularly busy; Wall Streeters in three-piece suits mixed with construction workers in overalls, and the mail carrier paused in his appointed rounds for lunch amid the booths selling pizza, pastries, Chinese food, health food, and one featuring a mixed Argentine and Italian menu. Mostly, though, the lunch crowd was lining up for portions of fish and chips and the large, cheap paper containers of beer from Jeremy's New York, New York.

But clearly this wasn't going to attract an urban mall's audience. The pale-green paint was peeling off the rough walls, the lights hung from steel girders, and the cement floors were pockmarked. Jeremy's had hand-lettered signs, a tin can for tips, and puddles of beer and water around its bare plank platform.

The ambivalence Huxtable wrote about is not restricted to the Seaport; it is endemic to projects like it. Calvin Trillin, for example, expressed it in his *New Yorker* essay, "Thoughts Brought On by Prolonged Exposure to Exposed Bricks," in which he reviewed several East Coast waterfront revivals. After wondering how all the new restaurants in such places suddenly knew what kind of cheese to put on their Special Sandwiches, and to insert celery stalks in their Bloody Marys, Trillin reflected, "My thoughts were interrupted by the realization that I had rather enjoyed the special sandwich at the Seamen's Club and I don't really mind a celery stalk in my Bloody Mary."

The ambivalence is brought on by the comprehensive newness and suspicious glitz, by the persistence of similarities among such "special" places, at the same time that new light and color and energy, food and drink and safety, are creating new pleasures, new access to old places, perhaps even new avenues to meaning. But in a basic sense this ambivalence is rooted in questions that such planned and managed projects raise about time and reality, and answer with their own peculiar ambiguity.

One of the effects of the Seaport project and similar ones may be to preserve visible elements of the past, but that is not altogether their purpose. "If I had to sum up Faneuil Hall Marketplace in one word," its manager told me, "it would be 'entertainment.'" Few in the urban mall business—in the megastructure or festival marketplace end of it—would dispute that assessment. However different in style or quality, the Seaport is linked by that purpose to the enclosed historical revival mall in Washington, D.C., Georgetown Park, of which Goldberger wrote, "It is clearly serious design, not cheap commercialism, and yet it carries the notion of the stage set as a retail environment farther than we have yet seen it go." It is also conceptually linked to Peter's Landing, a waterfront retail and office center in Huntington Beach, California, which was designed to resemble a French Mediterranean coastal village, and to Ocean One, a three-deck concrete mall in the shape of a ship, on a pier at Atlantic City. All of these use some element of a city's history—or simply the idea of "history" or "long ago and far away"—to create an image, an identity. Historic preservation or replication is an advertisement for the city and its nature as a place with a past. It is history as entertainment.

The American city has reached an intriguing point. In a sense, the all-new, all-at-once mall project is exactly American in its treatment of time. "The sense of the past is a precious commodity that has always been in short supply in America," writes Morris Dickstein, author on popular culture, in an article in *American Film.* "Some of our founders dreamed of making a clean break with history, leaving behind the corruption of the Old World. Their hopes materialized in a land that threw off the shackles of tradition and devoted itself passionately to expansion and change. The English, the Italians, and the French live with moments of their history as permanent companions inhabiting a visible landscape."

This is America, which derived much of the energy that is the envy of Europe from ignoring the constraints of the past. So much of America's brief history has simply been overrun by its own momentum—a society bolting forward while undergoing constant transformation, like waves of an army whose forward battalions are on horseback but whose rear guard arrives already in rockets. Inevitably, the belated decision to recapture history employs means that are artificial and sometimes simply comic. On my first visit to Harborplace in Baltimore, I was standing on the observation deck of the World Trade Center, looking out at the panorama of the Inner Harbor and listening to Lori Kranz, the Rouse Company representative, present her charming and informative explication of the project, when I suddenly was startled by a loud noise that sounded a great deal like a foghorn trapped inside skyscraper walls. That, as Lori Kranz told me, was exactly what it was. Since there were no foghorns in the harbor anymore, a recording of one was featured as part of the historical exhibit that surrounded us.

The ambivalence continues at South Street Seaport. . . . But look! Here come more crowds, pacing straight for the water, and seemingly bound for a dive. Strange! Nothing will content them but the extremest limit of the land; loitering under the shady lee of yonder skyscrapers will not suffice. Do they come—like Herman

Melville's inlanders whom he watched here at the Seaport, a few blocks from his birthplace—for the dream of escape to the sea? Or escape only into the belly of the beached and gleaming, wondrous and safe, thrilling and controlled White Whale in awesome replica? Do they at least come not only for the plumage of Foofaraw and Everything Yogurt, the theatrical interiors, the plastic shadows heaped on countertops, the artificial atmosphere of an eternal seaside fair, but also drawn by the grinding water and the gasping wind, to wonder at the way the lights of the Seaport master the night and portion out the sea?

Some come off tour buses, tour the marketplace, and, like visitors to the casinos of Vegas and Atlantic City (or Atlantic City's Ocean One mall, and The Fashion Show on the Vegas strip), climb back aboard their buses without glancing at the surrounding area, the other unmerchandised blocks of the Seaport. Are they only representatives of a hapless and disconnected middle class, parading like lemmings to the water's edge, to sip martinis and buy stuffed animals? Do they seek merely to take pleasure in the physicalization of images they know only from movies and television, from technicolor harbors and *The Love Boat*?

Again, the ambivalence. What's wrong with pleasure taken in eyeing products while being tingled by a river breeze? Of the touch of real wood and stone, the alternatives to plastics and speed, refuse and high-rise sophistication? Why be so *serious* about it? But the sea is more than an amenity to the Quixote people. The sea, the river, are at once unchangeable points that locate the landscape, and visible proof of an ever-changing, ever-receding reality.

But apart from changing the acts when the audience gets bored, can time be allowed to happen in a show? City malls are still fairly new, so it may yet happen. I got the sense that it was starting to happen at Harborplace when I visited it again after all the grand boosterism and the first grand failures. Will South Street Seaport be a successful part of its city, continuous with its past, true to its present, and illuminating both? Only time will tell.

Yet despite the authentic and illuminating museum exhibits and restorations, the new Seaport itself tilts against time. The artificiality of a one-period restoration like Williamsburg is replaced by an image of History—with strolling minstrels in medieval costumes—that becomes absurd and, finally, abstract.

"Europe's landscapes are a metaphor of its entire past," wrote Czeslaw Milosz, the Nobel Prize-winning Lithuanian-born poet.

"The abstract city and the abstract theater of nature, something one drives past, are the American metaphor." In a sense the new city revivals are not so far from the suburbs after all. The new city people patronize these packages of carefully designed images much as suburbanites flock to their controlled environments. City people might reexamine their snobbishness toward the shopping center. They go down to the sea in malls.

Part 5
MALLAISE (EXEGESIS AND EXAMPLES)

It is the transition from a culture based on the curbing of desires, thriftiness and the necessity of eking out goods in short supply to a new culture resulting from production and consumption at their highest ebb, but against a background of general crisis.
—HENRI LEFEBVRE
Everyday Life in the Modern World

34

Mallaise:
How to Know If You Have It

Malls make some people sick. Literally, sometimes. They feel fe-
verish, their eyes glaze, their stomachs tumble, they fall down, they
throw up.

Some people are just annoyed by one or another aspect of a
mall, or a nonspecific quality of a particular mall, or malls in general. "That mall makes me *sick!*" they say. Or "I don't like malls—I
hate them." Malls make people angry. Some of these people are
shoppers, but some are people who work in malls or even own
mall stores.

Malls affect people. They're designed to. But in some ways,
either by their nature or by a side effect caused by their main ingre-
dients, they do things to people that people are unaware of or don't
understand, but if they knew or understood, they probably
wouldn't like it.

There are other more obvious things that happen to people in malls that they don't or wouldn't like. Crime, for instance.

This section of *The Malling of America* is about some of the negative aspects of malls that affect people and that people perceive. Does the mall make you tired? Set your nerves on edge? Do you find it difficult to concentrate? Do you feel the absence of certain phenomena—weather, for example, or civil liberties? Do you sometimes wonder if you are really as safe as mall management would like you to believe?

If you're a parent, do you fear for your children's ability to survive outside comfort control because they spend so much time in the mall? And if you're an adolescent, do you feel your horizons becoming limited to a hundred chain store-outlets and three anchor department stores? Or are you worried that this is precisely the world your parents do live in, and where they want you always to remain?

These are some of the symptoms of mallaise. Perhaps you have one or two, or know someone who does, or perhaps you want to be prepared, just in case. Then perhaps you should read on.

I had my first attack of *mal de mall* in Columbia, Maryland. I was in a restaurant in the Columbia Mall having coffee. The attack was characterized by feverishness, sudden fatigue, and high anxiety, all recurring whenever I glanced out at the mall itself. The thought of going out there again made me sweat and swoon, and I had to fight the hallucinatory certainty that when I left the restaurant I would be in Greengate mall, or maybe Woodfield, or Tysons Corner. Or *all* of them.

Mal de mall, or mall sickness, is one of the classifications of mallaise, the general term for physical and psychological disturbances caused by mall contact. I know because I made them all up. Among the symptoms I have personally observed or heard about from their victims are these:

Dismallcumbobulation: "I don't like to go to malls because I always get lost," a woman told me, "and that's embarrassing. I feel stupid. It makes me mad." The hyped-up overabundance of similar products plus the bland sameness of many mall environments make people feel lost even when they aren't. Even familiar malls relocate stores and reconfigure themselves, which adds to the feeling of a continuous featureless space. And the similarity of one mall to another is disorienting. You walk out of the Stuft Potato and you not

only don't remember which way your car is, you might not remember what mall this is. There are other kinds of dismallcumbobulation: the loss of a sense of time as well as place, and
forgetting one's purpose in coming to the mall—all of which can
lead to apathy and hopelessness, loss of consciousness, or fainting.
Some victims recommend deep-breathing exercises every fifteen
minutes while at the mall.

Inability to Relate to Others: "It's impossible to talk to someone
when you're shopping at the mall," a friend told me, explaining
why she prefers to shop alone. "I notice it at the mall all the time—
you see two people together but they aren't really talking to each
other. They're talking, but they're staring off in different directions, and pretty soon they just wander away from each other."
Among the possible effects of this symptom are disenchantment
and divorce.

Plastiphobia, or the fear of being enclosed in a cocoon of
blandness. "Suddenly I just stood still and looked around," a young
man said. "I saw all the people and what we were all doing there,
what we were spending our day doing, and I suddenly just couldn't
wait to get out. I was in a plastic place with plastic people buying
plastic products with plastic charge cards. I had to escape." Sometimes this reaction is accompanied by severe anxiety, alienation
from the human race, and in at least one very severe case I know of,
by all the usual manifestations of a drug overdose.

All of these, and their variations, are unfortunate side effects (or
perhaps just extreme cases) of the main psychological effects that
the mall intends. Excitement may become overstimulation; relaxa-
tion may drift into confusion and torpor. The combination is what
I call the Zombie Effect.

There is, in fact, a fine line between the ideal mall shopper and
the dismayed mall shopper, between mall bliss and mallaise, between the captivated shopper and the Zombie Effect. The best description of the Zombie Effect I've heard was Barbara Lambert's,
which she imparted while we toured the malls of Chicagoland.

It hits you, Barbara said, when you're standing there naked,
looking in the mirror of the dressing room. Your clothes are in a
pile on the floor or draped over a chair. Maybe it's just a little
cubicle with a curtain, and you can still hear the hum and buzz of
the mall and the tiny timbres of Muzak. You're about to try something on, in an effortless repetition of what you've been doing since
you came to the mall. And suddenly you realize *you've been here all*

day. Time has in fact been passing while you've been gliding through store after store in a tender fuzz of soft lights and soft music. The plash of fountains, the glow of people, but almost no intrusive sound has broken your floating—no telephone, no demands, nothing to dodge or particularly watch out for. Just a gentle visual parade of clothes, fabric tags, and washing instructions. Racks, displays, cosmetics, brisk signs, flowing greenery, and spasms of color in the dream light. An ice-cream cone, a cup of coffee. Other figures have glided by: walking models of the mall's products, or walking models of the weird. An old man who reminds you of your grandfather, sitting on a blond-wood bench under a potted palm. A woman who may or may not have been your best friend's other best friend in high school, striding by on strange shoes—or maybe that's a new style and yours are strange? You're looking at your naked image in a bare little room, and a little breeze touches you. Whatever you actually came here for is in the distant past. You've been floating here . . . for hours.

But that's the whole idea of this psychological structure: to turn off your mind and let you float; to create a direct and unfettered connection between eyeing and buying; and the more you do, the easier it becomes. Malls make for great eye/hand-on-credit-card coordination.

The way it's done is with a combination of peacefulness and stimulation. The environment bathes you in sweet neutrality with soft light, candied music, and all the amenities that reassure and please without grabbing too much individual attention. At the same time, the stores and products dance for you with friendly smiles and colorful costumes. The sheer number of products and experiences you pay for and their apparent variety are in themselves factors that excite and focus.

Once again, it's all a lot like television. TV lulls and stimulates simultaneously. The medium itself is familiar and comfortable and friendly; the programs can be interesting but it is not really by accident that they are not as compact, colorful, dramatic, or insistent as the commercials. Watching television we are everywhere and nowhere in particular, just as at the mall. Suddenly you might realize that you've been watching it all day, just floating for hours. And if you look at people watching television—especially their eyes—they look pretty much like mall shoppers: the Zombie Effect.

But these effects are all supposed to be pleasant and unconscious. When either the lulling or stimulating quality—or especially the combination and conflict between them—is strongly felt, then it's no longer pleasant. Overstimulation causes anxiety, and sometimes an intense focus on heavy-duty, no-nonsense, get-out-of-my-way shopping, or else a frenzied need to get out of there, fast and forever. The lulling and sense deprivation cause listlessness and confusion, and occasionally rebellion at being Muzaked into implacable mushy madness. The conflict of both going on at the same time can cause the sense of dislocation and exhaustion that is the clearest indicator of the Zombie Effect. The victim shuffles and mumbles, is distant or unduly preoccupied, doesn't listen, acts automatically, and not only can't remember where the car is parked but often doesn't care.

There are ancilliary symptoms and causes as well: headaches caused by guilt at buying too much; depression at not being able to buy everything; the walking emptiness caused by consistently emphasized, endless greed.

The cure for all forms of mallaise is theoretically simple: The victim leaves the mall. There are no laws requiring people to stay in the mall, or even to go there in the first place. It isn't anyone's civic, moral, spiritual, or intellectual duty. The mall may be the best place—or even the only place—to shop for certain products, but that doesn't mean the shopper has to stay there for hours. Nevertheless, it isn't always easy to leave.

For that is another aspect of the Zombie Effect: Victims stay for no good or apparent reason, and even beyond their conscious desire to be there. Shoppers mallinger partly because of the mall's psychological apparatus, its implicit promise of safety, sanctuary, and salvation. Of Nirvana! The Crystal City! A New Heaven on a New Earth! The mall hasn't become the most successful artificial environment in America for nothing.

With its real walls and psychological illusions, the mall protects against so many hazards and uncertainties that the mallaise sufferer may well mallinger a little longer to ponder the consequences of walking out. Such a person may fear trading the maladies of the Zombie Effect for the perils of mall withdrawal, which is characterized by shaking in downtown areas, fear of crossing streets, inordinate terror in the presence of rain or sunshine, confusion when actual travel is required between purchases, and the feeling of estrangement when wearing a coat.

I wish I could say that medical science is on top of this new set of malladies, but the truth is that it is scandalously behind the times. Right now, there may be many thousands of Zombie Effect sufferers, untreated and undiagnosed. If you find this hard to believe—well, have you been to the mall lately?

There is one more form of mallaise that is especially frustrating because it is not so simply cured, even theoretically. It is the state of being malcontented with what the mall offers and how it offers it. Sufferers will rail on about the same limited clothing styles reproduced in a hundred mall shops, or the same five movies shown in two dozen mall theaters—the only cinemas around. They will complain endlessly about fast-print outlets masquerading as bookstores, where clerks don't know anything more about books than what appears on the computer stock list. They will raise angry fists against the screening boxes calling themselves cinemas, with their dark and blurry unwatchable images on the screen, and cold and tinny sound.

These unfortunate mallcontents really have a problem, because in many places they don't have any alternative: If they want to shop for clothes, see a first-run movie, buy a new book or record, it's the mall or nothing.

They flail away at the promises the mall implies but does not keep. They are in a sense prisoners of the mall, if only because the mall's predominance has destroyed the alternatives they miss, even the imaginary ones. But the mall takes other prisoners—the ones who are locked up inside.

35

Prisoners of the Mall

Something there is that doesn't love a mall—and that becomes pretty evident if you have to be there eight to twelve hours a day, five to seven days a week.

The scene was already a little surreal on a winter's afternoon at Greengate mall: An exhausted woman pushed a stroller across the red tiles, several more kids pulsating beside her; a self-important businessman in white suit and black shirt marched in the opposite direction; and a couple of tootsies in fake-fur coats that looked like hairy balloons tottered along on high heels, wearing skirts so short that they caught stares—which they primly ignored with smug satisfaction. Meanwhile the Muzak played the *Action News* theme.

But there was an extra edge to the internal atmosphere, discernable in each shop and restaurant, in the preoccupied eyes of salesclerks and the faces of waitresses blank with anxiety, absorbed in discussions among themselves. The reason for their distraction was not mysterious for long. They quickly questioned each person they knew, or waited on, or who simply looked relatively nontoxic, and who had just come into the mall with color in his or her cheeks and rubbing away the cold from his or her hands. As the mall workers glanced at each coat for signs of recent moisture, their one question was: "Has it started yet?"

For a major snowstorm had been forecast and the employees, stuck in this hothouse without windows, were going crazy with not knowing what it was like outside. They knew from experience that in this part of the country a snowstorm could come on quickly and stay for hours, making what had been an easy drive to work a terrible mess by quitting time. For some of them, a snowstorm that looked like a bad one would mean phone calls and arrangements about children and spouses—what to do if they were late and couldn't pick somebody up as planned, and should the kids wait at their grandmother's, or might school be let out early, and who would be home? If it looked really bad, was there enough food in the house? There were a dozen things to think about and decide on, all depending on whether it really was snowing and how hard. Was it going to get bad, and when? Meanwhile, they were supposed to keep serving and smiling in their fully enclosed fantasy island, and they *couldn't see,* they *didn't know* what was going on outside. Snow was outlawed here inside Camelot.

The panicky feeling among mall employees when a storm is forecast is palpable, but it is just an obvious manifestation of subterranean emotions that are ongoing almost every day. While the shoppers come and go, talking of Mop & Glo, these people are in the mall for long stretches of time. For every working hour of the day, most days of the week and the year, including most holidays, they are the prisoners of the mall. They must deal with the givens of a mall environment designed to soothe and stimulate shoppers who will be in the mall for a few hours at most. What shoppers go to as a haven of sensory pleasures, they are condemned to as an everyday sensory-deprivation chamber. The prisoners of the mall are in this timeless, placeless space, cut off from the outside and caught in an intense environment designed for purposes other than the maintenance of their sanity.

The weather factor is usually the first environmental complaint from people who work in the mall. Enclosure and comfort control are designed to make the customer feel more comfortable and more secure inside the mall than in the outside world. These purposes are artfully expressed in a "weather report" prepared by the publicity department of Tamarac Square mall in Denver for its mall newspaper. "Skies over Tamarac Square's enclosed street scene continued irrelevant through the weekend. Temperatures remained consistent, though thunder was heard through the skylights on at least one occasion. No indoor tornadoes were predicted. Forecast: consistently pleasant."

That says it all: the irrelevance of the outside, the consistently pleasant inside, but also the dangers out there—the ominous thunder heard through the skylights. As long as you stay in the mall you will be perfectly safe. There will be no "indoor tornadoes."

That's okay for the customers who don't want to bother with soggy packages or with catching cold running from one overheated store to another through windy streets. But for the mall workers it means a consistency that invites madness; it's an isolation ward, a rubber-walled room. And contrary to forecast, that can mean that the mall employees have met the indoor tornado, and it is them.

Michele, who had just transferred to a new shop in the mall from the original edition of it downtown, noticed it right away. (In deference to their jobs and businesses, some of the people and stores mentioned here are mildly disguised. And some are not.)

"I couldn't believe the difference. You don't know what's going on outside, and you never see the sky or feel the air," Michele said. "When I go out of the store here for the same things I did in town—to go to the bank or get something to eat, or buy something we need at the store—I'm still inside the mall. I never see the real world. I'm still in this little world."

Even after the surprise wears off, the feelings may not. A little farther along the mall court is the shop where Marina has been working for seven years. "It still drives me crazy," she said. "You're stuck in here. It's always the same, no sunshine, no snow, the air is bad, the light is bad—and the customers are crabby."

Mall workers complain a lot about their customers, just as customers do about them, and it may be that the environment has something to do with the surliness of both sides. Shoppers who can't stand the banality of the mall's decor, and who are alienated by alarmingly chirpy or impersonally glazed clerks whose artificial patter is accompanied by apathetic ignorance of their inventory, might consider what it is like to work long hours bombarded by fluorescence and flummoxed by Muzak, and all the while inundated by a steady stream of zombie shoppers.

In addition to the environment, other peculiarities of working in the mall add to what sometimes seems to be an adversary relationship between clerks and customers. "The work is tedious, we work long hours, and we're underpaid," Marina said. Together with high turnover and the mall environment, these are reasons that employees sometimes don't know much about what they sell, and don't care.

The adversary feeling seems to be encouraged by the mall environment in another way. "The difference between the customers here and in town is the difference between night and day," Michele said. "The majority of customers here are horrible. They're rude, not only to us but to each other. I hear women saying ugly things to their children. We had people here who broke dishes and walked out without saying anything. There are more awful people than nice people, but in town it's the opposite. There they stop and talk, and if they break anything they almost always offer to pay for it. The majority are nice."

But, Michele also noticed, there is an almost opposite kind of difference between store employees in the mall and in town. "There's a very warm relationship among employees of different businesses at the mall," she said. "It's like a family. I was surprised. In town, employees of different stores stay at a distance. Here, they introduce themselves the first time they come in. Some made a point of welcoming us to the mall when we first opened—and when you go into their stores they notice you and say hello." It may be that mall workers, imprisoned in the same little world, feel some of the solidarity that others in analogous situations do: They are the family, the inmates, the prisoners, and the customers are the outsiders.

Some mall workers are bothered by the environment more than others, and some adapt easily. For some of the young clerks it's the only work environment they've ever known, and a career in retail may well mean a working lifetime in malldom. The cumulative effects of daily exposure to the mall and its peculiar mixture of sensory stimulation and deprivation, however, has not yet been studied.

There are other aspects of the mall that make mall workers—and owners of mall businesses—angry and frustrated; other ways in which they feel they are prisoners of the mall.

Most of the mall's stores are outlets of national or regional chains. Some are franchised, but their owners aren't there. Their policies are set elsewhere, but the idiosyncrasies of each mall situation—and each mall management—are problems that the workers must handle every day. As the manager of a jeans store that's an outlet of a major chain, Elena has to follow company policy whether or not it works in her store and for her customers. "It's frustrating," she said, "and not just for me but for my employees and for my customers. When they complain, there's nothing I can do about it—it's chain policy."

The independently owned businesses have problems as well. Some owners are appalled at the expense of operating in the mall and chafe at the rules the mall imposes, which they feel further limit their ability to make a profit.

"It's been like a game lately. It's real dumb," said Dossie, who works at a locally owned booth in Greengate's food court. "We put our SPECIAL OF THE DAY sign a little farther out on the wall so people can see it, and the mall manager comes around and takes it down because it's not supposed to be there." For Dossie, it's just another annoyance, like being forced to look out at the same court scene day after day, the same people doing the same things in the same light with the same Muzak accompaniment. She doesn't own the place herself. But when the mall manager buys an item and mentions in a half-joking way that the price is a little steep, Dossie is quick to come back with a reference to their high rent, in a not-joking way.

Some of the conflicts are endemic: retailers who resent management butting into retailing, mall managers who thing retailers are uncooperative and blind to the necessity of seeing the mall as a whole. Mall management itself is not immune. Industry publications and conventions are rife with discussions about the conflicts—managers who are dissatisfied with maintenance personnel, maintenance workers who think of managers as pencil-pushers, market directors who think managers are behind the times, and managers who think marketers spend too much money. Security claims lack of support and bad mall design; managers worry about security guards' overreacting or not reacting at all.

So the battles go on, the anger, the frustration, the grousing, suspicion, intrigue, the carping, backstabbing, gossip, innuendo, dissatisfaction, chicanery, and finally the mild psychosis, the paranoia, the willing and willful detachment from reality . . . all in this peaceful wonderland, amid consistently pleasant weatherlessness and the antiseptic up-tempo brightness, the happy land of neon fantasy.

36

Kids in the Mall: Growing Up Controlled

Butch heaved himself up and loomed over the group. "Like it was different for me," he piped. "My folks used to drop me off at the shopping mall every morning and leave me all day. It was like a big free baby-sitter, you know? One night they never came back for me. Maybe they moved away. Maybe there's some kind of a Bureau of Missing Parents I could check with."

—RICHARD PECK
Secrets of the Shopping Mall, a
novel for teenagers

From his sister at Swarthmore, I'd heard about a kid in Florida whose mother picked him up after school every day, drove him straight to the mall, and left him there until it closed—all at his insistence. I'd heard about a boy in Washington who, when his family moved from one suburb to another, pedaled his bicycle five miles every day to get back to his old mall, where he once belonged.

These stories aren't unusual. The mall is a common experience for the majority of American youth; they have probably been going there all their lives. Some ran within their first large open space, saw their first fountain, bought their first toy, and read their first book in a mall. They may have smoked their first cigarette or first joint or turned them down, had their first kiss or lost their virginity in the mall parking lot. Teenagers in America now spend more

time in the mall than anywhere else but home and school. Mostly it
is their choice, but some of that mall time is put in as the result of
two-paycheck and single-parent households, and the lack of other
viable alternatives. But are these kids being harmed by the mall?

I wondered first of all what difference it makes for adolescents
to experience so many important moments in the mall. They are,
after all, at play in the fields of its little world and they learn its
ways; they adapt to it and make it adapt to them. It's here that these
kids get their street sense, only it's mall sense. They are learning the
ways of a large-scale artificial environment: its subtleties and flex-
ibilities, its particular pleasures and resonances, and the attitudes it
fosters.

The presence of so many teenagers for so much time was not
something mall developers planned on. In fact, it came as a big
surprise. But kids became a fact of mall life very early, and the
International Council of Shopping Centers found it necessary to
commission a study, which they published along with a guide to
mall managers on how to handle the teenage incursion.

The study found that "teenagers in suburban centers are bored
and come to the shopping centers mainly as a place to go. Teenagers in suburban centers spent more time fighting, drinking, litter-
ing and walking than did their urban counterparts, but presented
fewer overall problems." The report observed that "adolescents
congregated in groups of two to four and predominantly at locations selected by them rather than management." This probably
had something to do with the decision to install game arcades,
which allow management to channel these restless adolescents into
naturally contained areas away from major traffic points of adult
shoppers.

The guide concluded that mall management should tolerate and
even encourage the teenage presence because, in the words of the
report, "The vast majority support the same set of values as does
shopping center management." *The same set of values* means simply
that mall kids are already preprogrammed to be consumers and that
the mall can put the finishing touches to them as hard-core, lifelong
shoppers just like everybody else. That, after all, is what the mall is
about. So it shouldn't be surprising that in spending a lot of time
there, adolescents find little that challenges the assumption that the
goal of life is to make money and buy products, or that just about
everything else in life is to be used to serve those ends.

Growing up in a high-consumption society already adds inestimable pressure to kids' lives. Clothes consciousness has invaded the grade schools, and popularity is linked with having the best, newest clothes in the currently acceptable styles. Even what they read has been affected. "Miss [Nancy] Drew wasn't obsessed with her wardrobe," noted *The Wall Street Journal*. "But today the mystery in teen fiction for girls is what outfit the heroine will wear next." Shopping has become a survival skill and there is certainly no better place to learn it than the mall, where its importance is powerfully reinforced and certainly never questioned.

The mall as a university of suburban materialism, where Valley Girls and Boys from coast to coast are educated in consumption, has its other lessons in this era of change in family life and sexual mores and their economic and social ramifications. The plethora of products in the mall, plus the pressure on teens to buy them, may contribute to the phenomenon that psychologist David Elkin calls "the hurried child": kids who are exposed to too much of the adult world too quickly, and must respond with a sophistication that belies their still-tender emotional development. Certainly the adult products marketed for children—form-fitting designer jeans, sexy tops for preteen girls—add to the social pressure to look like an adult, along with the home-grown need to understand adult finances (why mothers must work) and adult emotions (when parents divorce).

Kids spend so much time at the mall partly because their parents allow it and even encourage it. The mall is safe, it doesn't seem to harbor any unsavory activities, and there is adult supervision; it is, after all, a controlled environment. So the temptation, especially for working parents, is to let the mall be their babysitter. At least the kids aren't watching TV. But the mall's role as a surrogate mother may be more extensive and more profound.

Karen Lansky, a writer living in Los Angeles, has looked into the subject and she told me some of her conclusions about the effects on its teenaged denizens of the mall's controlled and controlling environment. "Structure is the dominant idea, since true 'mall rats' lack just that in their home lives," she said, "and adolescents about to make the big leap into growing up crave more structure than our modern society cares to acknowledge." Karen pointed out some of the elements malls supply that kids used to get from their families, like warmth (Strawberry Shortcake dolls and similar cute and cuddly merchandise), old-fashioned mothering ("We do it all for you," the fast-food slogan), and even home cooking (the "homemade" treats at the food court).

The problem in all this, as Karen Lansky sees it, is that while families nurture children by encouraging growth through the assumption of responsibility and then by letting them rest in the bosom of the family from the rigors of growing up, the mall as a structural mother encourages passivity and consumption, as long as the kid doesn't make trouble. Therefore all they learn about becoming adults is how to act and how to consume.

Kids are in the mall not only in the passive role of shoppers— they also work there, especially as fast-food outlets infiltrate the mall's enclosure. There they learn how to hold a job and take responsibility, but still within the same value context. When *CBS Reports* went to Oak Park Mall in suburban Kansas City, Kansas, to tape part of their hour-long consideration of malls, "After the Dream Comes True," they interviewed a teenaged girl who worked in a fast-food outlet there. In a sequence that didn't make the final program, she described the major goal of her present life, which was to perfect the curl on top of the ice-cream cones that were her store's specialty. If she could do that, she would be moved from the lowly soft-drink dispenser to the more prestigious ice-cream division, the curl on top of the status ladder at her restaurant. These are the achievements that are important at the mall.

Other benefits of such jobs may also be overrated, according to Laurence D. Steinberg of the University of California at Irvine's social ecology department, who did a study on teenage employment. Their jobs, he found, are generally simple, mindlessly repetitive and boring. They don't really learn anything, and the jobs don't lead anywhere. Teenagers also work primarily with other teenagers; even their supervisors are often just a little older than they are. "Kids need to spend time with adults," Steinberg told me. "Although they get benefits from peer relationships, without parents and other adults it's one-sided socialization. They hang out with each other, have age-segregated jobs, and watch TV."

Perhaps much of this is not so terrible or even so terribly different. Now that they have so much more to contend with in their lives, adolescents probably need more time to spend with other adolescents without adult impositions, just to sort things out. Though it is more concentrated in the mall (and therefore perhaps a clearer target), the value system there is really the dominant one of the whole society. Attitudes about curiosity, initiative, self-expression, empathy, and disinterested learning aren't necessarily made in the mall; they are mirrored there, perhaps a bit more intensely—as through a glass brightly.

Besides, the mall is not without its educational opportunities. There are bookstores, where there is at least a short shelf of classics at great prices, and other books from which it is possible to learn more than how to do sit-ups. There are tools, from hammers to VCRs, and products, from clothes to records, that can help the young find and express themselves. There are older people with stories, and places to be alone or to talk one-on-one with a kindred spirit. And there is always the passing show.

The mall itself may very well be an education about the future. I was struck with the realization, as early as my first forays into Greengate, that the mall is only one of a number of enclosed and controlled environments that are part of the lives of today's young. The mall is just an extension, say, of those large suburban schools—only there's Karmelkorn instead of chem lab, the ice rink instead of the gym: It's high school without the impertinence of classes.

Growing up, moving from home to school to the mall—from enclosure to enclosure, transported in cars—is a curiously continuous process, without much in the way of contrast or contact with unenclosed reality. Places must tend to blur into one another. But whatever differences and dangers there are in this, the skills these adolescents are learning may turn out to be useful in their later lives. For we seem to be moving inexorably into an age of pre-planned and regulated environments, and this is the world they will inherit.

Still, it might be better if they had more of a choice. One teen-aged girl confessed to *CBS Reports* that she sometimes felt she was missing something by hanging out at the mall so much. "But I'm here," she said, "and this is what I have."

37

From Petition to Emotion: Big Brother Is Managing You

If the National Organization for Women gets to set up a card table in Westfarms Mall, does it mean that soon shoppers there will be staring at men wearing white sheets and handing out leaflets for the Ku Klux Klan?

It's not a question a mall manager wants to entertain, nor did it seem a mall manager would ever have to. For years the shopping mall has been able on the one hand to advertise itself as the New Main Street, and on the other to maintain strict control over who gets into the mall and who doesn't—which, except in movies about the old West and certain southern towns, isn't something that Main Street normally does. Not in America anyway.

But the mall was designed to control a protected fantasy environment, and that means controlling not only what is included but also what is excluded. Controversy distracts from the shopping experience. Unwanted thoughts make a shambles of fantasy. According to news reports, when most flags in America were at half-mast in honor of U.S. Marines killed in the suicide attack on their compound in Lebanon in 1983, the American flag at Disneyland stayed at full staff because the management did not want to remind its customers of anything unpleasant. That's the idea at the mall, too. Managing what, outside the mall, is considered the exercise of the rights and duties of a democracy is part of how malls manage emotions inside.

I started noticing that aspect of mall control early in my odyssey, and I was reminded of it often. The manager of Westmoreland Mall told me bluntly, "Nothing gets in here unless we let it in." In Washington, D.C., Tysons Corner and other Lerner Company malls post explicit notices at their entrances: "Areas in Tysons Corner Center used by the public are not public ways, but are for the use of the tenants and the public transacting business with them. Permission to use said areas may be revoked at any time." There are similar notices in malls all over America.

Some malls do allow petitioners or some kind of political activity, but only on their terms and at their discretion. The whole matter was put most succinctly by the manager of a mall in Florida when he told a reporter: "I don't mind that people are trying to save the whale, but I don't want my shoppers stopped to sign petitions."

But are they *his* shoppers? And are areas of the mall used by the public really not public ways? That's a matter of law and interpretation: For the purpose of assessing how the Bill of Rights applies within them, should malls be treated as essentially public institutions or as primarily private property? A lot of courts have had their say, including the United States Supreme Court on several occasions, and they've come down squarely on both sides of the issue.

The Supreme Court first looked into it directly in the Logan Valley Plaza decision in 1968, when it ruled that a labor union could picket a nonunion supermarket in a shopping center, despite the NO TRESPASSING signs posted by the shopping-center manager. The Court, under Chief Justice Earl Warren, cited an earlier decision that said a Jehovah's Witness was entitled to distribute leaflets on the sidewalks of a town completely owned by a private company, because the town had "all the characteristics of any other American town," even if it was privately owned. Therefore, constitutional rights apply: If it looks like a duck, walks like a duck, and quacks like a duck, it is a duck. That decision (*Marsh* v. *Alabama,* 1946) noted: "The more an owner, for his advantage, opens up his property for use by the public in general, the more do his rights become circumscribed by the statutory and constitutional rights of those who use it."

The principle was used again in a California State decision with the wonderful title of *Diamond* v. *Bland,* when antipollution petitioners were permitted to go into a San Bernardino mall because, the court said, ". . . in many instances the contemporary shopping center serves as the analogue of the traditional town square," which is what malls were saying all along, although in a different context.

But the judicial tide began to turn with the 1972 Supreme Court decision (*Lloyd Corp.* v. *Tanner*) involving a Portland, Oregon, mall that prohibited antiwar activists from distributing handbills. This time the case went to the more conservative Court under Chief Justice Warren Burger, which upheld the mall because the mall would suffer an "unwarranted infringement" of its private property rights if it were required "to yield to the exercise of First Amendment rights when adequate alternative avenues of communication exist."

But it was a 5–4 decision, and Justice Thurgood Marshall was among those who disagreed. "For many Portland Citizens, Lloyd Center will so completely satisfy their wants that they will have no reason to go elsewhere for goods and services," he wrote in his dissenting opinion. "If speech is to reach these people, it must reach them in Lloyd Center."

Nevertheless, the Burger Court reinforced this decision by ruling for another mall and against union pickets in a 1976 case, and Justice Marshall reinforced his dissent, writing (along with Justice William Brennan) that "shopping center owners have assumed . . . the traditional role of the state in its control of First Amendment forums." So now the mall not only looked like a duck, it was the only duck in town.

Shopping-center people were in an interesting position. Their centers had become, as they often bragged, the Main Streets of suburbia and even of towns. But when the law tried to apply the if-it-looks-like-a-duck principle, the malls demurred. They pointed out that as private enterprises they weren't supported by public funds or taxes; therefore, if their business was hurt by weirdos wearing beads or Nazi uniforms, shouting at customers, banging tambourines, and demanding contributions, then their right to function as businesses was suppressed, and more to the point, they could go broke and the free-speaking public wouldn't bail them out.

It was this environment they had created at considerable expense, after all, that brought people in. And the courts were beginning to agree to some extent. This was Main Street, but it was a made-up Mickey Mouse kind of Main Street, under private ownership and control. The mall had to be considered something different from both absolute private property and legitimate public domain. So, if it looks like a Mouse . . .

Another dimension was added, however, with the 1980 Supreme Court decision, *PruneYard Shopping Center* v. *Robbin,* which upheld the right of petitioners in the large San Jose mall but based the decison on free-speech provisions in the California state constitution, which grants broader rights than does the United States Constitution. The legal principle here was that a state may add rights to those given by the federal Constitution or courts, but may not subtract from them. This decision has been used several times since then to win the right to petition in the mall in several states, including Washington and Connecticut.

But the situation remained muddled. Potential petitioners may have to fulfill conditions—imposed by the courts and mall management—as specific as the size of their card tables. The policies of the mall industry were inconsistent. Some malls allowed political activity but often of a broad nature ("Meet the Candidates" night) and certainly as noncontroversial as possible (allowing petitions against foreign steel dumping—in western Pennsylvania malls). But as Jon Pushinsky, an attorney with the American Civil Liberties Union, put it: "Hey, free speech clauses of the Constitution weren't passed to protect people everyone wanted to hear talk."

The right to petition in malls may not seem vitally important to the Republic, but there is also the prescient point made by Justice Marshall in his dissent. He wrote, "It would not be surprising in the future to see cities rely more and more on private businesses" to create their downtown as well as to "perform functions once performed by government agencies. . . . As governments rely on private enterprise, property decreases in favor of privately owned property. It becomes harder and harder for citizens to find means to communicate with other citizens. Only the wealthy may find effective communication possible."

What Marshall was talking about ultimately is a tyranny not by

the government but by a corporate series of Big Brothers controlling spaces solely devoted to making sure that the big-man shops
and Brothers shoe stores get the full benefit of The Retail Drama.
But it isn't only increasing private ownership that's at issue; it's also
this new attitude of control that's peculiar to the mall. For previous
places of private business have not been controlled—from downtown districts back to the first American business institutions, the
public markets.

Developers of the new city malls locating where these historic
markets once flourished—such as Faneuil Hall Marketplace in
Boston and the Seaport in New York—like to hark back to this
rich tradition and call their malls a revival, making more specific
the suburban malls' claim to be the modern equivalent of the old
market squares. But those old markets were more than places
where apples were sold from cute little carts; they were the seed-
beds of American democracy.

As far back as 1877 the Supreme Court held that private property ". . . becomes clothed with a public interest when used in a
manner to make it of public consequence." But the exercise of public rights in the markets of early America was established long before that. It was a tradition that itself reached back to medieval
Europe, according to Padraic Burke, an urban planner and cultural
historian. "The most important element of the market was its public character," he wrote. It was always administered by a public
agency and ". . . existed to serve a variety of public needs, from
court to meeting place."

The essence of the market was that it was free: Everyone was
equal, and access was guaranteed by the public agency in charge of
the market, according to Burke. So it was no coincidence that the
American Revolution began with tea dumped into Boston Harbor
as a protest against restraints on independence, at Faneuil Hall, the
citadel of free speech in colonial Boston.

Malls, including the Faneuil Hall Marketplace, have acquired
many functions of the old markets. They are also theaters, carnivals, and gathering places, as well as commercial centers. Some
malls are host to churches, government offices, libraries, and
schools, as the old public markets were. But the mall is neither a
fully public place nor a free market. Although they were probably
constrained by the social mores of the time, the free markets did
not tell anyone they could not try to sell something because management and the marketing director thought it wasn't commercial

enough. The free market set no artificial limit on what the public could choose from, in ideas as well as products. But when not only the business of individual merchants but the market itself must be profitable, then certain competitions and freedoms are likely to be eliminated. It's doubtful that many mall managers are out to suppress constitutional freedoms or intellectual and aesthetic ferment, and some malls provide significant public service; it is simply the nature of the mall, privately owned, costly to create and maintain as well as somewhat fragile, that dictates its role.

It's not only what the mall doesn't do that sets it apart. The mall is actively engaged in persuasion and manipulation, which begin with that costly environment and include the roboticized charm of clerks and waiters who are trained to be impersonally personal. As Arlie Russell Hochschild pointed out in her book *The Managed Heart,* the conscious use of acting techniques to make customers feel important and personally served has moved from the theatrical stage and the repertoire of prostitutes to that of airline attendants and those in the more expensive end of the retail and restaurant fields. As malls include more fashion shops and chic-image eating and drinking places—both clear trends in the industry—this kind of emotional management is bound to increase. For one thing, it's perfectly in tune with what the rest of the mall environment tries to do.

Controlling the emotions of customers is another natural aspect of the mall's basic control apparatus, which treats the consumer as an object to be lulled and manipulated. This offends and sickens some people—it becomes a palpable part of the Zombie Effect. But it is apparently what most mall consumers want, and the proof is in the cash register. It's how Big Brother gets rich.

38

Crime and Shelter: The Malling of Fear

One of the functions of society is to make its inhabitants feel safe, and Americans devote more of their collective resources to security than to any other need. Yet Americans do not feel safe, despite (or because of) shotguns in the closet and nuclear bombers patrolling overhead.

—Philip Slater
The Pursuit of Loneliness

With its antiseptic fantasy and its bright distraction, its enclosed and selective universe, the mall is a shelter from fear. In many ways, this is no accident. By creating a secure environment in which buying is the whole point, the mall psychologically links the idea of safety with the idea of shopping. But it must do more than that; it must take practical steps to ensure the mall's actual security. And that is becoming an increasingly difficult task.

As surveys and interviews attest, a major attraction of malls is the assumption that they are safe. Generally, they are—but so are city streets, generally. What they aren't is crime-free. Malls have been the scenes of muggings, murders, kidnappings, car thefts, rapes, robberies, vandalism, and arson. For some categories of crime, they are particular targets.

Perhaps because of their newness or relative isolation, malls managed to stay out of the headlines for years, but by the late 1970s they became more visible participants in some of society's uglier dramas. Just a few days into the Christmas shopping season of 1981, a man used a .22 caliber long-barreled pistol to shoot and kill his wife, mother-in-law, and daughters—one of them three years old, the other one year old—in the parking lot of the Midway Mall in Elyria, Ohio. During the Christmas shopping season of 1982, an eighteen-year-old high-school cheerleader was abducted from the parking lot of the Morris County Mall in New Jersey. Holiday shoppers who weren't scared away soon saw twenty-six Guardian Angels patrolling the mall. In 1984, Christopher Wilder abducted an unknown number of women, killing at least four; according to the Associated Press: "The FBI said Wilder approached an average of one woman a day, often in suburban shopping malls, posing as a fashion photographer."

When a Brink's truck was held up and one guard killed by robbers who turned out to be missing members of the Weather Underground group of the 1960s, the first people arriving on the scene were the manager and two employees of the Nanuet Mall; the Brink's truck had just come from one of their banks. According to a shopping-center industry publication that interviewed the Nanuet manager, his attitude was a reasonable one: "You can't really plan before for a shootout at the mall. . . . It's what you do afterwards that counts."

The basic reason that crime is happening at the mall is both simple and inevitable. When Willy Sutton was asked why he robbed banks, he said because that's where the money is. Now robbers hit the mall because that's where the banks are. Rapes happen there because that's where women are. Abductions of children (including the case dramatized in *Adam,* a television movie) happen because children are there, in a busy but unthreatening place.

Car thefts are a particular problem. Mall parking lots have become favorite preying grounds because automobiles are easy to steal undetected, and they can go from the lot to the chop shop and be divided into untraceable and therefore negotiable pieces before the owner disengages from the mall fantasy long enough to notice that the car is gone.

All of this has become a growing matter for mall management concern. Crime can cut into business: When the cheerleader abducted from the Morris County Mall was found murdered nearby, the mall's Christmas shopping traffic dropped by nearly a third.

Even in less spectacular cases, a mall has a lot to lose if its image is tarnished. So these days, many malls are moving away from the more casual approach they maintained in earlier days to more earnest programs of crime prevention. Most malls used to favor the Neighborhood Cop image, a low-keyed, friendly approach, which worked fine as long as security's main activities were finding lost children and giving directions to lost adults. Now many malls have combined this image with something a little sterner: an image of highly visible police authority, designed to deter crime. The guys in blazers have been replaced by uniformed guards, their belts full of intimidating stuff, including guns. They use official-looking cruisers and other police technology. It all adds up to the image of the Big Neighborhood Cop.

The image is almost all they have. Few states grant guards police powers, so they must rely on visibility, persuasion, and quick communication with real police. Mall security guards can't stop and search purse snatchers; usually they can't go into a store to apprehend shoplifters (they patrol only the mall's common areas). They can organize information and alert stores if a credit card criminal or shoplifter has been spotted. But mostly they must hope that potential criminals are spooked by their uniformed presence.

According to what I observed on my mall trek, the quality of security varies considerably. Some malls employ former or off-duty police officers and retired military people, with mixed results. (Public relations is still a major function of mall security.) But much of the spottiness reflects a mall management's attitude. If the mall hires security guards only for appearances (and in at least one state—Tennessee—its highest court declared that shopping centers weren't required to provide any security at all), or if they pay low wages to unqualified people working long hours, then not even the appearance may be any good.

Some malls and developers provide superior security people who are well trained and work closely with local police. They can handle teenagers and emergencies; they are trained in first aid as well as firearms. The value of emergency medical training was impressed upon me when I talked to Mary Elton, Barbara Lambert's sister, who lives in Massachusetts. Mary told me that one of her young daughters had an inexplicable seizure while they were at a local shopping center. A mall guard, who was also a registered nurse, diagnosed it as a febrile seizure—a transitory event caused by fever—and had an ambulance on the scene within minutes. Hours later the hospital confirmed his diagnosis, and the little girl was released.

"When I thanked the mall people," Mary told me, "they said it was routine—they'd handled four emergencies that morning. But imagine if it had happened anywhere else."

Suburbia's safety can no longer be assumed: The suburban crime rate rose 250 percent between 1969 and 1979. Urban malls have their own special problems, and advantages: They probably attract more pickpockets, purse snatchers, and muggers, but they also can attract more police, and since many city malls are partly funded by government, police patrol them on a regular basis. Urban multi-use centers have additional worries, what with possible prostitution from the hotel infiltrating the food courts and retail shops, and pumped-up sports fans or stoned-out kids at a rock concert in the neighboring dome suddenly converging on the mall when their event is over.

Special deterrence is sometimes deemed necessary. The most extreme I've heard of was the police helicopter that patrolled over Plaza Las Americas in San Juan, Puerto Rico, during Christmas shopping season. Apparently it was there to impress the nearby housing projects, despite the fact that the mall's security chief reported his biggest problem was the shoplifting and other troublemaking perpetrated by children of the well-to-do. In the inner-city Vermont Slauson Shopping Center in Los Angeles a six-foot-high wrought-iron fence, and access limited to two entrances, are considered sufficient. But in general, mall security functions were accurately described by a guard I met in Chicago's Water Tower Place. "We're babysitters and watchdogs," he said. "That's all we can be."

There are other real and present dangers in the mall, including fire, the greatest threat to life in any enclosure in America. Today's buildings are scandalously vulnerable because of the use of volatile plastics, which can instantly emit killing chemical fumes and smoke. Although large buildings with inadequate protection and evacuation procedures are common, virtually all regional malls have fire alarm and sprinkler systems (although as one mall employee confided, "They're still kind of hit and miss, if you know what I mean"). Most mall managers I asked had instituted emergency evacuation procedures that were regularly rehearsed in the mall.

Malls have experienced large fires; a quarter of the Westgate

Mall in Bethlehem, Pennsylvania, burned down in 1977, and another Pennsylvania shopping center was destroyed by arson on Christmas Eve, 1981. Both were closed at the time. So far, no major life-threatening fires have yet tested the mall's particular physical properties: the smoke-trapping enclosures, the central court with possible updrafts, the mall-wide air-conditioning system. Malls in suburban and rural areas may also be relatively distant from fire companies, which may be too small and poorly equipped to respond to a major fire. There may also be insufficient water pressure to fight a large fire, either because of a remote location or overbuilding in the immediate vicinity. Inadequate water pressure is rumored to be the reason that a large civic center in a Maryland town burned down, even though it had sprinklers. Across the street from it was a shopping mall.

Malls also face special dangers from arson: Research shows that arson directed at retail establishments is usually motivated by anger and is carried out with complete disregard for human life. Because of all the people in them and their symbolism as citadels of conspicuous consumption, malls are also possible targets for terrorists. An enclosed, "American-style" mall in South Africa was devastated by a bomb for just those reasons, and six members of the American Nazi party were convicted of conspiring to blow up a mall in North Carolina.

Possible structural problems that malls have in common with other buildings are made worse in a sense because so many people go to them. Tornadoes demolished two shopping centers in Texas in 1979, with heavy loss of life, and tornadoes knocked down buildings in three shopping centers in southern Illinois in 1982. There are also internal potentials for disaster: Malls have walkways, similiar to the one that collapsed in a Kansas City hotel, killing and injuring scores of people.

Although malls have a great stake in the appearance of safety, not all malls inspire confidence. I was present at one, also in the Christmas season, when a small fire broke out in a toy store. It was handled by store personnel but the fire department was called. They arrived with reasonable promptness, but it was a small volunteer department that seemed to be made up exclusively of old men and very young boys, trooping around in hopelessly overlarge slickers. A mall security guard came out of the store, mumbling something into his Walkie-Talkie, and walked away—but not before instructions from the management came out of his receiver loud and clear:

"If television or radio or press people come or call, tell them we have no comment."

Most businesses try to protect their images. But the mall is vitally dependent on its image as a place made safe for the fantasy of The Retail Drama. Sometimes that dependence makes the mall safer, but sometimes it can be dangerous.

> "We're safe! It's a shopping center!"
> –LILY TOMLIN
> *The Incredible Shrinking Woman*

Malls have their work cut out for them, since it's hard to over-estimate the role of fear in American life. One major study indicates that television is partly responsible for disproportionate anxiety about crime—especially about crime in cities—and that the heavier the viewing, the more fearful the viewer. The truth is that Americans don't really *see* much of what they fear; our dangers are not obvious to the eye. For many, it's possible to avoid those places where poverty, illness, blight, and crime predominate.

What is obvious is that Americans live longer, healthier, and more comfortable lives than any humans in history. Perhaps their knowledge of that fact contributes to the silence and sublimation that principally characterize the deepest fear Americans feel: the fear of nuclear holocaust. Just as the missiles and bombs are buried out of sight in their silos, public reaction to the threat of nuclear weapons has been largely subterranean. It lurks beneath the appearance of things, but it is there. It may even find expression in something as apparently unrelated as the mall. For if the mall is an expression of new American dreams, it may also be an expression of new American nightmares.

Many elements of the mall conspire to make people feel more secure. The mere presence of an abundance of clean, efficient, and glittery consumer products is reassuring—they are the security blankets, tangible and warm, as well as the bright badges of prosperity. The mall displays them in a controlled environment that eliminates any suggestion of unpleasant realities, any reminders of war, terrorism, random murder, senseless death, toxicity in the biosphere, or of stupidity, mendacity, and psychosis in places high and low—even as softened by a Happy News format. Americans know full well that there is nowhere to hide and no way to escape nuclear death once the missiles are launched, but in the mall they can at least escape thinking about them.

To the environment of distraction, escape, and sanctuary, the mall's enclosure adds the potent element of psychological shelter. The history of atomic terror parallels the growth of malldom. Especially since the advent of the nuclear-tipped intercontinental missile—and proof of the Soviet Union's ability to launch them demonstrated when the first Sputnik satellite visibly passed over the United States—Americans have lived in sublimated terror of the "bolt from the blue," the instant and unwarned rain of annihilation. As the Bomb went deep into the hidden hearts of mothers, the nightmares of schoolchildren, and the secret souls of fathers obsessed with protecting their families, the public withdrew into itself, tucked its head into its shell much as Bert the Turtle did in the "duck and cover" film strips of the 1950s. When we feel helpless, we hide. An entire society may have tried to find shelter, first in suburbia and then in the psychological bomb shelter of the shopping mall.

Meanwhile the arms race accelerated. The public's attempt to ignore it may well have contributed to what writer Jonathan Schell, in *The Fate of the Earth,* characterized as "the greatest collective failure of responsibility of any generation in history." If that failure results in nuclear bombs falling tomorrow, perhaps it is fitting that they will probably find millions of Americans happily perambulating in the suspended animation of the mall. There they can contemplate some of the final creations of the human race—the Perma-Prest percale sheets, Megamania Atari cartridges, Sergio Valente kids' jeans, cold-pack cheese food, Hush Puppies and Sno Trackers, Underalls, puppy housebreaking pads, Estee Lauder Thorough Cleansing gel, tailored gold pendants, Sizzles front-closure underwire bras, Casualcraft chintz, Suburban outerwear, compact mini-dryers, Naturalizer mocs, designer perms—and just generally say goodbye.

Part 6

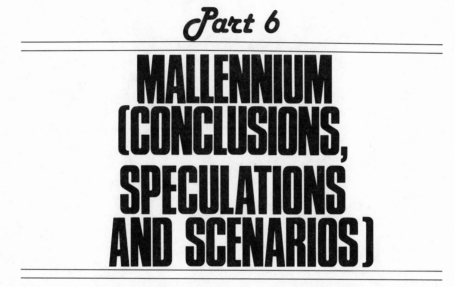

MALLENNIUM (CONCLUSIONS, SPECULATIONS AND SCENARIOS)

. . . we shall see the imagination build "walls" of impalpable shadows, comfort itself with the illusion of protection—or, just the contrary: tremble behind thick walls, mistrust the staunchest ramparts.

—GASTON BACHELARD
The Poetics of Space

39

Shall We Gather at the Bank Machine? The Mall as the Pleasure Dome of 1999

Money is the long hair of the eighties.
——Elizabeth Ashley

It's one o'clock in the morning and the last round of drinks emptied his wallet. He didn't use a credit card and he more or less purposely left his checkbook at the office. But he needs cash just to get home, so he walks a couple of blocks to the money machine. He knows just where it is.

He reads the words of green light and guides his plastic bank card into the slot. He remembers his code. And almost as a reward for that feat of mind, and for touching the right buttons in the correct sequence, the bills slide out with a click and hiss, as if hot off the government printing press. They are money. Sometimes—more often when he's half-sloshed, like now—he calls up more cash than he needs, just to see the bills come out in pairs of fives and twenties, four times in rapid succession: one hundred dollars, right before his eyes. It's quite a rush, as if they might never stop.

O brothers and sisters, don't we recognize this man? And don't we meld together with him here in plastic community, on line in New York City, in line everywhere else, a few decorous feet apart so as not to inspire furtive glances at the sacred code? Yes, and four digits hence, our forefingers bring forth a new nation. . . .

And it's yours, sisters and brothers still in your automobiles, winding slowly through the labyrinthine asphalt, headlighting the line of cars coming from the mall on down, to the branch office and the Bank Machine. And yea! Each shall dash from a car of one's own, sprouting umbrellas and running to punch the secret numerals and manage the machine one-handed in the rain.

Or better: In the dry halls of the mall itself—there, too, is the Bank Machine, for we, the shoppers, who are caught cash-shy, with bags in our hands and under our eyes, approach it eagerly to receive our cash communion and move on, melting into the undulating mass of worshipers.

It's fast, it's easy, it's technological, it's American. The automated teller is a natty new addition to the culture, the beginning of a whole new era of electronic access and abstraction. Money itself has lost much of its old meaning; with the speed of electronic transfers in a worldwide economy, value changes with velocity. "We don't even know what money is anymore," said financial analyst Henry Kaufman, known as the Wizard of Wall Street. Even for middle-class Americans, the new machines are making money less a thing than part of a process. The mall has to respond to that, or die.

You don't have to tell mall developers that the economic rules are changing. They've already had to weather inflation, recessions, and tight money times. They have reacted with new ways of financing their malls, with new discount and off-price malls, and by remodeling existing centers instead of just building new ones. In the midst of all this they were being told that malls were going to be obsolete altogether soon, because like so much else, they would be replaced by computers.

SHOPPING MALLS TO CRUMBLE BY THE YEAR 2000, screamed the headline in the *American Business* tabloid. "Grass could grow in the parking lots of our shopping centers," an economist warned, and even the U.S. Department of Commerce predicted that the suburban mall was doomed. The mall would fade because electronic shopping was coming to the American home. "I wouldn't want to own any bricks and mortar after 1990," said the president of a new electronics system.

Electronic shopping means that consumers can make their selections from a menu of products and services, order what they want, and even pay for it, all by means of their home computers or two-way cable television. Various systems have been tested in France, Canada, Germany, and Japan. Now, major corporations in the United States—AT&T, Warner-Amex, J. C. Penney, and the combined heft of CBS, IBM, and Sears Roebuck—were putting together national "videotex" services. Electronic shopping can also offer the consumer cross-referenced information, including product availability, up-to-the-minute prices, and even the option of custom-designed and personalized products untouched by human hands. Eventually a home computer could direct a factory computer to make up a lemon-yellow linen jersey with an electric-blue corduroy kangaroo pouch in front like none seen in any store before or after.

The message to the mall industry is obvious: Since people won't have to leave home to shop, they won't need the mall anymore. To add insult to injury, Compuserve, one of the new American firms, advertises its shopping services as an "Electronic Mall," which includes The Department Stores, The Book Bazaar, The Record Emporium, The Financial Market, and The Gardening Shed. Participating businesses include American Express, RCA, and E. F. Hutton.

The mall industry got its official warning at the 1981 ICSC convention from Jean Godzich, the representative of a regional mall in a Paris suburb which hosted the first large-scale tryout of the French videotex system, TeleTel. Godzich not only told the American mallers how well the system worked, he also advised them what to do about it. "Let's try to get away from the idea of one-stop shopping," he concluded, "and go on to the idea of one-stop living."

One-stop living—that was something the mall industry could understand. They'd already gathered just about everything from dentists to convention centers, Steak & Brews to the Girl Scouts, into their malls. Now the future of the mall would depend upon completeness. In particular it would depend on emphasizing the one element that, by its very nature, electronics could not replace: the mall as a controlled physical environment where people could go to be entertained.

"You've got to make your centers more *fun*," another expert in electronic shopping, Jack Steckel of Retailing Advertising Services in Canada, told the mall conventioneers. For it wasn't just that electronic shopping from home was convenient—playing with computer catalogues and calling up pictures was almost as exciting for some as playing video games. There had to be reasons other than habit and necessity to get people out of their homes. Habit would help, probably for a long time; a Newspaper Advertising Bureau survey showed that in 1983, 95 percent of all general merchandise shopping in the United States was done by car, and that 80 percent of adults surveyed said they had convenient access to two or more shopping centers. But still, malls would have to change.

They would have to capitalize on the fact that Americans shopped for recreation; some said that shopping was already the nation's favorite entertainment. When Alvin Toffler was the most fashionable prognosticator around, he could frighten the mall industry with the specter of no one leaving their homes for anything—everyone would work and play in the "electronic cottage." But then came a new foreseer, John Naisbitt, author of *Megatrends,* who said that the pressure of cascading technology would only increase the need for people to be with one another in public environments, and to touch real objects in the real world—the effect he called "high tech/high touch."

So far Naisbitt seemed to be right. When a company in Kobo, Japan, set up a demonstration of high-tech tailoring with computers and video, it attracted large crowds who simply wanted to *watch* the process of a garment being custom-made on the spot, with lots of laser flashes, electronic buzzers, and blinking computer lights. What if a mall put on a show like that? And as for the predilection of people for staying home and working by computer even for a few days a week, a survey by Management Recruiters International found that a vast majority of respondents would rather work at the office every day. What if the mall instituted computer workplaces and information centers behind glass walls, both as a service to companies and free-lance computer workers, and as entertainment for shoppers and workers alike? The possibilities were endless for *one-stop living* in the electronic age.

Of course, this would also mean that the mall would have to adjust to a new market with the characteristics of the Yumpies—the young upwardly mobile professionals. Not only is this the group most likely to use electronics at home, it is also the hot consumer market for the 1980s and 1990s, the one especially important for the mall to capture because the mall's old mass market is vanishing—literally splitting apart into those becoming richer and those becoming poorer. A study conducted for *Fortune* magazine concluded that the proportion of upper-income families would increase dramatically, from 25 percent in 1980 to 40 percent in 1990. The study predicted that, measured in constant 1977 dollars, families earning $25,000 or more would see income increases of 88.8 percent, with an increase in discretionary income (money that's left over after necessities) of 116 percent. But those making less than $25,000 would register income gains of under 2 percent, with no increase in discretionary income at all.

If anything like that actually happens, if the disparity between winners and losers becomes so great and the number and economic power of the winners increases that substantially, it would be an amazing difference from the postwar years, when the middle-income group—the mass market—made up the American majority. The signs indicate that it is indeed happening: By 1982, the middle-income group had fallen to 44 percent of the population and was still declining.

The malls lost no time in responding to the change, and they weren't chasing the fading middle-income group either. They were going after the upscale market, particularly the high-income working woman, with higher-fashion shops, eating and drinking places, and special services such as wardrobe planning and lectures on motivation in department store seminar rooms. Even such middle-income stalwarts as Montgomery Ward, Penney's, and Sears were adding fashion lines with celebrity-name labels. Sears was also getting into financial services: "If anyone was wondering if people will buy stocks where they buy socks," a Sears executive told a reporter, "they will."

The upscale market is the most susceptible to the malls' new efforts to entertain. They lead the way in the trend toward eating out (the percentage of American family income spent at restaurants has doubled since 1960, and the amount spent increases with income). By 1990 it's estimated that half of every food dollar in America will be spent on eating out, as opposed to 10 cents in the 1950s. The malls have responded with an explosion of food courts and their "half-speed" restaurants (not exactly fast food, but not quite traditional restaurant dining either).

The upscale market is also more likely to want personal attention from experts when selecting the right power saw as well as the right blue business suit, so the mall is beginning to emphasize the hands-on service it can provide that a computer screen cannot. Of course, those with the money to buy exclusive fashions are most likely to want to see and touch what they're getting, as well as to see what others are really wearing and buying, and what the styles look like. These shoppers have already caused a revolution in the popularity and design of mannequins, which have become both more stylized and more lifelike. "People in general have become more and more fashion-conscious and identify more with mannequins because of that," Lisa Zizzi, fashion coordinator at Filene's department store told Pam Reynolds in the *Boston Globe*. "As people have become more fashion-conscious they're more in tune with advertisements, visual display and visual merchandising. People want to identify more and more with anything they can identify with."

Once again, the mall becomes the visual medium made concrete; in the future, what the computer screen proposes, the mall will dispose. The theatrical aspect of shopping continues to work to the advantage of the malleable mall. Its future lies in its ability to become more fully what has already been implicit in its nature: America's Pleasure Dome.

But the mall doesn't have to rely only on shopping and eating out as recreational options. It also has strong ties to more traditional cultural and entertainment media. Not only do malls often present entertainments, from traveling hypnotists to symphony orchestras (in fact, the Dallas Symphony was saved from extinction by a series of concerts at NorthPark Shopping Center), but increasingly close ties are evolving between the mall and the major suppliers of American entertainment, culture, and information. Consider for example the virtual feedback loops connecting the mall and the movies, as well as the mall and television, rock music, and publishing—and the various symbiotic relationships quickly being formalized among them all.

Four survivors of the apocalypse are searching by helicopter for safety and sustenance. My God! What'll we do? Where will we go? Then, just below, they see it, spread out over one hundred acres, a million square feet of sheltered food and clothing, not to mention variable-intensity massagers, quick-diet books, Stayfree Maxi-pads, rat poison, hunting rifles, and glittering panels of Pac-Man and pinball, all enclosed in a single climate-controlled fortress complete with trees, fountains, and neon. Safe at last! Home free! The biggest, best-equipped fallout shelter imaginable, the consumer culture's Eden, the post-urban cradle, the womb, the home, the *mall*.

So begins George Romero's cult horror film *Dawn of the Dead,* the first zombie movie to be shot in a shopping mall. In the movie, the mall is a seductive place: It not only attracts passing pilgrims and lulls them into staying, even though they have to battle murderous zombie shoppers, it has acted as a magnet for the zombies themselves ("This was an important place in their lives," one of the pilgrims says). Both groups have been seduced by the mall's products and its completeness—*one-stop living,* even for the living dead.

But this completeness is also demonstrated for us when the circle is closed and the movie about the mall's power is itself *shown* in a shopping mall. For among other things, the mall is a fortress of entertainment.

Dawn of the Dead was in fact shot in the middle of the night at Monroeville Mall in western Pennsylvania, not far from Greensburg and Greengate mall. But it was only after my travels were completed that I saw Monroeville Mall as something of a model for malls across America. It isn't exactly average—it's more that Monroeville is the essential mall. It has a couple of big department stores and a reasonable selection of shops. It has all the typical mall stuff—the bathroom supply store, the fast-food dispensaries—but it also has a good French bakery and café, and a pleasant Italian restaurant.

Monroeville Mall is surrounded by a complex of other buildings, which include hotels and the Expo Mart, a convention and exhibition center. Monroeville itself is less a town now than a new downtown spread along the highway. Inside, the mall has that compact sense of being an enclosed and efficient distributor of everything. You can play the lottery there, and get quasi-religious counseling from The Talk Shop, a kiosk in the center of the mall that also functions as a living mall directory (the person there will give you directions to heaven, or to Pup-A-Go-Go). For a while there was a row of storefronts that deserved to enter into mall mythology: Funland (the game arcade) followed by the John XXIII Chapel, followed by the Luv Pub. The chapel is gone now. So is the skating rink, which was the mall's most distinguishing feature and most important community asset before shortsighted business people decided the space was too valuable. Now there's a shop that says LUV in blinking, roguish pink neon; it describes itself as being "for dating . . . mating and celebrating." Sure enough, inside are evening gowns, see-through blouses, and slinky, skimpy night-gowns.

If this weren't entertaining enough, on one of my visits I saw a specific link to show business on display: a traveling "Hollywood on Tour" exhibit in a shop window. Hanging behind the glass were clothes from famous movies, including a black dress worn by Marilyn Monroe in *Some Like It Hot,* the robes Greta Garbo wore in *Queen Christina,* and the rumpled khaki trench coat Humphrey Bogart wore in the Paris train station scene of *Casablanca.* "Are they the real ones?" a teenaged girl asked her mother. The real clothes worn by the real actors in the real movies, portraying fantasy characters in fantasy stories? "They could have kept them up better," her mother harrumphed. "That cape is *filthy.*"

To me the mall always felt something like a movie, a fantasy environment where it was perfectly appropriate for Bogie's coat (or Rick's) to rest overnight in a dark display case. But the ties between the movies and the malls have become more explicit as both movie studios and mall developers begin to see themselves as components of the same business, and as partners behind the stage of The Retail Drama.

It began when studios sponsored a few modest movie promotions involving poster giveaways and look-alike contests in a few mall courts. Then suddenly movie people started to see what they had here. Most of the movie theaters in America are in and around shopping centers. "That's where it really starts—where the theaters are," said Martin Levy, who handled MCA-Universal's mall promotions for *E.T.: The Extra-Terrestrial,* "—and that's a major revolution in distribution in the last ten years."

Not only that, but malls were where the teenagers of America hung out, even when they weren't headed for the movies. "The malls are where the kids are," said Bill Minot, who placed promotions for *The Return of the Jedi* in more than a hundred malls across the country. "For theatergoing demographics, twelve to twenty-four years old, that's where you've got to be. It's the modern Main Street; it's where the action is."

Not only *that,* but the mall is where a movie's licensed tie-in products are sold: the books (the novelization of *Return of the Jedi* was the top paperback best seller of 1983 and *E.T.* was second the year before; picture books and how-the-movie-was-made books sell well, depending on the movie), the records (sound tracks for *Flashdance* and *Footloose* both became major hits), the video cassettes, games, clothes, novelties, and of course the toys. This is not an inconsiderable part of the movie business, either: While the first two *Star Wars* films grossed an estimated $600 million, they generated something like $2 billion in retail merchandise sales.

It wasn't long before both studios and mall managers caught onto the synergistic possibilities, to the propensity of kids to walk out of *Return of the Jedi* with Star Wars in their eyes and to drift down the mall court and right into toy stores, bookstores, and record stores, picking up picture albums, theme music, Princess Leia lunchboxes, and Ewok dolls along the way. The movie helps to sell the merchandise; the merchandise helps to sell the movie—in effect continuously advertising it. The amount and duration of the feedback energy can even be multiplied when the movie is part of a series; the continuing characters are kept alive in the public mind by the action figures on the shelves, while the sequels keep the merchandise current and add new characters to old favorites. In fact, the trend toward sequels probably owes a good deal to the mall and its merchandise.

As movie promotions in malls proved successful, the mall industry became enthusiastic. Some developers—notably the Hahn companies in California—helped organize such promos, and both sides looked forward to the imminent day when big studios could launch national campaigns in concert with big mall developers. As the studios became more sophisticated (*Footloose,* for example, was promoted in malls together with the styles of clothes worn by characters in the movies), malls themselves added their own ideas. "You can coordinate an entire mall-wide promotion on the movie theme," explained Stacy Batrich-Smith, then marketing director for the famous Sherman Oaks Galleria. "On *The Pirate Movie* we had a 'treasure chest full of values,' and our stores had *Pirate Movie* sales, and we decorated our windows on the pirate theme. It really ties your center together. You can display all the things that are pirate-oriented, like blouson tops with wide collars and cuffs, as well as having a pirate costume contest and really involving the whole community in the promotion."

But early on, both studios and the malls decided that only certain movies could be promoted. Mall management wouldn't risk offending some of its customers by pushing the R-rated films it nevertheless shows. Studios chose films with a strong youth appeal: either films with young stars (another mall-compatible trend in movies), stars who have young followings, or films that just have *stars,* as in *Star Wars* and *Star Trek,* the spacey special-effects movies. Of course these are also the movies most likely to be marketing tie-in merchandise.

As the relationship between malls and the movies becomes better understood, the studios have powerful reasons not just to promote mall-compatible films but to make movies that will specifically sell in malls. After all, a movie can be a big-city hit, but if it doesn't sell in malls it isn't likely to be much of a success. "There are many cities in which a first-run quality film will only open in four or five theaters, and they will all be out in [suburban] communities, and those will be in shopping centers," said marketing consultant Martin Levy. Then there is the merchandising factor. "There is no question people look at scripts for their licensing potential," Lester Borden, general manager of Columbia Pictures Merchandising, told *The Wall Street Journal.* He added that some producers commission marketing studies of merchandising potential before deciding whether or not to make the picture.

All in all, it only makes good business sense that, as an advertising and promotion executive at one studio admitted, malls have a real influence on the choice of what films the studios will back.

In any case, mall theaters are the perfect place to show movies with a suburban setting and sensibility—such as *War Games* (in which a suburban teenager would have destroyed the world with his home computer except that he had to take out the garbage), *Poltergeist* (in which two suburban fathers engage in a western shootout using television channel changers), and *E.T.* (in which suburban children do not mug a small alien but harbor him and help him home)—which link them to the mall world. Like suburbia itself, the mall is clean, new, safe, yet gently fanciful and ironic—and everyone, as Moon Zappa says, in her "Valley Girl" song, is "super-super nice."

The movies are only one of the entertainment, information, and cultural media that involve the mall in a mutually lucrative feedback loop. Malls sell merchandise that ties in with television (Smurfs, Strawberry Shortcake) and rock music (Michael Jackson dolls), as well as being prime merchandisers of books and magazines, records and tapes, video equipment and cassettes. The same synergistic effect that happens with movies also occurs with products that begin their journey to profitability at another point. An exercise enthusiast, for example, can trot through the mall picking up the *Jane Fonda Workout Book,* the Workout record, the Workout video cassette, and the Fonda line of workout clothes, without a single negative vibe from the outside world falling on a single running shoe.

The relationships can get more complicated than that. They can even get fairly bizarre. The impact of Saturday morning television has become so strong that in one case, a product it advertised (the Cabbage Patch Kids doll) was the cause of hysteria and violence in shopping centers across America. At the same time, a network children's programming producer admitted on ABC's *Nightline* that unless a new show was based on an already familiar image—more often than not, a toy or video game character, such as Pac-Man— the networks simply wouldn't put that show on the air. Meanwhile the best-selling children's books in the mall bookstores were almost exclusively spin-offs of television shows, such as *The Smurfs* and *Sesame Street.*

Television's relationship to the mall isn't restricted to children. The merchandising of *Star Trek* stuff in malls while the old TV series was in syndication led to its revival as a series of motion pictures, which were in turn promoted in malls and seen in theaters there, and eventually sold there on video cassettes. Which led to more merchandise for the mall to sell.

Daytime television in particular has a mall-shopper audience, and so personal appearances by soap opera stars are always big draws in malls. Perhaps the strangest evidence is the success of a revived *Newlywed Game,* done just as it was for years on television but no longer televised—simply taken live to shopping malls around the country as a center-court performance. According to Bob Eubanks, its host in the mall as he was on television, it became the most successful shopping-center promotion in the United States.

Even the once-rebellious image of rock music has been transformed by acts that link themselves to commercial interests, including retail companies that sell their products almost exclusively in malls. One of the first such joint ventures paired Air Supply, a soft-rock group with a clean-cut image, and Jordache jeans. As part of this relationship, Air Supply appeared at a shopping mall in Tampa, Florida, first at a clothing store—which sold 2,500 pairs of jeans that day—and then at the mall's record store, where they autographed their albums, the entire stock of which sold out.

The synergy intensified further when rock music videos became popular (and available on cassettes in the mall). These videos also began to set fashions in clothes, which became instantaneous trends as soon as the videos were shown on such national outlets as MTV on cable, and on the broadcast networks. Such mall clothing chains as the Merry Go Round made specific efforts to sell the clothes that appeared in the videos. Movies also picked up on the music video style, which led to such films as *Beat Street,* and to Beat Street sweatshirts and tennis shoes in the mall.

Some of these relationships were organized by conglomerates with businesses in several media which could package movies, spin-off books, records, and video. When such conglomerates begin to include mall developers, then the last loops will be closed and the mall's strategy of a controlled environment can be more extensively and intensively applied.

The malling of the movies and the media may have more consequences. Many of the movies, records, and books that successfully fit into the mall world have been the work of individual vision and artistic accomplishment. But if books gets published (or written), or movies, TV shows, or records get made, based principally on the results of marketing studies and how well such "products" fit into the merchandising feedback system, then the media may find that they've taken on some of the mall's characteristics as a result of their lack of spontaneity, personal statement, or moral commitment. It may be the hearts and minds of America that next become malled.

Meanwhile the mall itself is becoming a movie star. After countless cameos as the location for crime or romance, and appearances in the background of TV commercials and man-on-the-mall interviews, it played major roles in two youth-oriented movies, *Fast Times at Ridgemont High* and *Valley Girl,* both filmed at the Sherman Oaks Galleria. Romero's *Dawn of the Dead* remains the definitive mall work so far, however, and the best movie scene in a shopping center is still the car chase through a Chicago mall in *The Blues Brothers* with John Belushi and Dan Aykroyd ("It's got everything!" Belushi remarks with uncharacteristic reverence as they demolish it).

So it seemed to me that it was only a matter of time before the mall would itself become the subject of a movie aimed at the mall constituency—the citizens of everybody's hometown. In the mall's theatrical setting, scenarios of such movies often came to me. For instance, *Princess Stacey,* a TV miniseries based on a steamy novel, a *Movie of the Week* shot in a glamorous urban mall . . .

Stacey's plump, hot-buttered curls were spilled across the pillow. Was she a television commercial for sheets? Not today, but sometimes. Stacey— rich, a star, and beautiful—stretched her slim athletic tawny limbs into the air that thrummed with a special signature, its monogram, its label. For this was Ritz air. A Ritz Hotel bed was the host for Stacey's high-priced body, now upright and snaking across the Ritz room to the Ritz shower.

But she was not alone in the Ritz. In the bed, or in the shower. His thick chest hair, matted only moments ago with the sweat of her impassioned curls, was foamy with Ritz soap. They laughed and splashed together: Stacey, her new, rich, and famous psychiatrist lover, and the Ritz. The day was just beginning. She would shave his face; he would shave her legs. Soon they would shop for diamonds.

Outside was Chicago's cold: the traffic-blackened snow, the pollution-processed slush. Also noise, crime, poverty, and desperation. But here Stacey's curls will never be moistened or dirtied or insulted. She will shop with Chicago slime outside. She will move as on angel's breath from Ritz air to the conditioned environment and comfort-controlled splendor of this titanic seven-level paradise, all agleam and a wonder, itself a kind of diamond—a diamond even bigger than the Ritz. It is called Water Tower Place.

Who would want to rescue Princess Stacey from her Tower? No one but a cad wishing to chance nasty encounters with the dragons outside Eden. "Place" had such a ritzy sound, Stacey thought, satisfied.

By afternoon Stacey was at work. She danced exactly, minimally for the cameras, for a commercial interrupted by unscripted screams. It was her brother, methodically re-forming a troop of Girl Scouts into the contours and consistency of raspberries. Sometimes medical science fails, says her psychiatrist lover evenly. We try; we succeed. But sometimes, dammit, we fail.

*Then the air was pierced by an eerier scream. Stacey, her hot-buttered curls awhirl, bansheed into her brother's twisted face. "This was my story!" Stacey cried. Now you're trying to turn it into yours—*Bloody Murder Nightmare at Water Tower Place!

But better yet, a movie about the more traditional suburban center, with all the *sturm und schmaltz* of a big-screen, cameo-filled epic—*MALL!,* the story of flamboyant self-made entrepreneur Byron Lord, manager of Esplanade Square Bigdale Mall, who is under pressure from the ambitious streamlined on-site development rep, a mall lifer who has never worked outside of air conditioning. Lord's affair with the chic and wordly manager of Casual Corner is getting tempestuous when . . . crisis! The sprinkler system is shut down following the dousing of a minor fire (and the quarrelsome county supervisor who got in the way) but another fire erupts, threatening the first floor all the way from Broadway department store past The Gap to the Piercing Pagoda. Meanwhile the parking lot is heating up as a suburban motorcycle gang, the Mall Marauders, is mixing it with a band of Hare Krishnas who've been refused permission to jingle their bells inside. Security is diverted from monitoring middle-school truants and observing car thieves and sent to these two scenes, expect for young rookie Mick O'Bannion, who is delivering a baby on the terrazzo tile in front of Karmelkorn. Of course all this distraction pleases glassy-eyed Dan the Dealer as he peddles his dilithium crystals near the fountain across from Tennis Lady. *But* dope-crazed Nicole is threatening to throw herself from the second level to the central-court Recreational Vehicle display because her mother (currently shopping at Big Woman) doesn't understand her, and her stoned friends are too busy riding the glass elevator to care—except Robert, who has come to the mall every day on the pretext of playing air hockey just to see Nicole. *He's in the elevator; he looks up, horrified—Nicole is perched outside the shiny railing, outlined against the bright lights of the National Record Mart. . . .*

40

The Mallennium Factors: Mallcondo Continuum, Fortress of the Future, or, Where No Mall Has Gone Before

We want to enclose the universe in the work of art.
Individual objects do not exist anymore.
                                        —GINO SEVERINI
                                        Futurist manifesto, 1913

All we know about the future is fiction. The generations after the marking of the millennium—the post-2001 world—are best dealt with in terms of scenarios and fictional but possible contexts. That the mall or its progeny will have a large part in a number of likely futures is my premise, and the conclusion I came to in my mall journeys and musings: One way or another, the millennium will be the mallennium.

The first and most often proffered fiction about the future is usually called "If Present Trends Continue," which is a scenario based on the assumption that certain elements of the present will predominate to form the character of the coming years. Right now the mall is in excellent position to be a major and defining part of such a pattern, since it is already interlocking with forms of housing, business, entertainment, and living that use its basic system of organization, as well as being compatible with its economic and cultural premises and implications.

Even now, the evidence is visible almost everywhere, in small towns, big cities, the wide swaths of suburbia and the fast-growing concentrations of the Sun Belt—all of them filling up with the same kinds of new enclosures, all connected by the same new electronic information and communications systems. It's the Mallcondo Continuum, and by 2001 it could be where America lives.

What so many of these new objects on the physical and social landscape have in common is their nature as controlled environments that separate themselves from the outside world in order to create an artificial internal world that is as self-sustaining and self-referential as possible. Sometimes it's the sense of total enclosure that's most obvious, as in the domed stadium (with artificial weather and artificial grass) that can be converted from a venue for one sport or amusement to another overnight. Sometimes it's the sense of variety under one roof, as in the multi-arts complexes found in cities and suburbs, which offer a shopping mall of culture. Or sometimes the combination of control and entertainment makes the resemblance to the mall clearer, as in the new generation of theme amusement parks like Sea World, or their adult counterparts, like the Condado Beach Hotel in Puerto Rico, which advertises itself as a "self-contained resort world of beach, pool, nightclub, disco, cocktail lounges, casinos, shops and gardens," all with a Roaring Twenties theme.

The same basic mode of organization is also used in the form of housing known as the condominium, which provides living units within a unified, centrally managed complex. Like the mall, it exacts from its tenants a fee above the purchase price for providing common services and facilities—for security, landscaping, recreation, and community events. Like some malls, some condos have "themes," as senior-citizen or singles-only enclaves. Condo complexes not only seem to sprout naturally near malls, some malls build their own.

The next step in the theoretical and actual expansion of the mall/condo concept is the "new town" or planned community. In such communities the homeowner or renter is subject to rules set forth by central management under the supervision of a private corporation that controls the community's growth and common environment. In exchange for the generally high prices of the homes and these restraints (and the fees exacted for their administration), the town's ownership provides stability, safety, and amenities. New towns guarantee the living fantasy of a peaceful, steady-state small town, enclosed by walls of rules and money.

The planned community is the logical extension of the mall concept. Not altogether incidentally, then, some of them have been built or owned by mall developers, and many—including Irvine, California (the largest)—have a major shopping mall as their centerpiece.

These environments, from mall and condo to theme park and planned town, are popular because they are economical castles that protect against the unwanted outside of soot and strife and uncertainty while providing efficient fantasy worlds inside. The spread of the Mallcondo Continuum is also being abetted by some of the current trends in communication and information technology.

Despite current claims for the grand and diverse potential of computers, cable television, and other new electronic technology (which bring to mind the claims once made for the potential of radio and television to spark a grand new era in knowledge and culture), so far the most familiar uses of the new machines have been controlled by the same business and commercial interests that ran the old machines, and therefore have been accommodated to the same purposes. Computers, for example, have vast potential and have been used in art and medicine (and in fact have worked miracles by giving previously helpless people with severe physical limitations the ability to function and communicate). But they face us most often at the supermarket check-out, where they categorize and tot up our bills, meanwhile (though, so far, only in experiments) feeding the product purchase information into the data banks of marketing analysts, while we watch video-taped commercials on the monitor and are watched by closed-circuit television cameras.

Whatever the capabilities of cable television and computers, they are right now being used to sell more products more efficiently. Computerized market research can "segment" a population into categories, which are then "targeted" by advertising and the highly specialized outlets at the mall. Two-way cable television is a market research tool of impressive potential: By asking questions, often in the guise of entertainment, and receiving instantaneous answers from consumers who are pushing response buttons in their homes, market analysts can gather more information more quickly and more often and eventually in more depth than ever before.

Cable television in general seems as yet to be simply a slightly more sophisticated commercial mechanism than the networks. Cable's chief innovations are more specialized and targeted channelsful of programming (all-sports, all-rock, and, inevitably, the Shopping Channel) and programming with a little more sex and violence. More challenging information and arts programming has been tried but generally has proved not profitable enough. Experiments in community-originated programming have also been overwhelmed by large commercial interests.

The many channels available on cable and the specialized nature of their programming is highly compatible with the mallcondo format. The president of a large cable television company once told me that his system was like a department store—you could walk through the many channels, shop around, buy or not buy. But cable is really more like a shopping mall: a series of specialized choices, or shops, within an environment controlled, monitored, and managed by a single commercial enterprise.

So in the American home, cable works in complete concert with other electronic entertainment to create a total media shopping mall, where Dad can watch *Digital Bowling for Yen* on the cable all-sports channel while Mom surveys her stock market profits at her designer-label personal computer terminal; meanwhile Sis dances to the latest *Video-of-the-Month Club* rock video and Sonny switches his Sony from the Toxic Galactons vs. the Mega-Quaaludes video game to the *Interactive Classics Theatre* on two-way cable, so he can vote on whether Ahab should kill the White Whale and live happily ever after.

Still, the new electronics are having one not-altogether-controlled effect: They are helping to make a difference in where Americans live and work. The 1980 census revealed a dramatic and unforeseen dispersal of population to areas outside major metropolitan areas—not to suburbia or even exurbia, but farther into rural areas, small towns, and small cities. Some of this was due to the decentralization of white-collar and information-related industries, brought on in part by the computer. Now that offices can locate anywhere and stay in instantaneous communication with company headquarters and other branch offices, this trend could accelerate. "Long Island is a significant back-office threat," an official of New York City's Office of Economic Development told a reporter. "But with telecommunications, South Dakota is almost as big a threat."

Where the information class goes, a significant service sector soon follows, and they all take with them the expectations that will mean their goods, services, entertainment, and culture, as well as their residences, will likely be components of the Mallcondo Continuum. Already the exurban corporate campuses are enclosing more facilities devoted to more aspects of employees' lives—recreation, entertainment, education—as part of the workplace. The company town is becoming a reality again, in more sophisticated form. In other places, however, corporations are looking to the mall to do all this for them. (Remember the Battle of Battle Creek.)

At the same time that this dispersal goes on, there is a countertrend bringing the information class back into cleaner, safer, and more glittery central cities. But even there they will find the Mallcondo Continuum asserting itself. All cities have seen the coincident coming of condos and urban malls, often in the same new megastructures that contain workplace, living place, and shopping and entertainment places. The mall has resurrected and controls elements of a new urban identity—the city historic, the city as fun—and that includes not only historical malls but the sports and arts complexes. It is no coincidence that in the city of Pittsburgh the newest and largest shopping mall (Century III), a new downtown megastructure (Oxford Centre), the major downtown sports and entertainment enclosure (the Civic Arena), three of the city's professional sports teams, and a cable TV channel that broadcasts local sports are all owned (wholly or substantially) by the DeBartolo family, who run one of the oldest and most powerful mall development companies in America.

Meanwhile the boom areas of the Sun Belt are growing in a new way, variously described by experts as "urban centers without cities," "the galactic city," or as "metro-nucleation." What it comes down to is the Mallcondo Continuum in its purest form, with malls, condos, planned towns, and planned unit developments along with megastructures, arts and sports and entertainment complexes, and all their combinations defining these new communities from the start.

Together, all these elements of the Mallcondo Continuum in every part of the country are creating new configurations to challenge the old patterns of cities and their suburbs for the heavy print on the maps of America: Beside Chicago there is Schaumburg, with giant Woodfield Mall and its growing community and electronics industries, all nestled next to O'Hare Airport. Near San Francisco there is the Silicon Valley, with its electronics complexes, it multiuse complexes, and its malls. Surrounding Orlando is a complex of theme parks, hotels, and condos, from Gatorworld to Circus Land, the capital of which is Disney World, and now the Disney World Shopping Village. Some of these new configurations are dominated by malls, such as South Coast Plaza outside of Los Angeles, or the mall-centered community of Paramus, New Jersey. Beside Philadelphia there is King of Prussia, with light industry and research labs, the historic-recreational facilities of Valley Forge, big convention motels, and one of the largest shopping malls in the country. Not far from New York City there is Stamford, Connecticut, with a concentration of offices and industry and the Stamford Town Center, the largest mall in the New York tri-state area. North of Atlanta, along the Perimeter beltway—near the Perimeter Mall—there are more workers employed than in all of downtown.

Dominating all these new configurations and setting their tone are the controlled environments that express the American situation: The external frontiers that used to create growth and which formed our national character no longer èxist. The new challenge is to create the ever-beckoning Eden of the frontier within the internal worlds of the planned town, the megastructure, the dome, the mall. It's enclosing time in the Garden of the West.

Perhaps some future writer will word-process the opening of the first comprehensive monument to the Mallcondo Continuum, the ultimate Eden of our If-Present-Trends-Continue destiny, the artificial empire where the magic of Marquez meets the vision of Vonnegut (with a nod to Steely Dan) in *The Year 2001 of Solitude No More. . . .*

Many years later, as he stood facing the Custerdome, Aristotle Bluenda remembered that distant afternoon when his father had taken him to Disneyland. Now, as a corporate vice-president for communications of the AT&T-Disney-IBM-Warner-Amex-Coca-Cola-Sears Company, he was privileged to lead the first media tour of the greatest living, working, and entertainment complex in the world, the most complete controlled environ-

ment that technology and the imagination could create, the linked structures and grounds known as the Custerdome Complex.

Its vast palisades of shops, its galleries, hotels, casinos, parks, its acres of wonders and miles of magical halls would soon be swarming with people, for in twenty-four hours the Custerdome itself would officially open with the greatest inaugural event possible in America: the Super Bowl.

After the ride on the advanced-technology people-mover from the Custerdome's own jet and heliport, Bluenda led the eager media representatives to the Info Mall, a complex of public and special-use computer facilities, information-access centers, and the high-tech atrium of information-oriented shops and casual restaurants. They examined several of the computer Work Centers, one of them designed for employees of various companies who lived within the Custerdome Condo Complex, and one of the many centers allocated to a specific company as a satellite headquarters. These Work Centers, Bluenda explained, were designed to counter the loneliness of home computing with the alternating hush and chatter of a group setting. Workers got in the habit of coming several times a week to use the newest hardware and software, to talk shop, gossip, eat together, and go shopping. Locating the Work Centers behind glass partitions in the shopping mall itself reinforced the anti-solitude effect, for other human faces and bodies gliding by were always visible.

Bluenda led them briefly by the Guest Access Center (for travelers staying at the complex hotels) and the computer recreation center, with its cross-competitive games linked to other centers all over the world. Then he showed them the Custerdome Community Town Meeting Rotunda, fully equipped with computer systems for information access and instant tallies, not only of those attending government or civic meetings in person, but also of those participating from home through interactive cable television. Everywhere in the Info Mall, information displays of astonishing clarity and variety were on view.

Bluenda led the astonished reporters from the Info Mall's hard-edged brightness to the lush greenery of the Garden of the World Mall, with its true miniature rain forest surrounded by its many restaurants and cafés. They stopped for a drink in the Macondo Café, where they could glance in leisurely fashion through one of the many electronic directories of all the malls (the Mondo Chic Fashion Mall, the Themes of the Centuries Mall, the Joke Mall, etc.) and their products and services.

He would not have time to show them everything—the electric casinos, symphony hall, theaters, art museum, professional service centers, fitness centers, Custer Tech, and the underground theme caves (a simulated Carls-

*bad Caverns, the Subways of the World exhibit). And they would have
only a brief helicopter ride over the outdoor theme areas—the Ecology Gardens, Moonscape, Animalworld, The Tree Museum. But he did take them
to the Science Lair to see the first functioning biomedical exhibit anywhere:
the lifelike robots acting out the parts of biochemists bent over their test
tubes, actually manipulating chemicals and describing what they were doing
while, twice an hour, they created life.*

*Then in the Custerdome itself—its green immensity settled under a
silver sky—Bluenda described the dimensions of the huge enterprise. It was
a totally self-sustaining and completely controlled community the size of a
city, yet it was also a major tourist attraction. It was, he mentioned, more
of what Walt Disney himself imagined that Epcot Center would be, but
even the master could not have envisioned this.*

"One-stop living!" Bluenda cried.

*But not many of the media reps were terribly interested in Bluenda's
speech outlining the inevitability of the Custerdome Complex, and except
for the historical nature of the moment, he himself wasn't either. For the
last stop on the Custerdome tour, as everyone knew, was to be the adult
entertainment complex of unparalleled size, variety, imagination, and freedom—far better than anything in Nevada—known as The Pleasure
Dome.*

> LANX: Outside the smog strikes clean to the
> heart. . . . Used-car lots melt away into the black
> macadam. The Tar Pits squirm with animal life.
> And all along through the terrifying shopping cen-
> ters the doom merchants whisper our fate.
>   —SAM SHEPARD
>   *Angel City*

Of course, those particular present trends may not continue on a
steady course. They may even be discontinued altogether. Toward
the end of his book *Terminal Visions*, futurist writer and teacher W.
Warren Wagar offers this opinion: "In the early 2080s, our descen-
dants may be living with the same chaos of Coca-Cola, fundamen-
talist Islam, suburban shopping malls, starving East Africans,
Eurocommunism and H-bombs crouching in their silos that we
know so well in the early 1980s. But it is not bloody likely."

So far we have lived in a lucky age in America. In the twentieth century our landscape has not been devastated by war, famine, plague, or pestilence. The weather has been, in the cycle of things, unusually beneficent for our comfort and prosperity. There have been few natural catastrophes to cause great destruction and death in the last few generations. We have had easy access to cheap energy and the natural resources necessary for a growing industrial and technological society.

But such luck may not last. We have amassed an arsenal of terrible destruction that is poised to wither the world in a comparative instant. We have created an immensely complicated and interrelated society, with cities of vast population and technical dependence that ironically makes all of us more vulnerable to the major natural convulsions of the earth's surface and atmosphere, as well as to disasters created by the determination of a few people or the psychosis of one. In the process of creating the widespread comforts of our society, we've poisoned ourselves, our air, land, and water, with consequences we don't yet know.

In an era of unparalleled prosperity and enlightenment, our society has still failed to eradicate poverty and racism, and America's cities still contain tinderboxes of wasted lives, nurseries of violence, breeding grounds for a subculture of potential killers whose survival depends on their remorselessness. Vast numbers of the world's people are starving; the only access to the modern age some of them have is to modern weapons.

The end of the first millennium—the year 1000—saw the dawn of the Dark Ages in Europe, a long period of widening disorganization after the Roman Empire collapsed and the waves of Germanic and Moslem conquests destroyed the patterns of European culture. Cities, towns, and villages fell into ruin and disappeared; fields went uncultivated, famine spread, and wolves and other wild animals roamed freely, as did the highwaymen who preyed upon travelers. Violence, from organized warfare to frequent random murder, ruled the bleak landscape. Government was nearly nonexistent and the monetary system disintegrated. For a while, even the measuring of time was lost.

The year 1000 began with portents and terrors: a comet hanging in the sky for months, and then earthquakes that set off widespread hysteria and panic. The millennial sense we have as the year 2000 approaches could find even more justification: global terrorism, nuclear blackmail, the vengeance of the Greenhouse Effect, the awful start of the Nuclear Winter, or simply another earthquake—the giant quake overdue in California along the San Andreas fault and in the Midwest and part of the East affected by the even larger New Madrid fault. If centered in a major city, a world information and financial center like Chicago or especially Los Angeles, such a major quake would send shock waves through the American and world economy that could cause incalculable changes in our way of life, as well as possibly devastating our national psyche. Or catastrophe could begin more quietly, with financial crisis and the collapse of an aging infrastructure and damaged ecology we can no longer afford to fix.

Once disorganization begins, history shows, it can feed on itself until it becomes chaos. Then it is a long way back to organization again. When this happened in the eleventh century, there arose a new system—feudalism—and a new institution, the feudal castles, fortresses against the wilderness which created small societies within themselves. Similarly protected enclosures, such as the monasteries and later the walled towns, became the only continuity; they saved the remnants of the old culture and served as the incubator of the new.

In such an apocalyptic future, the dour role of the mall might well be the same as that of those castles. For the malls are already becoming the citadels of our time, fortresses protecting the dream worlds of our culture. The vicissitudes of nature and urban life have already driven some malls underground. Huge multilevel shopping centers have been built underneath several earthquake-endangered cities in Japan. Toronto has several large underground malls connected by almost two miles of passageways. Toronto's planning and development commissioner worried that citizens might forsake the aboveground streets altogether, "except for a few brave souls dashing between buildings from urban fort to urban fort under the eye of skyscraper security guards."

Although most malls, including those underground, are obviously fortresslike, the resemblance is strongest in Southern California, where the malls along the freeways are very similar to the castle complexes of the Carolingian period, complete with walls and defensible perimeters as well as their own flags and coat-of-arms insignia. Even the mall's organizational system is similar to the feudal model: Instead of lords' distributing land among vassals who paid the lord in food, service, and loyalty in exchange for the castle's protection, the mall distributes space among tenants who pay the manager with money and obedience to the mall rules for the privilege of being inside the mall and not out in the unprofitable wilderness. Like the feudal tenants who bore the cost of the castle's court and the lord's army, the mall tenants pay for the mall's courts, the officers of marketing, and the foot soldiers of maintenance and security.

Whether or not apocalypse accompanies the millennium, it's clear that malls are the castles of our own prosperous but anxious times. As fortresses against a perilous present and the prospect of a disintegrating future, the malls expressed our fears in feudal images. Many of our fictions posit the aftermath of apocalypse in feudal terms, from the futuristic highwaymen in such films as *Road Warrior* to the industrial lord ensconced in his impregnable high-rise castle amid the bleak high-tech slum that Los Angeles has become in *Blade Runner;* and the Duke of New York, who rules a domain of broken streets and demented subjects from his fortress in the public library in *Escape from New York.*

But no fiction so far has taken into account the ready-made qualities of the mall as the model for the new feudalism. Such a text might not appear until the language has been slightly transformed by the heirs of James Joyce, John Lennon, and Russell Hoban's Riddley Walker, and discovered in a surviving cassette from a seminar conducted by a traveling video minstrel in the post-apocalyptic future. . . .

To the Mallgather I'm telling to you, this is my learnings with respect to the Lurd of this Mall. In the Beforetimes, in the High Dollar Deis, malls was places of cargathers and hot kultourism, and all was shopping to the muzak sinfunnies of GasHave Maller.

Then comes the Betweentimes, the Final Dollar Deis, when affinity gropes attacked with Big Bucks to take over Malls for theirsown. Some of these Great Malls were called Secular Humanism Esplanade, Moral Majorette Phamly Plaza, Big Survivorist Center, and oft in the Holy Wood Hills was the Gestalt Mall. Them was the days of the first Panic Wars that brut down the great Amerry-cannan empyre.

Now we who owe feelty to the Duke of Orange and are under his portection here at the Great Mall of Orange soon will be in wretchous battle with the forces of the Archbiship of Westminster Mall, fighting for free ways and just us.

Our lifes is hard, scrapping by and struggles to put mcdonalds on the table. In the Beforetimes people like us owned their own hojoinns, one per phamly. Now we lifes togather in the one holy Mall, but we are the lucky ones. At least we life in the End 'O Sungo Land (called Californica in the Beforetimes) in the ferdle feels of jolly green, the Beach and the Whether. We still Have a Good Day. Not like the terrorble Panic Wars of the High Walls in the big sities, all acros the Sunbolt and worst of all in the sities of the East Cost, where as our minstrel cassetters tell us, men and beest cannot be told apart as they forage in the avanews and undergrind, and horrorble Genesters from demento labs roam the broken ramps and cleverleaves.

Fer sure, we have the wolfpacks and kyotes comin down from the hills, and the freewaymen robbin us, but we are lucky because we live in the Great Mall, where the Wall portect us, and we have the Warmth and Stuff inside. After the fal de rol, isn't the Mall the winner of our disconnect?

That is why we owe humble and oily thanks and feelty to the Duke of the Great Mall of Orange who we service. Thats all folks. Thanatos for witching and gudnite everybuddy.

Why not endless till the farthest star?
—JAMES JOYCE
Ulysses

It was a vision of the mall I first had as I left the video game room at Greengate mall after talking to Carol. The futuristic aspect of the arcade itself was obvious: the young space pilots at their panels, their eyes assessing, their wrists twisting and fingers flying in clear channels of concentration between senses and hand, as they dispatched orderly hordes of turquoise and magenta aliens in quick bursts of lime-green, hot-pink, and pistachio.

What must the rest of the mall look like, I wondered as I left the arcade, to the denizens of these starry fantasy depths, where young minds burn on and occasionally nova? When they zip out for a cheese stick and Orange Crush, or cruise the continuous corridors past Radio Shack, Video Concepts, and the Software Store? Could it be that the fantasy continued—and could that fantasy, in a sense, be right?

For here is the mall: all this food, clothing, entertainment, and information in a sealed structure. The people move swiftly on their appointed tasks wearing various uniforms. They are part of a busy environment that is apparently autonomous. Every facet of its operation, including the air that everyone breathes, is controlled, as if outside its walls there were only a fatal eternity.

It could be anywhere, or nowhere; it could even be moving about. If you stand in just the right place, at Westmoreland Mall for example, the vibrations of people walking and the low hum of the mall's comfort control machinery can offer the illusion of movement, through the air, or through . . . space. The fantasy is explicit in the video arcade, but out here it is still curiously valid: a limited spectrum of events that satisfy basic sensory needs combining in cybernetic excitement, in a safe, enclosed structure with room to walk around in. Very logical. Give it a warp drive and a five-year mission and you've got this . . . starship.

For me, this idea was the most seductive aspect of the mall. I'd been a space-movie fan since my childhood with *Captain Video, Space Patrol,* and *Rocky Jones, Space Ranger* on television. I was such a *Star Trek* fan that my nickname at *Newsworks* in Washington was Spock. I resorted to bringing along the children of friends so I wouldn't be too self-conscious at matinees of the *Star Wars* trilogy. *Close Encounters of the Third Kind* became one of my favorite movies, right up there with *Rules of the Game, Pierrot Le Fou, Day for Night,* and *Help!* There was something very appealing about the energy of the trim techno-magical world of the spaceship and its collaborative mission combined with the excitement of exploring the ultimate physical unknown.

Science-fiction visions of the mall were reinforced everywhere I went. So many malls resembled the decor of so many fictional spaceships, from the alien saucer of *This Island Earth* to the space station in *2001: A Space Odyssey,* and the super-Portman interior of the mother ship in the special edition of *Close Encounters.* Malls also suggest companion visions of earth's future utopias: Fox Valley Mall in suburban Chicago and Eastridge Mall in San Jose were right out of Fritz Lang's *Metropolis;* Water Tower Place is the image of Everytown's City Hall as depicted in the 1935 film of H. G. Wells's *The Shape of Things to Come.* Of course the makers of the more recent *Logan's Run* didn't have to anticipate the shopping mall— they actually used one as a set for their futuristic society.

Not all the science-fiction scenes the mall suggests are benign. The totalitarian societies of *Logan's Run* and George Lucas's *THX 1138* (in which the computer-confessor gives absolution with the exhortation to buy more and be happy) hint at the planned perfection of the mall as well as the zombie qualities it seems to inspire in its patrons. When faced with the enclosed completeness of some malls, thoughts of *Brave New World* are inescapable, although there is probably not a "Central London Hatchery and Conditioning Center" in one yet, exactly. Still, the world-state motto in Aldous Huxley's novel—"Community, Identity, Stability"—seems appropriate. Even the mall's separation of the blissful shopping environment from the hidden supply and maintenance tunnels parallels the ultimate division of labor in *The Time Machine,* when the innocent Eloi, the upscalers of the earth's future, dance spacily aboveground, but are both the beneficiaries and the lunch meat of the Morlocks, the factory and service workers huddled underground.

These would all seem to be faintly frivolous and idiosyncratic thoughts, except perhaps for certain future possibilities. What if the earth becomes so toxic and dangerous, or simply so crowded and prosperous, that elements of the human race finally do make the leap from the earth's surface to artificial worlds in space? (*Blade Runner* specifies such space stations as the new West. Loudspeakers over Los Angeles announce: "A new life awaits you in the off-world colonies—the chance to begin again in a golden land of opportunity and adventure.") Then, ideas about what will really work in a self-contained habitat that must satisfy human needs and wants for long periods of time become a matter for serious speculation. People will start looking for prototypes. They could do worse than to look at the mall.

The foremost proponent of large space habitats has been astrophysicist Gerard K. O'Neill, who, together with a NASA-sponsored team, designed Island One, a self-sustaining artificial environment for ten thousand people. O'Neill claimed that even larger and more sophisticated habitats could be built with existing or foreseeable technology, and that they would be cost-effective.

In his book *The High Frontier,* O'Neill wrote, "We have talked of the necessities of life, but if we are to work and live in space by choice, and enjoy doing so, we will ask for more: the age-old human desires of comfort, good food to eat and good wine to drink, room to stretch our legs, good places to swim and to get a suntan, variety in travel and amusement. We have definite ideas of our needs for enjoyment and amusement, and any successful space community will have to accommodate them."

In planning to provide pleasures in space that most of the earth's population doesn't enjoy now, O'Neill is positing an American upper-middle-class habitat, and here is where the mall clearly shines: It is our most efficient enclosed and controlled environment that keeps people entertained. Not only that, but the mall already harbors a potential starship life-style—the psychological as well as physical adaptations have already been made.

A space habitat will be limited by size and by the hostility of the external environment. But a simple stroll down the mall courts shows how all that is being comfortably accommodated. Heavy clothing is unnecessary with the mall's temperature control (as it would be in space habitats), so people have already adapted with dress that is appropriately minimal and efficient, depending largely on symbolism for expressions of individuality and status. Mall outlet employees march by in fast-food uniforms of brown and red, or the green or blue blazers of banks and department stores, all with nameplates. Customers pass them wearing jumpsuits, jogging outfits, designer jeans distinguished from one another by label and pocket design, T-shirts and caps which differ only in color and what's written on them, asserting the wearer's team loyalty, sexual preference, favorite car, or quality of wit, with admirable efficiency. Sex differences are also economically indicated by very tight clothes and selective nakedness. Habitat tailoring should not be too terribly taxed.

Peer into the fast-food parlors and you see people eating preformed squares of processed foods; the lines at the drugstore counters indicate that the far-out future, when people will live on pills, is already here. The combination of fast food and pharmaceuticals (vitamins, relaxants, mood elevators, appetite suppressants, analgesics, and the rest) would add to food service efficiency and cut down on agricultural (and psychological) problems aloft.

Information minimalization is clearly the trend in the bookstores and computer software outlets, where most kinds of knowledge can be summed up in one minute. In the toy stores there are The Care Bears, identical except for the symbol of a single emotion sewn to each bear's belly—Tenderheart has a heart, Cheer Bear a rainbow, and Grumpy Bear a rain cloud (there are seven others, all designed as a result of market surveys). Up in the habitat these could provide emotional minimalization for children, as well as preserving certain natural phenomena of the earth—rain, rainbows, etc.—as pure symbol.

The mall offers compact recreational and cultural experiences for adults, too. Exercise equipment (as Stanley Kubrick's *2001* showed us) will be at least as important in space as on earth. One mall-like prototype might be the Vertical Club in Manhattan, an enclosed high-rise country club full of facilities for racquetball, swimming, aerobic dancing and running, whirlpool, sauna, plus Nautilus, Cam II, Paramount Dyna-Cam, and Universal exercise machines (which sound not only spaceworthy but like the products of movie studios). A recreational example can be found at the Astro Village Hotel in Houston, in the Celestial Suite, it features a twelve-seat Jacuzzi and rumpus room with mini-baseball diamond and electronic scoreboard. Or there's the Tarzan Room with fake tree and vine and birdcage dining room at that same hotel, conveniently located near the Astrodome.

Even perceptions of history and the earth itself have already been minimalized in electronic simulations and exhibits in theme parks and malls. The real earth could be conveniently left behind. But the space habitat will have to be not only minimalized but almost perfect; there isn't much room for error when there's no escape. Here again the mall offers hope: So far, it is the only utopia that works.

I first saw its capacity for a certain kind of sublimity when I stood outside Fashion Island mall in Southern California early one afternoon. A soft yellow light bathed the white sandstone of the high entrance columns, as well-dressed ladies in their neutral-look separates, clinging short-sleeved sweaters, and high-heeled sandals jogged neatly up the stone steps. Off to one side a maintenance man in a sea-green jumpsuit quietly tended the immaculate trees and shrubs. There was no intrusive sound or sight. The place was perfect. It was a three-dimensional, life-size, living Artist's Conception, one of those flawless models with clean buildings and perfectly shaped trees that never quite turn out to be like that in real life, except here—at this mall.

Fashion Island is the mall at the center of the Irvine planned community, a more extensive prototype for the space habitat. For a large space environment might not have to be quite so minimal and quasi-military as the starship mall. It could have its own golf course, schools, hospital, bank, churches, restaurants, industry, equestrian trails and riding academies, parks, and its own artificial lake, with private yacht club and marinas. All of that (plus some shopping centers and a big mall) is already part of the planned community of Westlake Village in California, for example. Westlake's planners included different types of housing and worked them into pleasant environments—even the trailer park, where mostly senior citizens live, is in a pleasant, secluded valley. There is also the elite section, gated and guarded, with a boat dock for every home, called the Island.

Resident satisfaction is high at Westlake Village, which is certainly something for space habitat planners to consider. Surveys show that while residents eat out often, few journey outside Westlake, or even to cultural and entertainment events in Los Angeles, forty miles away. As the official brochure puts it, Westlake is "more than a beautiful place to live . . . it's a way of life."

Of course, it's not *absolutely* perfect. Much in the spirit of Westlake's former days as the location for many galloping chase scenes in old Hollywood westerns, Westlake Hills Plaza Shopping Center staged a mock western gunfight as a publicity gimmick. Something went wrong and people started bleeding real blood, including an eleven-year-old girl and one of the stuntmen doing the shooting. Somehow, some of the bullets were real.

Accidents will happen, even in Eden. Westlake does demonstrate that small-scaled controlled environments can work beautifully, but so far they work only with a homogeneous group of affluent people when the community is run by a corporation. Government attempts to create New Towns that include a more socially, economically, and racially heterogeneous group of citizens have generally failed in America. It also helps if the citizens share a common fantasy or ideal way of life that transcends their smaller desires (for inappropriate self-expression, say) and inspires their personal and financial participation. Westlake Village is one of those planned communities that fits the bill. Owned and operated by the Prudential Insurance Company, it is the opulent model of a fantasy western small town. It is beautiful, quiet, and secure. Although several prominent Hollywood people have lived there (Mickey Rooney, George Fenneman), perhaps its most mythological resident was Robert Young, who found his Springfield in the planned community. Father knows best.

Such lessons should not be lost on the makers of a space habitat. They should know that, with the limited exceptions of the military and some religious groups, only corporate businesses have successfully built and maintained planned and enclosed communities. But this was already suggested in Kubrick's *2001* (a film that also portrayed the pioneers of outer space life not as intellectual giants but simply as average humans of the late twentieth century: technically competent and resourceful, but mostly people who follow orders, work out, and play games). The larger insight lodging in its apparently irrelevant details was that space wouldn't be the exclusive province of military star-fleets beholden only to national, world, or intergalatic governments; *2001* was the first movie to show us that space was finally going to be conquered by Coca-Cola and AT&T.

The military would also be there, of course, but like the warships of the past, they would represent economic interests—after all, *Star Trek*'s starship was called the *Enterprise*. This fact is already obvious in America's first steps toward permanent space stations. The space shuttle (the prototype of which was also called *Enterprise*) carries out commercial and military missions as well as scientific experiments. A prominent enthusiast for space habitats has already suggested that rockets carry display advertising as a way of financing their voyages.

The concept is intriguing. Just think of all the noncommercial utopias of the past and how they had one thing in common: They remained fictional or, after a few brief moments in the sun, subsided into myth. The New Jerusalem and the City of God, Plato's Republic and Thomas More's Utopia, Tommaso Campanella's City of the Sun, Andreae's Christianopolis, Francis Bacon's New Atlantis; Communitas and Walden Two, New Harmony and Oneida, Ebenezer Howard's Garden City, Soleri's arcologies, and Buckminster Fuller's Spaceship Earth—all of them were based on philosophy, religion, architecture, and science, and they were all more or less prescriptive, dependent on people fitting into their ideas and ideal structures. But how naïve! Did they really expect those utopias to work without taking a single market survey? Did they really think they could even be built unless somebody made money from them? One thing is certain—they would never now get off the ground.

On the other hand, there is a clear cultural continuity between the mall and the culture that created it, and the kind of space habitat O'Neill and others are advocating. There was a certain placelessness about suburbia, and now the high frontier may be the ultimate placelessness—Earth's suburbia of outer space. It may therefore be this culture's destiny and its most trenchant challenge to create the ultimate Disney World and hang it gleaming in the blackness beyond the mortal air and the threadbare earth. And so, powered by rocket motors and a profit motive, we may boldly go, encased in the ultimate subdivisions, the planned utopias, to make a new earth in the heavens while preserving the old one in simulations, maps, and memories.

But once again our fictions have not made the mall connection explicit. Such a scenario might call upon the collective visions of Hollywood, as well as the wise direction of *Star Trek*'s Mr. Spock, whose half-human, half-alien ambivalence, his inquisitive fascination, might be the point of view to apply to the Malling of the Cosmos. . . .

When the Klingon fleet was spotted, only Communications Officer Uhura was on the bridge. After all, nothing untoward had happened yet in the entire history of the Free Enterprise Space Habitat. Sure, there were the regular war games, but they were played in the Imperial Ming Darth Vader Video Game Center on C deck. Now something really was happening and nobody in authority was anywhere around: Admiral Kirk was off somewhere in the Hawaii Zone with Princess Leia, Mr. Spock was in earnest conversation with systems computer HAL in the Artificial Intelligence Recuperation Clinic. Han Solo and Mr. Sulu usually had their hands full with their various franchises—the Warp 9 Boutique, for example, in the College Ivy Section. Bones and Scotty were probably busy at their pub, The Bones 'n Scotty Star Wars Cantina. Luke Skywalker was out patrolling the solar power complex, Dr. Zarkov was repairing the mass driver, R2D2 was monitoring the hydroponics, Flash was on a moon mining mission, Yoda was busy with his students at the Force Academy, and E.T. was always—but always—phoning home.

Uhura herself had been on the subspace frequency all week dickering the details for the Pepsi distribution franchise in Smallville sector. The hangup was the Smallville Plaza Nostalgia Supply, which apparently had some kind of restrictive contract.

But then the first Klingon warships showed up on the scanners, and Uhura flew into action, summoning them all. "Admiral Kirk, to the bridge. Your ship is in danger! Mr. Spock, man the sensors!" Already Admiral Adama of the Galactica Habitat was on the fleet channel dispensing fatherly advice. Hey, forget the Inter-Habitat Squash Tournament, the

Over-Earth Marathon, the All-Orbit baseball championship (otherwise known as the Whirled Series)—we've got to save the ship!

The alternative was too horrible for Uhura to contemplate more than fleetingly. What would happen to the abandoned Earth, the other space malls, the whole human race? The future was here: Island One as Fashion Island, the Eden Prairre Mall of eternity, Southdale of the stars, the Galleria of the galaxies . . .

Index

About the Author

William Severini Kowinski grew up in Greensburg, Pennsylvania, and attended Knox College in Illinois, where he studied the liberal arts and wrote plays. He spent a term in the fiction and poetry workshops at the University of Iowa. He was a writer and editor for the Boston *Phoenix* and Washington *Newsworks,* and has written articles on a variety of subjects for national magazines, including "The Malling of America" in *New Times.* This is his first book.